THE PRINCIPLES OF
COMPUTER ORGANIZATION

THE PRINCIPLES OF COMPUTER ORGANIZATION

G. MICHAEL SCHNEIDER

DEPARTMENT OF MATHEMATICS AND COMPUTER SCIENCE
MACALESTER COLLEGE

JOHN WILEY & SONS
NEW YORK   CHICHESTER   BRISBANE   TORONTO   SINGAPORE

Production supervised by Ellen C. Baron
Cover and Text design by Karin Gerdes Kincheloe
Cover illustration by Steve Jenkins
Manuscript edited by Brenda Griffing under the supervision
of Martha Cooley

Library of Congress Cataloging in Publication Data:

Schneider, G. Michael.
    The principles of computer organization.

    Includes Index
    1. Computer architecture. 2. Assembler language (Com-
puter program language) I. Title.
QA76.9.A73S36 1985   001.64   84-20853
ISBN 0-471-88552-5

Printed in the United States of America

10 9 8 7 6 5 4 3 2 1

I dedicate this book to my wife, Ruthann, my son, Benjamin, my daughter, Rebecca, and my sister, Karen.

PREFACE

This book is intended as a one-semester text for the course entitled CS3, "An Introduction to Computer Systems," as described in Curriculum '78 of the Association for Computing Machinery (ACM). It also contains material from course CS4, "Introduction to Computer Organization," and it would be appropriate for course CS/IS 3, "Computer Organization and Assembly Language Programming," described in the recent ACM Report on Small College Computer Science Curricula.

A course in computer organization has two quite different and distinct goals:

- To study broad, general concepts related to the structure and organization of all computer systems
- To learn the assembly language and architecture of one specific system.

The main focus of such a course must be the first of these two points: the study of machine-independent concepts in computer organization. Technology is fleeting, and today's state-of-the-art computer system will be tomorrow's antique. During their professional careers, today's students will encounter computers from many different manufacturers, with quite different architectures and instruction sets. Concentrating too early on the unique hardware capabilities and ideosynchrasies of one machine can produce students with "tunnel vision" who feel comfortable with only one approach to computer design and are either uncomfortable with or ignorant of other structures. The ACM Report on Small College Computing Curricula alluded to this problem when describing the course entitled "Computer Organization and Assembly Language Programming." The report warned that "caution must be taken to avoid overemphasizing the particular hardware in use." Similarly, Curriculum '78, in its description of course CS3, stated that " . . . concepts and techniques that apply to a broad range of computers should be emphasized."

In light of this concern, Parts I and II of this text introduce the topics of information representation and computer organization in a machine-independent fashion.

Part I (Chapters 2–5), "The Representation of Information," discusses approaches for representing the four basic data types that exist on computer systems: unsigned binary, signed integers, characters, and floating point. The discussion includes a survey of a number of possible representational techniques, their theoretical underpinnings, and their advantages and disadvantages from the point of view of efficiency, accuracy, and ease of implementation. It concludes with a discussion of how higher-level data structures found in languages such as FORTRAN, COBOL, and Pascal can be realized in terms of these more elementary hardware data types.

Part II (Chapters 6–9), "The Design of an Idealized Computer," develops in step-by-step fashion the organization and structure of the well known and almost universally used Von Neumann architecture. Each large-scale functional component—memory, ALU, buses, I/O, and processor—is separately introduced along with important general concepts and principles associated with that functional unit. At the conclusion of this section, these separate pieces are combined and integrated into an idealized model of a Von Neumann computer of the type diagrammed in Figure 9-18. The text then introduces a range of different instruction formats and presents some typical instruction sets of the type that students are most likely to encounter. Finally, the overall fetch/execute instruction cycle of this idealized computer is described along with its realization in both hardware and microcode.

By the end of Parts I and II of this text, the student will have a solid grounding in the fundamental principles of information representation and computer structures as they apply to a wide range of different systems. However, computer organization is also an applied discipline, and it is important that students gain some experience in programming a real, rather than an idealized, computer system. This system will preferably have an interesting architecture and will be representative of what is currently available in the marketplace. For this text we have chosen the PDP-11 family of computers manufactured by the Digital Equipment Corporation. The PDP-11 is by far the most widely used minicomputer in the world today, and its architecture has influenced the design of a number of other systems. Its modest yet powerful basic instruction set is relatively easy for a student to learn and master in a one-semester course in assembly language. In addition, the PDP-11 instruction set can be executed by all members of the VAX-11 family of computers, using what is called "compatibility mode." The VAX-11 is one of the most popular of the group of "supermini" computers and is widely available in the computer science departments of colleges and universities. Therefore, by choosing the PDP-11, we have selected a computer that is interesting, important, and available to the widest possible range of students.

Part III (Chapters 10–18), "The Structure and Organization of an Actual Computer System," introduces the student to the PDP-11 and its assembly language, MACRO-11. These chapters cover virtually all MACRO-11 features, including the 90 or so instructions in the basic instruction set, all 12 addressing modes, interrupt-driven I/O (Chapter 15), subroutines and parameters (Chapter 16), macros and conditional assembly (Chapter 17), and the floating point instruction set (Chapter 18). The text contains a number of MACRO-11 programs and program fragments that illustrate the language feature under discussion. We have chosen to treat MACRO-

11 as a systems-oriented language rather than an applications programming language. We feel that this approach is more representative of the actual uses of assembly language and can better exemplify the capabilities of MACRO-11. Therefore, the examples presented in this section are primarily system-related and include such tasks as normalizing floating point numbers, multibuffering input/output, generating correct parity bits, performing extended precision arithmetic, managing a real-time clock, and producing a symbolic dump. In order to simplify input and output, which in assembly language can be quite complex, we have provided (in Appendix E) a set of prewritten MACRO-11 I/O routines that students may use until they are able to write their own I/O code.

Part IV (Chapters 19–20) is entitled "An Introduction to System Software." As everyone in computer science is well aware, an in-depth understanding of computer systems requires a knowledge of both hardware and software and the close relationship of the two. Of course, a thorough treatment of this complex topic is well beyond the scope of a single course in computer organization, and it will be the subject of a number of succeeding courses in computer science. In Chapters 19 and 20 we provide an introduction to some of the most common system software components that students have encountered, including scanners, one and two pass assemblers, linkers, and absolute and relocatable loaders. This material serves as both an introduction to the general concepts of system software and as motivation for material that will be presented in future courses, such as operating systems and compiler design. It also allows us to end the text by summarizing the life cycle of a process on a typical Von Neumann computer—from translation through linking, loading, and execution using the fetch/execute instruction cycle described in Part II. This discussion should clarify the close working relationship of hardware and software as well as demonstrate the steps needed to run computer programs.

There are essentially two different ways to approach a course in computer organization; this text will easily adapt to either one. The instructor who wishes to concentrate more on the general principles of computer organization and somewhat less on the assembly language of a specific system will want to spend more time on Chapters 1 to 9 and 19 to 20, and less time on the MACRO-11 material in Chapters 10 to 18. Because less time will be available to cover the language, the instructor may choose to omit some of the more advanced features of MACRO-11 such as conditional assembly, traps, or floating point instructions.

Conversely, the instructor who wants to concentrate more on assembly language programming may present the material in Chapters 2 through 9 more quickly so that time is available for a thorough presentation of all the features of MACRO-11. This instructor should find Chapters 10 to 18 a complete and self-contained introduction to assembly language programming in MACRO-11. This approach will allow the students to get into assembly language earlier and write more, and more complex, programs. However, we hope that adequate time will still be spent on the general concepts described in Parts I and II in order to give the student a firm grounding in the essential principles of computer organization.

I would like to thank a number of people who helped me in the preparation of this text. The faculty and staff of the Computer Science Department of the Hebrew University of Jerusalem provided me with both office and computer facilities during the writing of the original manuscript. Mr. Mark Wickham painstakingly and accurately coded, ran, and tested all of the MACRO-11 examples presented in the book. My students in the course CS30, "Computer Systems Organization," at Macalester College were the guinea pigs upon whom I tested the ideas contained in this book. A most important thank-you goes to Ms. Sandy Whelan, who edited, typed, and revised the manuscript and whose contribution to the success of this project was invaluable.

Finally, I wish to thank all of the wonderful people with whom I worked at John Wiley: Carol Beasley, Gene Davenport, Richard Bonacci, Lorraine Mellon, and Elaine Rauschal. This is the fourth book that I have completed for Wiley, and I have truly enjoyed every one.

G. Michael Schneider

Minneapolis, Minnesota

CONTENTS

APPENDIXES
495

CHAPTER 1

AN INTRODUCTION TO COMPUTER SYSTEMS

1.1
Introduction

In this text we will be studying the design, structure, and internal organization of computer systems. In this respect a computer is quite similar to a number of other large, complex systems, such as an automobile, a guided missile, or a telephone network. It can be studied at many levels of abstraction. People with different backgrounds and goals will examine a system in completely different ways and decompose it into totally different "building blocks."

We can clarify the last point by listing some of the ways that people view one well-known and widely used system—the automobile. To the casual *driver,* an automobile is simply a means of transportation. It can be driven from here to there at a certain speed, at a certain cost, and with a particular level of convenience. Technical questions about what is happening under the hood are irrelevant at this level of abstraction; the only things that matter are how to start and stop it and how to drive it.

From the viewpoint of an *automobile mechanic,* an automobile is a collection of major subsystems (e.g., engine, transmission, electrical, exhaust) that must function and interact properly to provide acceptable service.

The *automobile designer* is interested in the same collection of subsystems, but is also concerned about how to design them and put them together so that the finished product will meet the needs and desires of the user. The designer is concerned with marketplace demands, aesthetic appeal, convenience, reliability, and manufacturing costs.

An *automotive engineer* is concerned not only with these major functional subsystems, but also studies the design of more primitive and basic automotive building blocks such as valves, cams, gears, gaskets, and seals. The parameters of interest at this level may include stress, strain, tolerance, and strength.

Finally, a *chemist* or *metallurgist* considers a car at the lowest level of abstraction—as simply a collection of elements and materials such as iron, steel, aluminum, rubber, and glass.

This extended analogy should make you realize that when you study any large complex system, whether it be an automobile or a computer, the "pieces" you see and the approach you choose depend entirely on your purposes in studying the system, and the questions you wish to answer.

The viewpoint from which you decompose and study a system is called an *abstraction level,* and the components you study at that level are typically called the *building blocks* or *primitives* of the abstraction. At any given level of abstraction, the internal workings of the primitives at that level are hidden from view, and you see these building blocks only as indivisible entities that perform a given function. Likewise, any relationships that exist between these inner subcomponents are invisible, and the building blocks are viewed solely as "black boxes."

For example, in Figure 1-1a, you would study system S by studying its three components, A, B, and C, and the interactions between them, without concern for how A, B, and C themselves are constructed. If the inner workings of components A, B, and C were truly important to an understanding of system S, this level of abstraction would be inappropriate and you would have to choose a different abstraction level, such as the one shown in Figure 1-1b on the next page. Now you can view system S as being composed of components A, B, and C, as well as subcomponents A1, A2, B1, B2, B3, C1, and their interrelationships. You have gained some additional information about the internal construction of system S. However, you may also become enmeshed in a great deal of low-level detail that could inhibit your understanding of the operation of the overall system. Whether Figure 1–1a or 1–1b is the better way to view system S depends on what questions you wish to answer and what relationships you want to study.

In the next section, we show specifically how this generalized discussion of abstraction levels applies to the study of computers and computer systems. This allows us

FIGURE 1-1a   Abstraction Level 1.

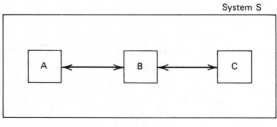

(a)

FIGURE 1-1b   Abstraction Level 2.

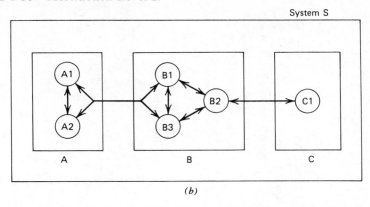

(b)

to explain in detail the material that is presented in the remainder of the text, and to explain the viewpoint from which we will be examining computer systems. This viewpoint will be quite different from the framework you may now be using.

1.2
The Hierarchy of Abstractions

There is no single, uniform way to classify the different ways of studying a computer system. Similarly, the terminology associated with these differing viewpoints is not totally standardized. Figure 1-2 presents a quite common and very popular set of abstractions of a computer system.

The very highest level of abstraction (level 1) is typically called the *operating systems level* or, more simply, the *systems level*. At this level of abstraction, you view a computer (or possibly a network of computers) as a "black box" that solves problems, much as the casual driver views a car merely as a means of transportation, without concern for the technical aspects of automotive engineering. At this level, you simply ask the computer to execute tasks, such as statistical packages, text processing, or graphic displays. You communicate with the computer through a high-level command language, which may be part of a program called the operating system or some other software system. This program interprets your request and either performs the desired task or schedules another program to execute it. Your interaction with the computer system is limited to entering these commands, providing data, and viewing the results. Typical primitives at this level include:

Log on/log off procedures
Account numbers, passwords, and billing procedures

FIGURE 1-2 The Levels of Abstraction in a Computer System.

Level		Deals With	View of a Computer
1	Operating systems level	Packages, jobs, canned routines	A black box that solves problems
2	Programming language level	Programs, statements, loops, conditions	A collection of problem-solving primitives in a high-level language
3	Functional organization level	Memory, processors, I/O devices, registers	A collection of major hardware subsystems
	Computer science / Electrical engineering		
4	Hardware design level	Gates, circuits, chips, boards	A collection of discrete electrical components
	Electrical engineering / Physics		
5	The laws of physics	Electrons, atoms, magnetism	A physical system composed of elemental particles

Listing of file directories
Running programs in your directory
Running special "packaged" programs
Entering data at the keyboard
Obtaining hard-copy results from a printer
Sending or receiving electronic mail

However, how operations concerning these primitives are carried out by the computer is completely hidden from you. At this level, the computer is simply a tool that provides services and solves problems in an unknown way.

This is probably the level at which you were introduced to computers. This is also the level of abstraction for the majority of computer users today: clerical staff, reservation clerks, data entry people, and automatic teller customers at banks. Much useful work can be done with a computer even if the user is totally unaware of how the equipment functions.

However, at some point this level of abstraction became inadequate, and you wanted to learn how the computer carried out the tasks you requested, and how it was able to perform such jobs as text editing or numerical integration. You also wanted to know what happens inside the machine while these operations were being performed. The view of the computer as an extremely fast, but totally mysterious, "black box" was no longer satisfactory. To answer your questions you probably took a course in computer programming (or studied it on your own), and you moved to a second level or abstractions called the *programming language level* (level 2 in Figure 1–2).

At this level the computer is no longer simply a black box. Instead, you study it as a collection of high-level problem-solving primitives expressed in the syntax of a special, high-level language. Exactly what these primitives are depends on which language you study: FORTRAN, BASIC, Pascal, and COBOL, are some of the most popular. However, regardless of which language you learn, the basic primitives are generally the same:

Programs and subprograms
Arithmetic and logical expressions
Assignment of value
Conditional branches
Unconditional transfer of control
Loops
Input/output
Simple data structures—integers, reals, characters
Higher level data structures—arrays, records

At this level of abstraction, you are able to understand the previously mysterious workings of level 1. You understand how a computer carries out numerical integration, because instead of simply entering the command:

>**execute integrate_program**

you actually write (or at least study) the program that performs this function.

However, you may again reach a point where this level of abstraction becomes inadequate to answer your questions. You now want to learn how a computer is able to execute typical programming language statements and produce correct answers. For example, when you write the following Pascal statement:

If $a > b$ **then** $c := 1$

you may wonder how the computer actually evaluates the relational operator "greater than," how it is able to carry out the assignment of the constant 1 to the integer variable c, and what happens inside the computer when the statement is executed.

To answer these questions, you must again move to a new level of abstraction, called the *functional organization* level, sometimes called the *conventional machine* level (level 3 in Figure 1-2). Here, you study a computer as a collection of major subsytems directed at managing the storage and flow of data and instructions along its internal communication paths. You learn how the computer actually carries out those high-level problem-solving operations written in FORTRAN or Pascal. At this level, the primitives you study are:

> Memory cells (e.g., words or bytes)
> Memory fetch/store operations
> Registers
> Adders, shifters, multipliers, and incrementors
> Machine-language instructions
> Addressing techniques
> Instruction decoding
> Processors
> Binary, octal, and hexadecimal representation
> Input/output controllers

This is the level of abstraction we assume in this text, and this is the view of computer systems that we will be taking. Specifically, we will answer the question: How is a computer able to interpret and execute the higher level problem-solving primitives of typical programming languages? This will be our task for the remainder of this textbook.

Two terms related to this level of abstraction are sometimes used interchangeably. However, *computer organization* and *computer architecture* do not mean the same thing.

Computer Organization: The computer system's resources; we study how these components are organized and integrated to form a correctly functioning computer system.

Computer Architecture: The computer system and the virtual or apparent set of resources as seen by the user of that system.

In computer organization, we study the actual (or physical) set of resources available on the computer. However, in many computer systems, we may choose either to hide from the user the existence of certain resources or to make a resource appear to behave in a way quite different from the way it actually behaves, possibly to make the computer appear less complex than it really is. For example, we may have a physical memory of 128,000 words on our system. For efficiency reasons, we may choose to partition this memory into four fixed-size banks of 32,000 words each and assign one user to each memory bank. Thus, each of the four users would see what appears to be a single-user computer with only 32,000 words of storage, instead of the four-user, 128,000-word computer that actually exists. This design may impart certain desirable performance characteristics that the computer architect was trying to achieve.

These and other similar architectural questions are treated in a separate and advanced computer science course typically called Computer Architecture and Design, which presupposes an organizational understanding of computer systems. This text is confined to the topic of *computer organization.*

We have now presented the necessary groundwork for the material to be covered in this text. For the sake of completeness, we will finish discussing the abstraction levels presented in Figure 1-2. Although this information is not covered in the text (except in a few explicitly marked examples), an understanding of the concepts that underlie the upcoming discussion will help you see the relation between computer science and other scientific disciplines. It will also help to explain the purpose of some of the courses that you may take later.

Just as before, the conventional machine level viewpoint may at some point become inappropriate for the questions you have. You may begin to ask questions about how such things as memory, processors, registers, and adders actually work. How is it possible to construct a device that fetches the contents of a memory cell? How are we able to build a decoder to determine which instruction the processor should execute? How can we build an adder to add two binary numbers? To answer these and similar questions, we enter the domain of electrical engineering and move to a level of abstraction called the *hardware design level* or, as it is sometimes called, *logic design* (level 4 in Figure 1-2). (In most modern computers there is an additional design level, between levels 3 and 4, called the *microcode* level or *firmware* level. We have more to say about this new view of computer systems in Chapter 9.) The exact boundary between computer science and electrical engineering is not fixed or well defined. Electrical engineers may perform computer architecture operations, and computer scientists may occasionally take soldering irons and build electrical circuits. The following discussion is meant only to be approximate.

At the hardware design level you study a computer as a collection of gates and discrete electrical components that manage the flow of data, timing, and control signals along internal circuits. The building blocks at this level are:

AND-gates	Resistors
OR-gates	Capacitors
NOT-gates	Control signals
Convertors	Timing signals and clocks
Transistors	Voltage and current levels

Study at this level of abstraction allows you to understand how to construct typical level-3 building blocks (e.g., a memory bank or a processor) and to explain how it operates internally.

Occasionally in this text we "drop down" to the logic design level and show the internal hardware design of a functional component. This is done only to remove some of the mystery associated with the underlying hardware and to introduce the reader to some of the basic principles of logic design. (See, for example, Figure 3-8 on page 43.) However, we have not assumed any background in either digital electronics or electrical engineering, and where we have presented such a discussion it is explained fully and is considered supplementary to the central discussion.

Following a course in electrical engineering and a study of discrete electrical components, you may still be unsatisfied with the understanding possible at that level of abstraction. A study of a 3-transistor circuit or a 1-out-of-N gate may still leave you with unanswered questions about how that circuit operates internally and about the principles according to which it is constructed. To answer these questions, you must enter into a study of the *laws of physics* (level 5 in Figure 1-2), in which you will learn about such building blocks as:

Electrons	Kinetics
Protons	Thermodynamics
Atoms	Magnetism
Forces and force fields	Conductivity

and you will begin to understand the physical principles on which the electrical components and gates of level 4 are constructed.

You have now reached the lowest level of abstraction in the study of computers, just like the chemist or metallurgist who sees a car not as a means of transportation or as an engine, or even as valves and gears, but simply as a collection of iron, aluminum, and steel. (If a student is *still* unsatisfied with this level of abstraction and is concerned with such questions as where electrons and atoms come from, a course in theology or metaphysics might be in order!)

1.3
Computer Organization

Computer organization is the study of the internal structure of a computer system: the hardware resources that are available, the purposes they serve, and the relationships between them. It is the express intent of a high-level language to *hide* from you virtually all of the "messy" low-level details of computer hardware. When a programmer writes and executes a Pascal program, he or she couldn't care less whether it is being run on an Apple Macintosh, a CRAY-1, a VAX-11/780, or a Whiz Bang 101. That is the beauty of high-level languages, and that is why high-level languages are a separate level of abstraction. Now, however, we want to demystify the process and see exactly what is going on internally during program execution.

As an example, let's study the seemingly simple fragment of Pascal code shown in Figure 1-3. This fragment is easy to understand, and its behavior could be explained by any student who has had an introductory programming course. It does not require any knowledge of the internal behavior of computer systems. But a detailed study of the internal operation of this little 5-line fragment opens up an enormous number of questions. Here are some of them.

1. How are numeric constants represented inside a computer?

In a high-level language we use numeric notational schemes chosen solely for their convenience to the programmer: the decimal numbering system, sign/magnitude notation for signed quantities, and decimal notation for fractional quantities. For example, in Figure 1-3, notice the easily recognized constants 2.0, 15.5, and −800. Is that how integers and real values are actually stored internally? If not, what representational scheme is used internally, and why does it differ from the external notation used in high-level languages? Related to these questions, although not apparent in the fragment above, is the question of how non-numeric data types (e.g., character, boolean, user-defined) are stored internally.

2. How are variables represented and stored inside a computer?

Instructors in introductory programming courses usually present a machine-independent definition of a variable. They use the analogy of a named "mailbox" or "slot,"

FIGURE 1-3   Sample Pascal Code Fragment.

```
x := sqrt(y + z/2.0);
if (x < 15.5) or (x > 222.2) then
    w := −800
else
    write ('HELLO');
```

into which numeric values can be stored and from which they can be retrieved. They draw little "boxes" like the following:

Name	*Contents*
w	-800
x	4.0
y	10.0
z	12.0

This type of explanation is completely adequate to explain variables in a programming language, but, quite obviously, computers don't have mailboxes or slots. They have addressable memory cells. How then are variables stored internally? How are they assigned to specific memory cells? How are the names that are used in the program (e.g., x, y, z) associated with memory addresses? What about variables that "appear" and "disappear" dynamically during execution, such as for-loop control variables, or local variables? Related to this, but again not illustrated by the preceding fragment, is the question of structured data types. How are such complex objects as multidimensional arrays, records, sets, and files implemented within the linear memory structure of a computer?

3.   How does the computer implement arithmetic, logical, and relational operators?

All programming languages provide a rich set of operators. For example, in Figure 1-3 we used arithmetic operators (sqrt, $+$, $/$), relational operators ($<$, $>$), and a logical operator (**or**). Pascal contains more than thirty others. Some languages, such as APL, contain hundreds of operators. These operators are indicated in our programs either by a special character (such as $+$, $/$, $>$) or by a reserved word (such as sqrt or **or**). In a high-level language, we are unconcerned about how these operations are carried out and what algorithms are used internally. We simply write down the special symbol or name and assume the operation corresponding to that symbol will be correctly interpreted and carried out by the hardware. What are the algorithms used in performing these operations? Are there internal representations that make these algorithms more or less efficient? What hardware is needed to implement these operations? What errors can occur when these operations are carried out?

4.   How do we implement the normal sequential flow of control?

You know that after completing one statement, the computer executes the next one in sequence. As a programmer, you are able to physically locate the next statement by looking for the semicolon (in PL/1 or Pascal), looking at the next non-comment line (in FORTRAN), or looking for the next higher line number (in BASIC). Is this how a computer implements a sequencing operation? How does a computer identify the separate statements within a program and properly proceed from one to the next? How is the equivalent of a STOP or END statement handled internally?

5.   How do we alter the flow of control to implement conditional branching and iteration?

In an introductory programming class we usually explain the flow of control of loops and conditionals by using a flow diagram:

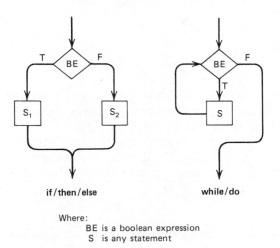

if/then/else   while/do

Where:
    BE is a boolean expression
    S is any statement

In the Pascal fragment in Figure 1-3, if x has the value 4.0, then we will perform the assignment statement, skip the next two lines, and begin again with the statement immediately following the write command. How does the computer internally alter the normal sequential flow of control? What are the internal primitives used for conditional testing and iteration? Are they similar to what is available in high-level languages, such as **if/then/else** and **while/do**? If not, why are the internal conditional and looping primitives different from those in higher level languages?

6.   How is input/output implemented?

Input and output are two areas in which the greatest number of messy details are hidden from the programmer's view. The programmer simply says input x or write (y), and it happens. However, if you think about it, that's pretty spectacular! You may be sitting at a terminal miles from the main computer, and dozens of other people may be in the same room using the same computer for totally different operations. Your terminal could be from Hewlett-Packard, your computer from IBM, and the communications equipment may be supplied by AT&T. And on top of all that, the phone line connecting you with the computer may run next to a noisy interstate highway! Yet, in spite of all that, if you were to execute the fragment in Figure 1-3 with a value of x = 24.0, the five characters "HELLO" would correctly appear on your screen 99.9999 percent of the time. How is input/output implemented? What steps are needed to overcome the problems of distance, multiple users, incompatible equipment, differing representations, and speed differentials to provide virtually error-free input and output?

7. How are the statements of a high-level language stored internally and how are they actually executed?

The primitives of the fragment in Figure 1-3 are typical of those found in high-level languages:

Assignment statement
Function call
If/then/else
Output

Can a computer directly execute statements like these? If not, what is the internal representation of the langauge that is directly executed by the hardware? How is the translation between these two languages performed?

These are just some of the questions that we address in this text. After reading this book, you should be able to look at the simple 5-line Pascal fragment in Figure 1-3 (or any piece of high-level code), and explain, in great detail, what happens inside the computer when that code is executed.

One last question: Why study computer organization? After all, until now you have been able to write programs and perform useful operations without any real understanding of the hardware, just as you can drive a car without any knowledge of the workings of the internal combustion engine.

First of all, an understanding of computer organization will allow you to intelligently evaluate, compare, and select computer equipment and peripherals. More and more, computer equipment is being purchased directly by the user. Scientists, business people, and college students, for example, are purchasing micro- and minicomputers for use in their work and their personal lives. This selection process is much more difficult if the user knows nothing about hardware. (What do you say to the computer vendor who tells you that this computer has 256K of RAM, 4K of ROM, and a microcoded 12-MHz 80286 processor?) Today, with the rapid growth of personal computers, it is important to be familiar with *both* hardware and software.

Second, a knowledge of computer organization and the underlying hardware will allow you to understand how to write optimized and more efficient programs. When you actually see how the program you are writing is translated and executed by the computer, you can begin to write code that runs faster and occupies less memory space. Even more important, you begin to learn which resources on a computer are the most valuable and should be utilized most efficiently. For example, should you write your program to minimize the number of write operations to a file or to minimize the number of arithmetic operations to be evaluated? Does it make a difference whether you use integer or real data types? Without an understanding of what a computer is and how it operates, you will find these and similar questions difficult to answer.

Finally, and most important, almost every branch of computer science other than simple applications programming requires a background in computer organization. You need an in-depth introduction to the functional organization and internal structure of computer systems to work in any of the following areas of computer science: operating systems, compiler design, computer architecture, networks and data communications, database design, computer graphics, and systems analysis. The material in this text is a prerequisite for study in any of these fields.

Part I of this text discusses the internal representation of information (integers, characters, floating point) in a computer system. Part II develops, step by step, a model (or paradigm) of an idealized hypothetical computer. This simplified model allows us to study the general characteristics and principles that are common to all computers, without getting bogged down in the messy details of a specific system manufactured by one particular company. In Part III we take our idealized knowledge of computer organization and see how these concepts are realized in one family of computers, the PDP-11 and VAX-11 systems manufactured by the Digital Equipment Corporation (DEC) of Maynard, Massachusetts. Finally, Part IV is a brief introduction to the topic of systems software. These critically important system software packages are integrated with and operate in conjunction with the hardware to produce an efficient and useful computer system.

PART ONE

THE REPRESENTATION OF INFORMATION

CHAPTER 2

UNSIGNED BINARY REPRESENTATIONS

2.1
The Binary Numbering system

When we study the representation of information, we must be very clear in distinguishing between *external representations* and *internal representations*.

> An *external representation* is the way information is represented and manipulated by a programmer in some programming language or command language notation.

> An *internal representation* is the way information is actually stored and manipulated internally on the computer system.

These two representations need not be, and in fact are rarely ever, the same. External representations, as we saw in Chapter 1, are chosen to maximize convenience for the programmer, the language designer, and the user. Therefore, external representations are usually based on well-known standard algebraic notations such as decimal numbering and sign/magnitude representation of integers. Internal representations, on the other hand, are chosen to facilitate the construction of computer hardware, to maximize efficiency, to minimize cost, and to make the hardware as reliable as possible. If these two representations are not the same, two translations will be necessary: one from the external to the internal representation so processing can be started, and a second from the internal to the external representation when processing is finished so that the results can be presented in a more convenient and natural format. This is what is done in all computer systems.

Internally, all computers built today store information using the *binary numbering system*. Binary is a base-2 positional numbering system. A *positional numbering system* is one in which the value of a digit depends not only on its absolute value but also on its position within the number. If d_i ($i = 0, 1, \ldots, n$) represent digits in a positional numbering system, then the interpretation of the following whole number:

$$d_0 d_1 d_2 \cdots d_n$$

is:

(2.1) $\qquad d_0 r^n + d_1 r^{n-1} + d_2 r^{n-2} + \cdots + d_n r^0$

where r is called the *radix* or *base* of the numbering system. The value r also specifies exactly how many unique symbols exist in that system. A base-r numbering system will always contain exactly r digits. For example:

Decimal:	$r = 10$	$d_i \in \{0,1,2,3,4,5,6,7,8,9\}$
Binary:	$r = 2$	$d_i \in \{0,1\}$
Quarnery:	$r = 4$	$d_i \in \{0,1,2,3\}$

Figure 2-1 on the following page shows the binary representation of the first twenty-two non-negative decimal integers. To determine the decimal value of a binary number not in that table (or, indeed, the decimal equivalent of a number in any other base), simply evaluate expression 2.1 using the appropriate radix r.

EXAMPLES

(a) $11101_2 = ?_{10}$ (Note: The subscript indicates the base.)

$(1 * 2^0) + (0 * 2^1) + (1 * 2^2) + (1 * 2^3) + (1 * 2^4) =$
$\quad 1 \quad + \quad 0 \quad + \quad 4 \quad + \quad 8 \quad + \quad 16 \quad =$
29_{10}

(b) $3012_4 = ?_{10}$

$(2 * 4^0) + (1 * 4^1) + (0 * 4^2) + (3 * 4^3) =$
$\quad 2 \quad + \quad 4 \quad + \quad 0 \quad + \quad 192 \quad =$
198_{10}

(c) $77_8 = ?_{10}$

$(7 * 8^0) + (7 * 8^1) =$
$\quad 7 \quad + \quad 56 \quad =$
63_{10}

To convert a number from decimal to binary, or to any other base, we use a technique called *division by radix*. We initially have a number N_R in a base R for which we are able to do simple arithmetic (decimal, in our case), and we want to determine the representation of N in a different base r. That is, we want to determine the unknown digits d_i in the following formula:

$$N_R = d_0 r^n + d_1 r^{n-1} + \cdots + d_{n-1} r^1 + d_n r^0$$

To do this, we first divide N_R, and then the remaining quotients, by the base whose representation we desire, namely r. (Remember that we do the arithmetic in base R.

FIGURE 2-1   Decimal-to-Binary Conversion Table.

Decimal	Binary	Decimal	Binary
0	0	11	1011
1	1	12	1100
2	10	13	1101
3	11	14	1110
4	100	15	1111
5	101	16	10000
6	110	17	10001
7	111	18	10010
8	1000	19	10011
9	1001	20	10100
10	1010	21	10101

Thus, if we are converting numbers into other bases, we do the arithmetic in base 10.) This division is shown below:

$$(2.2) \qquad N_R' = \frac{N_R}{r} = d_0 r^{n-1} + d_1 r^{n-2} + \cdots + d_{n-1} r^0 \qquad \text{Remainder} = d_n$$

$$(2.3) \qquad N_R'' = \frac{N_R'}{r} = d_0 r^{n-2} + d_1 r^{n-3} + \cdots + d_{n-2} r^0 \qquad \text{Remainder} = d_{n-1}$$

$$(2.4) \qquad N_R''' = \frac{N_R'}{r} = d_0 r^{n-3} + d_1 r^{n-4} + \cdots + d_{n-3} r^0 \qquad \text{Remainder} = d_{n-2}$$

As you can see, the remainders from the division operation are equal to the digits of the desired representation of N in base r *in the reverse order of the representation;* that is, the lower order digits are generated first. Thus, to convert a decimal value into any other base r, we divide repeatedly by r and save the remainders. These remainders, read in reverse order, form the desired representation.

EXAMPLES

(a) $53_{10} = ?_2$

$2\underline{|53}$

$2\underline{|26}$ Remainder $= 1$

$2\underline{|13}$ 0

$2\underline{|6}$ 1   ↑

$2\underline{|3}$ 0   Representation

$2\underline{|1}$ 1

  0   1

$53_{10} = 110101_2$

(b) $99_{10} = ?_4$

4 | 99

4 | 24   Remainder = 3

  4 | 6   0   ↑

    4 | 1   2   Representation

     0   1

$99_{10} = 1203_4$

(c) $50_{10} = ?_8$

8 | 50   Remainder = 2   ↑

  8 | 6   6   Representation

   0

$50_{10} = 62_8$

We now have a way to convert a number N from decimal into any other base and from any other base back into decimal. However, after working with binary numbers or other bases for a while, you should no longer find it necessary to explicitly apply conversion formulas like those in expressions 2.1–2.4. Instead, you will become comfortable working with these numbers directly just as you are now comfortable working in decimal. (Note that the division by radix technique can be used to convert a number in *any* base into any other base. For example, to convert a base-7 number into base-3, you repeatedly divide by 3 and save the remainders. The problem is that you must do the arithmetic in base 7, which is difficult for most people. A simpler way would be to convert the original base-7 number to decimal using expression 2.1, and then use the division-by-radix technique to convert that decimal value to base 3.)

Before we go on to discuss some additional numbering systems, there is one fundamental question we must answer: Why is binary used for the internal representation of information? Since all the familiar programming languages use decimal, wouldn't it be more convenient to build computers that store decimal values directly and avoid the two translation steps described earlier? There is no theoretical reason for not building computers to store decimal (or base-4 or base-19) values. The algorithms for conversion between bases in positional numbering systems work for *all* bases, not just binary. (A number of exercises at the end of this chapter ask you to apply the conversion algorithms just described to other bases.)

The reason for the universal use of binary is *reliability*. If we were to construct a "base-10 computer," we would need to have ten distinct energy states (e.g., voltage or current levels) that would correspond to the ten digits (0–9) of the decimal system. Each distinct energy state would correspond directly to one of these ten digits. However, as electrical components age, they become somewhat unreliable, and they may slowly *drift,* or change their energy state slightly over time. As shown in Figure 2-2a, a drift of as little as 10 percent could cause us to misinterpret the value stored in a location. In this case, the digit 6 might incorrectly be interpreted as the digit 5.

Electrical systems operate best in what is called a *bistable environment,* in which there are only two energy states, separated by a large energy barrier. In this case, it would take a great deal of drift to misinterpret the value stored in a location. Exam-

FIGURE 2-2a   Reliability Problems with a Decimal
Computer.

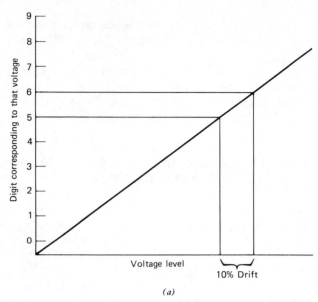

(a)

FIGURE 2-2b   Increased Reliability of a Binary
Computer.

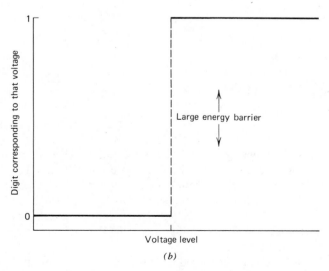

(b)

ples of such bistable states include full on/full off, charged/uncharged, positive/negative, and magnetized clockwise/counterclockwise. This condition is diagrammed in Figure 2-2b.

In the binary numbering system, one energy state represents the digit 0, and the other represents the digit 1. The use of binary greatly increases the internal reliability of the computer. The advantages of this system make it worth the extra time needed to convert to binary for internal storage and then back into decimal.

2.2
Shorthand Representations of Binary Numbers: Octal and Hexadecimal

There is one drawback to the binary number system: it is too *wordy*. That is, it takes many more digits to represent a quantity in binary than it does to represent the same quantity in decimal, because each binary digit contains less information than does each decimal digit. For example, the decimal number 5,000 is represented in four decimal digits, but the same quantity in binary is 1001110001000, which requires thirteen bits. (The word *bit* is a contraction of the two words *bi*nary dig*it*.)

In a positional number system with radix R and D digits, the largest number that can be represented is $R^D - 1$. If we change to a second base r, approximately how many digits d will it take to represent the same range of numbers in the new base r? We can answer that by solving the following expression for the value of d, the number of digits needed.

$$r^d - 1 = R^D - 1 \qquad \text{(We disregard the } -1\text{s, since we only want an approximation to the value of } d.)$$

$$r^d \approx R^D$$

(2.5) $d \approx D \log_r R$

In our case $R = 10$ and $r = 2$

$$d \approx \log_2 10$$
$$d \approx 3.3D$$

This means that on the average, it will take about 3.3 times as many digits to store a value in binary as it does to store the same value in decimal. This is one of the minor disadvantages of the binary numbering system. We must build our memory cells about 3.3 times larger to store the same range of values. If, for example, we wanted to store integers in the range 0–999,999 using decimal, we would need to build a memory with six digits of storage per cell. With binary, we would need to store about twenty digits per cell (6 * 3.3).

There is nothing we can do to reduce the amount of internal storage needed because this is an inherent characteristic of the binary system. But there is something we can do to reduce the excessive number of digits that would be printed out when we wish to examine what is stored in the computer's memory. We can use a more convenient representation, or *shorthand notation,* to eliminate long strings of binary digits.

The development of this shorthand notation is based on the fact that if two bases, R_1 and R_2, are integral powers of one another, there is a trivial conversion mechanism back and forth between numbers in R_1 and R_2. Specifically:

> If a base R_1 is an integral power of another base R_2, such that $R_1 = R_2{}^d$, then each group of d digits in base R_2 maps directly into one digit in base R_1, and each digit in base R_1 maps directly into d digits in base

This means that, in this special case, you do not have to apply complex conversion algorithms like those shown in expressions 2.1 to 2.4. Instead you simply cluster together d digits in the old base and replace them with one digit in the new base, or vice versa. The new number will take up only $1/d$th as much space.

For example, since $100 = 10^2$, conversion of a number from decimal to base 100 is very easy. We simply take each *pair* of decimal digits and map them into one base-100 digit. Since the base-100 numbering system has one hundred unique symbols, these would correspond directly to the values 00–99 in decimal. Conversion of the number $12,345_{10}$ to base 100 would be:

$$\begin{array}{c|c|c} 1 & 2\ 3 & 4\ 5 \\ D_1 & D_2 & D_3 \end{array}$$

D_3 The base-100 digit corresponding to 45

D_2 The base-100 digit corresponding to 23

D_1 The base-100 digit corresponding to 01

In binary, we have a choice of shorthand notations. We could use base 4 (quarnery) since $4 = 2^2$. Then every pair of binary digits would convert directly into one quarnery digit. (See Figure 2-3a.) Quarnery is never used, however, because it would

FIGURE 2-3a   Binary-Quarnery Conversion Table.

Binary	Quarnery
00	0
01	1
10	2
11	3

reduce by only one-half the length of the numbers produced, and the resulting strings of quarnery digits would still be quite long.

We could also use base 8, which is called *octal*, since $8 = 2^3$. Then every group of three binary digits would convert to one octal digit. Figure 2-3b shows the complete octal conversion table for all combinations of binary digits from 000 to 111. To convert a binary number to octal, simply cluster the digits into groups of three, beginning with the low-order digits. Then replace each three-digit cluster with the corresponding octal digit shown in Figure 2-3b.

Octal is a very commonly used shorthand for two reasons. First, it requires only one-third as many digits to represent a value in octal as it does in binary. Second, its closeness to base 10 makes the resulting numbers intuitively meaningful. Octal is the shorthand notation used in all PDP-11 software, and we use it throughout this text.

EXAMPLES

(a) $110001_2 = ?_8$

110	001
6	1

$= 61_8$

(b) $10001101110_2 = ?_8$

10	001	101	110
2	1	5	6

$= 2156_8$

(Note: If necessary, add enough high-order zeros to fill out the binary number to an even multiple of three digits.)

(c) $477_8 = ?_2$

4	7	7
100	111	111

$= 100111111_2$

There is one additional possibility for a shorthand notation. We could use base-16, called *hexadecimal,* or more simply *hex* ($16 = 2^4$). Each group of four binary digits converts to one hexadecimal digit. However, there is one minor problem. A base-16 numbering system requires sixteen unique symbols. We can use the digits 0–9 to represent the first ten symbols in base 16, but we also need unique symbols to represent the decimal quantities 10, 11, 12, 13, 14, and 15. Traditionally, the first six letters of the alphabet have been used for this purpose, so that $A = 10$, $B = 11$, $C = 12$, $D = 13$, $E = 14$, and $F = 15$. In hexadecimal, the digit pair 10 has the decimal value 16 ($10_{16} = 16_{10}$). The decimal quantity 10 is represented in hexadecimal by the symbol "A" ($10_{10} = A_{16}$). Figure 2-3c on page 26 shows the complete hexadecimal conversion table for all groups of binary digits from 0000 to 1111.

FIGURE 2-3b   Binary-Octal Conversion Table.

Binary	Octal
000	0
001	1
010	2
011	3
100	4
101	5
110	6
111	7

EXAMPLES

(a) $10001111_2 = ?_{16}$

1000	1111
8	F

$= 8F_{16}$

(b) $10011101011_2 = ?_{16}$

100	1110	1011
4	E	B

$= 4EB_{16}$

(Note: If necessary, add enough leading zeros to fill out the binary number to a multiple of four digits.)

(c) $1D9C_{16} = ?_2$

1	D	9	C
1	1101	1001	1100

$= 1110110011100_2$

We cannot stress strongly enough that both octal and hexadecimal are only *external representations,* used to avoid printing out long strings of binary digits when the computer displays the internal contents of memory cells or registers. The computer always stores the values *internally* in binary. It *displays* them in octal (or hexadecimal) only to make it more convenient for you.

You might be wondering why we don't simply print out internal binary values in decimal as we have always done in high-level programming languages. There are two reasons. First, the conversion from binary to decimal (expression 2.1) is more difficult and time-consuming than either binary-to-octal or binary-to-hexadecimal conversion. The former involves multiplication, exponentiation, and addition; the latter requires a simple translation using the table in Figure 2-3b or 2-3c.

FIGURE 2-3c   Binary-Haxadecimal Conversion Table.

Binary	Hexadecimal
0000	0
0001	1
0010	2
0011	3
0100	4
0101	5
0110	6
0111	7
1000	8
1001	9
1010	A
1011	B
1100	C
1101	D
1110	E
1111	F

There is a more important reason, however. In an applications programming environment, we usually care only about the final answers and getting them in the most convenient format possible. The internal processes involved in producing the answers are less important. When studying computer organization, we care more about what is happening inside the computer and the internal processes that are occurring. We want the output to be in a format that is most convenient for conveying this information. We want a representation that is closely related to the internal structure of the computer. Of course, we could use binary directly, but it is too long and cumbersome. That is why we choose to use octal or hexadecimal shorthand notation. It is an ideal compromise; it is compact and easy to use, but at the same time it is closely related to the actual binary digits being stored internally.

As an example, assume that we have a computer that stores six binary digits per memory cell, numbered left to right 0–5. We have reason to believe that bit number 3 in memory cell 500 is causing trouble or may be defective, and we want to know what is stored in that bit position right now.

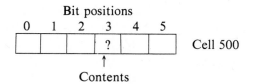

If we ask the system to "dump" (i.e., display) the contents of memory cell 500, and it prints out the decimal value "35," this doesn't tell us anything directly about the value of bit 3. To determine that value, we have to convert the number 35 to binary using the division-by-radix technique described in the previous section. This would be time-consuming and cumbersome, especially if we had to do it hundreds or thousands of times a day. If, instead, the computer printed out the octal value "43," we could easily and immediately convert it to 100011 binary, and it would now be obvious that the current value of bit number 3 is "0."

Decimal can be thought of as an *applications-oriented notation,* while octal and hexadecimal are *systems-oriented notations.* Octal and hexadecimal are used whenever we need to study the internal contents of a computer system. Octal and hexadecimal would be appropriate notations for the following situations.

Dumps: Printed listings of the contents of all, or some portion of memory.

Machine-Language Listings: Listings of machine-language code produced by a compiler or assembler while translating high-level programs written by the user.

Debugging Tools: Tools used to debug programs "on-line," that is, while they are being executed.

Operator Console Display: Displays to the operator what is happening inside the computer.

Although we will be using octal throughout the remainder of the text, a number of exercises at the end of the chapter use hexadecimal. Hex is a very popular scheme used on a number of computers, and you should become familiar with that notation also.

2.3
Summary

We have now developed a way to internally represent the unsigned natural numbers, 0, 1, 2, . . . If we use m digits to store our binary numbers, we can represent values in the range:

$$\underbrace{000 \ldots 0}_{m \text{ digits}} \quad \text{to} \quad \underbrace{111 \ldots 1}_{m \text{ digits}}$$

or

$$0 \leq I \leq 2^m - 1$$

This data type is called *unsigned binary,* and it is the first of the four major internal data types that we present in Part I. All computers have the ability to directly process (e.g., store, retrieve, compare, add) information represented in unsigned binary notation.

How can we extend this unsigned representation to include both positive and negative values, and thus be able to store signed integers? We answer this important question in the next chapter.

Exercises for Chapter 2

1. Convert the following values into decimal.
   a. 1332 (base 4)
   b. 555 (base 7)
   c. 1001110 (base 2)
   d. 1776 (base 8)
   e. ABC (base 16)
   f. ABC (base 13)

2. Convert the following decimal values into the indicated base.
   a. 1,000 into base 8
   b. 913 into base 16
   c. 1,234 into base 7
   d. 199 into base 2
   e. 163 into base 5
   f. 10,000 into base 13

3. Convert the following values into the indicated base.
   a. 400 (base 6) into base 8
   b. A92 (base 16) into base 12
   c. 222 (base 3) into base 4

4. On the average, how much longer (i.e., how many more digits) is an octal value than a decimal value?

5. Could base 32 be used as a shorthand notation for binary numbers? What would be the advantages? The disadvantages? How much shorter would the base-32 number be?

6. Assuming that you designed and built a computer that stored values internally in base 3 (a *ternary* computer), what base would you most likely use as a shorthand representation for base-3 numbers? Make a conversion table for converting ternary digits to this shorthand representation.

7. Convert the following octal numbers to binary.
   a. 17670
   b. 4005
   c. 1010
   d. 212077

8. Convert the following binary numbers to both octal and hexadecimal.
   a. 111011
   b. 10000000
   c. 1010101110100
   d. 1111111111
   e. 110101111110

9. Convert the following hexadecimal numbers to binary.
   a. 1A2B
   b. 9C
   c. 77760
   d. FEED

10. Your computer stores numbers internally using twenty binary digits. The bit positions are numbered left to right beginning with 0. The rightmost bit is bit 19. What is the internal value of bit position 7 if the decimal contents of the cell is 94,275? What is the internal value of bit postion 9 if the hexadecimal contents of the cell is 2E6A5? How easy were these two operations? What does this tell you about the major use of hexadecimal (and octal)?

11. Could the division-by-radix technique be used for conversion of Roman numerals into binary? Explain why or why not.

12. Write a high-level language procedure called "convert" that converts a decimal number D into base N, where both D and N are parameters to the procedure. The procedure should write out the new value and return. For example, if D = 17 and N = 2, then the call:

$$\text{convert}(D,N)$$

should produce the output 10001 which is the base 2 representation of the decimal quantity 17.

13. Even though octal and hexadecimal are considered "system-oriented" representations, many high-level languages allow you to print answers in either or both of these formats. Find out whether the language you are most familiar with has this feature, and if it does, generate the conversion tables shown in Figures 2-3b and 2-3c.

CHAPTER 3

SIGNED INTEGER REPRESENTATIONS

3.1
Introduction

With m binary digits, we can represent the 2^m unique patterns, from $000 \ldots 0$ to $111 \ldots 1$. In Chapter 2 we used these 2^m patterns to store the natural numbers 0, 1, $\ldots, 2^m - 1$. When we try to represent signed quantities in the same m digits, we still have only 2^m patterns to work with. Unless we increase the number of digits available for our representation (i.e., make m larger), the representation of signed numbers will involve deciding how to divide up these 2^m available patterns into positive and negative portions. There are three widely used techniques for doing this: sign/magnitude, complementation, and binary coded decimal.

3.2
Sign/Magnitude Notation

Sign/magnitude notation is the simplest and most obvious encoding scheme for representing positive and negative numbers. It is identical to the way signed quantities are represented in algebra. We assign the high-order (leftmost) bit to be the sign bit. By convention, we let 0 be the positive sign $(+)$, while 1 represents the negative sign $(-)$. The remaining $(m - 1)$ bits represent the magnitude of the number in the unsigned binary notation described in Chapter 2.

EXAMPLE

Assume $m = 4$.

Binary	Value	Binary	Value
0000	0		
0001	+1	1001	−1
0010	+2	1010	−2
.	.	.	.
.	.	.	.
.	.	.	.
0111	+7	1111	−7

In general, for a given m, the range of values that can be represented using sign/magnitude notation is:

$$(3.1) \qquad -(2^{m-1} - 1) \le I \le +(2^{m-1} - 1)$$

The major advantage of sign/magnitude notation is *familiarity*. Numbers in this notation are easy to interpret because they mimic the way we write signed numbers in everyday life. The first digit is the sign, and the next $(m - 1)$ digits are an unsigned binary quantity of the type described in Chapter 2. However, in spite of its familiarity, this technique is not widely used because it suffers from one major problem, which was not apparent in the previous example. We intentionally omitted one particular bit pattern: namely, 1000. According to the interpretation of sign/magnitude notation, this pattern represents the value "negative zero." Sign/magnitude notation suffers from the problem of having two distinct patterns for a single quantity—zero.

$$000 \ldots 0 = +0 \qquad 1000 \ldots 0 = -0$$

The problem occurs when we ask the following question: "Are $000 \ldots 0$ and $1000 \ldots 0$ equal?" Numerically, the answer is yes, since 0 is not a signed quantity and $+0 = -0$. However, computers usually test two values for equality by comparing each bit positition of the two numbers. If all bit positions are identical, the two values are said to be equal. If we build our computer to work this way, it will say that $+0 \ne -0$.

The existence of the pattern -0 causes the computer designer a good deal of irritation, because this one special case requires special circuitry to be sure that it is handled correctly. This can be done, and a number of computers do use the sign/magnitude method. However, in the next section we look at another encoding scheme that eliminates the problem of "negative zero."

3.3
Radix Complementation (Twos Complement)

Radix complementation is a technique used for representing signed quantities. (Note: The method is usually referred to by replacing the word "radix" with the number of the base in which you are working. In decimal it is called *tens complement;* in binary it is called *twos complement.*) The technique is based on the ideas of *modular arithmetic.*

In modular arithmetic there is a value called the *modulus* (M) which, when added to or subtracted from a number, does not change its value. That is, if A and B differ only by a multiple of M, we would say that:

$$A = B \,(\text{mod } M)$$

A simple way to understand modular arithmetic is to think about the standard 5-digit odometer on an automobile. Regardless of its current reading, if you drove exactly 100,000 more miles, or any multiple of 100,000, the odometer reading would be exactly the same. In this case $M = 100,000$.

In a computer that stores m binary digits per memory cell, the modulus would be $M = 2^m$. That is:

$$M = \underbrace{1000 \ldots 0}_{m \text{ zeros}}$$

This value is one unit larger than the largest quantity that can be stored in a single m-bit memory location, which is:

(3.2)
$$\underbrace{111 \ldots 1}_{m \text{ ones}} = 2^m - 1 = M - 1$$

The technique of twos-complement representation is based on the following principle: Positive numbers are represented by counting *up* from 0 the amount of the number, and negative numbers are represented by counting *down* from the modulus M the amount of the number. That is, $+5$ is represented by counting up five units from 0, and -4 is represented by counting down four units from the modulus, or, in other words, by computing the value $M - 4$.

The twos-complement representation can be defined symbolically:

(3.3)
$$+X = X$$

(3.4)
$$-X = M - X$$

or pictorially, as shown in Figure 3-1 on the next page.

EXAMPLES

Assume $m = 4$.

(a)   What is $+6$ in twos-complement representation?
      $+6$ would be represented by simply counting up six units from 0, or

0110

FIGURE 3-1   Pictorial Representation of Twos-
Complement Values.

0	Positive values		Negative values	M − 1
Smaller	Larger	Larger		Smaller
+	+	−		−
numbers	numbers	numbers		numbers

As you can see, in twos complement, positive numbers have the same representation they would have in unsigned binary.

(b)   What is −7 in twos-complement representation?
To represent a negative number, we count down from the modulus. $M = 2^m = 2^4 = 16$
Therefore, $-7 = 16 - 7 = 9 = 1001$

However, there is ambiguity in both examples a and b. In Example a, the number 0110, which we said was +6, could also be interpreted as −10, since 16 −10 = 6 = 0110. Likewise, in example b, the number 1001, which we said was −7, could also be interpreted as +9. Referring to Figure 3-1 or expressions 3.3 and 3.4, we see that every binary number has two possible interpretations, depending on whether you assume it was counted up from 0 or down from *M*.

To resolve that ambiguity, we will adopt the following rule: If a number begins with a 0, it is given a positive interpretation. It is assumed to be a positive quantity whose magnitude is simply the unsigned binary value of the number. If a number, *X*, begins with a 1, it is given a negative interpretation. It is assumed to be a negative number whose magnitude is given by the value of the expression $M - X$.

With this rule, we can now unambiguously interpet any twos-complement value. Figure 3-2 shows both the twos-complement and the sign/magnitude representation for all integers that can be represented in four binary digits.

The operation of *complementing* a number is equivalent to taking the negative of a value. To find the complement of any number, *X*, we can use expression 3.4. However, this extremely cumbersome technique, which we applied in example b, involves subtraction and borrowing. There is a much easier way if we just make a small change in the formula $M - X$. If we simply add 1 and subtract 1, we can rewrite that expression in the following way:

(3.5) $-X = (M - 1) - X + 1$

FIGURE 3-2   Table of Twos-Complement and Sign/
Magnitude Values.

Decimal	Twos Complement	Sign/Magnitude	(m = 4)
+0	0000	0000	
+1	0001	0001	
+2	0010	0010	
+3	0011	0011	
+4	0100	0100	
+5	0101	0101	
+6	0110	0110	
+7	0111	0111	
−0	does not exist	1000	
−1	1111	1001	
−2	1110	1010	
−3	1101	1011	
−4	1100	1100	
−5	1011	1101	
−6	1010	1110	
−7	1001	1111	
−8	1000	cannot represent in 4 digits	

The quantity $(M - 1)$ is a string of exactly m 1 bits, as we demonstrated in expression 3.2. Therefore, subtraction of a number, X, from $(M - 1)$ will be trivial because there are no borrows. Moreover, look what happens when we subtract a binary digit from a 1:

$$\frac{\begin{array}{r}1\\-0\end{array}}{1}) \qquad \frac{\begin{array}{r}1\\-1\end{array}}{0})$$

Subtracting a 0 produces a 1, and subtracting a 1 produces a 0. Thus the quantity $(M - 1) - X$ can be evaluated without subtraction by simply changing all 0s to 1s and all 1s to 0s. Then, referring back to expression 3.5, we see that we must add a 1 to get the correct result. To summarize, to negate a twos-complement value, do the following:

1. Change all 0s to 1s, and all 1s to 0s.
2. Add 1 to the result.

You will obtain the negative equivalent of the quantity you started with.

EXAMPLES

Assume $m = 5$.

(a) What is -5_{10} in twos complement?

$$+5 = 00101 \qquad \text{Now change all 0s and 1s}$$
$$= 11010 \qquad \text{and add } +1.$$
$$= \underline{11011}$$
$$= 11011_2 \qquad \text{This is } -5 \text{ in twos complement.}$$

(b) What is the decimal value of the twos-complement binary value 11100_2?

   The quantity must be interpreted as a negative number because it begins with a 1. To determine its magnitude, take the complement using the two-step process just described.

$$11100 \implies 00011 \implies 00100.$$

The complement is a $+4$, so the original value is a -4. (You can check this by computing $M - 4$).

(c) If the computer printed out that the contents of a 5-bit memory location was 27_8, what would that value be in decimal, assuming it is a twos-complement value?

$$27_8 = 10111_2 \qquad \text{This is a negative number.}$$
$$10111 \to 01000 \to 01001$$

The complement is $+9$, so $27_8 = -9_{10}$ in twos complement.

Everything we have described so far applies to *all* bases, not just binary. For example, we could use tens complement to represent positive and negative decimal quantities. If we had two digits available to store our signed decimal numbers (i.e., $m = 2$), then we could store the one hundred unique patterns 00–99, and the modulus M would be 100. Positive numbers would be counted up from 0, as before, while negative values would be counted down from 100.

EXAMPLES

Tens complement, $m = 2$.

(a) $+8 = 8$
(b) $-23 = 100 - 23$
   $\qquad = 77$

However, just as with binary, there is an ambiguity that must be cleared up. Every number has two possible interpretations, depending on whether you assume that it was counted up from 0, or down from $M = 100$. For example, the quantity 8 in example (a) could represent either a $+8$ as shown, or a -92 ($100 - 92 = 8$).

   To resolve this ambiguity, we must adopt a convention to determine whether we use the positive or negative interpretation. One possible convention is to say that numbers beginning with 0, 1, 2, 3, or 4 are to be given a positive interpretation, and numbers beginning with 5, 6, 7, 8, or 9 are to be given a negative interpretation. This would give us forty-nine positive and fifty negative values:

Positive numbers: 01, 02, . . . , 49 (from $+1$ to $+49$)
Negative numbers: 99, 98, . . . , 50 (from -1 to -50)

There are a number of exercises at the end of the chapter that examine in more detail radix complementation in other bases.

3.4
Arithmetic on Twos-Complement Values

Learning the rules of binary arithmetic is much easier than learning the rules of decimal arithmetic. Instead of having to memorize 10×10 addition and subtraction tables, you only need to learn a 2×2 table. Figure 3-3 shows the addition table for binary. To add two binary numbers, you simply apply the addition table to each column, compute the sum, and determine whether there is a carry to the next column. This is exactly what the functional unit called an *adder* does: it takes in two binary numbers, a and b, and adds them bit by bit according to the addition rules in Figure 3-3.

EXAMPLES

Assume $m = 5$.

(a)   00101 $(+5)$
     $+$ 00110 $(+6)$
          01011 $(+11)$

(b)   00111 $(+7)$
     $+$ 11110 (-2)
     ①$|$ 00101 $(+5)$
      Discard

FIGURE 3-3   Binary Addition Table.

+	0	1
0	0	1
1	1	0*

* = includes a carry to the next column

In the second example, we discarded the 1 bit that was carried into the column beyond the last digit. After discarding it, we ended up with the correct answer (00101). Why can we do that? How can we throw away a digit and end up with the correct result?

The explanation is that the 1 in the column to the left of the high-order digit is simply the value 2^m, or M, the modulus. Remember that adding or subtracting the modulus will not change the value of a number. Discarding that 1 bit is exactly the same as subtracting the modulus, and it is a perfectly legal operation. The bit that is carried into the position just beyond the most significant digit is called the *carry bit*. Even though the carry bit does not affect the result and can be discarded, there are times when it is important to know whether there was a carry. Therefore, instead of actually discarding the bit, we usually store it in a special location called the *carry register*. The specific uses for this register and for the carry bit itself are discussed later.

(c)
$$\begin{array}{r} 11011 \ (-5) \\ +\ \underline{11100 \ (-4)} \\ \textcircled{1}|\ \ 10111 \ (-9) \end{array}$$
Carry register

(d)   What is the twos complement of 0?
$$\begin{array}{r} 00000 \Rightarrow\ \ \ \ 11111 \\ +\ \underline{\ \ \ \ 1} \\ \textcircled{1}|\ \ 00000 \end{array}$$
Carry register

As you can see, the complement of 0 is still 0. There is no -0 in twos-complement representation. The pattern 100 ... 0, which in sign/magnitude was the quantity -0, now represents the largest negative number (in absolute value) that can be stored in our system.

The range of values that can be represented in twos-complement notation is:

(3.6) $-(2^{m-1}) \le I \le +(2^{m-1} - 1)$

As the above formula shows, there is one more negative value than there are positive values.

(e)
$$\begin{array}{r} 00101(+5) \\ +\ \underline{01110(+14)} \\ 10011(-13) \ \ \ \ ???\end{array}$$

Something strange happened in example e. We added two positive quantities and produced a result that has a negative interpretation in twos-complement representation. This happened because we tried to represent a value that was too large to be represented on this computer. Referring to expression 3.6 and letting $m = 5$, we see that the range of values that can be correctly represented is -16 to $+15$. In this example, we tried to generate a result of $+19$, which is too large. That was the cause of the error.

This is called an *overflow condition*. We must be warned that this condition has occurred so that we do not improperly try to use the result that is produced (10011 in example e). All computers have an *overflow register* or an *overflow switch* that is turned ON if the previous arithmetic operation resulted in an overflow condition. Fortunately, it is quite easy to detect this condition: If you add two positive numbers and produce a negative result, or if you add two negative numbers and generate a positive result, you have an overflow. (You cannot generate an overflow when adding a positive and a negative quantity.) For an alternative definition of overflow, see Exercise 18 at the end of the chapter.

Figure 3-4 summarizes our discussion of twos-complement addition and shows a functional diagram of its operation.

To perform twos-complement subtraction, we could follow the same line of reasoning that we developed for addition. We could build a 2×2 subtraction table analogous to Figure 3-3, and then build a subtractor unit to implement it, complete with borrow and overflow registers. However, computer designers don't like to add new pieces of hardware to a computer if they can get by with what they already have, because adding features increases the cost of building and maintaining the computer. In this case, it is possible to avoid this expense by defining subtraction in terms of existing operations. Subtraction of two twos-complement integer values can be expressed completely in terms of addition and complementation. Instead of performing the following subtraction:

$$D = Y - X$$

we can compute instead:

$$D = -X + Y$$

FIGURE 3-4   Functional Organization of Twos-Complement Addition.

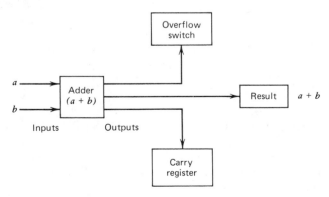

We negate the subtrahend (this does not involve subtraction as we mentioned earlier, but only changing 0s and 1s and then adding 1), and then add in the minuend. The result will be the desired difference.

EXAMPLES

Assume $m = 4$.

(a)   0010 $(+2)$
       $-$0001 $(+1)$

         0010
       $+$1111   Complement the subtrahend and add.
    (1)| 0001   Result is a $+1$
    ↳Carry register

(b)   0010 $(+2)$
       $-$0011 $(+3)$

         0010
       $+$1101   Complement of $+3$.
         1111   Result is a -1.

(c)   1110 (-2)
       $-$1011 (-5)

         1110
       $+$0101   Complement of -5.
    (1)| 0011   Result is $+3$.
    ↳Carry register

Building a device to do twos-complement subtraction involves using many of the same devices that were used for addition. Note the similarity between Figure 3-5, which shows the functional organization of a subtraction unit, and Figure 3-4. The PDP-11 and VAX-11 computers use twos-complement representation for signed integer quantities. This is the signed encoding scheme that we use throughout the remainder of this text.

3.5
Implementation of a Twos-Complement Adder

(Note: This section describes the implementation of the adder box shown in Figures 3-4 and 3-5. It is optional, and you may skip to Section 3.6 without a loss of continuity.)

FIGURE 3-5   Functional Organization of Twos-
Complement Subtraction.

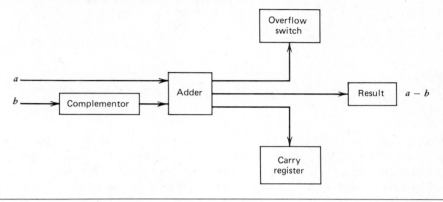

Figures 3-4 and 3-5 are typical diagrams at the level of abstraction that we have
called functional organization (see Figure 1-2). They display the major functional
components of a computer without indicating how they are implemented internally.
It is at this level that we want to study computers here. Most of the time we will not
want to get involved with the lower level details of electrical circuitry.

However, just for a moment, let's "drop down" one level and attempt to construct
the box labeled "Adder" in Figures 3-4 and 3-5, simply to see what questions and
issues exist at the abstraction level below our own level of study. We will also try to
eliminate some of the mystery surrounding those "black boxes" shown in Figures 3-
4 and 3-5.

Initially, we are not going to build a complete adder, but only a one-bit adder that
adds two binary digits and produces the sum bit and carry bit described in Figure 3-
3. This table is shown in Figure 3-6 on the following page.

Now, if we refresh our knowledge of boolean logic and remember the definition of
the logical operations and, or, and not, we see that expressions for the columns
labeled Sum and Carry in Figure 3-6 can be described in terms of these logical operators ($\cdot$ = and, + = or, $\tilde{}$ = not).

(3.7) $sum = (a \cdot \tilde{b}) + (\tilde{a} \cdot b)$

(3.8) $carry = a \cdot b$

(If you are not convinced that these are indeed correct formulas, work out the values
of sum and carry for each of the four possible cases to verify that they produce the

FIGURE 3-6 Detailed Binary Addition Table.

a	b	Sum	Carry
0	0	0	0
0	1	1	0
1	0	1	0
1	1	0	1

correct results.) Now, let's assume that we are able to construct three types of electrical circuit, called *gates,* that correspond directly to the definition of the three logical operators and, or, and not. For example, the "and circuit" or "and gate" would have two input leads and one output lead. Each lead can be in one of two states corresponding to the two logical values TRUE and FALSE. (These states could correspond to either current levels or voltage levels; it doesn't matter for this discussion.) The value coming out on the output lead would correspond to the TRUE state if and only if the values coming in on *both* input leads corresponded to the TRUE state. Otherwise, the value appearing on the output lead would correspond to the FALSE state. Thus, the and gate behaves electrically in exactly the same way as the and operator does logically. Similar conditions hold for the "or gate" and the "not gate."

Pictorially, we would represent these gates as shown in Figure 3-7.

If we assume that these three types of electrical gate actually exist (and they do), then we can use them to construct the one-bit adder described by expressions 3.7 and 3.8. This device is shown in Figure 3-8.

The circuit in Figure 3-8 does not implement the full adder operation displayed in Figure 3-4 or 3-5, because it adds only one bit and does not include the effect of the carry bit that propagated from the previous column. The simple circuit in Figure 3-8 would be appropriate only for adding the two rightmost low-order bits of the number for which there is no carry.

FIGURE 3-7 Pictorial Representation of Electrical Gates.

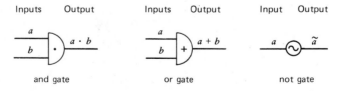

| Inputs | Output | | Inputs | Output | | Input | Output |

and gate · · · or gate · · · not gate

FIGURE 3-8   Logic Design Description of a One-Bit
Adder.

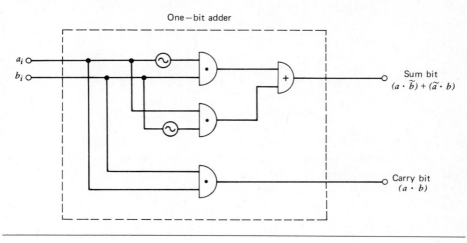

One—bit adder

a_i

b_i

Sum bit
$(a \cdot \tilde{b}) + (\tilde{a} \cdot b)$

Carry bit
$(a \cdot b)$

To describe the addition of the remaining bits of the two operands, we need to use
a table that includes the effect of the carry bit. This table is shown in Figure 3-9.

Now we can perform the same operations as before. We must describe the sum
bit and new carry bit columns in terms of logical expressions of the three inputs a_i,
b_i, and the previous carry bit. We could then construct a circuit out of our and, or,
and not gates to realize those two expressions. (Optional Exercise 19 at the end of
this chapter asks you to complete this circuit synthesis.)

FIGURE 3-9   Binary Addition with a Carry Bit.

a_i	b_i	Carry from Previous Position	Sum Bit	New Carry Bit
0	0	0	0	0
0	0	1	1	0
0	1	0	1	0
0	1	1	0	1
1	0	0	1	0
1	0	1	0	1
1	1	0	0	1
1	1	1	1	1

When we complete this operation, we will have a circuit, let's call it C, that properly adds one binary digit to another, including the effect of any previous carry, to give the correct sum and new carry bit:

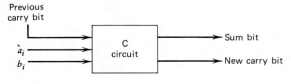

One–bit adder with carry

Now, to add two binary numbers, each containing m digits, we simply "daisy chain" m of these C circuits together. For example, if we want to add the numbers a and b, each with m bits, to get an m-bit result called s, as in:

$$
\begin{array}{r}
a_m \ldots a_1 \\
+\ b_m \ldots b_1 \\
\hline
s_m \ldots s_1
\end{array}
$$

it would be done as shown in Figure 3-10, where each individual C circuit is the circuit that realizes the table described in Figure 3-9.

This brief discussion of an extremely important and quite complex subject has, of necessity, omitted a great number of key details (e.g., the adder circuit in Figure 3-10 does not detect overflow conditions. This is done in optional exercise 20). It simply introduces the types of operation that characterize the next level of abstraction in the study of computers. Other courses in computer science and electrical engineering address the issue of logic design in much greater detail.

FIGURE 3-10 The Internal Structure of a Full Adder.

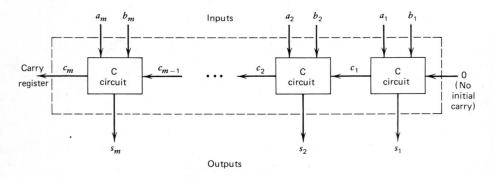

3.6
Diminished Radix Complementation (Ones Complement)

There is a minor variation of the radix complementation technique called *diminished radix complementation.* Again, the term is a generic name; in practice we usually replace the words "diminished radix" with the integer one less than the base in which we are working. In decimal, we would call this technique *nines complement;* in binary, it is called *ones complement.* It is not a new technique at all, but a slight variation of twos complement, designed to make the computer a little easier to construct.

The difference between twos complement and ones complement lies in how the complement of a value is formed. Expression 3.5 shows the formula for the twos complement of a value. In ones complement, we delay adding in the $+1$ when forming the complement. Thus the definition of the ones complement of a negative integer value X is:

(3.9)
$$-X = (M - 1) - X$$

(Note: The representation of positive quantities is the same in both ones and twos complement.)

As we discussed earlier, the operations in expression 3.9 can be carried out by simply changing all 1s to 0s and all 0s to 1s. This makes complementation extremely easy with this method.

The range of values that can be represented in m digits, and ones-complement representation is:

(3.10)
$$-(2^{m-1} - 1) \leq I \leq +(2^{m-1} - 1)$$

EXAMPLES

Assume $m = 6$.

(a)   What is the ones-complement representation of -20_{10}?

$$+20_{10} \text{ would be } 010100$$

The ones complement would be 101011 (change all 1s to 0s and 0s to 1s)

$$-20_{10} = 101011_2$$

(b)   What is the ones complement of 0000111_2?

$$= 1111000_2, \text{ which is, by the way, } -7.$$

The advantage of using ones complement is simply the ease of forming the complement of a number. You don't have to add on a $+1$; instead you simply "flip" the 0s and 1s. The $+1$ is added back in later when you perform arithmetic operations on ones-complement values, and this is where the "games" that computer designers play come in.

At the end of an arithmetic operation on a negative value, we need to add the $+1$ that we didn't add in when we formed the complement. But in Section 3.4 we showed how arithmetic operations using complementation could generate an extra 1 bit, called the carry bit, which is simply discarded or put in the carry register. It is wasteful during addition or subtraction to throw away a 1 (the carry bit) and then add in a 1 (the 1 not added when forming the complement). So, in ones complement, we combine these steps by simply adding the carry bit back into the result to get the correct answer. This is sometimes referred to as an *end-around carry*.

EXAMPLES

Assume ones complement, $m = 5$.

(a)
```
      00111   (+7)
  -   00011   (+3)

      00111
  +   11100   Complement the subtrahend and add.
 ① |  00011
    |    → 1  Add in the carry bit.
      00100   (+4)
```

(b)
```
      10101   (−10)
  +   11100   (−3)
 ① |  10001
    |    → 1  Add in the carry bit.
      10010   (−13)
```

(c)
```
      10000   (−15)
  +   10000   (−15)
 ① |  00000
    |    → 1  Add in the carry bit.
      00001   (+1) ???
```

In this example, we have an overflow condition. We added two negative numbers and got a positive result. Overflow can occur in ones-complement representation just as it can with any of the other techniques we have described so far.

(d)   00111   (+7)
       − 01011   (+11)

         00111
       + 10100   Complement the subtrahend and add.
         11011

When performing ones-complement subtraction, if there is no carry bit, the result is negative and it is the correct ones-complement representation of the result.

$$11011 \Rightarrow 00100 = 4_{10}$$

So the result is −4.

(e)   What is the complement of 000 . . . 0?
      The ones complement of +0 = 000 . . . 0 is 1111 . . . 1. We are again back to the problem of −0. This is the one major drawback to the use of ones-complement representation.

Like sign/magnitude, ones-complement representation requires special circuitry to look for and correct the problems associated with −0. For this reason, radix complementation (twos complement) is a much more popular technique than ones complement, although the latter is occasionally used on some systems (e.g., the Control Data Cyber series of computers).

3.7
Binary Coded Decimal (BCD)

The last representational method we describe is the least used and can almost be thought of as a special technique for use in one specific situation. In certain applications, there are massive amounts of input and output data, but very little numeric processing is done on the data, and the total number of arithmetic operations is small. The best example of this is found in such business data-processing applications as payroll or inventory. A user might have a big inventory, but the extent of the numeric processing might be simply adding or subtracting a few numbers. In this special case, the designer may not want to use time converting large quantities of input data from decimal to twos complement and then back to decimal. For this situation, there is an alternative representation called *binary coded decimal,* usually abbreviated BCD.

In BCD, instead of converting the entire number into binary, we convert it one digit at a time. We use four binary digits to represent each decimal digit, and convert each decimal digit using the decimal-to-BCD conversion table shown in Figure 3-11. To translate a number from decimal to BCD, we simply translate one digit at a time using the values in Figure 3-11.

FIGURE 3-11   Decimal-to-BCD Conversion Table.

Decimal Digit	BCD Code
0	0000
1	0001
2	0010
3	0011
4	0100
5	0101
6	0110
7	0111
8	1000
9	1001

EXAMPLES

(a)   What is $1{,}234_{10}$ in BCD?

$$1{,}234 = \underbrace{0001}_{1}\underbrace{0010}_{2}\underbrace{0011}_{3}\underbrace{0100}_{4}$$

The comma is not translated.

(b)   What is -567_{10} in BCD?

A negative sign can be implemented in BCD in a number of ways. For example, the currently unassigned bit patterns 1010 can be used for a "+" and 1011 for a "−". If we use this technique, then:

$$-567_{10} = \underbrace{1011}_{-}\underbrace{0101}_{5}\underbrace{0110}_{6}\underbrace{0111}_{7}$$

The major advantage of using BCD is the ease and speed with which decimal numbers can be converted into BCD representation. The disadvantage is that BCD arithmetic usually takes longer than arithmetic on either sign/magnitude or ones- or twos-complement values. In BCD you add the numbers, one decimal digit at a time, and generate a decimal carry (exactly the way you learned decimal arithmetic as a child). The BCD addition tables are not 2×2 (like Figure 3-3) but 10×10.

EXAMPLE

```
(0001)   (0001)          ← carry
          0110  0011    (+63)
        +0100  1001    (+49)
 0001     0001  0010    (+112)
  ‿        ‿     ‿
   1        1     2
```

However, if very little arithmetic is being done, then slower performance is a less serious drawback, and BCD is a possible choice for an integer representation. Some computers that are used extensively in commercial areas provide BCD representation and BCD arithmetic as an option that can be purchased at extra cost.

EXAMPLES

Assume $m = 12$ for the first three examples.
What is the value of -250_{10} in sign/magnitude, twos complement, ones complement, and BCD?

(a)   Sign/magnitude: 100011111010

   Sign   Magnitude

(b)   Twos complement: $+250$ = 000011111010
   Complement = 111100000101
   Add 1   = 111100000110

(c)   Ones complement: $+250$ = 000011111010
   Complement = 111100000101

(d)   BCD: 1011001001010000   Note: We need sixteen bits for
                                 this representation.

   $-$ 2   5   0

3.8
Summary

The second basic data type that exists on all computer systems is called signed integers. All computer systems have machine-language instructions to manipulate (store, retrieve, add, subtract, compare, etc.) values in one or more of the following notational schemes: sign/magnitude, twos complement, ones complement, or BCD. Each technique has its own distinct advantages and disadvantages, and it is up to the computer designer to select the representation technique that best fits the needs of the user.

In special cases, a computer system may provide more than one integer representation technique. For example, the PDP-11/44 uses twos-complement integer arithmetic as its "normal mode"; however, you can purchase (at extra cost) the Commercial Instruction Set (CIS), an option that provides BCD representation and twenty-seven new machine-language instructions for doing BCD arithmetic and BCD-decimal conversion.

In addition to supporting more than one integer representation, many computers also support integers of differing *size*. That is, there may be multiple values of m, the number of bits used in the representation of integer values. For example, a computer may have a *short-integer* representation using $m = 16$, which would allow values up to $2^{15} = 32767$. For work with larger numbers, the system may support a *long-integer* (or *extended-precision integer*) with $m = 32$. This would allow integer values up to about $2^{31} \approx 10,000,000,000$. The disadvantage of these enlarged ranges is the increased time needed to perform arithmetic operations on the larger values.

Exercises for Chapter 3

1. Show how to represent the following decimal values in sign/magnitude notation. Assume $m = 8$.
    a. $+66$
    b. -7
    c. -101
    d. -201

2. Show how to represent the following decimal values in twos-complement representation. Assume $m = 10$.
    a. -201
    b. $+199$
    c. -15
    d. $+700$

3. Give the decimal value of the following binary quantities assuming first that they are in sign/magnitude notation and then in twos-complement notation. Assume $m = 6$.
    a. 100001
    b. 111100
    c. 011111
    d. 100000
    e. 111111
    f. 000000

4. Is the following statement true or false? Explain why.

    Any representational system for integers that uses binary numbering for storage and has only a single 0 cannot have an equal number of positive and negative values.

5. The rule given in this chapter for interpreting a twos-complement value (if it starts with a 0 it is $+$; if it starts with a 1 it is $-$) produces approximately equal numbers of positive and negative quantities. Is that equal division necessary? Can you think of a different rule for interpreting twos-complement values that produces a highly uneven number of positive and negative values?

6. If $m = 12$, what is the largest (in absolute value) positive and negative quantity that can be represented in sign/magnitude notation and twos complement?

7.   Using *tens-complement* representation for decimal quantities, ($m = 3$), show the representation of the following decimal values.
   a.   5
   b. -1
   c. -123
   d.   99

   What assumptions did you have to make to answer this question?

8.   Perform the following binary additions in twos complement. For each one, state whether there is a carry, an overflow, or both. Convert both operands and the result back to decimal as a check. Asusme $m = 5$.

   a.   00110
      +01110

   b.   10111
      +11110

   c.   00001
      +01010

   d.   10100
      +01111

   e.   10000
      +10000

   f.   11111
      +11111

9.   Perform the following binary subtractions in twos complement. Do the subtraction using the "complement-and-add" algorithm described in Section 3.4. For each one, state whether there is a carry, an overflow, or both. Convert both operands and the result back to decimal as a check. Assume $m = 5$.

   a.   00111
      $-$00101

   b.   00101
      $-$00111

   c.   10011
      $-$01011

   d.   00001
      $-$11111

   e.   10000
      $-$11111

   f.   11110
      $-$11111

10.   Show the 2×2 binary multiplication table similar to the 2×2 addition table in Figure 3-3. Use that table to perform the following multiplication operation. Assume twos complement values and $m = 6$.

$$11011$$
$$\times\ \underline{1001}$$

Check your answer by converting the operands and the result back to decimal.

11.   Show how to represent the following decimal values in ones-complement notation. Assume $m = 6$.
    a. -22
    b. $+23$
    c. -32

12.   What is the decimal value of the following binary quantities, assuming they are
in ones-complement notation. Assume $m = 4$.
    a.   1110
    b.   1000
    c.   0111
    d.   1111

13.   Perform the following ones-complement binary additions. Use the "end-around
carry" method described in Section 3.4
    a.   00111   c.   10101
        $+01100$ $+11100$

    b.   01100   d.   11001
        $+10001$ $+10111$

14.   Does the BCD representation technique have the value -0? If so, how is it
represented?

15.   If $m = 8$, what are the largest (in absolute value) positive and negative numbers that can be represented in sign/magnitude, twos complement, ones complement,
and BCD?

16.   Show the representation of -200_{10} in all four representational schemes: sign/
magnitude, twos complement, ones complement, and BCD. Assume $m = 10$.

17.   Take the complement of the twos-complement binary value 10000000. Explain
what happened.

18.   Is the following a valid alternative definition of *overflow* in twos-complement
arithmetic?

    If the exclusive-OR of the carry bits into and out of the leftmost column
    is a 1, then there is an overflow condition. Otherwise, there is not.

19.   *(Optional)* Develop logical expressions for the sum and new carry bit columns
in Figure 3-9. Then construct the C circuit in Figure 3-10 from and, or, and not
gates. Try to do it with the smallest possible number of gates, since the expense of a
circuit is directly proportional to the number of gates in the circuit.

20.   (*Optional*) Modify circuit C (let's call it C*) so that it correctly detects overflow. That is, circuit C* will have three inputs: a_i, b_i, and the previous carry bit. It will have three outputs: The new sum bit, the new carry bit, and an overflow indicator which is 0 if there is no overflow and 1 if there is an overflow. Now the full adder of Figure 3–10 would be constructed by chaining together $(m - 1)$ C circuits and one C* circuit in the leftmost bit position.

CHAPTER 4

CHARACTER DATA TYPE

4.1
Introduction

It may seem a bit strange to describe the *character data type* at this point in our discussion of the representation of information, before such other well-known data types as floating point or boolean, which you may consider "more important." However, characters (also called *bytes*) and their associated character-manipulation operations are the third primitive data type that exists on every computer system (along with unsigned binary and signed integer). Byte-oriented instructions exist even on computers that do not directly support other common data types such as real or boolean.

This is not because character-oriented applications such as text formatting or electronic mail are so important. Rather, characters are always included as a primitive data type in computer hardware because all low-level input and output is character oriented. Therefore, we must have character-oriented operations (also called byte-oriented operations) to be able to implement input and output at this level of abstraction.

Let's explain this point a little more fully. When you sit down at a terminal and enter the decimal number 123, you think of that value only as a 3-digit integer. Your high-level language, whether it is Pascal, FORTRAN, or BASIC, allows you to think at that high level by providing you with language primitives to input, directly as an integer, the value entered at the terminal:

      a)   readln (x)

      b)   read (5,100)m
          100 format (i3)

      c)   input x%

However, when we work at a lower level of abstraction (as we are doing here), we can no longer treat the input string as the integer 123. Instead, we see only what was actually entered at the terminal: the character '1', the character '2', the character '3', and finally, the character 'carriage return'. If we want to interpret this character string as the signed integer value +123, we must manipulate these characters *ourselves* and perform the desired conversions using the character-oriented instructions available on the computer at hand. This facility is no longer provided automatically.

Similarly, if we wish to output the integer quantity +123, we cannot simply say:

a)   writeln (x)

b)   write (6,100) x
      100 format (i3)

c)   print x%

Instead, we must convert the signed integer value into the 4-character string—'+', '1', '2', '3'—before printing. This is why all computers have internal character representations and machine-language instructions for working with and manipulating character-sized quantities. (Exercises 1 and 2 ask you to write some of these conversion routines.)

Our discussion used characters entered at a terminal as an example. However, the character-oriented nature of input/output is exhibited by virtually all other input/output devices: printers, disks, tapes, hard-copy terminals, and video display terminals (VDTs). They all transmit and receive character-based quantities. Even if the actual quantities stored on these devices are not characters, they will typically be transferred to and from the device in "character-size" chunks, using character-oriented or byte-oriented instructions. Thus, a 32-bit signed integer stored on a disk would likely be transferred as four 8-bit bytes rather than as a single 32-bit integer quantity.

4.2
Character Codes

Internally, all computers represent characters by storing them as the non-negative integers: 0, 1, 2, ... A mapping of characters into the integers is called a *character code*. Two important decisions must be made concerning these character codes: the *size* and the exact *collating sequence* (i.e., the specific internal integer value of each character).

The first question has to do with the number of bits that should be used to represent a character. The earliest alphabetic codes were telegraphy codes, and they used a maximum of five bits (e.g., dots and dashes). This 5-bit encoding allowed up to 2^5 (32) unique characters. Since this was not enough to represent the full complement of letters and digits in English, these codes used a special character, called an *escape character,* which changed the meaning of the other thirty-one characters. This change remained in effect until the occurrence of another escape character. (In a sense, it works just like the shift key on a typewriter, which changes the meaning of all the keys until you "unshift.")

However, this 5-bit encoding scheme was insufficient for computer use, and the earliest computers used 6-bit character codes. This allowed 2^6 (64) unique characters, which was enough for twenty-six uppercase letters, ten digits, and up to twenty-eight special characters, including:

$$, . ( ) : ; - + * /$$

needed by high-level languages like FORTRAN, COBOL, and BASIC. There are many examples of these early 6-bit encoding schemes, including:

1. Display code (used on Control Data equipment).
2. Fielddata (used on Univac equipment).
3. BCD.
4. MIX (a hypothetical computer used to teach the principles of computer organization).

However, it soon became obvious that a 6-bit encoding scheme was still inadequate for representing all of the characters that would eventually be needed on modern computer systems. A number of forces were pushing computer designers toward a significantly larger character set. Among these forces were:

1. The rapid growth of text processing, which demanded unique character codes for both upper- and lowercase letters. A 6-bit code did not have enough room for twenty-six uppercase letters, twenty-six lowercase letters, ten digits, and fifteen to twenty special symbols.
2. The desire to add non-English alphabets to our computer system, which increased the number of characters needed. Codes were needed for such symbols as tilde, umlaut, accent grave, and circumflex, as well as new alphabets such as Hebrew, Greek, and Cyrillic.
3. The desire to add graphical (picture-drawing) capabilities to computers. A character code might be assigned to a pattern not because it represents a character of an alphabet, but because its shape is needed for graphic displays.

Because of these and other forces, the size of character codes needed to be increased. Seven bits per character might have been adequate (since it would allow 2^7 [128] characters), but seven was considered inappropriate and inefficient because it is not a power of 2. Therefore it was decided to adopt the *8-bit byte* as the standard encoding of character data. Each character was to be represented as a string of eight binary digits, and there are a total of 2^8 (256) unique characters available.

There are two distinct approaches for using these eight bits and the 256 possible character codes, which are exemplified by the two most popular 8-bit codes: ASCII and EBCDIC.

ASCII: *A*merican *S*tandard *C*ode for *I*nformation *I*nterchange.

EBCDIC: *E*xtended *B*inary *C*oded *D*ecimal *I*nterchange *C*ode.

ASCII is a character code that was intended to be an international standard for representation of textual data. It is certainly the most widely used code set, but the existence of many other character codes, such as EBCDIC, prevents us, as yet, from calling ASCII an international standard. ASCII is, in reality, only a 7-bit character code; its collating sequence is shown in Figure 4-1.

There are two classes of characters in ASCII. The *printable characters* (40_8–176_8) are the ones that can be printed on all (or almost all) output devices. Characters 0– 37_8 and 177_8 are called *control characters*. When transmitted to or received from an I/O device, they do not cause a character to be printed but instead initiate some action (e.g., form feed, tab) or convey status information. Figure 4-2 shows a more detailed definition of the purpose of some of the widely used control characters.

FIGURE 4-1   Collating Sequence for the ASCII Code.

Left 2 Octal Digits	Right Octal Digit								
	0	1	2	3	4	5	6	7	
00	NUL	SOH	STX	ETX	EOT	ENQ	ACK	BEL	↑
01	BS	HT	LF	VT	FF	CR	SO	SI	
02	DLE	DC1	DC2	DC3	DC4	NAK	SYN	ETB	Control characters
03	CAN	EM	SUB	ESC	FS	GS	RS	US	↓
04	Blank	!	"	#	$	%	&	'	↑
05	(	)	*	+	,	—	.	/	
06	0	1	2	3	4	5	6	7	
07	8	9	:	;	<	=	>	?	
10	@	A	B	C	D	E	F	G	
11	H	I	J	K	L	M	N	O	Printable characters
12	P	Q	R	S	T	U	V	W	
13	X	Y	Z	[	\	]	∧	_	
14	`	a	b	c	d	e	f	g	
15	h	i	j	k	l	m	n	o	
16	p	q	r	s	t	u	v	w	↓
17	x	y	z	{			}	⌐	DEL	←Control character

FIGURE 4-2   Some ASCII Control Characters.

Octal Code	Abbreviation	Meaning
004	EOT	End of transmission
007	BEL	Ring a bell
010	BS	Backspace character
011	HT	Horizontal tab character
012	LF	Line feed character
013	VT	Vertical tab character
014	FF	Form feed
015	CR	Carriage return
033	ESC	Escape character
177	DEL	Delete/rub out character

The ASCII code uses only seven bits, although these 7-bit characters are stored right-justified within a standard 8-bit field (Figure 4-3). The eighth bit can be used in one of two ways: for *character set expansion,* or for *error checking.*

When we wish to do character-set expansion, we consider the characters shown in Figure 4-1 to be the 128 characters that can be represented in seven bits with the high-order bit set to 0. That is, the 128 characters in Figure 4-1 correspond to the codes for:

$$00000000 = 000_8$$
$$\vdots$$
$$01111111 = 177_8$$

The "other" 128 characters, which correspond to:

$$10000000 = 200_8$$
$$\vdots$$
$$11111111 = 377_8$$

FIGURE 4-3   The 7-Bit ASCII Code in an 8-Bit Field.

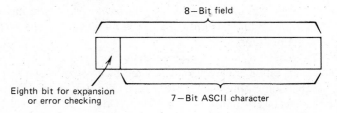

8—Bit field

Eighth bit for expansion or error checking

7—Bit ASCII character

can either be left unused or set by the user as desired: new letters, new alphabets, or special graphical symbols. The ASCII code set does not define these 128 codes. This usage is called character-set expansion.

A second approach is to consider ASCII as *only* a 7-bit code with a maximum of 128 characters exactly as shown in Figure 4-1. The eighth bit is used not for new characters, but for *error checking* on the other seven bits. Error checking is especially important in input/output operations that take place across great distances and along channels with very high error rates, such as telephone lines. An error is much more likely to occur during an I/O operation than during an arithmetic operation.

When used for error checking, this eighth bit is called a *parity bit*. It is set to a 0 or a 1 so that the total number of 1 bits in the representation of that character is either odd, if we are using *odd parity,* or even, if we are using *even parity*.

EXAMPLES

(a) Using ASCII and odd parity, how would we represent the letter 'A'?
In ASCII,

$$\text{'A'} = 101_8 = 1000001_2$$

The total number of 1s in the 7-bit value 1000001 is 2, an even number. Therefore, the eighth bit would be set to 1, to make the total number of 1 bits odd.

$$\text{'A'} = 11000001_2 = 301_8 \quad \text{in odd parity.}$$

(b) Using ASCII and even parity, how would we represent the character '$'?
In ASCII

$$\text{'\$'} = 044_8 = 0100100_2$$

Since the total number of 1s in the 7-bit value 0100100 is even, the eighth bit is set to 0, to leave the total number of 1 bits an even number.

$$\text{'\$'} = 00100100 = 044_8$$

If we use the eighth bit as a parity bit, then we can begin to detect certain types of errors. For example, if the rightmost bit of the letter 'A' in example a above were accidentally changed from a 1 to a 0, we would receive the bit pattern 11000000. If we had agreed to represent characters using odd parity, we would know that there was an error, since this 8-bit pattern has an *even* number of 1 bits. We would not accept or process that character.

Note that parity checking is only an *error-detection* mechanism; it does not allow us to determine what bit or bits were changed and do *error correction*. It only allows us to determine that something went wrong. Also note that if two bits in the representation are changed, we will still have the correct parity and we will be unable to detect an error condition. Exercise 8 at the end of the chapter deals with this problem.

When the eighth bit is used in this way, it is *not* part of the character code itself; it is only an error-detection mechanism. When interpreting the code, you look up only the rightmost seven bits in the ASCII code table. For example, given the code 301_8, you would use only the low-order seven bits (101_8) to determine what character it represents, namely the character 'A'.

The PDP-11 and VAX-11 families of computers use the ASCII character set, storing each character as a 7-bit value right-justified in an 8-bit field. Therefore, we use this character code throughout the remainder of the text. Unless stated otherwise, the representation of a character will be as shown in Figure 4-1, with the leftmost bit set to 0.

The other major character code, EBCDIC, is a true 8-bit character code. The definition of the collating sequence for EBCDIC uses all eight bits, although not all 256 patterns have been defined. Only about 95 have been assigned to printable characters. The collating sequence for EBCDIC is shown in Figure 4-4: entries not filled in are either control characters or unassigned.

EXAMPLES

(a) What does the string 'Cat' look like in ASCII (assume no parity)?

$$01000011\,01100001\,01110100$$

$$103_8 \quad 141_8 \quad 164_8$$
$$\text{'C'} \quad \text{'a'} \quad \text{'t'}$$

(b) What does the string '= 1' look like in EBCDIC?

$$01111110\,11110001$$

$$176_8 \quad 361_8$$
$$\text{'='} \quad \text{'1'}$$

(c) What is the internal ASCII code for the character string '123' (assume no parity)?

$$00110001\,00110010\,00110011$$

$$061_8 \quad 062_8 \quad 063_8$$
$$\text{'1'} \quad \text{'2'} \quad \text{'3'}$$

Example c points up an important representational difference that is easy to overlook. The internal representation of the character string '123' is quite different from the representation of the signed integer $+123$. The character string '123' corresponds to the twenty-four bits shown above. Using sixteen digits, the integer $+123$ is:

$$0000000001111011_2 (= 1 + 2 + 8 + 16 + 32 + 64 = 123)$$

FIGURE 4-4   Collating Sequence for EBCDIC Code.

High Order Two Octal Digits	Low-Order Octal Digits							
	0	1	2	3	4	5	6	7
10	Blank							
11			¢	.	<	(	+	|
12	&							
13			!	$	*	)	;	¬
14	-	/						
15				,	%	_	>	?
16								
17		'	:	#	@	'	=	"
20		a	b	c	d	e	f	g
21	h	i						
22		j	k	l	m	n	o	p
23	q	r						
24		~	s	t	u	v	w	x
25	y	z				[		
26				]				
27								
30	{	A	B	C	D	E	F	G
31	H	I						
32	}	J	K	L	M	N	O	P
33	Q	R						
34			S	T	U	V	W	X
35	Y	Z	\					
36	0	1	2	3	4	5	6	7
37	8	9						

4.3
Summary

This brief but important chapter has introduced the internal representation of characters, the third fundamental data type that exists directly on the hardware of all computers. We now have three classes of data:

1.   Unsigned binary values.
2.   Signed integers.
3.   Characters.

Surprisingly, on many computer systems, that's all there is. Only these data types can be directly manipulated by the computer hardware. If other data types are needed, they must be simulated using one of these three primitive data types and subroutines that provide, in software, operations on these new data types. This situation can be somewhat disheartening to a person who has been programming in a high-level language (like Pascal) and is accustomed to having a wealth of data-structuring facilities. At this lower level of abstraction, most of these data types do not exist directly. In fact, one of the major reasons for the construction of higher level languages in the first place was to expand the range of available data structures and to allow the programmer to code on a "virtual" machine that appears to have such powerful data types as boolean, complex, strings, arrays, sets, pointer, and records. (Now you may begin to see the importance of studying computer organization. It can explain the need for and the design of high level programming languages.)

In Chapter 5 we introduce a fourth data type that is implemented in hardware on some (but not all) computer systems. We also have much more to say about other data types such as arrays, and how they can be implemented in hardware.

Exercises for Chapter 4

1.   Write a procedure in any high-level language that takes as input an array of characters corresponding to a syntactically valid integer and converts those characters to their equivalent integer values. The syntax of the characters is:

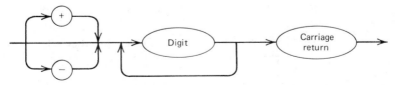

Assume that there is a carriage return character (octal code 15) at the end of the digits.

The output of your procedure should be the equivalent integer value. For example:

Array of characters

Input: | '+' | '9' | '8' | '7' | cr |

Output: The integer value 987

2.   Write a procedure to do the exact *opposite* of the operations described in Exercise 1. That is, the procedure gets as input a signed integer value, and produces as output an equivalent array of characters in the syntax of Exercise 1, including the carriage return at the end. Write your procedure in any high-level language.

Input: −5   An integer

Output: | '−' | '5' | cr | An array of characters

3.   If we use nine bits, rather than eight, to represent each character, how many unique characters will we be able to represent? How might we choose to use this ninth bit?

4.   Show the representation for the 3-character string 'YES' in:
   a.   ASCII, no parity (i.e., the eighth bit is 0)
   b.   ASCII, odd parity
   c.   ASCII, even parity
   d.   EBCDIC
Write out your answers in octal.

5.   Using ASCII and odd parity, what character does each of the following 8-bit binary patterns represent?
   a.   01000011
   b.   10111111
   c.   10001010
   d.   00110100

6.   If the 2-character string '12' were incorrectly interpreted as a sixteen-bit, signed twos-complement integer, what value would it be? (Assume ASCII, no parity.)

7.   Using sixteen bits and twos complement, show the internal representation of −1 as both an integer and as characters. (ASCII, no parity.) Give your answers in hexadecimal.

8.   Describe the types of error that would *not* be detected using only the 1-bit parity checking discussed in this chapter. Describe a possible variation of this technique that would allow you to detect more errors.

CHAPTER 5

FLOATING-POINT REPRESENTATIONS AND OTHER DATA TYPES

5.1
Floating-Point Representations

5.1.1 Introduction

We know that binary is a positional numbering system. In expression 2.1 we showed how the value of a digit in a positional system depends both on its absolute value and on its position within a number. The same positional interpretation holds true for a fractional quantity for the digits to the right of the binary point. (Note that in base 2, when the symbol "." appears in a floating-point value, it is called a *binary point,* not a decimal point.)

$$(5.1) \quad d_0 \ldots d_n \cdot d_{n+1}d_{n+2} \ldots = d_0r^n + \ldots d_nr^0 + d_{n+1}r^{-1} + d_{n+2}r^{-2} + \ldots$$

In decimal, the value of the positions to the right of the decimal point are tenths, hundredths, thousandths, and so on. In binary, the positions to the right of the binary point are halves, quarters, eighths, and so on. In general, for any base r, the value of the digits positions to the right of the radix point (i.e., the ".") are $r^{-1}, r^{-2}, r^{-3}, \ldots$.

EXAMPLES

(a) What is the decimal value of 110.01101_2?

$$110.01101 = 1 * 2^2 + 1 * 2^1 + 0 * 2^0 + 0 * 2^{-1} + 1 * 2^{-2}$$
$$+ 1 * 2^{-3} + 0 * 2^{-4} + 1 * 2^{-5}$$
$$= 4 + 2 + \frac{1}{4} + \frac{1}{8} + \frac{1}{32} = 6\frac{13}{32}$$
$$= 6.40625_{10}$$

(b) What is the binary representation of the decimal fraction 0.375_{10}?
To convert a decimal fraction to a binary fraction, we use the inverse of the

division-by-radix technique introduced in Section 2.1. We multiply the fractional part of the number by 2 and save the digit (or digits if the base is greater than 10) that is carried to the left of the binary point. We then repeat the process by multiplying the remaining fractional part by 2. In this way, we generate the binary digits in the correct order of their representation.

$$
\begin{array}{r}
.375 \\
\times\,2 \\
\hline
\textcircled{0}.750 \\
\times\,2 \\
\hline
\textcircled{1}.500 \\
\times\,2 \\
\hline
\textcircled{1}.000
\end{array}
$$

Binary representation

Therefore, $0.375_{10} = 0.011_2$

This technique will allow you to convert a decimal fractional quantity into *any* other base r. Simply multiply by the appropriate radix value r and save the digit or digits to the *left* of the radix point. Keep multiplying the remaining fractional quantity by r. (Exercise 3 asks you to explain mathematically why this method works.)

(c)   What is the value of 0.3_{10} in base 4?

$$
\begin{array}{r l}
& 0.3 \\
& \times\,4 \\
\hline
1\ | & .2 \\
& \times\,4 \\
\hline
0\ | & .8 \\
& \times\,4 \\
\hline
3\ | & .2 \\
& \times\,4 \\
\hline
0\ | & .8
\end{array}
$$

Correct
base-4
representation

So, to 4-place accuracy,

$$0.3_{10} = 0.1030_4$$

(d)   What is the decimal value of 1.234_5?

$$
\begin{aligned}
1.234_5 &= 1 * 5^0 + 2 * 5^{-1} + 3 * 5^{-2} + 4 * 5^{-3} \\
&= 1 + \tfrac{2}{5} + \tfrac{3}{25} + \tfrac{4}{125} \\
&= 1\tfrac{69}{125} \\
&= 1.552_{10}
\end{aligned}
$$

(e)   What is 0.984_{10} in base 16 (to 4-place accuracy)?

$$
\begin{array}{rr}
 & .984 \\
 & \times\ \ 16 \\
\hline
15 & .744 \\
 & \times\ \ 16 \\
\hline
11 & .904 \\
 & \times\ \ 16 \\
\hline
14 & .464 \\
 & \times\ \ 16 \\
\hline
7 & .424
\end{array}
$$

base-16 representation

Using the standard hexadecimal notations for the digits 10–15:

$$0.984_{10} = 0.\text{FBE7}_{16}$$

5.1.2 Scientific Notation

Inside the computer, *floating-point numbers, R,* are not represented in the positional notation of expression 5.1. Rather, they are expressed in *scientific notation,* as shown in expression 5.2.

(5.2) $$R = \pm M * B^{\pm E}$$

where M is called the *mantissa*
E is called the *exponent*
B is called the *base of the exponent*

This can also be written in the following format:

$$R = (\pm M, B, \pm E)$$

where the three values M, B, and E are to be interpreted as in expression 5.2.

The value B in expression 5.2 should *not* be confused with the base of the numbering system that we are using to store the numbers internally. This base is *always* binary. Here B is the base of the exponent we are using to represent real quantities; B may be 2, but it may be a different value entirely.

EXAMPLES

(a)   What is 1,228.8 in scientific notation, using an exponent base (B) of 10, and giving the answer in decimal?

$$1{,}228.8 = 1.2288 * 10^3$$

Where

$$M = 1.2288$$
$$E = +3$$
$$B = 10$$

The base of the numbering system for writing out the answer (decimal) and the base of the exponent ($B = 10$) are the same in this example.

(b)   What is 1,228.8 in scientific notation using an exponent base of $B = 8$?

$$1,228.8 = 2.40 * 8^3$$

Where

$$M = +2.40$$
$$E = +3$$
$$B = 8$$

Now the base of the numbering system for writing out the answer (decimal) and the base of the exponent ($B = 8$) are different.

On all computer systems, the exponent base B is set by the hardware of the system and cannot be changed by the user. Therefore, it is omitted from the explicit representation of a real number and is not stored internally. A real number, R, on a computer is represented as the following two fields:

$$R = (\pm M, \pm E)$$

and interpreted as $\pm M * B^{\pm E}$, where B is the fixed exponent base of the system on which you are working. For example, on the PDP-11 and VAX-11 systems, the exponent base $B = 2$. On the IBM-360 and 370, $B = 16$. On the Burroughs B6500 system, $B = 8$. The advantages and disadvantages of different exponent bases are discussed in the next section.

5.1.3 Normalization

In the example showing the scientific representation of 1,228.8, the answer was given as $1.2288 * 10^3$. But that is only one way to represent this number. The following representations are also correct.

$$.12288 * 10^4$$
$$.012288 * 10^5$$
$$.0012288 * 10^6$$
$$\vdots$$

In fact, there is an infinite number of representations in scientific notation for the quantity 1,228.8.

To avoid confusion, we should agree on a single standardized representation for a floating-point number. The process of putting a number into a standardized format is called *normalization,* and the standard representation is called the *normalized form.* In principle, we could choose any format for our normalized form, but we should choose one that maximizes the accuracy of our representation. This is achieved when the binary point is immediately to the left of the first significant digit so that no space is wasted on nonsignificant leading zeros.

For example, assume that we have only five decimal digits in which to represent the mantissa of 1,228.8. Look what happens to our accuracy level as the digits move to the right:

$$.12288 * 10^4$$
$$.01228 * 10^5$$
$$.00122 * 10^6$$

Significant digits are lost, and the value becomes less precise. To minimize this problem, we always normalize a floating-point number so that the binary point is immediately to the left of the first significant digit. This means that the first "base-B" digit of the mantissa M will be nonzero and will satisfy the following relationship.

(5.3)
$$\frac{1}{B} \le |M| < 1$$

where B is the base of the exponent
When a floating-point representation satisfies the relationship in expression 5.3, it is said to be *normalized*.

EXAMPLES

(a)   Normalize 103.5_{10} ($B = 10$).

$$103.5_{10} = 0.1035 * 10^3$$

This is normalized since $\frac{1}{10} \le |M| < 1$. Notice that the first decimal digit is nonzero. (It is a 1.)

(b)   Normalize 0.000011101_2 ($B = 2$).
To normalize, we must move the binary point four positions to the right, that is, immediately to the left of the first '1'. This is equivalent to multiplying by 2^4, or 16. Therefore, we must decrease the exponent by 4, which is equivalent to dividing by 16.

$$0.000011101 = 0.11101 * 2^{-4}$$

(c)   Normalize $10011.110 * 2^{10}$ ($B = 2$).
Move the binary point five positions to the left and increase the exponent by 5.

$$10011.110 * 2^{10} = 0.10011110 * 2^{15}$$

(d)   Normalize $.000011_2 * 8^2$ ($B = 8$).
This is a little more tricky. The base of the exponent is $B = 8$. Therefore, we must normalize the mantissa so that it is between $\frac{1}{8}$ and 1. We cannot move the binary point one place at a time because that is equivalent to multiplying or dividing by 2; changing the exponent by 1 is equivalent to multiplying or dividing by 8. Therefore, we can move the binary point only three binary digits at a time ($2^3 = 8$).

$$0000.011 * 8^2 = 0.011 * 8^1$$

This mantissa value, 0.011, is normalized because the first *octal* digit (011) is nonzero, and the mantissa is between ⅛ and 1.

(e) Normalize $0.0001_2 * 16^5$ ($B = 16$).
This value is already normalized. The first hexadecimal (base-16) digit (0001) is nonzero.

Examples d and e illustrate the advantages and disadvantages of different exponent bases. With bases like $B = 8$ and 16, we can represent much larger numbers than we can with an exponent base of $B = 2$. For example, with a 6-bit exponent field, we can represent signed exponent values of (approximately) -32 to $+32$. If our exponent base is 2, we can represent exponent values between 2^{-32} and 2^{+32}. However, if our exponent base is $B = 16$, that same 6-bit field would allow representation of exponent values from 16^{-32} to 16^{+32} or 2^{-128} to 2^{+128}. Thus, a larger exponent base results in a larger *range* of real numbers.

However, to achieve this larger range, we may have to accept a decreased level of *accuracy*. In example e, the 4-digit normalized mantissa (0001) contains only one significant digit. We cannot get more significant digits because we can move the binary point only four places at a time to the right or left. This is equivalent to multiplying or dividing by 16, which we can then balance out by increasing or decreasing the exponent by 1. Thus, a base-16 mantissa may have anywhere from zero to three nonsignificant leading zeros that cannot be removed by normalization. A base-2 mantissa will not have *any* leading zeros because we may move the binary point one unit at a time to the right or left, and we can therefore always position it immediately to the left of the most significant digit.

EXAMPLE

Show the normalized representation of 7.5 (decimal) as a real number using a base-2 and base-16 exponent and a *4-digit* mantissa field.

$$7.5_{10} = 111.1_2$$
$$111.1_2 = 0.1111 * 2^3 \quad \text{Base-2 exponent}$$
$$111.1_2 = 0.0111 * 16^1 \quad \text{Base-16 exponent}$$

Notice that with the base-2 exponent we were able to keep four significant digits in the 4-bit field and thus represent the desired quantity *exactly*. With the base-16 exponent we could maintain only three significant digits and were thus not able to represent 7.5 exactly in the given field. (The quantity represented above is 7.0, not 7.5.)

A computer designer's decision about which exponent base to use depends on whether it is more important to maximize the *range* of real numbers that can be represented or to maximize the *accuracy* with which the system can represent any one particular value.

To summarize: Floating-point numbers are represented as a pair of signed values corresponding to the mantissa and the exponent of the number in scientific notation. The mantissa is normalized, and the exponent represents the power of a base B, which is set by the system.

5.1.4 Other Representational Issues

Floating point is a much more complex representation than the other three types we have discussed. There are a number of other questions that must be answered before we can begin to show the internal representation of floating-point numbers. In this section we identify these questions and, as examples, show how they have been answered for the PDP-11 and the VAX-11 systems.

1. What signed representation scheme should we use to represent the mantissa?

The mantissa is a signed value. It will be normalized with an implied binary point immediately to the left of the field.

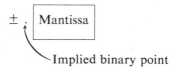

To represent the mantissa field we could use any of the four integer schemes (sign/magnitude, ones complement, twos complement, BCD) discussed in Chapter 3. They would work equally well. The PDP-11 and VAX-11 use sign/magnitude notation to represent the mantissa field.

2. What signed representation scheme should we use to represent the exponent?

Again, we could use any one of the four representation techniques discussed in Chapter 3. However, in almost all modern computers, an entirely different technique is used. This technique is called *biased notation,* or *excess-n notation.* (The letter n is frequently replaced by the actual numerical value of the bias, such as excess-64, or excess-128.)

In biased notation, the true exponent, e, is stored in a b-bit field as a *biased exponent, e',* defined as:

$$(5.4) \qquad\qquad e' = e + 2^{b-1}$$

Simply put, we add the *bias value* 2^{b-1} to the actual exponent, and store the sum in the exponent field. Figure 5-1 shows the biased exponent values for a 5-bit exponent field (bias = $2^{5-1} = 2^4 = 16$.) The range of exponent values, E, that can be represented with biased notation and a b-bit exponent field is:

$$-2^{b-1} \le E \le +(2^{b-1} - 1)$$

Biased notation is commonly used in floating-point exponents because of one very important characteristic: the ordering of the binary representation actually stored in

FIGURE 5-1   Biased Exponent Value in a 5-Bit Field.

True Exponent	Biased Exponent	Binary Representation
+15	31	11111
+14	30	11110
.	.	.
.	.	.
.	.	.
+1	17	10001
0	16	10000
−1	15	01111
−2	14	01110
.	.	.
.	.	.
.	.	.
−15	1	00001
−16	0	00000

the computer, when considered as an unsigned quantity, is the same as the signed ordering of the true exponent. That is, if a true exponent E_1 is larger than a true exponent E_2, then the internal biased representation of E_1 (when interpreted as a simple unsigned binary value) will be larger than the internal biased representation of E_2. (Look at the ordering of the three columns in Figure 5-1 to confirm this fact.) This characteristic gives us a quick way to compare the magnitude of two floating-point numbers. To determine whether floating-point value, R_1, is bigger than floating-point value, R_2, we simply compare their respective exponents, using an unsigned binary compare. If the exponent field of R_1 is bigger than the exponent field of R_2 in an unsigned binary sense, then $R_1 > R_2$.

The PDP-11 and VAX-11 use 8 bit-fields and excess-128 notation as their standard representation for exponents of real values. Figure 5-2 describes two *optional* representations also available on the VAX.

FIGURE 5-2   Size of the Mantissa/Exponent Fields on the PDP-11 and VAX-11.

Format	Mantissa (bits)	Exponent (bits)	Total Length (bits)
F	24	8	32
D	56	8	64
G*	53	11	64
H*	113	15	128

*VAX only

3.   How many bits should be allocated for the mantissa and exponent fields?

The larger we make the mantissa field, the greater will be our *precision,* the number of significant digits we can keep. The larger we make the exponent field, the larger will be our *range,* the distance between the smallest and largest possible values. Because priorities change depending on circumstances, many computer systems have more than one format for floating-point numbers. These formats may use a different number of bits for representing a floating-point quantity, and differ in their allocation of bits between the manitssa and exponent fields. Figure 5-2 shows the four floating-point formats available on the PDP-11 and VAX-11 computers.

In F format, the 24-bit mantissa allows for approximately seven decimal digits of accuracy. The 8-bit exponent field allows exponents up to about $2^{\pm 128}$. This is equivalent to decimal exponents of $10^{\pm 38}$. The D format (for *d*ouble precision) mantissa yields about sixteen significant decimal digits. The H format (available only on the VAX) allows you to maintain an accuracy of about thirty-four decimal digits and a range of numbers $-10^{480} <= R <= 10^{480}$.

Trying to represent a value that is too large to be stored in the exponent field produces an error called *floating-point overflow.* Trying to represent a value that is too small (i.e., too close to zero) results in an error called *floating-point underflow.* For example, given the F format described in Figure 5-2, the value $\frac{1}{2} * 2^{200}$ would result in floating-point overflow, while $\frac{1}{2} * 2^{-200}$ would produce a floating-point underflow, because the possible range of exponents is -128 to $+127$. Floating-point overflow is a fatal error, but floating-point underflow can sometimes be handled by resetting the real number to 0.0, since it is so close to 0 anyway.

4.   Where should the mantissa and exponent fields be located?

A floating-point quantity has three components: the sign of the mantissa, the mantissa itself, and the exponent field. The sign of the mantissa, which represents the sign of the entire number, is always stored in the leftmost bit of the representation, so that the sign of either an integer or a floating-point quantity is always in the same location. However, the remaining two fields (the mantissa and the exponent) may be in either order, without affecting the efficiency of the representation.
Figure 5-3 shows the bit layout for the F and D formats for the PDP-11 and VAX-11. Different systems may change either the size or order of these fields. Figure 5-4 shows the floating-point format on the IBM 370.

5.   Are there any other special "games" or "tricks" associated with floating-point. representations?

Computer designers love to find ways to increase the efficiency, speed, or precision of a computer. The PDP-11 and VAX-11 systems have been modified to increase the precision of the representations just described. If we look back at expression 5.3 (and remember that $B = 2$), we see that the mantissa of a floating-point quantity on the PDP-11 or VAX-11 will always be greater than or equal to $\frac{1}{2}$. This means that the high-order bit of the mantissa will *always* be a 1. Since we know that it is

FIGURE 5-3   Field Layout for Floating-Point Numbers on the PDP-11 and VAX-11.

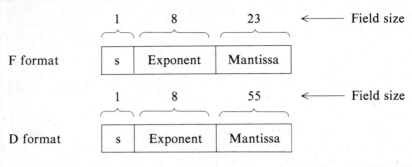

a 1, there is no need to store it. On the PDP-11 and the VAX-11, the high-order digit of the mantissa is *not* explicitly stored in the computer. Instead, it is implied to be there and to have the value 1. This allows the designers to achieve $N + 1$ bits of significance in an N-bit mantissa field.

With this modification, however, it is no longer possible to tell the difference between the value 0 and a number whose mantissa is exactly ½. The mantissa value ½ would be represented in binary as:

$$100 \ldots 0$$

But because the leading digit is not stored, it would appear internally as:

$$000 \ldots 0$$

which is indistinguishable from 0. To solve this problem, the designers of the PDP-11 and VAX-11 eliminated the floating-point value zero, 0.0. Instead, 0.0 is stored

FIGURE 5-4   Field Layout for Floating-Point Numbers on the IBM 370.

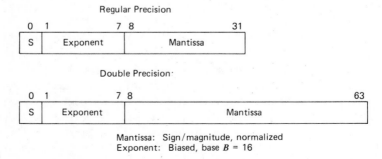

internally as the integer value 0. This type of optimization is typical of the "real-world" pragmatic changes made by computer designers to enhance speed, precision, and efficiency. You will probably see similar modifications on your own system.

EXAMPLES

(a)   How would the PDP-11 store the decimal value $-\frac{3}{16}$ in F format?
   (1)   Normalize: $-\frac{3}{16} = -\frac{3}{4} * 2^{-2}$
   (2)   Bias the exponent: $e' = e + 2^{b-1}$

$$e' = -2 + 2^{8-1}$$
$$e' = -2 + 128$$
$$= 126$$
$$= 01111110_2$$

   (3)   Represent the mantissa in sign/magnitude notation:

$$-\frac{3}{4} = \qquad 1 \mid 11000 \ldots 0$$

Sign $\quad$ Mantissa

   (4)   Remove the high-order 1 bit:

$$= 1 \mid 10000 \ldots 0$$

Final representation $= 1011111101000000000000000000000000$
$$= 27720000000_8$$

(b)   How would the PDP-11 store the decimal value $+200.0$ in F notation?
   (1)   Normalize: $+200 = +\frac{200}{256} * 2^8$
$$= \frac{25}{32} * 2^8$$
   (2)   Bias the exponent: $e' = e + 2^{b-1}$
$$= 8 + 128$$
$$= 136_{10}$$
$$= 10001000_2$$
   (3)   Represent the mantissa in sign/magnitude notation:

$$+\frac{25}{32} = \qquad 0 \mid 1100100 \ldots$$

Sign $\quad$ Mantissa

   (4)   Discard the high-order 1 bit:

$$= 0 \mid 100100 \ldots 0$$

Final representation $= 0100010001001000000000000000000000$
$$= 10422000000_8$$

(c) Assume that the internal representation of a 32-bit real value in PDP-11 F format is:

$$27734000000_8$$

What decimal floating-point quantity does that represent? (The layout of the F format is shown in Figure 5-3.)

(1) Determine the sign.

Sign bit = 1. It is a negative quantity.

(2) Evaluate the exponent field.

Biased exponent = 01111110_2 = 126_{10}

True exponent = $126 - 2^{b-1}$

$$= 126 - 128$$

$$= -2$$

(3) Evalute the mantissa field.

Mantissa = 1110000 . . . 000

$$= \tfrac{1}{2} + \tfrac{1}{4} + \tfrac{1}{8}$$

$$= \tfrac{7}{8}$$

(4) Final decimal representation = $-\tfrac{7}{8} * 2^{-2}$

$$= -\tfrac{7}{8} * \tfrac{1}{4}$$

$$= -\tfrac{7}{32}$$

$$= -0.21875_{10}$$

There are numerous other representations and formats, and Exercises 10–15 at the end of the chapter ask you to work out floating-point representations for a number of these different alternatives.

Figure 5-5 lists the floating-point characteristics of a number of popular and widely used computer systems.

FIGURE 5-5   Floating-Point Characteristics of Some Popular Computers.

System	Total Width	Mantissa Width	Mantissa Representation	Exponent Width	Exponent Representation	Exponent Base	Normalized
Burroughs B5500	48	41	Sign/ magnitude	7	Sign/ magnitude	$B = 8$	Yes
CDC Cyber-70	60	49	Ones complement	11	Excess-1,024	$B = 2$	Yes
Sigma 7	32	25	Twos complement	7	Excess-64	$B = 16$	Yes
Univac 1100/80	36	28	Ones complement	8	Excess-128	$B = 2$	Yes
Cray 1	64	49	Sign/ magnitude	15	Excess-2^{14}	$B = 2$	Yes
Hewlett-Packard 3000	32	24	Twos complement	8	Twos complement	$B = 2$	Yes
DEC System 10	36	28	Sign/ magnitude	8	Excess-128	$B = 2$	Yes

5.2
Floating-Point Errors

The integer representations in Chapter 3 are all *exact*. Within the range of values that can be represented on the computer, all decimal integer quantities convert exactly to their binary equivalent, but this is not the case for floating-point representations. Given a finite number of digits with which to represent a number, we may not be able to represent it exactly. We have this problem in all bases, including decimal. For example:

$$\tfrac{1}{3} = 0.33333\ldots._{10}$$

No matter where we truncate the representation of $\tfrac{1}{3}$, we will have induced an error. The error that may be caused by attempting to represent a real value in a finite number of significant digits is called *round-off error*.

For example, in binary the fraction $\tfrac{1}{5}$ is a nonterminating value and cannot be represented exactly:

$$\tfrac{1}{5} = 0.2_{10} = 0.0011001100110011\ldots._2$$

If we try to represent the value of 0.2 in a 12-bit sign/magnitude mantissa field and a 6-bit biased exponent field, we get the following:

$$+0.2 = +0.8 * 2^{-2}$$

$$= 0 \quad 011110 \quad 110011001110$$

Sign   Exponent   Mantissa

This quantity is not 0.2; it is equal to approximately 0.19995, so we have induced an error of about 0.02 percent. Increasing the size of the mantissa field will reduce the magnitude of the error, but it will never eliminate it. Round-off error is an inherent problem in any finite representation of real quantities.

The existence of round-off errors explains why results are occasionally off by one digit in the last place. That is, you expect your program to print the answer $5,000.00, but instead you get $4,999.99. The discrepancy is caused by the small round-off errors that occur when decimal quantities are converted to binary.

This is also why you were taught in introductory programming classes never to check real values for exact equality. For example, using the previous representation of $\tfrac{1}{5}$ (0.19995), the sum:

$$\tfrac{1}{5} + \tfrac{1}{5} + \tfrac{1}{5} + \tfrac{1}{5} + \tfrac{1}{5}$$

would be 0.99975, not 1. Comparing the sum for exact equality to the real value 1.0 will yield false.

There is another type of error that occurs when arithmetic operations are performed on floating-point numbers that differ greatly in the magnitude of their exponents. The algorithm for addition of real values involves first *scaling* the exponents, that is, making them identical. After the exponents are scaled, we can properly add the mantissa and renormalize the result. For example:

$$
\begin{array}{c}
\text{(Scale)} \\[4pt]
\begin{array}{ll}
0.38 * 10^4 & \\
+ \ 0.00713 * 10^6 & \Rightarrow
\end{array}
\qquad
\begin{array}{ll}
0.00380 * 10^6 & \\
+ \ \underline{0.00713 * 10^6} & \\
0.01093 * 10^6 & \text{unnormalized} \\
0.10930 * 10^5 & \text{normalized}
\end{array}
\end{array}
$$

This looks fine, but what happens when the following algorithm is implemented internally? Let's use a 6-bit sign/magnitude mantissa (five bits plus the sign), and a 4-bit biased exponent, and perform the decimal addition (11 + ¼).

$$
\begin{array}{c}
\phantom{+11 = +^{11}/_{16} * 2^4 = 0|} | \qquad | \\
+11 \ = \ +{}^{11}/_{16} * 2^4 \ = \ 0\,|\,1100\,|\,10110 \\
\phantom{+11 = +^{11}/_{16} * 2^4 = 0|} | \qquad | \\
+¼ \ = \ +½ * 2^{-1} \ = \ 0\,|\,0111\,|\,10000 \\
\phantom{+11 = +^{11}/_{16} * 2^4 = 0|} | \qquad | \\
\text{Sign} \quad \text{Exp} \quad \text{Mantissa}
\end{array}
$$

Now, to form the sum (11 + ¼), we must scale the exponents. We must increase the exponent −1 in the representation of ¼ up to the exponent +4. This is equivalent to multiplying by 2^5. Therefore, we must shift the digits of the mantissa field of the value ¼ five places to the right to balance things. But when we shift the mantissa (10000) five places to the right, we lose all of the significant digits and end up with 0. So, with the mantissa and exponent sizes used in this example, the sum (11 + ¼) is 11! This error occurs because the values 11 and ¼ differ greatly in the magnitude of their exponent fields, which causes the loss of significant digits when we try to scale the two operands. The problem is not limited to addition; the algorithms for subtraction, multiplication, and division may also cause the loss of significant digits because of scaling or other internal arithmetic operations.

The condition is called *propagation error*. As is the case with round-off error, increasing the size of the mantissa and exponent fields can reduce the problem, but it cannot eliminate it. It is inherent in our finite representational method for real numbers and the algorithms we use to manipulate them. The area of computer science that studies the causes and magnitude of these errors and their effect on subsequent arithmetic operations is called *numerical analysis*. It is a very important and interesting area of study in the field of computer science.

5.3
Summary of Floating-Point Representations

This completes our discussion of the fourth and final data type available on the hardware of most computers. However, not all computers have floating-point hardware. In fact, most inexpensive microcomputers do *not*, because it is much too costly in relation to the price of the computer itself. If you need to perform real arithmetic on a microcomputer, you may have to use software routines to simulate (using integer arithmetic) the existence of the real data type. This type of "software floating point" typically operates twenty-five to fifty times slower than "hardware" floating point.

Most larger minicomputers and mainframes have a hardware floating-point data type available, either standard or as a very expensive option. This option provides the functional units needed to perform, directly in hardware, the floating-point operations discussed in this chapter, such as:

Normalization
Exponent biasing
Exponent scaling
Floating-point addition, subtraction, multiplication, and so on
Conversion of integers to floating points, and vice versa
Floating-point error handling (underflow or overflow)

Optional hardware floating-point processors are available for all members of the PDP-11 family except the smallest one, the PDP-11/04. Hardware floating point is standard on all models of the VAX-11.

5.4
Other Data Types

Before we move on to consider the structure of an idealized computer system, let us comment on the absence of the other data types (boolean, arrays, sets, pointers, complex numbers that are used in Pascal, FORTRAN, and BASIC. These other data types do not actually exist on the hardware of a computer. They are all "created" by the language from one of the four primitive data types—unsigned binary, integer, character, floating point—that do exist.

To create a new data type, a representation is chosen that utilizes one of the existing data types. Then the operations on this new type are described in terms of the operations available on the actual internal representation. Finally, programs are written to perform these operations in software, using existing machine-language instructions. All this is accomplished by the high-level language to make it seem as though the machine has many interesting data types when, in fact, it usually has only the four described in Chapters 2 to 5.

For example, Pascal provides a data type called boolean, which contains two constants, true and false. We can declare objects to be of type boolean and perform logical operations on boolean variables, such as:

```
var a,b,c : boolean;
    .
    .
    .
if a then . . .
while (not a) do . . .
c := (a or b)
```

When you program in Pascal, boolean appears to be a primitive data type of the computer. But, as we have shown, it is not. What has happened is that the boolean constants true and false, which you are using in your program, have been mapped into one of the available data types, probably the integer constants 0 (for false) and 1 (for true). All logical operations on boolean variables are converted by the Pascal compiler into integer operations on the constants 0 and 1. For example:

> **if a then** . . . becomes if "a = 1" then . . .
> **while (not a) do** . . . becomes while "a = 0" do . . .
> c := (a **or** b) . . . becomes c: = a+b;
> **if** c = 2 **then** c: = 1

To be sure, we could do the mapping ourselves (and in fact that is exactly what we must do in BASIC, which does not directly provide type boolean). However, the purpose of high-level programming languages is to create an idealized "virtual" programming environment that is rich in interesting data structures, and allows the programmer to think, design, and code directly in terms of these structures. The literal absence from hardware of such structures is totally irrelevant at the programming-language level of abstraction. However, now that we are taking a different (and lower level) view of computer systems, we no longer have this helpful and supportive "virtual" programming environment to enhance our problem-solving abilities. Instead, we have available only the data types that are indeed supported by the underlying hardware. All others must be realized by the programmer or language designer from

FIGURE 5-6   Realization of High-Level Data Types in Hardware.

High-Level Type	Low-Level Realization
boolean	the integers 0, 1 (0 = false, 1 = true)
user-defined scalar types	the integers 0, 1, 2, 3 . . . , N
complex numbers	pairs of floating-point values (r_1, r_2)
strings	sequences of individual characters preceded by a 1-byte unsigned binary value that specifies the length of the string
pointers	unsigned binary memory addresses
arrays of real	a block of sequential memory addresses filled with floating-point values
sets	unsigned binary values, with each bit corresponding to the presence or absence of a member in a set
double-precision	a floating-point representation with a larger mantissa and larger exponent

the four primitive types described in Chapters 2–5. Although the desire to create these "virtual" data structures was one of the major reasons for the development of high-level programming languages, there were many other reasons, which we will mention later.

Figure 5-6 lists some of the more better known high-level data types and their possible low-level realization on the hardware of the computer.

In our discussion of the representation of information, we have focused on the four basic data types that can be manipulated directly by the hardware of a computer system, and how these data types are represented internally. In Part II we describe how to build a computer system to manipulate the data objects we have just created. In addition, we introduce one more primitive data type that exists on all computers: information of type "instruction." It may seem strange to refer to an instruction as a data type, but at this lower level of abstraction we can treat an instruction exactly as if it were data and operate on it exactly as we operate on numbers, addresses, or characters.

Exercises for Chapter 5

1. Convert the following fractional binary values to decimal.
   a. 0.110010
   b. 0.000001
   c. 0.1110001
   d. 0.101

2. Convert the following fractional decimal values to binary.
   a. 0.75
   b. 0.001
   c. 0.4
   d. 0.153827

3. Show (mathematically) why multiplying a decimal quantity by r (the radix) and saving the first digit to the left of the radix point produces the correct digits of the representation of that number in base r. (Hint: Start with the definition of a positional number given in expression 5.1)

4. Convert the following fractional decimal values to the indicated base.
   a. 0.55 to base 5
   b. 0.102 to base 8
   c. 0.99 to base 3
   d. 0.6 to base 16

5. Normalize the following binary values so that they meet the definition of normalization given in expression 5.3.
   a. 0.00001 ($B = 2$)
   b. 110.01 ($B = 2$)

    c.   1111.0 ($B = 2$)
    d.   .0001101 ($B = 4$)
    e.   .0101 ($B = 4$)
    f.   101.101 ($B = 8$)
    g.   1.001011 ($B = 8$)
    h.   .001001 ($B = 8$)
    i.   .00000001 ($B = 16$)

6. What would be the bias value of a base-2 exponent (i.e., $B = 2$) in a 6-bit field?

7. What would be the bias value of a base-8 exponent (i.e., $B = 8$) in a 7-bit field?

8. Assume that base-2 exponents are stored as biased values in an 8-bit field. Show the internal binary representation of the following exponents.
    a. 2^{+15}
    b. 2^{+63}
    c. 2^{-1}
    d. 2^{-100}
    e. 2^{+130}

9. Using the information given in this chapter about how the PDP-11 and IBM 370 store floating-point values (see Figures 5-2, 5-3, and 5-4), show the internal representation of the following decimal values on both a PDP-II (F format) and IBM-370.
    a. 1.25
    b. −8.5
    c. −0.0125
    d. 200.0
    e. 0.0001

10. Assume a computer with the following floating-point representation:

S	Mantissa	Exponent
1	10	5

Mantissa: Sign/magnitude, 11 bits (10 bits plus the sign bit), normalized, all digits are stored.

Exponent: Biased, base $B = 8$.

Show the internal representation of the following decimal values. Give your final answers in hexadecimal notation.
    a. +12.25
    b. −0.55
    c. −0.001
    d. 0.0

11. Using the floating-point representation described in Exercise 10, compute the decimal values that are equivalent to the following internal representation. (Note: If any of the values are not normalized, state that fact, and work out the internal value anyway.) All values below are given in *hexadecimal*.
   a. 6012
   b. 9A13
   c. B00F
   d. 0030

12. Assume a computer with the following floating-point representation:

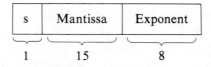

s	Mantissa	Exponent
1	15	8

Mantissa: Ones complement, 16 bits (15 bits plus the sign), normalized. Assume that when complementing, you complement *only* the mantissa.

Exponent: Biased, base $B = 16$.

Show the internal representation of the following decimal values. Give your final answers in octal.
   a. 1.5
   b. −0.75
   c. 24.25
   d. −0.0125

13. Using the floating-point representation shown in Exercise 12, compute the decimal values that are equivalent to the following internal representation. (Note: If any of the values are not normalized, state that fact, and work out the equivalent decimal value anyway.) All values below are given in *octal*.
   a. 30000203
   b. 41777601
   c. 03000177
   d. 76777600

14. Try to represent the decimal quantity +0.4 in the following floating-point representation:

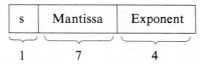

s	Mantissa	Exponent
1	7	4

Mantissa: Sign/magnitude, normalized.
Exponent: Biased, base $B = 2$.

Is your representation exact? If not, what is the closest decimal value that can be represented internally? What is the percentage of error induced by your representation?

15. Using the floating-point representation in Exercise 14, show the internal representation of the decimal quantity $+2.0$. Then perform the following addition, using the values you obtained here and in Exercise 14. Use the "scale and add" algorithm described in section 5.2 to do the addition.

$$2.0_{10} + 0.4_{10}$$

How many significant digits were discarded during the scaling operation? What answer do you obtain for the sum? What is the percentage of error in this final answer? Compare the magnitude of error in the final sum with the magnitude of error in each of the two original operands.

16. You want to provide a boolean data type in a high-level language you are designing, but boolean is not available on your machine. Therefore, you decide to create the boolean data type from the integer data type that does exist, using the integer constants -1 and $+1$ for false and true, respectively. Using these constants, show how you would implement the following logical operations (a, b, and c are boolean variables). Use any high-level algorithmic notation to write out your answer. Assume that the only operations you have available are *integer addition* and *comparison* of two integer values.

$$c := a \text{ and } b$$
$$c := a \text{ or } b$$
$$c := a \text{ xor } b \quad (\text{exclusive-OR})$$
$$c := \text{not } a$$
$$c := a \text{ implies } b$$

PART TWO

THE STRUCTURE OF AN IDEALIZED COMPUTER SYSTEM

CHAPTER 6

MEMORY

6.1
Introduction

Part II treats the *functional organization* of a typical modern computer system. Instead of looking at a specific machine manufactured by a particular company, we first study an idealized hypothetical computer called a PVM (for *primitive Von Neumann machine*). This acronym honors the famous mathematician John Von Neumann who, in 1946 presented the structure for a computer that is still valid today. Von Neumann laid out some of the fundamental concepts inherent in the design of computer systems, including:

1. The use of the binary numbering system.

2. A single, sequentially addressed memory.

3. A separate arithmetic/logic unit for performing arithmetic and logical computations.

4. The *stored program concept,* in which both the program and its data are stored in memory.

5. A controller that fetches instructions from memory and executes them.

6. The overall functional organization of computers, and how the major pieces fit together.

There have been a number of alternative architectures proposed since 1946, and a few such experimental computers have been built, but the overwhelming majority of modern computers are based on the classic "Von Neumann architecture" presented almost four decades ago. There is more than a little truth to the saying that, in the area of computer organization, "There is nothing new since Von Neumann."

By studying our idealized PVM, we will be able to concentrate first on the important general concepts of computer organization without becoming bogged down in innumerable "real-world" details. (In Part III we address the organization and structure of a "real" system.)

The Von Neumann architecture divides a computer into five major functional components:

1. Memory.
2. Arithmetic/logic unit.
3. Interconnect network.
4. Input/output.
5. Control unit.

In the next four chapters we introduce each of these functional components. We then show how the five major subsystems work together to execute instructions and solve problems. In this chapter we will be examining the *memory subsystem.*

6.2
The General Structure of Memory

Memory is the subsystem that stores and retrieves information. It is divided into *cells,* and data are accessed by means of the unique *address* of the cell in which the data are contained. A memory *fetch* from address N will simultaneously fetch all of the binary digits stored in location N. A memory *store* into address N will simultaneously store new binary values into all of the bit positions of that location. Figure 6-1 provides a pictorial view of memory.

The individual memory cells or locations in Figure 6-1 are sometimes called memory *words.* However, we will not use "words" as a general term for an addressable

FIGURE 6-1 Logical View of Memory.

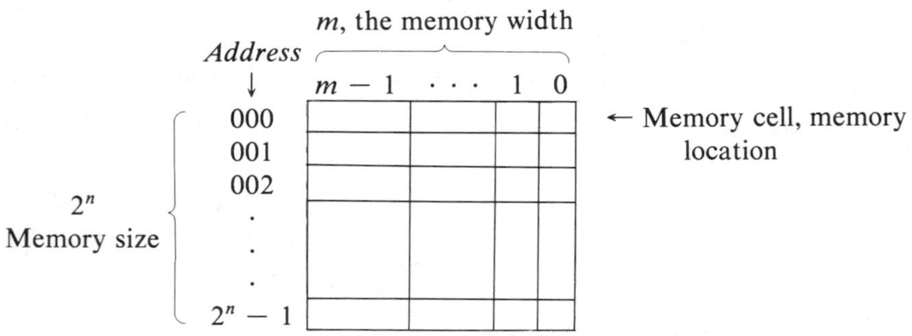

cell because it has another meaning on the PDP-11 and could cause confusion. The number of bits in each location (the symbol m in Figure 6-1) is called the *memory width,* sometimes called the *cell size* or *word size.* The individual bits of each memory location are usually numbered from right to left beginning with 0 and ending with $m - 1$. Although this is not a universal standard, we adopt this numbering convention throughout the text.

Each memory cell in the computer has a unique unsigned binary address, beginning with 0. The maximum possible number of memory cells is called the *memory size* or the *address space;* it will always be a power of 2 because the internal representation of the memory address is binary. If we use n bits to represent the unsigned binary address, then we will have a maximum of 2^n memory cells, and their addresses will be the values $0, 1, 2, \ldots, 2^n - 1$.

In early computers, all memory cells were the same size, and all accesses to memory either fetched or stored a cell of that one fixed size. However, it quickly became apparent to computer designers that this memory organization could be quite inefficient. If we want to access a character, we probably want to fetch 8 bits of information (see Chapter 4). If we want to fetch an integer, we probably want 16 or 32 bits (see Chapter 3). Finally, referring to Figure 5-2, we see that if we want to fetch a floating-point value, we may need 32, 64, or even 128 bits. If we can access only 8 bits at a time, we may have to do as many as sixteen separate fetches to get the necessary information. On the other hand, if we had a large cell size (e.g., 32 bits) many times we would fetch much more information than we actually needed.

To solve this problem, we should no longer think of memory as being composed of units of only one size. Instead, we first define a *minimum-sized addressable unit.* This is the smallest unit of memory that has a unique address and can be fetched or stored as a unit. We refer to the size of this minimum addressable unit as m. On most modern machines, $m = 8$ and the minimum-sized addressable unit is the *8-bit byte.* (There are computers for which m has other values. On some computers, $m = 4$ and we can directly address a *half-byte,* usually called a *nibble.* On the Burroughs B1700, $m = 1$ and every bit in the computer is uniquely addressable.)

We then define clusters or multiples of these minimum addressable units that can be stored or retrieved *as a unit* in a single operation. This clustering allows us to retrieve from memory exactly as much information as we need, and it eliminates the problem of getting too much information or having to make many memory accesses to get what we need. The terms for these "clusters" are not standard. Figure 6-2 lists the memory-cluster terminology for three popular computers. On all of these the minimum addressable unit is the 8-bit byte.

It is important to realize that these larger clusters are not separate entities with unique addresses. Rather, they represent clusters or multiples of the minimum addressable units. For example, on the VAX-11/780, the 16-bit word with address 0 corresponds to the two addresses 0 and 1, each of which is an 8-bit byte. The 32-bit "longword 0" corresponds to the four consecutive 8-bit addresses 0, 1, 2, and 3. Actual physical addresses are associated only with minimum addressable units. It is the computer's responsibility to figure out that, when you ask for "longword 0," you

FIGURE 6-2   Terminology for Memory-Cluster Sizes.

	Number of Bits	Terms*		
		Intel 8086	VAX-11/780	IBM 370
Minimum → addressable unit	8	Byte	Byte	Byte
	16	Word	Word	Halfword
	32	—	Longword	Word
	64	—	Quadword	Doubleword
	128	—	Octaword	—

*The "—" means that memory cannot be accessed in size unit so designated.

want address 0, 1, 2, 3; then it should fetch all four locations for you automatically. This memory organization allows you to get exactly as much information as you need with a single memory access. Otherwise, you would need to make several separate fetches, getting one 8-bit unit at a time, which would be significantly slower. Figure 6-3 summarizes the layout of these cluster units for the VAX-11.

6.3
The Implementation of Memory

6.3.1   Storage of the Individual Bits
Because computers always store data internally using the binary system, the memory itself can be constructed from any physical device capable of storing two values, corresponding to binary 0 and 1. Specifically, a storage device must have:

1. Two stable states separated by a large energy barrier as diagrammed in Figure 2-2b.

2. The capability to switch between these two states a virtually infinite number of times.

3. Some way of determining which state it is in without permanently destroying information.

Theoretically, any device that meets these three cirteria, even an on-off light switch, is a candidate for use in constructing a computer memory. In reality, however, we must consider not only theoretical constraints, but also such pragmatic concerns as manufacturing cost, reliability, power demands, and availability.

Until about 1975, the most popular device was the *magnetic core,* shown in Figure 6-4a. This "doughnut" of ferric oxide, with an internal diameter of about ½₀ of an

FIGURE 6-3   Memory Units on the VAX-11 Computer.

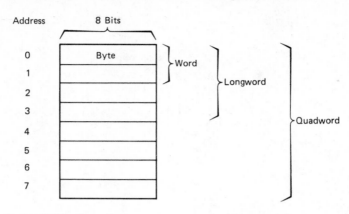

inch, had a wire running through it, called a *selection wire* (actually, as we will show later, there are two selection wires). The selection wire could carry an electric current, which was sent through the wire in either direction. Depending on the direction of the current, the core became magnetized in the clockwise or the counterclockwise direction. These two states corresponded to 0 and 1. The rule for determining the direction of the magnetic field is called the "right-hand rule." If you point the thumb of your right hand in the direction of the current, the fingers will curl in the direction of the magnetic field.

To determine what value is stored in a core at any given time, we send a current through the selection wire in a preset direction—for example, in the direction corresponding to binary 0. If the core is already in the 0 state, nothing will happen. If it currently contains a 1, the core will be changed to the 0 state. The changing magnetic field induces a small electric current that can be picked up on a second wire, called a *sense wire*. The presence of this current indicates that the original value stored in the core was a 1. In this case, it is necessary to immediately rewrite the core back to its original 1 state so that no changes will remain (otherwise condition 3 above would be violated). This is accomplished by simply sending a current through the selection wire in the proper direction to write back a 0.

Magnetic cores were by far the most popular method of constructing memory (so popular, in fact, that the term "core" is still used as a synonym for memory, regardless of whether cores are actually being used). However, since about 1975, core technology has been completely replaced by *semiconductor memories,* in which the two states 0 and 1 are represented by two differing voltage levels across a transistor. Figure 6-4b shows a schematic diagram of a simple 1-transistor semiconductor memory cell.

Semiconductor memories offer enormous advantages over cores. They are signifi-

FIGURE 6-4   Devices for Constructing Memory: (a) Core Memory and (b) Semiconductor.

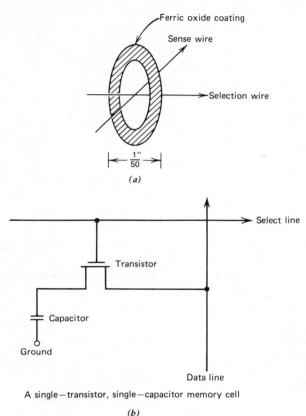

cantly faster, switching states in 10–200 nanoseconds (nsec: billionths of a second) rather than the 0.5–3 microseconds (μsec: millionths of a second) for magnetic cores. They are much smaller than cores: approximately 64,000 bits of semiconductor memory can be placed on a 0.25-inch-square chip. Newer manufacturing methods are being developed to increase that capacity to 256,000 or more bits per chip. In fact, the only major disadvantage of semiconductor memories is their *volatility*: if power is lost, the entire contents of memory are lost. Cores are nonvolatile and maintain their magnetic states even in the absence of power.

All computers today are constructed with some type of solid-state semiconductor memory. There is a great deal of research under way to design better solid-state memories with higher speeds, improved efficiency and reliability, and lower costs. An "alphabet soup" of memory technologies has emerged from this research, and acronyms like TTL, ECL, PMOS, NMOS, and CMOS all represent slightly different technologies to achieve the same end: the efficient and cheap storage of a 0 and a 1. Other courses in hardware design and solid state physics describe in greater detail the underlying technology of semiconductor memory devices and other memory technologies. For the remainder of this chapter, we simply assume that there is a device, a "black box," that meets our original three conditions and can fetch and store the two binary values 0 and 1.

6.3.2 Putting the Bits Together

We must now organize these individual bits into an integrated *memory unit.* All memory units are constructed of *memory planes,* two-dimensional $k \times k$ arrays of binary storage elements, as shown in Figure 6-5 (where $k = 4$). A memory plane contains the same numbered bit (i.e., the same bit position) from a sequence of consecutive memory addresses. For example, if we have a 4×4 plane as shown in Figure 6-5, that plane might contain all of the bit 0s from sixteen consecutive locations (addresses 0–15 in Figure 6-5). This organization is used because memory is accessed by memory cells, and there will be only one bit from each cell on a plane; therefore, every memory reference (fetch or store) will reference one and only one bit on a plane.

Because of the two-dimensional structure of our memory planes, we now must have two selection lines per storage element, called the x- and y-selection lines, instead of a single one as shown in Figure 6-4a. The *x*-selection line and the *y*-selec-

FIGURE 6-5   Organization of a Memory Plane.

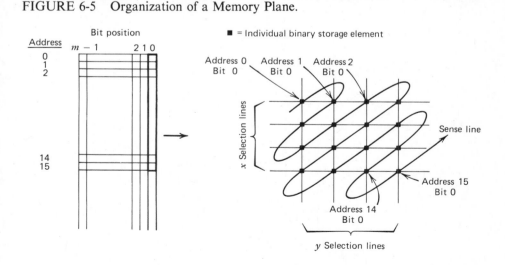

tion line in Figure 6-5 can be activated simultaneously to select the one bit on the plane on which we want to operate. Only the one storage element at the intersection of the activated (x,y) wires will be fetched or stored during this cycle. The single sense line shown in Figure 6-5 running through all of the storage elements will be used to sense the contents of that one cell. (Exactly how the selection and sense wires operate depends, of course, on the particular technology that is being used.)

Figure 6-5 shows the organization of only a single plane. However, that gives us only one bit per location. As we showed in Figure 6-1, a memory cell is made up of m bits. To achieve this cell size, we must "stack up" exactly m of these $k \times k$ planes, and let each plane correspond to one bit within our cell. This organization is shown in Figure 6-6.

A memory location now corresponds to a "vertical axis" cutting through the planes, that is, one bit in the same (x,y) position in each of the m planes. If we want to access a word from memory, we determine its (x,y) position within the plane and then, simultaneously on all m planes, activate the same (x,y) selection lines. Coming out on the sense line of plane 0 will be bit 0 of that word. Coming out on the sense line of plane 1 will be bit 1 of that word, and so on, up to plane $(m - 1)$, which will provide bit $(m - 1)$ of that word. A complete set of k^2 memory locations, each containing m bits as shown in Figure 6-6, is called a *memory bank*. If we want more memory, we must purchase another bank, up to some physical limit (which we describe shortly).

At current levels of technology, typical values for k are 128 and 256, and it is possible to purchase memory planes (usually called memory *chips*) with 16K–64K

FIGURE 6-6   A Memory Bank.

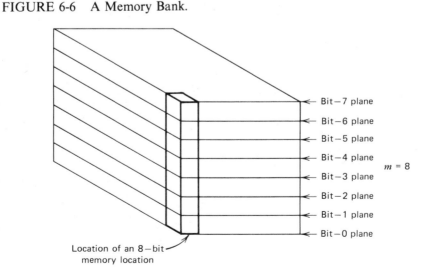

Bit–7 plane
Bit–6 plane
Bit–5 plane
Bit–4 plane
$m = 8$
Bit–3 plane
Bit–2 plane
Bit–1 plane
Bit–0 plane

Location of an 8–bit
memory location

FIGURE 6-7   A Computer Memory.

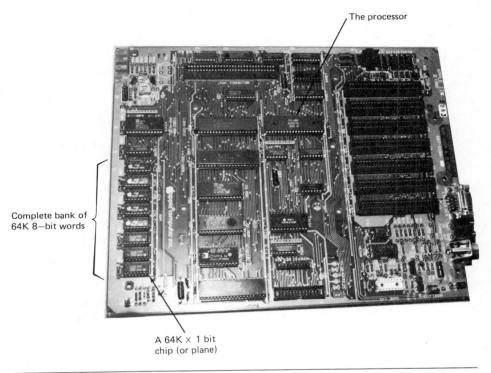

The processor

Complete bank of
64K 8—bit words

A 64K × 1 bit
chip (or plane)

bits per plane ($K = 2^{10} = 1,024$). To construct the typical byte-oriented memory that we have described, we would need eight chips per bank. Larger planes containing 256K, or 1,024K bits of memory are being developed. Figure 6-7 shows a photograph of an actual microcomputer system, identifying the individual memory chips. Notice that instead of being stacked up, as in Figure 6-6, they are laid out end to end.

6.4
Memory Registers

Figure 6-5 and 6-6 showed how memory is organized, but they do not tell us where the information necessary to operate this memory comes from or where the results go. For these details we need two critically important registers: the *memory address register* (MAR) and the *memory buffer register* (MBR).

The memory address register contains the *address* of the word we want to store or fetch. We must always be careful to distinguish between an *address* and its *contents*.

A	B

The address of the above cell is A. The contents of cell A, sometimes abbreviated CON(A) are B. If we want to fetch the contents of this cell, we must load the MAR with the value A.

The size of the MAR (i.e., the number of bits) is a very important quantity. It determines the maximum amount of memory that can be put on the computer. We can fetch from or store into a memory location only if we can place its address in the MAR. Recall from Figure 6-1 that our computer has 2^n words of memory, with addresses from 0 to $2^n - 1$. To reference that much memory, our MAR must be n bits wide. This maximum memory size (2^n words with an n-bit MAR) is called the *address space* of the computer.

The second major register, the *memory buffer register* (MBR), contains the *contents* of the location we want to store or fetch. If we read or write memory in m-bit units, the MBR must be m bits wide. As we described in Section 6.2, computers frequently have the ability to directly access memory units that are multiples of m. In such cases, the MBR must be large enough to hold the largest unit of information that is transferred to or from memory (e.g., $2m$ or $4m$ bits). In our description of a simplified and idealized computer, we assume that memory is accessed only in units of m bits and that the MBR is exactly m bits wide.

To go from an address in the MAR to the corresponding signals on the proper (x,y) selection lines in the proper memory bank, we need a device called a memory *decoder*. This memory component interprets the address currently stored in the MAR and converts it into the output signals to select the correct storage elements. It sounds difficult and somewhat mysterious, but it is actually quite simple. (We are again going to drop down one level to discuss the implementation of a decoder. You may skip the remainder of this discussion without loss of continuity.)

A decoder interprets memory addresses much as you might "decode" a street address to find the right house. You decompose the house number into component parts, each of which provides an additional piece of information about the location. For example, in the address 12345 Elm Street, the first three digits (123) might tell you that the nearest cross street is 123rd Street. The next digit (4) might tell you that the house is the fourth one from the intersection, and the next digit (5) might tell you that it is on the odd side of the street. Together, the five digits uniquely identify a specific location.

A memory decoder does the same thing by decomposing the address in the MAR into its component pieces. Let's work through an example. Let's say that we have 128 memory locations each containing eight bits. The memory unit contains eight banks, and each bank contains sixteen locations. There are eight planes per bank corresponding to the eight bits in each memory cell. The MAR must contain at least seven bits so that it can reference all 128 (2^7) addresses. This situation is depicted in Figure 6-8.

The addresses in the first bank are 0–15. In binary, this is 0000000 to 0001111. Notice that the first three bits of every address in bank 0 are always 000. Likewise,

FIGURE 6-8   Process of Address Decoding.

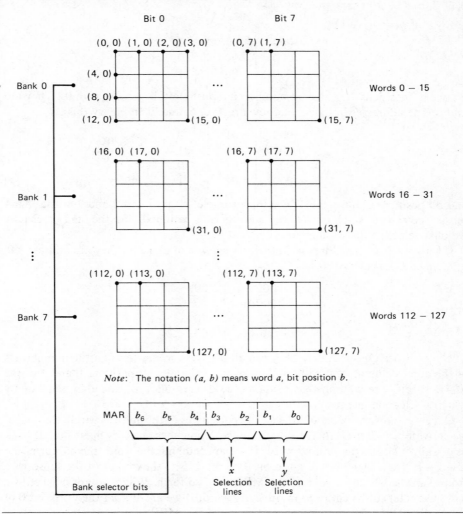

Note: The notation (*a, b*) means word *a*, bit position *b*.

the second bank contains addresses 16–31. In binary, this is 0010000 to 0011111. The first three bits of every address in bank 1 are always 001. If you work out the address representations for the remaining banks you will see that for all banks, the first three bits of the MAR tell which bank contains the desired address. These three bits can be used as the *bank selector.*

Having selected a bank, how can we identify the correct (*x,y*) position of that address within a plane? The addresses along the first *row* of plane 0 in bank 0 are 0, 1, 2, and 3. In binary this is:

000	00	00
000	00	01
000	00	10
000	00	11

Notice bit positions 2,3 (bits are numbered right to left, beginning with 0.) They are all 00. The addresses in the second row are 4, 5, 6, and 7. In binary this is:

000	01	00
000	01	01
000	01	10
000	01	11

and bit positions 2,3 are all 01. For this example, bit positions 2 and 3 of the MAR tell us the *row* in which the desired address is to be found, and they tell us exactly which x-selection line to activate.

Finally, look at the addresses in the first *column* of plane 0. They are addresses 0, 4, 8, and 12. In binary this is:

00000	00
00001	00
00010	00
00011	00

Look at bit positions 0 and 1. They are all 00. By working through the numberings of the other columns, you will see that, in this example, bit positions 0 and 1 of the MAR specify the column that contains the desired address, and they tell exactly which y-selection line to activate.

Once we know the bank and the (x,y) coordinates of the address within that bank, we activate *simultaneously* the same (x,y) selection lines on every plane in that bank to get all m bits of the desired word. If we are fetching the word, the output of the sense wire from plane 0 will go to bit 0 of the MBR, the output of the sense wire from plane 1 will go to bit 1 of the MBR, and so forth. When we are finished, we will have fetched the entire m-bit memory word. If we are storing the word, bit 0 of the MBR will be written into plane 0, bit 1 of the MBR will be written into plane 1, and so on. When we are finished, we will have stored the entire m-bit memory word.

We have only one component left to complete the pieces of our memory organization: the *read/write control lines*. The memory unit we are describing has no control function. That is, although it is capable of performing a fetch or store operation, it cannot initiate one. It will perform an operation only when given an explicit signal from a centralized control. When the signal is received, the operations described will begin. The read/write control lines provide that signal. These two lines may be in the following states.

1. READ: If in the ON state, initiate a memory fetch from the address currently in the MAR during this memory cycle. Otherwise do not perform a read.

2. WRITE: If in the ON state, initiate a store into the address currently in the MAR during this memory cycle. Otherwise, do not perform a write.

This start signal comes from the centralized "control unit," which we describe later.

We have now seen how a complete memory unit can be implemented out of $k \times k$ memory planes containing k^2 binary storage elements. The next section explains how the overall memory unit is organized, how the various memory components work together, and how the operations of memory read and memory write are carried out.

6.5
Overall Memory Organization

Figure 6-9 shows the overall organization of a typical Von Neumann memory. The five components of memory are:

1. 2^n words of m-bit memory with addresses $0, 1, \ldots, 2^n - 1$.

2. Memory address register (MAR).

3. Memory buffer register (MBR).

FIGURE 6-9   Overall Memory Organization.

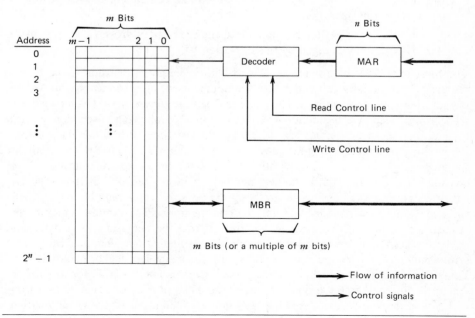

4.   Decoder.

5.   Read/write control lines.

The two operations that can be performed are a *memory read* and a *memory write*. A memory read proceeds in four steps:

1.   An (unsigned binary) address is loaded into the MAR. This value must be between 0 and $2^n - 1$, where 2^n is the total amount of memory available on the system.

2.   A READ signal is initiated along the READ control line.

3.   The address in the MAR is translated by the decoder into the proper signals on the "bank select" and (x,y) selection lines. (The contents of the MAR are not changed by this operation.)

4.   The m-bit contents of that address are placed in the MBR.

A memory write proceeds in the following five steps:

1.   An (unsigned binary) address is loaded into the MAR. This value must be between 0 and $2^n - 1$, where 2^n is the total amount of memory available on the system.

2.   The m-bit quantity to be stored is loaded into the MBR.

3.   A WRITE signal is initiated along the WRITE control line.

4.   The address in the MAR is translated by the decoder into the proper signals on the "bank select" and (x,y) selection lines. (The contents of the MAR are not changed by this operation.)

5.   The m bits in the MBR are copied into the specified address. (The contents of the MBR are not changed by this operation.)

The most important parameter associated with a memory operation is the time it requires. Two memory terms that are sometimes used interchangeably but are not in fact identical are *memory access time* and *memory cycle time*. (Note: read and write times need not be identical. However, in the following discussion we will assume that these two values are the same.) Access time is the time elapsed from the issuance of a read or write request until that value is in the MBR and available for processing. Cycle time, on the other hand, is the time elapsed from the start of one memory operation until another memory operation can be initiated. The two times are not identical because even though the desired value may be in the MBR, there may still be some "cleaning up" to do in memory. For example, remembering our earlier discussion about magnetic cores, it may be necessary to go back and restore values that were changed by the process of finding out what was there. In a semiconductor memory, we may have to wait for certain electrical or magnetic transients to disappear. During this period, the memory is not available for use and we cannot begin another fetch or store operation. This interval is called *restore time,* and in some technologies it may be quite significant. Figure 6-10 shows the relationship between access time and cycle time.

FIGURE 6-10   Relation Between Access Time and Cycle
Time.

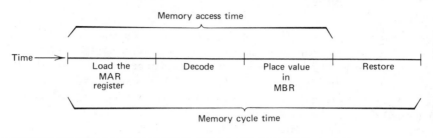

Since we usually care about the speed of memory over a long period of time rather than the time it takes to fetch or store a single value, cycle time is considered to be more important than access time as a measure of memory speed. Cycle times for semiconductor memory are 10–300 nsec, with typical times being 50–100 nsec. Core memories had cycle times that were usually in the range of 0.3–2 μsec. Thus, the change to semiconductor memories has produced a tremendous increase in speed.

The time it takes to fetch or store a word from or into memory is independent of its address. Regardless of whether you are reading the contents of memory location 00000 or 77777, the time will be the same. This characteristic is called *random access,* and the memory organization that we have described in this chapter is called random-access memory (RAM). The main memory of all computers is constructed of random-access memory. However, other memory structures do exist, and in the next section (and in Exercises 9–11), we will briefly discuss some of these alternatives.

6.6
Alternative Memory Structures

One of the most popular alternatives to RAM is *read-only memory,* usually abbreviated ROM. A ROM is similar to RAM except that the write command on the read/write control lines is disabled. We can read the contents of memory, but we cannot make any changes to the contents. ROMs are used to hold critical information that must be protected from accidental or intentional changes by the user. The information is loaded into the ROM by the manufacturer before the system is delivered. (Occasionally there are procedures that allow a user to load a ROM after delivery.) Note that a ROM is also random access.

The typical types of information that might be placed in a ROM are:

1.   Critically important library routines.
2.   The loader program that loads all other programs.

3. The compiler or interpreter for a high-level language.

4. Important error-recovery procedures.

5. Portions of the operation system of the computer.

Other types of information, introduced later, may also be candidates for storage in a ROM. The characteristic they share is critical importance to the proper operation of the computer; they all must be protected from change or destruction.

A variation of the ROM is the erasable, programmable read-only memory (EPROM). The EPROM is similar to a ROM in that it cannot be written into during normal operation. However, unlike the ROM, the EPROM does not prevent writing via an irreversible physical modification such as breaking a connector. When the EPROM is removed from the computer and inserted in a special device, new information can be stored in it.

All of these memory types—RAM, ROM, and EPROM—have one thing in common. They access memory through addresses. A totally different memory organization is based on accessing by *contents* rather than addresses. For this reason, it is called *content-addressable memory* (CAM). With CAM, you do not ask, "What are the contents of address A?" Instead you ask the exact opposite question: "Is there any location that contains the value *x*?" All memory locations are searched *in parallel* to see whether any contain the desired value. Any location that has the desired value emits a signal indicating that the value was found. In certain situations, such as table look-up operations, a CAM can be a very useful alternative memory organization.

ROM, EPROM, and CAM are just a small set of the possible alternatives that are available on many real-world computers. Some other interesting possibilities are discussed in the exercises at the end of the chapter, including *multiport memory* (Exercise 9), *interleaved memory* (Exercises 10 and 11), and *cache* or *buffer memory* (Exercise 12).

For our idealized PVM computer, however, we temporarily ignore these other interesting but often confusing real-world options. We assume that our PVM has a

FIGURE 6-11   Organization of a Content-Addressable Memory (CAM).

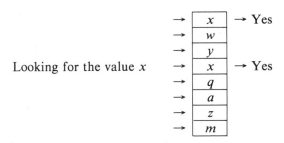

Looking for the value *x*

simple random-access memory with the structure shown in Figure 6-9. The memory has 2^n addressable memory locations, each containing m bits, and it can read from or write into any of those locations in the same amount of time. In Parts III and IV, where we begin to discuss a "real-world" computer, we look in more detail at these alternative organizations and see how they can be used.

In the next chapter, we add arithmetic and logic capabilities to our PVM.

Exercises for Chapter 6

1.   On a computer with 64K (2^{16}) 32-bit memory cells that are divided into four separate 16K banks, give the most likely size of:

a.   The MAR
b.   The MBR

How many banks would you need for a 96K memory?

2.   Assume that you have a memory unit with twenty-four distinct memory banks. Each bank is composed of sixteen identical planes containing 64×64 binary storage elements. What is the most likely value of the *cell size* of this computer? What is the *total number* of memory cells? How many banks would you have if you had constructed the memory from planes containing 128×128 storage elements instead?

3.   Show the physical organization of a memory unit with 65,536 ($64K = 2^{16}$) words of sixteen bits each. Diagram the structure of the memory planes and banks. Assume that the memory is constructed of memory planes that have 128×128 bits of storage in each plane. (Use the type of notation shown in Figure 6-8.)

4.   How many bits are needed in the MAR for the memory organization described in Exercise 3? How many bits in the MBR? Which bits of the MAR would correspond to the bank select bits? The x-selection line bits? The y-selection bits?

5.   Most microcomputers today typically have 64K, 128K, or 256K memory locations, each of which holds an 8-bit byte. In Chapter 4, we saw that it takes eight bits to store one character. Estimate (very roughly!) the number of characters contained in this textbook and determine whether a typical 128K memory would be sufficient to store the entire book.

6.   If the cycle time of a memory unit is 25 nsec, how many memory locations can be fetched per second? Using your rough estimate (from Exercise 5) of the number of characters in this book, determine how long it would take the memory unit to fetch all of the characters in this text, one byte at a time.

7.   Why would a computer have 524,288 memory locations instead of a nice round number like 500,000 or 550,000?

8.   Assume that you built a ternary (base-3) computer rather than a binary one. Each storage element could store a 0, a 1, or a 2. How large would the address space be if the MAR held eight ternary digits *(trits)*? How large would you need to make the MBR if you wanted to store numbers from 0 up to $99,999_{10}$?

9.   An MAR, an MBR, and a decoder together are called a *port* into memory. When constructing a memory unit, you can place all memory locations in one big "box" with one port, or you can split them into two boxes, each containing half the available addresses and each with a separate port. The second option is called a *multiport memory*. For example, the sketches show two different ways to construct a 16K memory.

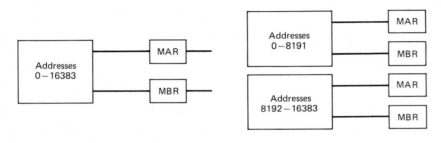

(a) Single-Port Memory   (b) Multiport Memory

Discuss the advantages of a multiport memory over a single-port memory. How could you take the best advantage of this organization? How could you best partition the information to be placed in the two banks?

10.   A variation on the multiport memory is called *interleaved memory*. Instead of putting addresses 0, 1, 2, . . . , 8191 in box 1, and addresses 8192, . . . , 16383 in box 2, you could put addresses 0, 2, 4, 6, 8, . . . , 16382 in box 1 and addresses 1, 3, 5, 7, 9, . . . , 16383 in box 2. Do you think this would help make the multiport memory more useful? If so, why?

11.   The interleaving described in Exercise 10 is called *two-way interleaving* because the addresses are alternately placed in two different banks. Assume that you had a memory unit with four different banks. Describe two different approaches to interleaving the addresses among these four memory banks. Which of your *four-way interleaving* schemes do you think is best?

12.   One final variation of memory is to have a very small amount (i.e., 10–1,000 locations) of very high speed memory, typically an order or magnitude faster than regular random-access memory. This high-speed memory is typically called a *cache memory* or *buffer memory*. How might you take best advantage of this type of memory? What type of information would you put in it? (Assume that the total amount is too small to hold an entire program.)

CHAPTER 7

THE ARITHMETIC/ LOGIC UNIT

7.1
Introduction

The *arithmetic/logic unit* (abbreviated ALU) is, as its name implies, the functional unit that carries out all of the arithmetic operations (e.g., add, subtract, multiply, divide, shift) and logical operations (e.g., AND, OR, complement) within the computer. The ALU has two parts: the *functional units* themselves (e.g., adder, multiplier, complementor), which perform the operations, and *registers,* which hold operands, results, and error and status information.

Before we discuss these two components in detail, we should mention one important point. In modern computer systems, the ALU is not considered to be a separate and distinct functional component. The ALU and the control unit (described in Chapter 9) are treated as a single subsystem, the *processor* (usually called the *central processing unit,* or *CPU*). However, for our purposes, it is easier to discuss these two components separately.

7.2
The Functional Units

The functional units are the "black boxes" that perform arithmetic and logical operations. Figure 7-1 lists some typical arithmetic and logical functional units that exist on most computers.

All of the operations performed by the units listed in Figure 7-1 can be carried out directly in hardware by most computers (although BCD and floating-point operations are frequently options on smaller computers).

105

FIGURE 7-1   Some Typical Arithmetic/Logical
Functional Units.

Arithmetic	Logical
Integer adder	AND unit
Integer subtractor	OR unit
Integer multiplier	Complementor (NOT)
Integer divider	Exclusive-OR unit
Arithmetic shift unit	Logical shift unit
Incrementor/decrementor	Comparator
BCD arithmetic units	
Floating-point arithmetic units	

Although the units listed in Figure 7-1 perform a wide variety of hardware oper-ations, most of them behave in a similar fashion. Figure 7-2 shows a functional dia-gram for an arbitrary binary operation.

The typical binary operation proceeds in five steps.

1.   Move the left operand from holding cell X into the functional unit.

2.   Move the right operand from holding cell Y into the functional unit.

FIGURE 7-2   General Block Diagram of a Binary
Functional Unit.

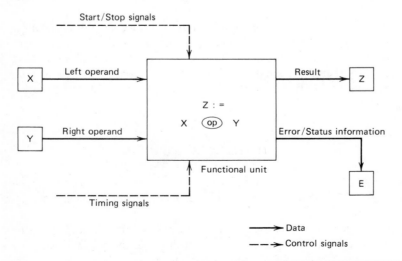

3. Send a START signal along the START control line. This begins the computation of the desired result Z.

4. Wait a fixed interval based on the operation being performed.

5. Place the result (X ⊚ Y) in holding cell Z. (Note: holding cell Z might be identical to either X or Y, and X or Y might be modified during this operation.) Move status and/or error information (e.g., overflow, underflow) to a special location E.

The length of the time interval in step 4 obviously depends on which operation is being performed and on what computer. Figure 7-3 gives the time needed for some typical arithmetic and logic operations for a PDP-11/44, a VAX 11/780, and an Intel 8086 microprocessor. It also lists some of the errors that will be detected by the hardware during the operation.

The internal implementation of these functional units is not described here (although we very briefly commented on the logic design of a twos-complement adder in Section 3.5 and in Exercise 19 in Chapter 3. If you did not read that section earlier, you may wish to go back and read it now). That subject is more properly handled in a course on hardware design. However, there are two additional remarks concerning the list in Figure 7-1.

First, some of the functional units included in Figure 7-1 may seem redundant and unnecessary. For example, why have both an incrementor unit (A + 1) and a general binary adder (A + B)? We could increment by simply keeping the constant +1 somewhere in memory, and then performing a regular binary addition using the value we want to increment and the constant +1 stored in memory. However, incrementing by 1 is such a common operation, and it is so critical to the efficient oper-

FIGURE 7-3   Times Required for Some Typical Operations.

Operation	Intel 8086	PDP-11/44	VAX-11/780	Detected Errors
Integer Add, Subtract	3.0 μsec	1.4 μsec	0.6 μsec	Arithmetic overflow
Integer Multiply	18 μsec	6.6 μsec	1.0 μsec	Arithmetic overflow
Integer Compare	3.0 μsec	1.4 μsec	0.6 μsec	Arithmetic overflow
OR	3.0 μsec	0.36 μsec	0.2 μsec	None
Floating-Point Add	Not available	8.9 μsec	2.0 μsec	Overflow, underflow

ation of the machine, that a special functional unit is often provided to minimize the time needed to increment or decrement. For example, on the PDP-11/44, an add takes 1.4 μsec, whereas an increment takes 1.1 μsec, a reduction of about 20 percent.

The inclusion of functional units to perform arithmetic shift operations may also seem redundant. An arithmetic left shift of an integer value is equivalent to multiplying by 2. An arithmetic right shift is equivalent to dividing by 2. Obviously, we could easily omit arithmetic shifting by simply using the multiply and divide operations instead. However, it is much more efficient to implement a multiply or divide by a power of 2 with shift commands than with the direct arithmetic equivalent. For example, on the PDP-11/44, a 1-bit arithmetic shift takes 1.59 μsec, whereas a multiply takes 6.6 μsec, and a divide takes 11.01 μsec.

You should be aware that functional units are not selected solely on the basis of their need or their importance to the "applications level," or to directly mimic the operators that are available in high-level languages like Pascal or FORTRAN. Rather, they are selected on the basis of machine-level efficiency and their usefulness in implementing other primitive operations.

A second point about the functional units listed in Figure 7-1 is that there may not be a distinct and physically separate hardware unit, or "box," for each operation. For example, in Section 3.4 we showed how subtraction in radix-complement notation can be defined in terms of addition and complementation (see Figure 3-5). Thus, we do not have to pay for the construction of a separate "subtractor unit." We can use the adder and complementor units that we already have. Likewise, many other primitive operations can be defined in terms of existing functional operations. Let's take a look at integer multiplication.

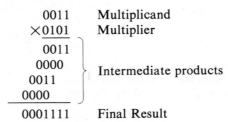

When we multiply by a 1 in the multiplier, the intermediate product is exactly the same as the multiplicand. When we multiply by a 0, the intermediate product is all 0s. Each time we move to the next digit in the multiplier, the intermediate product is shifted left one more position. The final result is the sum of all of the intermediate products. Thus, an algorithm for integer multiplication can be defined solely in terms of integer addition, arithmetic shifting, and integer compares.

If the multiplicand is called A and the multiplier is called B (with the individual bits of B labeled $B_0, B_1, B_2, \ldots, B_N$), then a possible algorithm for multiplication is shown in Figure 7-4. (Note: This algorithm omits any consideration of the sign; it is only concerned with the magnitude of the result.)

Looking at the algorithm in Figure 7-4, we see that multiplication is being carried out using only addition (line 10), left shifting (line 9), and comparing (line 6).

FIGURE 7-4 Algorithm for Binary Multiplication.

```
START
    result : = 0
    for i : = 0 to N do
        begin
        digit : = B₁
        if digit = 1 then
            begin
            partial product : = A
            shift the partial product left i bit positions
            result : = result + the shifted partial product
            end { if statement }
        end { for loop }
END OF ALGORITHM
```

The point of this discussion has been to demonstrate that arithmetic and logical operations may not be implemented using the "classical" methods you learned in high school algebra. They may instead be defined and implemented in a manner that maximizes their ability to use other functional units already on the system and so reduce the cost of manufacture.

7.3
Registers

In Figure 7-2, we showed the operands and results of an arithmetic operation placed in "holding cells." Those holding cells, or *registers,* are special-purpose storage locations. A register is similar to a memory cell in that it can store and retrieve information, but it differs in a number of important ways.

1. Registers are not referenced by unsigned binary addresses 0, 1, 2, . . . , but by a special alphanumeric identification such as A, R0, PSW, or I2.

2. They are usually faster than regular memory cells (i.e., they have a lower memory cycle time). This is because registers are so closely involved in the execution of virtually every operation that they must work extremely fast to ensure efficient machine operation.

3. They may be assigned special purposes. All memory locations are generally identical and serve the same purpose: to store and fetch data. Registers are generally not identical and may be assigned unique roles in the operation of the computer.

4. There may be special data paths associated with the registers (see Section 7.4).

There are three types of register. The first type, *accumulators,* are used in performing the arithmetic and logical operations described in the previous section. Accumulators typically hold arithmetic and logical operands and results, so their size is related to the size of a memory word (m bits in our discussion). There will always be at least two accumulators, because the multiplication of two m-bit operands will produce a product that is up to $(2m - 1)$ bits long. If each accumulator holds m bits, then we may need two to hold the result. Similarly, the operation of division produces two results—an m-bit quotient and an m-bit remainder. Most computers have many accumulators.

A second class of registers, called *index registers,* hold operands that are unsigned binary memory addresses and hold the results of arithmetic operations on addresses. The size of an index register is likely to differ from the size of an accumulator. As we have mentioned, the size of an accumulator is related to the size of the data representations on the computer, which is the value we have been referring to as m (see Figure 6-1). However, an index register, which holds addresses, only has to be large enough to hold all possible addresses. Referring to Figure 6-1, we see that on a computer with 2^n memory locations, the index registers would require n bits.

However, on most newer machines the distinction between an accumulator and an index register has disappeared, and instead of these two distinct register classes, there is now only a single class of *general-purpose register* that may hold any type of operand: integer, character, or unsigned binary address. (The only exception to this is that general-purpose registers usually are not large enough to hold floating-point values, which usually are placed in a separate and distinct set of floating-point registers.)

The number of general-purpose registers is an important parameter of a computer system. If more registers are available, more operands can be kept in these higher speed locations and fewer transfers between registers and memory will be necessary. For example, evaluating the following assignment statement:

$$X := (A + B) * (C + D)$$

is easy if we have four registers available. We load the four operands A, B, C, and D into the four registers and perform the necessary operations. If we have only two registers, then we will have to do some juggling of operands and results. For example, if we had only two registers called R0 and R1, we would have to do the following:

Move A to register R0
Move B to register R1
Add R0,R1 and put result in a temporary memory location T1
Move C to register R0
Move D to register R1
Add R0,R1 and put result in a temporary memory location T2
Move T1 to register R0
Move T2 to register R1
Multiply R0,R1 and put result in memory location X

In general, increasing the number of registers will simplify the resulting code and speed up execution. Figure 7-5 shows the number of general-purpose registers on some well-known computers.

FIGURE 7-5   Register Structures of Some Typical
Computer Systems.

System	Number of General-Purpose Registers	Register Size (bits)
Intel 8086	8	8
PDP-11	8	16
Motorola MC68000	16	32
VAX-11/780	16	32
IBM 370	16	32
Cray 1	64	64

In addition to general-purpose registers, every computer has a machine-dependent set of *special-purpose registers* to meet its specific needs. These special-purpose registers generally belong to the following types:

Overflow registers (as described in Section 3.4)
Carry registers (as described in Section 3.4)
Shift registers
Scratch (or temporary) registers
Stack pointers
Floating-point registers
Status information registers

Because these registers are so highly machine specific, we postpone a detailed discussion of them until Part III, where we describe a specific computer system. For the sake of our discussion of an idealized PVM computer, all we need to assume is the existence of an arithmetic/logic unit with two components:

1.   A set of $k + 1$ general-purpose registers labeled R0, R1, R2, . . . , Rk ($k \geq 1$). The registers will be large enough to hold either an address or the contents of a single memory cell. That is:

$$\text{size} \geq \max\ (m,n)$$

where m is the size of a memory cell, and n is the number of bits needed to hold the largest memory address.

2.   A set of functional units for implementing the arithmetic and logic operations referred to in Figure 7-1.

7.4
The Interconnect Network

We have described a significant number of components that will be included in our hypothetical PVM computer: general-purpose registers, special-purpose registers,

FIGURE 7-6a   A Serial Bus.

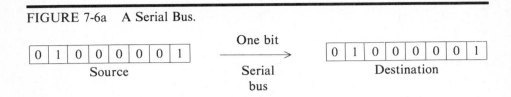

memory cells, functional units, and the like. However, we have not yet discussed the connection of these components so that data can flow from one unit to another. In the study of computer organization, the data path connecting two or more functional units of a computer system is called a *bus,* and the number of buses that exist, and their types, is called the *bus structure* of the computer.

Buses can be either *unidirectional,* which means that transfers can proceed in only one direction, or *bidirectional,* which means that transfers can proceed in both directions, but not at the same time.

Buses also come in two quite different forms depending on the nature of the transmission. These two forms are called serial and parallel.

In a *serial bus* only one binary digit at a time can be transmitted. Therefore, a collection of binary digits would need to be transmitted sequentially, each one following right after the previous one. Transmission of the 8-bit ASCII character 01000001 (the letter 'A') would involve eight separate 1-bit transmissions as shown in Figure 7-6a.

A *parallel bus* transmits information simultaneously along a number of parallel paths. If we had an 8-bit parallel bus between the source and the destination, the value 01000001 would be transmitted as in Figure 7-6b.

A serial bus is usually slower than a parallel bus because it transmits only one bit at a time. For the same reason, it is frequently much cheaper. The speed of a bus is usually measured by the number of *bits per second* that can be transmitted along the bus. Typical speeds for serial buses are in the range of 100–50,000 bits per second.

Since speed is so important, all buses inside the computer are parallel. The number of bits that can be transmitted simultaneously along the bus is called the *bus size* or the *bus width,* and depends on the size of the units that it is connecting. A bus connecting two *m*-bit registers must be at least *m* bits wide. In reality, the bus width is frequently much larger than just the size of the registers to which it is connected.

FIGURE 7-6b   A Parallel Bus.

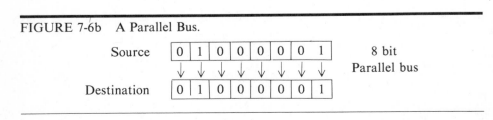

This is because in addition to transmitting binary data, the bus will also simultaneously transfer control and timing information that this discussion has omitted. For example, the main bus on the PDP-11 has fifty-six parallel lines, even though the largest register holds only sixteen bits. The main parallel bus on the VAX-11/780 has a maximum transmission rate of 2 million bits per second.

A parallel bus can be constructed as an integral part of the frame of the computer, much like a plugboard, into which other functional components are inserted. This construction is usually called a *backplane.* Alternately, portable and flexible parallel buses can be purchased by the running foot. This type of bus, usually referred to as a *ribbon cable,* is shown in Figure 7-7.

Serial buses are usually reserved for *external communications* (communication to devices that are located away from the main processor). The use of serial communications usually lowers costs considerably. For example, a printer located 1000 meters from the computer could be attached with the parallel ribbon cable shown in Figure 7-7. However, at $5/meter, this would be an extremely expensive approach! A simple serial connection using a single twisted pair of copper wires would be much cheaper. For long-distance communications using telephones or microwaves, all transmission is serial. In our discussion of the bus structure of our hypothetical PVM computer, we assume the use of bidirectional, parallel buses.

Once we have decided what type of bus to use, we must determine *how many* buses we need. The straightforward approach is to have a data bus placed along every path where a transmission could possibly take place. If register R_i could possibly transmit

FIGURE 7-7   Parallel Bus Implemented as a Ribbon Cable.

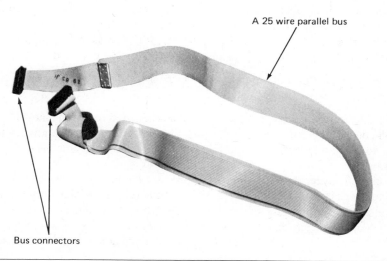

A 25 wire parallel bus

Bus connectors

FIGURE 7-8   Typical Fully Connected Bus Structure.

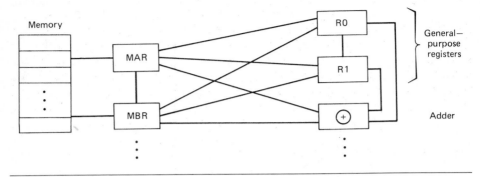

its contents to register R_j, we place a bus between them. This creates a *fully connected bus structure* (Figure 7-8), which has some very distinct advantages. First, there is never a queueing delay; that is, you never have to wait for a bus to become available because, in a sense, there is no competition for that resource. If, in Figure 7-8, we want to transfer the contents of register R0 to the MAR, we use the R0-MAR bus, which exists for that purpose only.

There is an even more important advantage to this bus structure. For the past few years, computer engineers have been able to make computers work faster and faster. This has been accomplished by building faster electrical circuits, using newer and faster technologies (e.g., semiconductors instead of cores), and putting components closer together so the signals do not take so long to propagate between them. However, it may no longer be possible to maintain this rapid increase in computer speeds solely on the basis of hardware improvements, because designers are beginning to confront insurmountable constants—like the speed of light!

However, there is still a way to achieve dramatic increases in computer speeds, and it is based on the following principle:

> If you can't build something to work twice as fast, make it do two
> things at once.

The implementation of this principle, called *parallelism,* is one of the most important developments in modern computer organization, and designers are always looking for ways to overlap two or more operations to reduce the total time needed for their performance.

The fully connected bus structure in Figure 7-8 offers a great number of opportunities to overlap operations, since each bus can handle a transfer during the same cycle (as long as we don't try to perform an operation that might lead to unpredictable behavior, like transferring something into and out of the same register at the same time). For example, let's try to execute the following pair of instructions within our program.

1. Move the contents of R0 into register R1.
2. Add +1 to the contents of register R1.

These two operations would normally be executed by sequentially fetching each instruction in turn, and then carrying it out.

1. Get instruction 1.
2. Carry out instruction 1.
3. Get instruction 2.
4. Carry out instruction 2.

However, looking at steps 2 and 3, we see that carrying out the first instruction (R0 → R1) and getting the second instruction (which is stored in memory) do not directly affect each other. Perhaps we could overlap these two steps by using different buses to implement them. In fact, this is possible, and if separate buses are available, the two operations could be carried out in the following way.

1. Get instruction 1.
2. Carry out instruction 1 *and* fetch instruction 2.
3. Carry out instruction 2.

The total time needed would be reduced by about 25 percent.

When designing a computer, we almost always benefit by looking for ways to perform operations simultaneously. However, we must be very careful when we perform operations in parallel instead of sequentially. Some very subtle, time-dependent errors are possible. For example, if the first instruction of a 2-instruction pair had said, "Modify the next instruction," and we did them simultaneously, we would have executed the unmodified rather than the modified instruction.

In spite of its advantages, the fully connected bus structure has some major disadvantages, which are obvious from the number of lines in Figure 7-8. Theoretically, if we have n components, each of which must be connected to all or nearly all other components, the number of connections will grow at the rate of n^2. In real machines the number of components (registers, processors, etc.) is very large and the complexity of the potential interconnectivity is astronomical. It becomes very difficult and very expensive to build a computer with that many wires and connections. A fully connected bus structure (or even a highly interconnected one) is appropriate only for very large and expensive computer systems. (If you have ever been in a computer room where a large, expensive "supercomputer" was operating in its own computer room, you probably noticed that it had a raised floor. Under this false floor are the thousands or even hundreds of thousands of cables connecting the different functional units of the system.)

There is another drawback and that is the problem of *wasted capacity*. Even if parallelism can be implemented, it typically involves performing two or possibly three operations simultaneously. If there are twenty separate and unique buses, even at the highest possible utilization, only 10 or 15 percent of their capacity can ever be fully utilized at once. Thus 85 or 90 percent of the transmission capabilities of the computer will be idle.

Now let's look at the interconnect network from the other extreme. Instead of having the maximum number of buses, we could have the minimum number, namely, one. All functional components will hang on this bus, and all transfers will take place along it. Typically, this is called a *common bus structure* (Figure 7-9).

Whenever we wish to effect a transfer we must request ownership of the bus for a specific time period. If another operation is also trying to request the bus, *arbitration* is required. A decision has to be made about who will get the bus and who will wait. No overlapping is possible, and a queueing delay occurs because of the waiting time involved. The arbitration policy is usually carried out by a centralized device called a *bus controller* or *bus master* and is based on a scheme in which priority levels are assigned to each device on the system. The request with the highest priority always gets control of the bus. Alternatively, we could use a decentralized arbitration scheme and let the individual units decide among themselves who will gain ownership of the bus during the next cycle.

Such an architecture has the advantages of simplicity and low cost. There is, in effect, only a single parallel bus in the entire system. Such a device is relatively inexpensive and easy to manufacture. If one isn't careful, however, and the bus transfer times are too slow, the common bus can become a bottleneck. In extreme cases, the queueing delays can become much longer than the actual processing times. In addition, no overlapping transfers of data are possible. Therefore, a common bus scheme is probably appropriate only for small and inexpensive micro- or minicomputers in which extremely high system throughput is not the central concern.

FIGURE 7-9   Common Bus Structure.

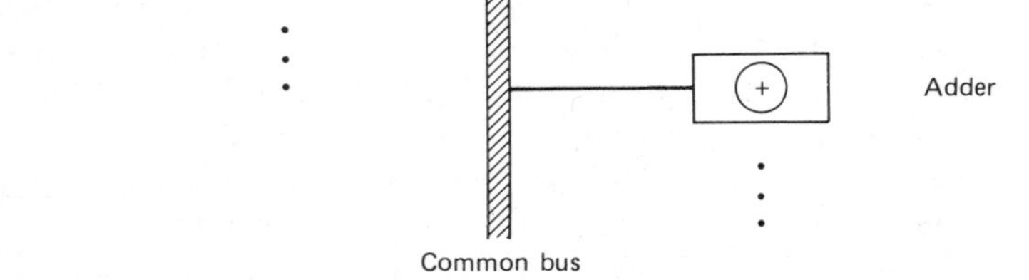

In reality, the bus structure of most computers represents a compromise between the two extremes shown in Figures 7-8 and 7-9. Most systems, except the very smallest and the very largest, have a few buses (say, 2–4). These buses can be organized in a number of ways, and there is no clear categorization of these compromise bus structures.

The system in Figure 7-10 has two buses, one m bits long, used as a *data bus,* and one n bits long, used as an *address bus.* Data transfers, such as moving an m-bit twos-complement integer from R0 to the adder, could take place along the data bus. Address transfers, such as moving an n-bit unsigned binary address from R1 to the MAR, might take place along the address bus. Since we have two buses, a modest amount of parallelism is possible. For example, the two transfers (R0 $\rightarrow$ adder and R1 $\rightarrow$ MAR) could be accomplished simultaneously along the two buses.

The three buses shown in Figure 7-11 are broken up into *input/output buses* and *memory buses.*

FIGURE 7-10   A Two-Bus Structure Using an Address and a Data Bus.

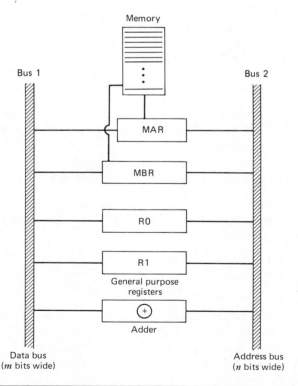

FIGURE 7-11   A Three-Bus Structure Using Input/
Output Buses and a Memory Bus.

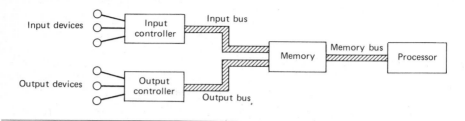

Now there is one bus, called the *memory bus,* for handling all transfer between memory and the internal components of the computer, much like the common bus of Figure 7-9. There are also second and third buses specifically for handling the direct transfer of information between input/output devices and memory. Again, some modest level of parallelism is possible. An I/O operation can be transferring characters into memory while the computer is executing other operations that are unrelated to the I/O operation taking place.

The VAX-11 has a special bus, called a *mass bus,* specifically for supporting transfers between memory and the mass storage subsystem.

Currently, there is a move to standardize the electrical, mechanical, and physical characteristics of buses. The following standardized bus structures are extremely popular and widely used.

S-100 bus	A 100-wire parallel bus used on many microcomputers.
Unibus	A 120-wire parallel bus used on many minicomputers.
RS-232C	A standardized interface for transmitting data serially along external communication paths.
IEEE-488	A 24-wire bus that transmits data in a byte serial mode.

Standardization brings the advantage of allowing many manufacturers to produce computer components (e.g., memory banks, I/O controllers) that will plug directly into the standardized buses.

7.5
Summary

In this chapter, we introduced the arithmetic/logic unit, the second component of our ever-growing hypothetical computer. In addition, we explored some basic principles of bus structure associated with interconnecting components. In real life, we would have a set of functional units to implement the operations referred to in Figure 7-1, a large number of general-purpose registers (e.g., 8, 16, 32), and a multibus architecture something like the one in Figure 7-10 or 7-11.

However, to keep our PVM simple, we will limit it to the following components.

1. Two m-bit general-purpose registers called R0 and R1.
2. The following functional units:
   a. Adder (given a,b computes $a + b$).
   b. Subtractor (given a,b computes $a - b$)
   c. Incrementor (given a computes $a + 1$)
   d. Decrementor (given a computes $a - 1$)
   e. Multiplier (given a,b computes $a \times b$)
   f. Integer divider (given a,b computes a/b)
3. A single common bus, as shown in Figure 7-9, which connects all of the components just named.

Our PVM is not very realistic but it is sufficiently realistic and complex to let us study the operation and behavior of computer systems.

In the next chapter we add to our PVM yet another component: input and output.

Exercises for Chapter 7

1. Develop an algorithm for integer division that uses only integer addition, subtraction, and comparison. How efficient would this algorithm be in general?

2. Using your algorithm from Exercise 1, determine how long it would take to perform the following operation:

$$23 \div 2$$

Compare that to the time it takes to perform a division directly in hardware which, on the PDP-11/44 is 11.01 μsec.

3. Modify the multiplication algorithm in Figure 7-4 so that it will properly multiply *signed* values. Assume that the technique for representing the signed operands is sign/magnitude.

4. If you already have hardware functional units for performing the logical AND, OR, and NOT operations, is it necessary to build a separate functional unit for the exclusive-OR operation, defined as follows?

		A	
X-OR		0	1
B	0	0	1
	1	1	0

5. Show the sequence of operations necessary to evaluate the expression:

$$A := ((B + C) * D) + (E/F)$$

Assume that all operands must be in general-purpose registers before they can be operated on, and that the result may be placed anywhere. Assume:

    a.   Two general-purpose registers called R0, R1.

    b.   Four general-purpose registers called R0, R1, R2, R3.

How much more "juggling" of numbers is necessary in case a than in case b?

6.   If you placed a bus between register R1, which is 15 bits wide, and register R2, which is 18 bits wide, how large would that bus have to be? What design decision would we have to make concerning how to move information between the two registers.

7.   How might you exploit the concept of parallelism if you had two adder units instead of one? How much of an increase in speed would result when evaluating the following expression?

$$A := (B + C) * (D + E)$$

8.   When you have a common bus, you must decide who gets it for any one cycle. Discuss criteria for establishing priority among functional units on a common bus.

CHAPTER 8

INPUT/OUTPUT AND
MASS STORAGE

8.1
Introduction

Input/output (I/O) is a difficult topic to discuss in general terms because it is by far the most machine-dependent operation performed by a computer. I/O is usually carried out by a highly specialized method implemented by only one particular manufacturer, and understanding it requires familiarity with the organizational structure of that particular computer. This is exactly what we wanted to avoid in this general discussion of the organizational structure of computers.

I/O is also difficult to discuss because it is changing so rapidly. New gear is being introduced all the time, and the number of different products on the market is overwhelming. Currently, there are over fifty companies that manufacture disk drives, and over two hundred companies that make VDTs, each with its own unique combination of capabilities, options, advantages, and disadvantages. Figure 8-1 lists just some of the currently available types of I/O equipment that can be added to computer systems.

For now, we shall not consider how I/O is accomplished on any one particular computer system. (That topic is addressed in Part III.) Instead, we introduce only the characteristics that are common to all I/O devices, regardless of manufacturer, and that will contribute to a broader understanding of input/output in general.

Furthermore, we do not distinguish between the following classes of I/O devices:

1. Devices that record information in a machine-readable form, such as magnetic encoding, generally for the purpose of long-term storage of information. These devices are usually called *mass storage devices* and include disks, tapes, and cassettes.

2. Devices that record information in a form that is easily understood by a human being: alphabetic, pictorial, or spoken. These devices are sometimes referred to, by themselves, as *input/output devices.*

121

FIGURE 8-1   Types of Input/Output Device.

Input	*Output*
Keyboard	Video display terminal
Touch panel	Hard-copy terminal
Light pen	Graphics terminal
Voice input unit	Plotter
Digitizer	Voice output unit
Analog input device	Environmental controls
Punched card	Analog output
Mark sense reader	Phototypesetter
Optical scanner	Line printer
Badge reader	Braille printer
Fingerprint reader	Disk (input and output)
Telephone buttons	Tape (input and output)
Cash register controls	Cassette (input and output)

Regardless of whether we record information as bits on the surface of a device coated with ferric oxide, or as letters on a piece of paper, both of the above classes and, indeed, all of the devices listed in Figure 8-1, fall into the domain of the subsystem called input/output.

8.2.
Access Mechanisms

In Chapter 6 we defined a *random-access memory* (RAM) as a storage mechanism in which all information is uniquely addressed, and for which the same amount of time is required to locate all pieces of information. In general, input/output devices are not random access. Instead, they use two different types of access mechanisms, called *direct access* and *sequential access.*

In a direct-access device, we eliminate the second characteristic of random access listed above: namely, the requirement that all data be accessed in the same amount of time. Information is still uniquely addressed and we can go directly to it, but the time it takes to fetch any one piece of information is not a constant; it depends on the location of the information sought. There are many types of direct-access storage device (DASD) available, such as floppy disks, hard disks, drums, and addressable cassettes. The following illustration uses a disk, but the discussion is valid for any other type of DASD.

Figure 8-2 shows the organization of the surface of a typical disk. The disk surface is coated with ferric oxide, and information is recorded magnetically in concentric circles, called *tracks,* on the surface of the disk. Each track is divided into a number of fixed-size units called *sectors,* each of which has its own unique address. For exam-

FIGURE 8-2   Layout of the Surface of a Disk.

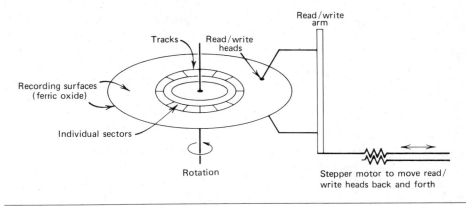

ple, if our disk has 100 tracks (numbered 00–99), and 500 sectors per track (numbered 000–499), then the sector address 23456 might mean track 23, sector 456 from the start of that track. (Each track contains a starting indicator where we begin numbering the sectors.) Typical disks have many surfaces (not the single surface shown in Figure 8-2), and each surface may have 100–500 tracks with 10–100 sectors per track. A sector itself may contain 128–1,024 individual bytes of information. Disk capacities vary widely; some disks may hold as few as 100,000 bytes, while others may store as many as 500,000,000 bytes per disk unit.

Fetching a particular sector on the disk involves three steps.

1.   Move the read/write head to the correct track *(seek time)*.

2.   Wait for the correct sector to rotate under the read/write head *(latency)*.

3.   Read the entire sector *(transfer time)*.

The total time required to read any one sector on the disk is then:

(8.1)   total time = seek time + latency + transfer time

Obviously, the total time depends on exactly which sector we are accessing. If it is a sector located on the same track as the current position of the read/write head, then no head movement is necessary and the seek time will be 0. Otherwise, we must move the read/write arm, and the time required will be a function of how far the arm has to travel. Likewise, if we are accessing a sector that is just about to pass under the read/write head, the latency will be approximately 0. Otherwise we must wait for up to one full rotation.

Figure 8-3 shows some simple best-case/worst-cast timings for a typical disk,

FIGURE 8-3   Typical Time Requirements (msec) for Disk Accessing.

	Seek Time	Latency	Transfer Time	Total Time
Best case	0	0	1	1
Worst case	100	50	1	151
Average case	50	25	1	76

assuming 100 tracks, 1 msec to cross a track, 50 sectors per track, and a rotational speed of 1,200 rpm. All times are in milliseconds (thousandths of a second).

As we can see from Figure 8-3, the access times for our hypothetical disk are definitely not constant; in fact, they can differ by as much as two orders of magnitude, depending on which sector is being accessed. This is a typical characteristic of direct-access storage devices.

There are a great many other direct-access storage devices, and our previous discussion addressed only one type, a disk. Figure 8-4 shows a second possibility, called a *drum*. With a drum there is one read/write head for each track. Therefore, there is never any need to move a read/write head, and the seek time on a drum is always 0. There will still be delays caused by rotation and transfer, but because of the elimination of seek time, drums usually have a lower overall access time than disks.

Regardless of the mechanics of the device, however, a DASD always has the following two characteristics.

1.   All information is identified and accessed through a unique address.

2.   Access time is dependent on the location of the information being retrieved.

The second basic access mechanism for I/O devices is called *sequential access*. With sequential access, we relax both of the original requirements of random access. We

FIGURE 8-4   A Magnetic Drum.

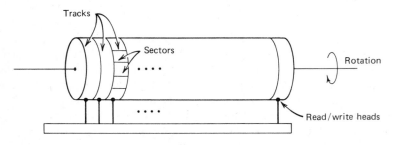

FIGURE 8-5 Layout of Information on a Magnetic Tape.

One character (101_8 = 'A')

Ferric oxide coating

Channels

							0								
							0								
							1								
							0								
							0								
							0								
							0								
							0								
							1								

Number of characters per inch = tape density

no longer require that information be accessed through a unique address. Instead, to locate a piece of data, we must search sequentially all of the information stored on the device until we find what we are looking for. The best known example of a *sequential-access storage device* (SASD) is reel-to-reel magnetic tape. Figure 8-5 shows the layout of information on the surface of a tape. As with the disk, the surface of the tape is coated with ferric oxide, and information is magnetically recorded in rows called *channels*. Most modern tapes contain nine channels, to allow the storage of an 8-bit character and a parity bit for error checking (see Section 4.2). The number of characters that can be packed together in a specified amount of space is called the *tape density,* and on most current machines it is either 800 or 1,600 characters per inch. Since a typical tape is about 2,200 feet long, it could theoretically hold about:

$$2{,}200 \text{ ft} \times 12 \text{ in/ft} \times 1{,}600 \text{ chars/in} = 42{,}240{,}000 \text{ chars}$$

However, that limit is unattainable because we must allow space for the tape drive to come up to speed and stop. We must place unused space, called an *interrecord gap* or *tape gap* between each chunk of data to be read, as shown in Figure 8-6.

FIGURE 8-6 Record Gaps on a Magnetic Tape.

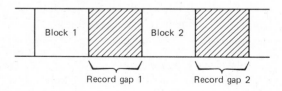

Block 1 | Block 2

Record gap 1   Record gap 2

Gap 1 in Figure 8-6 will allow space for stopping the tape drive after reading block 1, and for starting it up to begin to read block 2. The exact size of these gaps depends on the characteristics of the particular tape drive, but they can easily occupy 30, 50, or even 70 percent of the entire tape, reducing the effective storage per reel to 10 million to 20 million characters rather than the 42 million characters computed earlier.

There are a number of other classes of SASD but they all share one characteristic: Information is not uniquely addressed. To locate a specific piece of data, we must search sequentially through all items until the desired one has been found.

8.3
Record Sizes and Blocking Factors

In high-level languages like Pascal, FORTRAN, and BASIC, we specify input/output operations only in terms of how much information we need within our program. For example, if we are reading a 3-digit integer from a disk file, we think only about the three digits that we need, not the size or physical layout of the sectors of the disk:

read(textfile, i:3)

read(1,100) i
100   format (I3)

The information format, as seen by the user, is called a *logical record*. High-level languages allow you to think about and program in terms of logical records.

However, at the level of computer organization, there are no longer any logical records. All input/output is done in terms of fixed-size units called *physical records* whose size is an inherent physical characteristic of a particular device. (Magnetic tapes do not have a fixed physical record size. Instead, they allow the user to specify the physical record size when first writing on the tape.) All transfers to and from an I/O device take place in units of one or more physical records. Looking at Figure 8-2, we see that a physical record on a disk is a sector. In Figure 8-6, we see that the physical record size of a magnetic tape is equal to the area occupied by all of the information contained between two record gaps. Other common physical record sizes are:

Card reader/punch	80 characters (one card)
Line printer	132 (or 136) characters (one line)
VDT (line oriented)	80 characters (one line)
VDT (screen oriented)	1,920 characters (an 80 × 24 screen)

Whenever you perform an I/O operation at this level, you must work in terms of the physical record size of the device, regardless of the logical record size that exists within your program. You must always transfer one physical record unit to or from the I/O device. So, for example, to print a 3-digit integer on one line of a 132-character line printer, in a high-level language, you would write:

writeln (i:3)

write(6,100)i
100   format(I3)

But at the functional organizational level, it would have to be carried out as follows.

1. Allocate 132 characters of space for this line.
2. Move the 3 characters of the number into positions 1, 2, and 3 of the line.
3. Move blanks into positions 4, 5, . . . , 132.
4. Print the 132-character line.

The number of logical records contained in a single physical record is called the *blocking factor*. There are a number of advantages to having a large blocking factor. Let's say, for example, that we had a blocking factor of 5, as shown below:

One physical record

LR	LR	LR	LR	LR
1	2	3	4	5

↑
An individual logical record

The first time our program requests a logical record (via a read operation), we will go to the input device and get one physical record, which contains five logical records. We will then pass logical record LR1 to the program. The next four times our program requests input, we will not need to perform an input operation because the data are already in memory and can be given to the program immediately. Since inputting data from a disk is a relatively slow operation, this elimination of input operations will result in a significant speed-up of program execution.

In addition, a large blocking factor can increase the utilization of a magnetic tape device. Referring to Figure 8-5, we see that each physical record is bounded on both sides by interrecord gaps. If we assume that the gap is ¾ in. (a typical value), the tape density is 800 characters per inch, and the logical records are 80 characters each, then if we store the logical records unblocked, each one will occupy only ⅒ in. The tape will look like this:

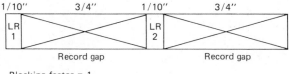

Blocking factor = 1

The utilization of the tape will be about 12 percent. If, instead, we block ten logical records per physical record, the tape will look like this:

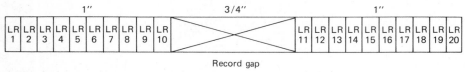

Blocking factor = 10

and the tape utilization will be increased to 58 percent.

The only limit to increasing the blocking factor is the amount of available memory on the computer and the amount of space that can be allocated to an input operation. Remember that we must always read or write one complete physical record. That means that we must allocate enough memory space to hold all of the bytes that will be transferred into or out of memory by this operation. The memory used to hold the information transferred in or out by an I/O operation is called a *buffer*.

In the example where the logical record was 80 bytes and the blocking factor was 1, we would need a memory buffer containing at least 80 bytes. If the blocking factor were increased to 10, our buffer would have to be enlarged to 800 bytes. If we increased the blocking factor to 100, our buffer would need to hold 8,000 bytes. At some point we simply would not have enough available memory to create a buffer large enough to hold the contents of a physical record.

Because logical record sizes are not necessarily related to physical record sizes, it is also possible that one logical record will occupy more than one physical record. In this case, a single read statement in a high-level language may ultimately require more than one I/O transfer. However, even in this case, the unit of transfer will still be the physical record.

8.4
The Character Orientation of Input/Output

As we first mentioned in Chapter 4, all I/O transfers are byte oriented (i.e., the unit of transfer is the 8-bit byte), even if the information itself is not in character format. The user is responsible for converting data into or out of character form for its correct transmission. Assume, for example, we were inputting the following 80-character line from a VDT:

$$+123 \;\; \text{(CR)} \quad (\text{(CR)} \;\; = \text{carriage return})$$

we obviously mean to input the positive integer quantity 123. What we would get instead are the following 80 characters in our 80-character input buffer (assume an 8-bit ASCII code without parity):

	1	00101011	A + sign
	2	00110001	The character '1'
	3	00110010	The character '2'
	4	00110011	The character '3'
80-Character input buffer	5	00001101	The character 'carriage return'
	6	00100000	The character 'blank'
	7	00100000	The character 'blank'
	.	.	
	.	.	
	.	.	
	80	00100000	The character 'blank'

If the computer stored integers using sixteen bits, the user would be responsible for the conversion of the above information into the proper 16-bit representation of $+123$:

$$0000000001111011$$

(Exercise 11 asks you to develop this algorithm.)

Similarly, one of the most common errors people make when first programming in machine or assembly language is forgetting that information must also be converted *into* character representation before it can be printed or displayed on most output devices. Assume that you have just completed an algebraic operation, and now have the following 16-bit sign/magnitude integer result sitting in a register:

$$0010100001100001 = 024141_8 = 10,337_{10}$$

If you try to print this 16-bit integer value directly, you will not get the integer value 10,337 as expected, but rather the rather cryptic character pair:

(a

This is because the sixteen bits have not been interpreted as integers but as the two 8-bit ASCII characters 050 and 141, which are "(" and "a", respectively.

$$
\begin{array}{c|c}
00101000 & 01100001 \\
050 & 141 \\
\text{"("} & \text{"a"}
\end{array}
$$

Things can actually get quite a bit worse. As shown in Figure 4-2, certain ASCII codes represent control signals rather than printable characters, and their transmission causes certain operations to occur at the input or output device. For example, the code 007 causes a bell to ring on some terminals. The code 004 can cause an immediate termination of output. So, if you try to print, without conversion, the decimal value 1,796, which in binary is:

$$0000011100000100$$

the sixteen bits will be interpreted as the two ASCII characters 007 and 004, possibly causing a bell to ring and the terminal to shut off!

The discussion in Chapters 6 and 7 points out yet another major advantage of high-level languages: the ease and simplicity of I/O. Low-level input/output is difficult, messy, confusing, and highly machine dependent. It requires the user to be very familiar with the physical characteristics of the device being used. High-level languages conceal all this mess and allow you to view I/O in terms of a few simple problem-oriented commands, like read, write, open, and close. Such useful user-oriented commands do not exist at the level at which we are working, and when studying a specific computer, we will have to learn the low-level details of I/O processing. This is another example of how a high-level language can be used to create a friendly, user-oriented *virtual machine*.

8.5
Modes of Transfer

The final topic of discussion about I/O is probably the most important. How is information transferred between an I/O device and the memory of the computer? All I/O devices are composed of two distinct parts, the *I/O mechanism* and the *I/O controller*. The mechanism is simply the mechanical, electrical, and/or optical components that make up this device: keys, paper feeders, screens, tape heads, and so on. The I/O controller is the component that manages the flow of information between the I/O device and the computer.

The I/O controller contains a buffer to temporarily hold the data being transferred to or from the computer. The controller also accepts control signals (e.g., START) from the computer and activates the proper I/O mechanism in response. When the operation is complete, the controller can transfer the contents of the buffer to the primary memory of the computer. It may also return a simple set of control signals, such as DONE or ERROR, describing the status of the I/O operation just completed. Figure 8-7 shows the general structure of I/O devices.

FIGURE 8-7   Structure of an I/O Device.

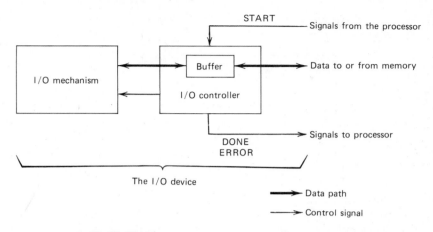

There are a number of well-known and standardized classes of I/O controllers. The acronym PIO (parallel input/output) refers to a wide class of controllers that can handle the parallel transfer of an 8-bit byte between a data bus and an I/O device. This is shown in Figure 8-8a. The acronyms USART and UART—for universal (Synchronous and) Asynchronous Receiver and Transmitter—refer to a class of controllers that can take an 8-bit byte of data and transmit it serially to an I/O device, one bit at a time, as shown in Figure 8-8b.

The simplest technique for transferring data between an I/O device and a computer is called *programmed input/output*. With this technique, the process simply activates the I/O device directly (typically with some kind of START signal), and waits until the I/O device signals DONE, at which time the character is in some

FIGURE 8-8a   A Parallel I/O Controller.

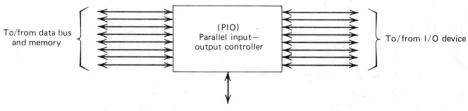

FIGURE 8-8b   A Serial I/O Controller.

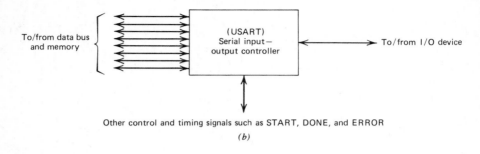

Other control and timing signals such as START, DONE, and ERROR

(b)

special register within the I/O controller or the processor. The processor checks for an error and moves the character into memory if no error is found.

The problem with programmed I/O (Figure 8-9) is that I/O operations are usually very, very slow in comparison with the internal speed of the computer. Computers execute instructions in one or two microseconds or even a few hundred nanoseconds, while I/O operations can take milliseconds, seconds, or even minutes to complete. Appreciating the difference between nanoseconds, milliseconds, and seconds is quite difficult because these are such small units of time. To give you a better idea of just how slow I/O can be in comparison to internal processing speeds, let's assume that we could slow down a computer so that it executed an instruction once every second instead of once every microsecond. If this were the case, a 30 characters per second VDT terminal would print one character every 9½ hours! Displaying a full 80-character line would take a month. Filling up an entire 80 × 24 screen would

FIGURE 8-9   Programmed I/O.

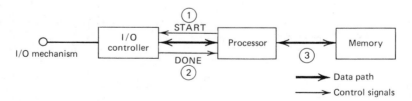

1.   Processor issues a START command to begin the I/O operation.

2.   Processor waits until I/O controller issues a DONE signal, which means that the operation is finished.

3.   (If input) Processor moves the character into the proper memory location.

take about 2 years. Even at the more typical high-speed terminal rate of 9,600 bits per second (1,200 characters per second), filling up an 80 × 24 screen would still take about 18 days!

We must compensate for this enormous speed disparity between computer processing and I/O. Otherwise, the system will become horribly inefficient. Looking back at Figure 8-9, we see that the computer is likely to spend 99.99 percent of its time at step 2 ("Wait until the DONE signal") doing no useful work. Overcoming the disparity between computer processing speed and the slowness of I/O devices is one of the major problems in computer design.

One of the most common solutions of this problem calls for the use of *interrupts*. An interrupt is a signal to the processor that a specific event has occurred. When an interrupt signal is generated, the processor must stop what it is doing and handle the event. It is not unlike setting an alarm clock to remind you to finish a task at a particular time, go off to work on something else, and return immediately to complete the original task when the alarm sounds.

Specifically, when an interrupt signal arrives, the processor does the following.

1. Interrupts the task T that it is currently executing.

2. Saves the state of the machine (registers, memory, etc.) so that T can be restarted at a later time.

3. Checks to see what event caused the interrupt.

4. Executes a special program associated with this specific event (called an *interrupt handler*).

5. When the interrupt handler is finished, restores the state of the machine to its pre-interrupted conditions.

6. Restarts task T from exactly the point at which it was interrupted.

In this case, we are concerned about the completion of the I/O operation, and the interrupt signal would correspond to the arrival of the DONE signal generated by the I/O controller. Our *interrupt-driven I/O* would proceed as shown in Figure 8-10.

Now there is no waiting or wasted time except for the overhead time needed for servicing the interrupt. This overhead will correspond to steps 2 and 5 in the description of interrupt processing: namely, saving and restoring the state of task T. The processor is free to do useful work (e.g., working on someone else's program) instead of idly waiting for the completion of a relatively slow operation.

An interrupt is one of the most important concepts in computer architecture, and interrupts are used in many areas other than I/O processing. Interrupts are used to signal that a fatal error has occurred in a program, that there has been a power failure, or that a ticking clock needs to be advanced. This brief discussion of interrupts has pointed out their existence and their purpose. Further courses in computer architecture and operating systems will discuss this topic at much greater length. In addition, in Part III we describe how one computer system, the PDP-11 family, implements interrupt-driven I/O.

FIGURE 8-10 Interrupt-Driven I/O.

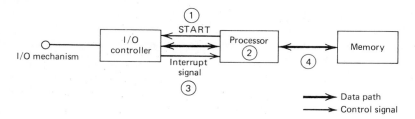

1. Issue START command for I/O operation.
2. Processor now free to handle other computations.
3. When interrupt signal occurs, telling processor that I/O is done, stop whatever it is doing.
4. Move character to memory.

One problem remains with both programmed and interrupt-driven I/O (Figures 8-9 and 8-10): in both cases the processor is responsible for moving the newly received character into memory, because the only path into memory is through the processor. If we were reading a disk sector containing 512 bytes of information, the processor would be interrupted 512 times, once for each byte. If the bytes were coming in moderately fast, the processor might end up spending a significant part of its time doing the relatively low-level operations of processing interrupts and storing characters in a buffer.

In general, a processor is a valuable resource, and we would like to see it spend its time doing more important work than I/O processing. We can achieve that end by creating a second path into memory. A path into computer memory is called a *port*. (As Figure 6-9 showed, a port into memory consists of the MAR and MBR registers, and a decoder). In Figures 8-9 and 8-10, the only port into memory is through the processor. However, we could add a second port into memory directly through the I/O controller. An I/O controller of this type, called a *direct memory access* (DMA) controller (Figure 8-11), is much more sophisticated than the kind we have been talking about.

The DMA device can place the individual characters into memory directly and so eliminate that overhead from the processor. There is a special register in the DMA controller called a *DMA address register* (DAR). This is the address of the first byte of the memory buffer that will hold the data. Now when we issue the START operation, the DMA device will cause a physical record to be read in, and without processor assistance, it will store the characters in memory locations A, A + 1, A + 2, ..., where A is the address in the DAR. (Some DMA controllers contain a second

FIGURE 8-11   Input/Output via a DMA Device.

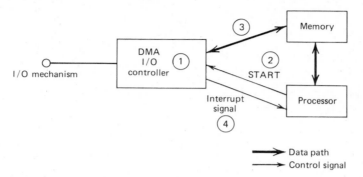

1. Load the memory address of the buffer into the I/O controller.
2. Issue START command to initiate the I/O operation.
3. The DMA controller transfers an entire physical record directly into the specified memory addresses.
4. The processor is interrupted when the *entire* physical record has been transferred and the I/O operation is complete.

register, called a word count [WC] register, that allows you to specify exactly how many bytes will be stored in memory. One physical record will be read, but only WC bytes are stored in the buffer. The remainder are discarded.) When all i characters have been transferred (where i is the physical record size of the device), an interrupt is issued to the processor that the *entire* transfer is complete. This reduces the number of interrupts that must be handled by the processor from i (the number of characters per physical record) to 1.

A slight variation of Figure 8-11 is shown in Figure 8-12. Here again we have a DMA controller, but there is only a single port into memory for which the I/O controller and processor compete on an independent and asynchronous basis. If both the DMA controller and the processor attempt to access memory at the same time, the memory unit will be given to the I/O device, and the processor will have to wait for one cycle. This is because I/O is a time-dependent operation. There may be a punched card, tape, or disk arm in motion that cannot be stopped. Failure to service the device within a fixed time period may cause a loss of information. This method of transfer is called *cycle stealing* because the DMA controller occasionally "steals" a memory cycle from the processor.

We can continue this process of "off-loading" more and more of the work of I/O away from the processor and onto a separate I/O controller. For example, the DMA device handled the problem of storage of characters into memory, but other I/O-

FIGURE 8-12   DMA Controller Using a Cycle-Stealing
Transfer Method.

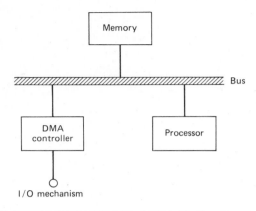

related tasks that are handled by the processor could be handled elsewhere, leaving
the processor free to do useful work. Some of these mundane I/O tasks include:

1. *Code conversion:* For example, converting punched-card code or paper tape code
   to ASCII.
2. *Echoing:* Displaying on the screen the character just typed at the keyboard.
3. *Parity checking:* Checking the parity of the incoming character and handling it
   if it is incorrect.
4. *Editing:* Handling special editing characters (e.g., BACKSPACE, DELETE,
   RUBOUT).
5. *Optimization:* Operating the I/O device to ensure that it is used as efficiently as
   possible.

I/O controllers that can perform such a wide range of complex I/O operations are
called *I/O channels.* These channels can execute special I/O programs and, in many
ways, are like small special-purpose computers. If an I/O device is extremely fast,
then only one device at a time will be able to use the channel. For a short period of
time, the channel will dedicate its entire transmission capacity to servicing that one
I/O device.

Alternatively, if the channel is controlling relatively slow devices, like VDTs, it
may be able to handle many devices simultaneously. For example, if a VDT can
transfer a character every 2 msec (the equivalent of 500 characters per second), and
it takes the channel 100 μsec to fully process and store that character, then the channel could handle twenty terminals in rotation, and guarantee that it could get back

FIGURE 8-13   Multiplexor Channels.

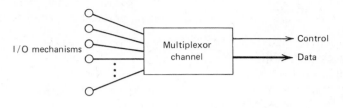

to the first terminal before it had another character to transmit (since 20×100 μsec $= 2$ msec). This is called a *multiplexor channel,* and the process of interleaving the transmissions from a number of devices is called *multiplexing.* If the interleaving is done on a byte-by-byte basis, it is called *character multiplexing.* If the interleaving is based on a larger unit of data, it is called *block multiplexing.* This type of multiplexed channel is diagrammed in Figure 8-13.

We can continue this trend to its ultimate and logical conclusion. Instead of making the I/O channel a special-purpose device, we can make it a separate general-purpose computer in its own right; in effect, an independent *I/O computer.* Attached to many large computer systems are one or more minicomputers or microcomputers to handle every facet of input/output. This frees the main processor (which on a large, sophisticated computer is a very expensive device) to work solely on user programs without having to worry about input/output at all.

8.6
Summary

In this chapter, we have surveyed some of the general principles of I/O processing and have presented a broad overview of the subject area. In no other area of computer organization are there so few general concepts and so much dependence on the design specifications of one specific machine.

When you begin to study the I/O structure of a specific system, you will probably find it quite different from, and a lot messier than, our simple and idealized discussion had led you to expect. You will probably never see a computer that handles I/O transfers exactly as we have described. Instead, you will encounter hardware that is unique and quite specialized for each system.

For our idealized PVM computer system, we do not assume any specific set of I/O devices or any specific modes of transfer. The upcoming discussion of the operation of the PVM computer involves no detailed discussion of the operation of the I/O component. We merely assume that our idealized system has an adequate complement of mass storage devices and input/output units to let it communicate with the "outside world."

Exercises for Chapter 8

Exercises 1 to 7 assume a disk with the following physical characteristics:

> 2 Surfaces (1 platter, top and bottom).
> 64 Tracks per surface.
> 64 Sectors per track.
> 256 Characters per sector.
> 1,200 Revolutions per minute.
> To move the read/write arm x tracks ($x \geq 1$) takes $(5 + 0.5x)$ msec.

1. How many characters can be stored on this disk unit?
2. What is the physical record size of this disk unit?
3. How many addressable units are there on this disk?
4. What is the fastest retrieval time possible for a single sector?
5. What is the slowest retrieval time possible for a single sector?
6. What would the average retrieval time be?
7.   Assume that you added a read/write head for every track (in essence, making it a drum). Recompute the best-case/worst-case condition and average retrieval times for a single sector.

Exercises 8 to 10 assume a magnetic tape with the following characteristics:

> Tape density: 1,600 characters per inch
> Tape length: 2,200 feet
> Physical block size: 800 characters
> Record gap: 1 inch

8. How many characters can be stored on this tape?
9. What percentage of the tape is being utilized to store meaningful information?
10.   Assume that the block size is tripled. Recompute the number of characters being stored and the utilization percentage. What negative consequence could this change have?

11.   Develop an algorithm that takes an array of ASCII characters in the following syntax:

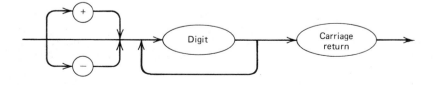

and converts it to the corresponding decimal integer value. For example, if the array contained the characters

'-' '7' '8' 'CR'

your algorithm would return the result

-78

12. Develop the exact opposite algorithm from the one in Exercise 11. That is, your algorithm accepts a signed decimal integer in the syntax shown in Exercise 11. It returns as a result an array of ASCII characters corresponding to that integer. For example:

Input: 129

Output: | '1' | '2' | '9' | 'CR' |

13. Assume that you are reading one sector from the disk described for Exercises 1–7. If you are using the interrupt-driven I/O technique shown in Figure 8-10, whereby the processor is interrupted for each character, how often will the processor be interrupted? If it takes 2.5 μsec to process each interrupt, what percentage of the time will the processor spend handling I/O? (Disregard the seek and latency times.)

14. If you change the I/O technique described in Exercise 13 to a DMA device that only generates an interrupt when the entire sector is read, how often will the processor be interrupted?

15. Assume that we are using a character-oriented DMA controller which transfers characters to memory using a cycle-stealing approach. The controller is connected to a terminal transmitting at 9,600 bits per second, and the processor is fetching instructions and data on the average of once every 1 microsecond. By how much will the processor be slowed down because of interference with the DMA channel?

CHAPTER 9

THE CONTROL UNIT

9.1
Introduction

All of the subsystems discussed in the past three chapters are able to perform a specific function (e.g., add, read, store), but they lack a *control capability*. That is, they cannot execute their specific function until told to do so by the *control unit*. It is the job of the control unit to obtain instructions from memory in the proper order, decode them, and then issue the necessary timing and control signals to all other devices so that the instructions can be executed correctly.

The control unit and the arithmetic/logic unit together are now considered as a single functional unit, the *processor*. On older machines, there was only one processor, and it was the most valuable and critical resource of the computer system. Much time and effort were devoted to ensuring that the processor was never idle and was being utilized to the highest possible degree. A computer was generally seen as a "processor-oriented" device, with the processor at the center of the system and all other components subservient to it (see Figure 9-1).

This view changed as hardware costs came down and processors became significantly cheaper. To be sure, large special-purpose processors, like those found on high-speed supercomputers, are still expensive and valuable resources, but small microprocessors—like the Zilog Z80, Intel 80286, and Motorola 68020—have a great deal of processing capability and cost as little as $5 or $10. Figure 6-7 shows a picture of a typical microprocessor found on today's microcomputers.

The result of this change is that most modern large-scale computer systems contain more than one processor. Some of the largest systems have dozens. These processors may be allocated specific tasks, like I/O (see Section 8.5), or they may all be identical, with each processor working on a different user program. A system with more than one processor is called a *multiprocessing system*. As we mentioned earlier,

FIGURE 9-1   Processor-Oriented View of Computer
Architecture.

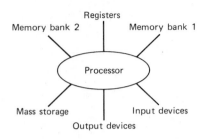

if we can't make a computer work twice as fast, we should make it do two or more things at once. The result is the same. Hence the advantage of a multiprocessing system is that it can do more work in a given period of time.

The general view of computers today is no longer processor oriented. Memory is the critical resource, and the processor is just another device on the system. This memory-oriented view of computer resources is diagrammed in Figure 9-2.

However, the cost of memory is dropping, and today most computers are constructed with maximal memory capacities well into the millions of bytes. Since a 64,000-bit memory chip only costs about $200, the optimal utilization of memory is not as important an issue as it once was.

Already, a new view of computers is beginning to emerge, in which the most critical resource on the system is *information.* For as hardware costs decrease, the resources that will most need optimization are the technical staff, and the collection, storage, and dissemination of information. This information-centered view of computers is depicted in Figure 9-3.

FIGURE 9-2   Memory-Centered View of a Computer.

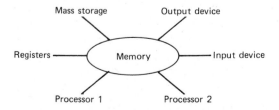

FIGURE 9-3   Information-Centered View of a Computer System.

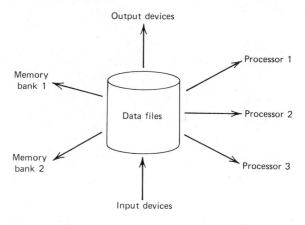

9.2
Instruction Formats

Before we begin to describe the operation of a processor, we must look at the format of *machine language instructions*.

A machine-language instruction has two fundamental components: the *operation code*, almost always called the *op code*, and some optional *address fields* (Figure 9-4). All "real" machine-language instructions also contain other fields, called *modifiers*, specific to their particular architecture. Because the number and interpretation of these modifier fields is highly machine specific, we delay their discussion until Part III.

The op code is a unique unsigned binary value indicating the operation that is to be carried out. The set of all op codes that can be executed directly by a processor is called the *instruction set* or *machine language* of the computer. If the instruction allocates i bits for the op-code field, we can have a maximum of 2^i unique op codes, numbered $0, 1, 2, \ldots, 2^i - 1$.

FIGURE 9-4   General Layout of a Machine-Language Instruction.

Op code	Address field	Address field	. . .

The address fields, also called the *operands,* are the addresses of the information upon which the processor will perform the specified operation. Instruction sets are typically characterized by the number of operands allowed per instruction. In the sections that follow we briefly describe the five possible instruction formats.

9.2.1   Four-Address Format

The 4-address format allows us to put up to four addresses in a single instruction. These addresses can be used to identify the location of:

1. The left operand of a binary operation.
2. The right operand of a binary operation.
3. The result.
4. The next instruction to execute when the current one is finished.

For example, to execute the following assignment statement:

$$A := B + C - D;$$

using a 4-address format, would be done as shown in Figure 9-5. The two instructions in Figure 9-5 effectively perform the following two steps.

1) $B + C \rightarrow$ Temp;   Then go to step 2
2) Temp $- D \rightarrow A$

In spite of their power, 4-address instruction formats are never used because the instructions would be too big. If we wanted to have 2^i different operation codes and 2^n possible memory locations, the total length of each instruction would be:

(9.1)   instruction length $= i + 4n$

FIGURE 9-5   Example of a 4-Address Instruction Format.

Address	Op Code	Left Operand	Right Operand	Result	Next Instruction
100	ADD	Address of B	Address of C	Address of temporary location T	101
101	SUB	Address of T	Address of D	Address of A	Address of next instruction

For typical computers, $i = 6$ to 8 (allowing 64–256 op codes), and $n = 16$ to 24 (allowing 64K–16 million storage locations). Therefore, the size of each instruction would be about 70–100 bits, or about 9–12 bytes. This is a very large instruction. To reduce the size, our first step will be to eliminate field 4 above, the address of the next instruction. This will produce a 3-address format instruction.

9.2.2 Three-Address Format

A 3-address instruction format allows up to three addresses per instruction. They are the addresses of:

1. The left operand of a binary instruction.
2. The right operand of a binary instruction.
3. The result.

Since we no longer specify the address of the next instruction, we must have an implicit convention to specify its location.

The convention for all computers is to complete the instruction located in address L and then execute the instruction in the next sequential memory location, L + 1, unless the current operation specifies otherwise. If an instruction occupies more than one memory location, the next instruction will come from location L + k, where k is the number of memory locations occupied by one machine-language instruction.

Our previous example (A := B + C − D), coded into a 3-address format, would appear as shown in Figure 9-6.

In Figure 9-5, the two instructions were placed in locations 100 and 101. But they could have been placed in *any* pair of locations, since the first instruction points to the location of the second. In Figure 9-6, the two instructions *must* be placed in sequential storage locations. After completing the instruction in location 100, the processor will automatically proceed to the next sequential location, 101.

The elimination of the "next address" field has a number of implications in the design of a computer. First, programs will generally be stored in a sequential block of memory.

FIGURE 9-6   Example of a 3-Address Instruction Format.

Address	Op Code	Left Operand	Right Operand	Result
100	ADD	Address of B	Address of C	Address of temporary location T
101	SUB	Address of T	Address of D	Address of A

This sequential storage would not be necessary if each instruction pointed to the next one, much like a chain.

Second, a special register will be needed in the control unit to keep track of the address of the instruction to be executed next. For example, in Figure 9-6, while executing the ADD instruction in location 100, this register would hold a 101. When the computer finishes executing the ADD instruction, it will examine the register, see the 101, and begin executing the SUBtract instruction in location 101. While that instruction is being executed, the register will contain a 102. This special register, which holds the address of the next instruction to be executed, is called the *program counter* (PC).

Third, some instructions are needed in the instruction set to be able to override the convention of fetching the instruction in the next sequential operation. These instructions will say, "Don't go to the next location; instead get the next instruction from address A." In machine language, these are called *branching instructions.* They are roughly analogous to the control statements of a high-level language (e.g., **if/then/else, while,** and **goto**), which alter the normal sequential flow of execution.

Although smaller than the 4-address format, the 3-address format still results in a large instruction size, namely, $i + 3n$. Using our previous values for i and n, these 3-address instructions may be between fifty-four and eighty bits long, or seven and ten bytes. This is still quite large, and although 3-address machine formats have been built, no modern machines use this layout. Instead, we eliminate one more address field—the address of the result—to produce a *2-address instruction format.*

9.2.3   Two-Address Format

The 2-address format allows up to two addresses per instruction—typically the address of:

1.   The left operand of a binary instruction.
2.   The right operand of a binary instruction.

This format does not provide an address in which to specify the location of the result; so we automatically imply that the result is placed in some fixed and known location, not specified in the instruction itself. For example, the result of an ADD operation could, by convention, always be placed in register R0. The result of a SUBtract operation could always be placed in memory location 50.

Most 2-address computers use the convention that if a result address is needed, it is implied to be the same address as either the left or right operand. Thus, if we assume that the second operand field corresponds to both the address of the right operand and the address of the result, then the machine-language instruction:

ADD	Address of A	Address of B

would correspond to the assignment statement:

$$B := A + B;$$

The original content of memory location B is destroyed when the result, A + B, is stored in it. Similarly, we could have assumed that the result went into the left operand instead. Then the ADD instruction would correspond to the statement:

$$A := A + B;$$

In a 2-address instruction format, you must always be very careful not to accidentally destroy one of your operands by storing an intermediate result in the same location. You can usually avoid this risk by using temporary memory locations to hold these intermediate values. In 2-address format, the assignment statement $A := (B + C) - D$ might be coded as shown in Figure 9-7. (There are other and possibly

FIGURE 9-7   Example of a 2-Address Instruction Format.

Address

100	MOVE	Address of C	Address of T_1	$\{ T_1 \leftarrow C \}$
101	ADD	Address of B	Address of T_1	$\{ T_1 \leftarrow B + C \}$
102	MOVE	Address of D	Address of T_2	$\{ T_2 \leftarrow D \}$
103	SUB	Address of T_1	Address of T_2	$\{ T_2 \leftarrow (B + C) - D \}$
104	MOVE	Address of T_2	Address of A	$\{ A \leftarrow T_2 \}$

better ways to encode this assignment statement.) Notice the use of temporary variables T_1 and T_2 to hold the intermediate computation. This is necessary to ensure that the operands B, C, and D are not affected or changed by the computation.

Two-address instruction formats are quite common on many machines, including the PDP-11 and VAX-11 families of computers.

Figure 9-8 lists some instructions that might exist on our typical PVM computer if it used a 2-address format. Notice that not every operation uses both address fields. A 2-address format does not mean that every instruction must contain two address fields; it means only that the instructions *may* contain up to two address fields. Some operations can completely specify what needs to be done with a single address. In that case, the second address field is simply not used.

EXAMPLES

Assume that you may use the symbolic names A, B, C, and D to refer to memory locations in the computer and that branching addresses are specified by symbolic labels. Translate the following high-level language fragments using the 2-address instructions in Figure 9-8.

(a)   A := (A − B) * (C − D)

```
        MOVE    B,T1
        SUB     A,T1
        MOVE    D,T2
        SUB     C,T2
        MUL     T1,T2
        MOVE    T2,A
```

(b)   If A = B then
           C := D
       else
           C := 0

```
            COMP    A,B
            BEQ     L1
            MOVEI   0,C
            BR      DONE
     L1:    MOVE    D,C
  DONE:
```

(c)   D := 0;
       for A := B to C do
           D := D + A

```
            MOVEI   0,D
            MOVE    B,A
```

FIGURE 9-8   Typical 2-Address Instruction Set.

Instruction*	Meaning
MOVE s,d	CON(s) → CON(d)
MOVEI v,d	v → CON(d)
ADD s,d	CON(s) + CON(d) → CON(d)
INC s	CON(s) + 1 → CON(s)
SUB s,d	CON(s) − CON(d) → CON(d)
DEC s	CON(s) − 1 → CON(s)
MUL s,d	CON(s) * CON(d) → CON(d)
DIV s,d	CON(s)/CON(d) → CON(d)
COMP s,d	Compare CON(s) to CON(d) Set EQ, GT, LT flags based on the value of the compare. Do not change the contents of either s or d.
BEQ address	Branch to address if EQ flag is ON
BLT address	Branch to address if LT flag is ON
BGT address	Branch to address if GT flag is ON
BR address	Branch to address
INP address	Input a single character and store it in the indicated memory address
OUT address	Output the contents of the indicated memory address in a proper character-oriented format

*Where s and d are the source and destination addresses, and v is an octal integer constant. The notation CON(x) means the contents of memory address x.

```
LOOP:   COMP    A,C
        BGT     DONE
        ADD     A,D
        INC     A
        BR      LOOP
DONE:
```

Exercises 1–7 ask you to write some additional instruction sequences using the 2-address instructions in Figure 9-8.

We can continue this process of eliminating instruction fields even further and eliminate the address of one of the two operands. We will then have a *1-address instruction format*.

9.2.4   One-Address Format

We now have a single address field in each instruction. If we have a binary operation, we must imply the location of both the second operand and of the result. Usually, the second operand and the result fields are implied to be in a specific general-purpose register. For example, if the ADD instruction implies that the right operand and the result are in general register R0, then the 1-address instruction:

ADD	Address of A

would mean:

CON(memory location A) + CON(register R0) → CON(register R0)

Figure 9-9 shows a possible 1-address encoding of our assignment A := B + C − D.

The 1-address instruction format is the one most commonly found on modern computer systems. Even computers that utilize a 2-address format will include a number

FIGURE 9-9   Example of a 1-Address Instruction Format.

LOAD	Address of B	{ R0 ← B}
ADD	Address of C	{ R0 ← B + C }
SUB	Address of D	{ R0 ←(B + C) − D }
STORE	Address of A	{ A ← R0 }

of 1-address instructions in their instruction set. For example, the PDP-11 contains nineteen 2-address instructions and forty-seven 1-address instructions. The INTEL 8086 microprocessor also uses a mixture of 1- and 2-address instruction formats with a total of about three hundred different operation codes.

The advantage of the 1-address instruction format is that the instructions are short and concise. If we assume that we have 2^i different operation codes and 2^n memory locations, then a 1-address instruction will require only $i + n$ bits. Using the values of i and n given earlier, this will require only about 16–32 bits per instruction, much less than the 2-, 3-, and 4-address formats.

Figure 9-10 lists some typical 1-address machine-language instructions that might exist on a hypothetical PVM computer with one general-purpose register called R. This set is not intended to be complete, but it should give you a feeling for the style of 1-address instructions.

EXAMPLES

Assume that you may use the symbolic names A, B, C, and D to refer to memory locations in the computer and that branching addresses are specified by symbolic labels. Translate the following language fragments using the 1-address instructions shown in Figure 9-10. The text material following the instructions is just explanatory comments.

(a)
$$A := (A - B) * (C - D)$$

```
LOAD    B
SUB     A       ;R0 now holds A — B
STORE   T1      ;Save it in T1
LOAD    D
SUB     C       ;R0 now holds C — D
MUL     T1      ;R0 now holds the correct expression
STORE   A       ;Save the answer in A
```

(b)
```
                    if A = B then
                        C := D
                    else
                        C := 0
```

```
        LOAD    B
        SUB     A
        BEQ     L1      ;Branch to L1 if A = B
        LOADI   0
        STORE   C       ;Set C to zero
        BR      DONE    ;And finish up
L1:     LOAD    D
        STORE   C       ;Set C to D
DONE:
```

FIGURE 9-10   Typical 1-Address Instruction Set.

Instruction	Meaning
LOAD a	$CON(a) \rightarrow CON(R)$
LOADI v	$v \rightarrow CON(R)$
STORE a	$CON(R) \rightarrow CON(a)$
ADD a	$CON(a) + CON(R) \rightarrow CON(R)$
INC a	$CON(a) + 1 \rightarrow CON(a)$
SUB a	$CON(a) - CON(R) \rightarrow CON(R)$
DEC a	$CON(a) - 1 \rightarrow CON(a)$
MUL a	$CON(a) * \mathbf{CON(R)} \rightarrow \mathbf{CON(R)}$
DIV a	$CON(a) \div CON(R) \rightarrow CON(R)$
BPOS address	Branch to address if $CON(R) > 0$
BEQ address	Branch to address if $CON(R) = 0$
BNEG address	Branch to address if $CON(R) < 0$
BR address	Branch to address
INP address	Input a single character into the specified memory address
OUT address	Output the contents of the indicated memory address in the correct character-oriented format

Where a represents a memory address and v represents an octal integer constant. The notation $CON(x)$ means the contents of memory address x.

(c)

```
D := 0;
for A := B to C do
    D := D + A
```

```
LOADI    0
STORE    D        ;Initialize D to zero
```

```
            LOAD    B
            STORE   A          ;Initialize A to the value B
   LOOP:    LOAD    C
            SUB     A
            BPOS    DONE       ;Test if A > C. If yes, we are done
            LOAD    D
            ADD     A
            STORE   D          ;Compute D := D + A
            INC     A          ;Increment loop counter
            BR      LOOP       ;And do the loop again
   DONE:
```

Exercises 1–7 ask you to write some simple instruction sequences using the 1-address instructions in Figure 9-10.

You may think that we have eliminated as many address fields as possible, but not so. We can eliminate the last address field to create a very interesting instruction format called *0-address instructions*.

9.2.5 Zero-Address Format

A 0-address instruction has no address fields at all. Obviously, we cannot eliminate all of the address fields from all instructions; if we did, we could never reference a memory location or a register. Instead, in some instructions, all of the operands are assumed to be in specified locations, and for these instructions there is no address field. The specified locations for the operands and results in a 0-address instruction are a special set of registers called a *stack*.

A stack is a set of registers in which additions or deletions can be made only at one end, the *top*. A special register, called the *stack pointer* (or TOP), points to the top item in the stack. (Alternatively, it can point to the location just above the top item in the stack. In this case it is pointing to the next available slot.)

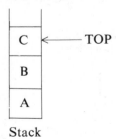

Stack

The only item that is immediately accessible is the item on top of the stack, C in the diagram above, and a new item can only be placed on top of the top item.

The two basic operations that can be performed on a stack—namely, putting a new item on top of the stack and taking the top item off the stack—are called "push" and "pop," respectively. Figure 9-11 diagrams the behavior of these two operations.

A 0-address instruction operates by assuming that both of the desired operands are currently on the stack, and that the result is to be placed back on the stack. For

FIGURE 9-11   Behavior of the Push and Pop Operations.

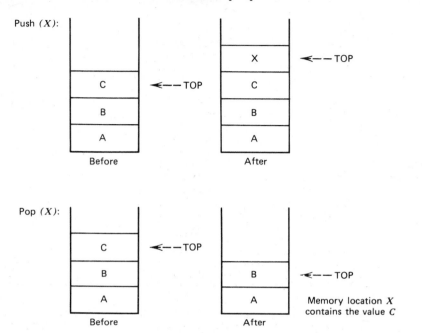

FIGURE 9-12   Operation of a 0-Address Add.

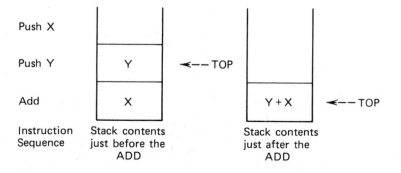

example, the 0-address instruction ADD might mean to remove the top two items on the stack, add them together, and put the result back on the stack. This operation is diagrammed in Figure 9-12.

Using this type of 0-address instruction, our assignment statement A := (B + C) — D might be coded as follows:

FIGURE 9-13   A 0-Address Instruction Sequence.

Push	Address of D	
Push	Address of C	
Push	Address of B	{ Stack now contains D, C, B }
Add		{ Stack now contains D, B + C }
Sub		{ Stack now contains B + C − D }
Pop	Address of A	{ Stack is now empty. }

A stack can be an extremely useful tool, and many types of operation can be more easily translated with 0-address stack-oriented commands than with the 1- or 2-address commands described earlier. For example, stacks can allow for the rapid evaluation of arithmetic expression. To achieve this speed-up, however, we must change the way we write our expressions. instead of using *infix notation,* in which the operator appears between the operands, as in:

$$A + B - C * D / E$$

we must write it in *prefix notation,* in which the operator appears immediately before the two operands. (This is also called *Polish notation.*) In prefix notation, the previous expression would be written as follows (assuming a strict right-to-left evaluation):

$$+ A - B * C / D E$$

Once the expression is in this form, its evaluation is trivial. Just work your way from right to left and use the following two rules.

1. Every time you see an operand, put it on the stack using a push command.

2. Every time you see an operator, perform that arithmetic operation immediately on the current contents of the stack.

When you are finished, the desired result will be on top of the stack. So, looking back at the preceding prefix expression and applying the two rules, the 0-address code to evaluate that expression would be:

```
PUSH    E
PUSH    D
DIV             ;Stack now holds D / E
PUSH    C
MULT            ;Stack now holds C · D / E
PUSH    B
SUB             ;Stack now holds B − C · D / E
PUSH    A
ADD             ;Stack now holds A + B − C·D / E
```

The ease of evaluating arithmetic expressions is one of the main reasons that many programmable pocket calculators are frequently based on a 0-address, stack-oriented architecture.

Stacks are also used to handle subroutine linkage. In a subroutine we can call another subroutine, and then another, and so forth. When we finally execute a RETURN (or come to the END of the subroutine) we must return to the proper address.

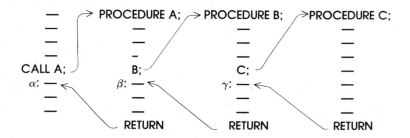

Given that procedure calls can be nested ten or fifteen levels deep, you might think that subroutine linkage would be a complex operation. However, with a stack it becomes trivial. Every time we execute a procedure call, we push the return address onto the stack. Every time we execute a return, we pop the stack and return to the address that we just removed.

For example, when we are inside procedure C, we will have executed three procedure calls to procedures A, B, and C. Each call will push the return address onto the stack. At this point, the stack will contain the following values in the following order.

When we execute the RETURN in procedure C, we will pop the address "γ" off the stack and begin executing from there. This is the correct return address in procedure B. The next RETURN will pop the address "β" off the stack, which will correctly return us to procedure A. The final return operation will pop off the address "α" and return us to the correct location in the main program. Thus, a complex series of calls and returns becomes a simple series of PUSH and POP operations on the stack.

A stack mechanism is useful in other areas as well. It is so useful, in fact, that even machines that are not 0-address, "stack-oriented" computers include a stack to facilitate the kinds of operation we have described. For example, the PDP-11 is a 1- and 2-address machine, but it has a stack mechanism available to the programmer. The instruction set does not directly include PUSH and POP operations, or 0-address ADD, SUB commands, but they can be effectively simulated by means of other instructions in the PDP-11 instruction set.

Figure 9-14 shows some typical stack-oriented instructions that we might find on our PVM computer if it were a stack-oriented 0-address computer.

EXAMPLES

Assume that you may use the symbolic A, B, C, and D to refer to memory locations in the computer and that branching addresses are specified by symbolic labels. Translate the following language fragments using the 0-address instructions in Figure 9-14.

(a)

$$A := (A - B) * (C - D)$$

In prefix notation the expression is $* -AB-CD$.

```
PUSH    D
PUSH    C
SUB             ;Stack now holds C − D
PUSH    B
PUSH    A
SUB             ;Stack now holds A − B on top of C − D
MULT            ;Top of stack is now the correct expression
POP     A       ;Put the answer away in A
```

        If A = B **then**
            C := D
        else
            C := 0

```
PUSH    B
PUSH    A
SUB             ;Top of stack now holds A − B
TEST            ;Test if A = B
BEQ     LOOP    ;If it does branch to LOOP
```

FIGURE 9-14   Typical 0-Address Instruction Set.

Instruction	Meaning*
PUSH a	CON(a) → Top of stack
PUSHI v	v → Top of stack
POP a	Top of stack → CON(a)
ADD	CON(Top) + CON(Top-1) → Top of stack The original operands are removed
SUB	CON(Top) − CON(Top-1) → Top of stack The original operands are removed
MULT	CON(Top) *CON(Top-1) → Top of stack The original operands are removed
DIVIDE	CON(Top)/CON(Top-1) → Top of stack The original operands are removed
TEST	Check the top of the stack. Set the EQ, GT, and LT indicators if the top item is zero, greater than zero, or less than zero, respectively. Do not change the value on top of the stack.
COMPARE	Compare the top two items on the stack. Set the EQ, GT, and LT indicators if the top item is equal to, greater than, or less than the second item on the stack. Remove the two operands from the stack.
BEQ address	Branch to address if the EQ indicator is ON
BGT address	Branch to address if the GT indicator is ON
BLT address	Branch to address if the LT indicator is ON
BR address	Branch to address
INPUT address	Input a single character from the terminal and store it in the indicated memory address.
OUTPUT	Output the value contained on top of the stack in the correct character-oriented format. Then pop the value off the stack.

*Where a is a memory address and v is an octal integer constant. The notation CON(x) means the contents of memory cell x.

```
              PUSHI    0
              POP      C        ;Set C to zero
              BR       DONE     ;We are all done
      LOOP:   PUSH     D
              POP      C        ;Set C to D
      DONE:
```

(c)   D : = 0;
       For A : = B to C **do**
          D := D + A

```
              PUSHI    0
              POP      D        ;Initialize D to zero
              PUSH     B
              POP      A        ;Initialize A to the value of B
      LOOP:   PUSH     C
              PUSH     A
              COMPARE           ;Test if A > C
              BGT      DONE     Yes it is. We are all done
              PUSH     D
              PUSH     A
              ADD
              POP      D        ;Compute D := D + A
              PUSH     A
              PUSHI    I
              ADD
              POP      A        ;Increment the loop counter A
              BR       LOOP     ;Start the loop again
      DONE:
```

9.3
The Storage of Instructions

Machine-language instructions, in one or more of the formats described in Section 9.2, are stored sequentially in memory. Together, they make up the *machine-language program,* also called the *object program.* Even though a *source program* was originally written in Pascal or FORTRAN, it must be translated into machine-language instructions of the type shown in Figures 9-8, 9-10, or 9-14. This translation is the job of a program called the *compiler.* Figure 9-15 shows the translation of a fragment of Pascal code into some hypothetical 1-address instructions. As Figure 9-15 shows, compilation is a difficult task, and designing and developing compilers for high-level languages like Ada, Pascal, or FORTRAN can take years.

FIGURE 9-15   Compilation of Source Program to Object Program.

Pascal Source Program		Object Program		
If a > b then		LOAD	B	
c := c + d		SUB	A	**(Is A > B?)**
else	Compiler	BNEG	YES	
c := c − d;	⟶	LOAD	C	**(No, it is not)**
		SUB	D	
		STORE	C	**(C := C − D)**
		BR	DONE	
	Yes :	LOAD	C	**(Yes, it is)**
		ADD	D	
		STORE	C	**(C := C + D)**

After the machine-language instructions have been produced by the compiler, they are stored in memory. One of the most fundamental aspects of the design of a Von Neumann computer is the rule of *interchangeability of instructions and data:*

> There is no distinction in memory between instructions and data. An instruction may become a piece of data, and a data value may be executed as if it were an instruction.

This rule effectively says that a binary string in memory has no a priori interpretation or preset meaning. A set of binary digits takes on a meaning only when you use it. Then it assumes *whatever* interpretation is appropriate for its use. If you use the binary value:

$$10010000$$

as an address, it will be interpreted as the unsigned binary value of 144. If you use it as an operand in an integer ADD (assuming twos-complement representation), it will become the signed decimal quantity -112. If you try to execute this value, it will become an instruction; part of it will become the op code, and part of it will become the address field(s).

This is why an instruction is really just another type of data, and the instruction format on a particular computer is just another format for the representation of information. We can now, in a sense, complete the discussion begun in Part I and list the *five* basic classes of data that exist at the machine level.

1. Unsigned binary (Chapter 2).
2. Signed integers (Chapter 3).
3. Characters (Chapter 4).
4. Floating point (Chapter 5).
5. Instructions (Chapter 9).

This is quite different from high-level languages, which rigidly enforce the distinction between instructions and data. In a high-level language environment, it would be foolish to talk about executing the constant $+3$, or subtracting 1 from an **if** statement. This distinction between instructions and data is yet another service provided for you by high-level languages to create an environment conducive to programming. The language allows you to think in terms of conceptually distinct code and data, and prevents you from intermixing the two, either accidentally or intentionally.

However, this is not the case at our level of discussion, and the implications are enormous. First of all, errors that would be fatal in a high-level language may not be immediately fatal in machine language. For example, in machine language, if you fail to stop at the end of your program, you may begin to execute your data structures with unpredictable results. Similarly, if you overrun the bounds of an array, you may accidentally fetch an instruction and process it as if it were data. In machine language, neither of these situations would immediately be recognized as an error because there is no "watchdog" or "proofreader" in the form of a language translator ensuring that the instructions you are performing are meaningful and consistent. Thus, debugging in machine language can be extremely difficult, since the cause of an error and its eventual detection can be separated by a good deal of time and space.

A second major implication is that you can intentionally modify a program as if it were a piece of data. For example:

```
        LOAD   X
        ADD    Z
        STORE  X
          .
          .
    X:  SUB    Y
```

The first group of instructions is changing the SUBtract command into something else. When that instruction is actually executed, it may no longer operate on address Y; in fact, it may no longer be a subtract instruction. This ability to modify a program also makes debugging difficult because the instruction you see in the program listing is not necessarily the one that is ultimately executed.

Throughout this text, we avoid the intentional modification of instructions and try to clearly delineate and separate values that are to be used as data from those that are to be used as instructions. A program that does not modify itself in any way is called a *reentrant program,* or *pure code.*

9.4
The Components of the Control Unit

We have already introduced one component of the control unit, the *program counter* (PC), which contains the address of the next instruction to be executed. Since we execute instructions sequentially, the PC will usually be incremented by 1 (or by a constant, k, if it takes k memory locations to hold one instruction). Therefore, associated with the PC is an *incrementor,* a functional unit that adds 1 to the value sent to it. We represent this functional unit in the following way.

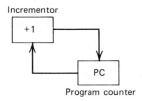

We also need a register to hold the actual instruction that is being executed. This is called the *instruction register* (IR). The layout of the IR will be identical to the structure of a machine-language instruction. That is, if the machine language contains two address fields, the IR will be a 2-address register.

IR | Op code | Address 1 | Address 2

Finally, we need a functional unit that determines the type of operation currently in the IR and sends out the necessary timing and control signals to implement that operation. This device is called the *instruction decoder.* The instruction decoder is connected to the op-code portion of the IR, and it determines which op code is being indicated. This organization is shown in Figure 9-16.

One and only one of the output lines of the decoder shown in Figure 9-16 will be "ON," depending on whether it is an ADD, SUB, MOVE, and so on. These output lines will be connected to the actual hardware circuits that open and close gates, perform transfers along buses, and otherwise carry out the ADD, SUBtract, or MOVE instruction.

FIGURE 9-16   The Instruction Decoder.

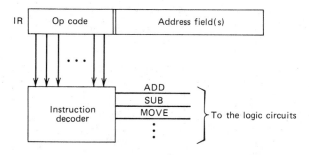

Like the memory decoder, an instruction decoder may initially seem like an extremely complex functional component, but it is quite simple. All it really does is implement the following nested **if/then/else** statement.

if op-code = 0 **then**
   we have an ADD   {Assume ADD = op code 0}
else
  if op-code = 1 **then**
    we have a SUB   {Assume SUB = op code 1}
  else
    if op-code = 2 **then**
      we have a MOVE   {Assume MOVE = op code 2}
    else
     .
     .
     .

If we assume a 3-bit op-code field (which is unrealistically small since it would only allow 8 unique op codes), the same operation codes shown above, and the symbols for AND, OR, and NOT gates shown in Figure 3-7, then an instruction decoder would be implemented as shown in Figure 9-17. By tracing through the logic of the

FIGURE 9-17   The Instruction Decoder (Internally).

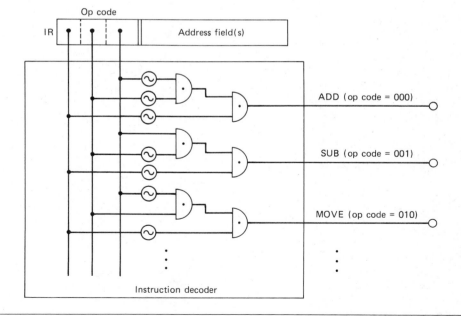

decoder circuit you will see that one and only one of the output lines will be "true" corresponding to the operation code currently in the instruction register. (You may disregard Figure 9-17 without any loss of continuity.)

We have now completed the description of the control unit and, indeed, of our entire hypothetical PVM computer. Figure 9-18 summarizes and displays all of the components of this PVM. This is an important diagram and you should understand

FIGURE 9-18   Overall Diagram of a PVM Computer.

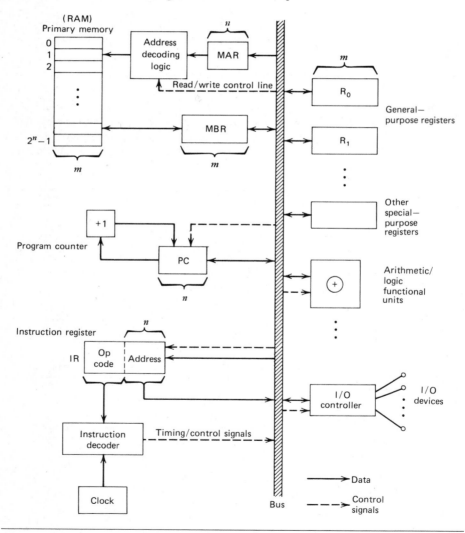

it fully before going on. Although Figure 9-18 does not represent any particular computer, it does represent the concepts that are common to *all* computers. (Figure 9-18 assumes a PVM with a single-bus architecture and a 1-address instruction format.)

9.5
The Overall Operation of a Computer

The execution of a computer program is nothing more than a repeated sequence of fetching and executing individual instructions, either until the program executes a halt instruction or until it encounters a fatal error that prevents it from continuing. Algorithmically, this can be represented as:

> Repeat
>   Fetch phase
>   Execute phase
> Until (halt) or (fatal error)

During the *fetch phase,* we fetch the next instruction to be executed and place it in the IR. (Chapter 20 explains how the address of the first instruction in the program is initially loaded into the PC, and how the whole process of program execution is begun.) The fetch phase is the same for all instructions. We go to memory and fetch the instruction whose address is currently in the PC, because the PC contains the address of the next instruction to be executed. When the memory READ is completed, the instruction is sitting in the MBR. We then move the instruction into the IR. Finally, we increment the PC by 1 so that it will correctly point to the next instruction when we get to the next fetch phase.

If we use the notation A ← B to mean that we transfer the contents of register B into register A, and READ, WRITE to mean memory read and write signals along the read/write control line, the operation of a fetch phase can be summarized simply (Figure 9-19) (Note: We have included data transfers only, not timing signals. The sequence shown is timing independent.)

During the *execution phase,* we determine what instruction is in the IR and issue

---

FIGURE 9-19   Formal Description of the Fetch Phase.

1. MAR ← PC   {Move the PC to the MAR.}
2. READ   {Fetch the instruction.}
3. IR ← MBR   {Move it into the IR.}
4. Incrementor ← PC
5. PC ← Incrementor {Incrementor PC.}

FIGURE 9-20   Execution Phase of a Load Instruction.

1. MAR ← IR$_{address}$
2. READ
3. R0 ← MBR

the commands needed to carry it out. Naturally, the exact sequence of signals will be different for every instruction. For example, the 1-address instruction:

LOAD   address   {CON(address) → CON(R0)}

may cause the sequence of transfers shown in Figure 9-20 (where subscripts indicate the various subfields of the instruction register).

The address field of the instruction register is transferred to the MAR, and the contents of that cell are READ and placed in the MBR. Finally, the MBR is moved to register R0, completing the LOAD instruction.

The 1-address add instruction:

ADD   address   {CON(address) + CON(R0) → CON(R0)}

might result in the sequence of transfers shown in Figure 9-21.

We fetch the contents of the address in the address field (steps 1–2) and move them to the adder (step 3). We also send the contents of register R0 to the adder (step 4). These two operands are added (step 5) and the result is placed back in register R0 (step 6). This completes the ADD instruction.

Finally, the unconditional branching instruction:

JUMP   address

would be carried out by the single transfer shown in Figure 9-22.

To carry out the branch instruction, we simply move the branch address to the

FIGURE 9-21   Execution Phase of an Add Instruction.

1. MAR ← IR$_{address}$
2. READ
3. Adder ← MBR
4. Adder ← R0
5. ADD
6. R0 ← adder

FIGURE 9-22 Execution Phase of a Jump Instruction.

1. $PC \leftarrow IR_{address}$

program counter. Then during the next fetch phase, we will fetch the instruction whose address is in the PC, which is now the address of where we want to branch (see Figure 9-19).

There are basically two ways to implement the signal sequences that occur during the execute phase. One is to do it in hardware. That is, all of the transfer and control sequences shown in Figures 9-20 to 9-22 are implemented in terms of fixed electrical circuits. The result is called a *hard-wired processor,* and most early computers were built this way.

However, most modern computers implement the processor in a different way. Just as a high-level language is translated into machine language, machine language can be translated into an even lower level language called *microcode,* sometimes called *firmware* because it is midway between hardware and software. The meaning of a machine-language instruction is specified by a program written in microcode that defines exactly what should happen inside the machine when that machine-language instruction is encountered.

The types of instruction that exist in microcode are very low level and are directly related to the circuitry of the computer:

1. Open a gate/close a gate (from the register to the bus).

2. Transfer data along a bus.

3. Initiate a control signal (e.g., READ, WRITE, ADD).

4. Send a timing signal.

5. Wait a fixed unit of time.

6. Test certain bits within a register.

The sequences of microcode instructions that define a machine-language instruction are called *microprograms,* and a processor that works this way is called a *microprogrammed processor.* These microprograms are stored in a special *control memory,* which is usually a read-only memory of the type described in Section 6.6. When an instruction is placed in the IR, we decode it and then fetch and execute the microprogram that defines it. This organization is diagrammed in Figure 9-23.

The microprograms would look very similar to the instruction sequences shown in Figures 9-19 to 9-22. These low-level instruction sequences would be fetched, decoded, and executed, one line at a time, in very much the same way that we have been describing for machine-language instructions. For example, if the machine-language instruction in the IR were an ADD, we would execute something like the 6-line microprogram shown in Figure 9-21, which would be stored in control memory.

FIGURE 9-23   Structure of a Microprogrammed Processor.

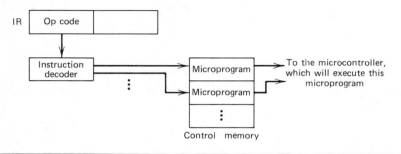

When the sequence was finished, we would have successfully performed an addition. In effect, we have created an entirely new level of machine organization (complete with a new language) beneath the machine-language level we have been discussing.

If we return to Figure 1-2, we see that there is another complete level of abstraction between level 3 (the functional organization level being studied in this text) and level 4 (the hardware level). This level is frequently called the *microprogramming* or *firmware* level. The primitives at this level are microprograms, control memory, and the microcontrollers that execute these microprograms. And, just as we were able to understand high-level language primitives such as if/then, assignment, and while loops by studying the underlying machine language, so we can begin to understand machine-language primitives by studying the underlying microcode. This is summarized in Figure 9-24.

In the early days of microprogramming, the existence of these microprograms was completely hidden from users, who could not tell whether their computer was hardwired or microprogrammed. Newer machines, however, sometimes allow the user to

FIGURE 9-24   Three Levels of Abstraction of Computer Programs.

High-Level Language Abstraction	*Machine-Language Abstraction*	*Firmware Abstraction*
A := B + C $\longrightarrow$	LOAD B $\longrightarrow$	MAR ← IR$_{address}$
	ADD C	READ
	STORE A	R0 ← MBR

have access to the microcode. Instead of being implemented using ROM, the control memory is frequently implemented instead using RAM, and it is called a *writable control store* (WCS). Users can then write, develop, and store their own microprograms. This allows them to:

1. Optimize the execution of certain operations to take advantage of new hardware.
2. Simulate, in firmware, the instruction set of a different computer. (This is called *emulation.*)
3. Define new operation codes.

For example, the following microprogram, called ADDI (for ADD Immediately), defines an instruction that adds *the address field*, rather than the contents of that address, to the contents of R0.

$$\text{ADDI} \quad \text{address} \quad \{\text{address} + \text{CON(R0)} \rightarrow \text{CON(R0)}\}$$

$$\begin{array}{ll} \text{ADDI:} & \text{adder} \leftarrow \text{IR}_{addr} \\ & \text{adder} \leftarrow \text{R0} \\ & \text{ADD} \\ & \text{R0} \leftarrow \text{adder} \end{array}$$

Thus,

$$\text{ADDI} \quad 5$$

would add the integer value 5, rather than the contents of memory cell 5, to R0.

Microprogramming allows a user to build the optimal instruction set for a particular application. The user is no longer restricted to the machine-language instructions provided by the manufacturer. Instead, machines can be customized and optimized for specific needs. Microprogramming is an extremely important topic in the field of computer design. Other courses in computer architecture discuss this interesting subject at great length.

9.6
Summary

In our development of a hypothetical PVM computer, we have discussed each individual component that went into the model of Figure 9-18, and we have shown how that PVM machine would execute a program via the fetch/execute cycle diagrammed in Figures 9-19 to 9-22. You should now have a general understanding of what happens to your Pascal (or FORTRAN or BASIC) program from the time you submit it for compilation and execution until you get either the correct answers or error messages.

We have spent a good deal of time describing the Von Neumann model of a computer, culminating in the structure shown in Figure 9-18. Although the real computers you encounter in the future may not look or behave exactly like this idealized model (e.g., they may have more registers, additional buses, or alternate instruction formats), the overwhelming majority of modern computers do adhere very closely to the ideas and principles presented in Part II. Certainly most of today's computer systems are classic Von Neumann machines.

This is not to say that alternate computer architectures do not exist. There is a good deal of research under way in the design of machines quite different in structure and behavior from what was described here. Many of these *non-von Neumann architectures* are either experimental or one-of-a-kind machines, but actual computer systems have been constructed and such machines do exist. Exercise 21 at the end of this chapter describes one of the more common of these special architectures called an *array processor*.

Another alternative structure is called a *pipeline processor*. In this type of processor an instruction is decoded and carried out in stages, as shown in the diagram below. When a functional unit S finishes its task in the partial execution of an instruction, it immediately starts working on the next instruction. Therefore in a pipeline processor there will always be N partially executed instructions in the "pipeline."

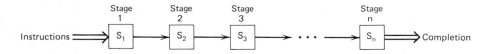

As an example, let's look at floating point addition as described in Section 5.2. That operation is composed of four or five distinct and sequential steps. Instead of building a single, monolithic floating point addition unit which can work on only one pair of values at time, we could construct it to operate in stages, as shown in Figure 9-25. The advantage of the pipelined structure shown in Figure 9-25 is that we can increase the throughput of the functional unit by letting it work on more than one operand at a time.

As this all too brief discussion has shown, the major thrust in computer architecture research is directed at breaking out of the linear, sequential method of programming and problem solving imposed by the classic Von Neumann design. These newer architectures are investigating methods for effectively using parallelism, concur-

FIGURE 9-25   Pipelined Implementation of a Floating
Point Adder.

rency, and operation overlap to increase system throughput and enhance problem solving capabilities.

These and other unique computer structures are an important area of research in computer science, and these systems will become essential for solving special classes of problems or translating certain types of programming languages. The topic of non-Von Neumann architectures can be studied in depth in advanced courses in computer design.

It is now time to leave the world of general discussions, broad overviews, and idealized computers, and look at a real-life, wire-and-steel, built-for-profit computer. In Part III we introduce the PDP-11 and VAX-11 families of minicomputers.

Exercises for Chapter 9

Use the 2-address instructions in Figure 9-8, the 1-address instructions in Figure 9-10, and the 0-address instructions in Figure 9-14 to translate the high-level language sequences in Exercises 1–7. You may use the same symbols that appear in the high-level language fragment as addresses. Thus, to translate A := B + C, you may use the symbols A, B, and C to represent the desired addresses. To branch to an address, simply label the desired instruction and branch to that label.

1. A := B + 1;

2. C := (A/5) * (E − F);

3. if A < 0 then
        e := f * g;
        write (e)
    else
        e := f/g;

4. a := 0; sum := 0;
    while (a < 10) do
        begin
        a := a + 1;
        sum := sum + a
        end;

5. if (a > 100) and (b > 50) and (c > 20) then
        d := 0
    else
        d := 1;

6. case i of
            1: d := a;
            2: d := b;

```
      3: d := c;
         otherwise: d := 0
   end;
```

7. **sum** : = 0;
    for i := 1 to 200 **do**
        sum := sum + (i * i);
    write (sum)

8. Using the 0-, 1-, or 2-address instruction format, write a complete program to print out the first twenty Fibonacci numbers. Fibonacci numbers are defined in the following way.

$$F_1 := 1, \quad F_2 = 1$$
$$F_i = F_{i-1} + F_{i-2} \qquad i = 3, 4, 5, \ldots$$

9. Using either the 0-, 1-, or 2-address instruction format, write a complete program to find all integer solutions to the equation:

$$x + 3y + 9z = 126 \qquad x \ge 0, y \ge 0, z \ge 0$$

10. Assume that you have a computer that uses a 2-address format, has 50,000 (decimal) words of memory, and 100 unique operations. How large would the instruction register be?

11. Is the following computer organization consistent and meaningful? If not, explain what is wrong and correct it.

A memory with 65,536 (2^{16}) 24-bit words
A processor with a 1-address instruction format and 256 unique operations
A 24-bit MAR register
A 24-bit MBR register
A 16-bit instruction register

12. Do you agree or disagree with the following statement?

At the end of the fetch phase, the program counter will always contain the address of the next instruction to be executed.

13. Discuss the problems you would encounter trying to debug a nonreentrant program. Give some examples of these difficulties. Can this problem occur in Pascal or FORTRAN?

14. If the execution phase of some machine-language instruction is described by the following 1-line microprogram,

$$R0 \rightarrow PC$$

what type of instruction must this be?

15.   One of the problems with the 0-address examples b and c given in Section 9.2.5 is that they leave "junk" on the stack. Rewrite these two examples so that no unnecessary information is left on the stack.

16.   Rewrite the following expression in prefix notation and then show the 0-address machine-language instructions that evaluate it.

$$A := ((B + C * (C/(D * E))) - 1$$

17.   Show the sequence of operations that would occur during the execution phase of the following hypothetical 1-address instruction.

SEND val   Send the value "val" directly to register R0

18.   Assume that you added the following "microinstruction" to your microinstruction set.

TEST   register, bit position, value, skip-count

This microinstruction says: test the specified bit position in the indicated register to see if it has the specified binary value; if it does, skip the next "skip count" microinstructions; if it does not, go on to the next microinstruction. For example:

TEST   R0, 13, 1, 2

Test bit position 13 of register R0 to see if it is a 1. If it is, skip two microinstructions. Using this new instruction, show a microprogram that would correctly carry out the following instruction.

BNEG address {Branch to address if CON(R0) < 0}

(Assume that register R0 is sixteen bits wide, and that the bits are numbered right to left, 0 to 15.)

19.   Throughout this chapter we have implied that the size of the operation-code field is fixed for all instructions (see Figure 9-4). However, on some computers, the size of the op-code field is variable and could be, for example, four, eight, or twelve bits long. This scheme is called a *variable-length op code* or an *expanding op code*.

   a.   Describe a scheme whereby you could unambiguously determine the size of the op-code field for any arbitrary instruction.

   b.   Assume that you have a 2-address machine that stores instructions in a 16-bit word using the following format:

Op code	Address 1	Address 2

4 bits   6 bits   6 bits

Furthermore, assume that you want to implement on your computer fifteen 2-address instructions and twenty-five 1-address instructions. At first, it seems impossible to fit forty op codes into a 4-bit field. Describe how it would be possible to implement these forty op codes using a *variable-length op-code approach*.

20. Assume that you have a computer that uses the following conventions:

    a. 16-bit sign/magnitude for integers

    b. ASCII characters, no parity

    c. 4-bit op codes, one 12-bit address field

If a memory location contains the following bit pattern:

$$415F_{16}$$

what are all the possible meanings of that bit pattern?

21. A variation on the Von Neumann structure is the simultaneous operation of a single instruction (e.g., ADD, SUB, MULT) on many different pieces of data via replicated arithmetic/logic units:

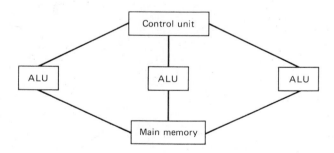

A single instruction decoded in the control unit would be applied to all of the ALUs, which would be fetching different operands from main memory. This type of architecture is called an *SIMD machine* (single instruction/multiple data) or an *array processor*. For example, the instruction:

    ADD   s,d,N   (∗ N simultaneous additions ∗)

$$
\left.\begin{array}{l}
\text{CON(s)} \quad\ + \text{CON(d)} \quad\ \rightarrow \text{CON(d)} \\
\text{CON(s+1)} + \text{CON(d+1)} \rightarrow \text{CON(d+1)} \\
\text{CON(s+2)} + \text{CON(d+2)} \rightarrow \text{CON(d+2)} \\
\qquad\qquad\quad\ \cdot \qquad\qquad\qquad \cdot \\
\qquad\qquad\quad\ \cdot \qquad\qquad\qquad \cdot \\
\qquad\qquad\quad\ \cdot \qquad\qquad\qquad \cdot \\
\text{CON(s+N)} + \text{CON(d+N)} \rightarrow \text{CON(d+N)}
\end{array}\right\} \text{This all happens concurrently.}
$$

Describe some applications for which an array processor would be a very useful architecture, superior to the more traditional Von Neumann structure.

PART THREE

THE STRUCTURE AND ORGANIZATION OF A COMPUTER SYSTEM: THE PDP-11 FAMILY OF COMPUTERS

CHAPTER 10

INTRODUCTION TO THE PDP-11 AND MACRO-11

10.1
Introduction

In this chapter, we begin our discussion of a real computer system, the PDP-11 manufactured by the Digital Equipment Corporation of Maynard, Massachusetts. The PDP-11 is the most popular minicomputer ever manufactured. Over 200,000 units have been sold since the introduction of the PDP-11/Model 20 in 1970. Today there are over a dozen models of the PDP-11, ranging in size from the tiny PDP-11/04—a single-board microcomputer costing just a few thousand dollars—to the VAX-11/782 "supermini" which can cost, in a full configuration, over $400,000. In this section, we will introduce you to the hardware features that are common to all models of the PDP-11 and to MACRO-11, the assembly language of the PDP-11.

Of course it is impossible to cover every detail of this highly complex computer system and the complete language specification. If you wish to study this topic at greater length, consult the following reference books, available from the vendor.

    The PDP-11 Processor Handbook
    The PDP-11 MACRO-11 Language Reference Manual
    The VAX Software Handbook
    The VAX Hardware Handbook
    The VAX Architecture Handbook

10.2
The PDP-11 Family

The PDP-11 is not a single computer, but a *family* of computer systems. PDP-11 models are *upwardly compatible*. That is, the more powerful members of the family can perform every operation that the simpler models can, but they also have advanced features not available on less powerful models. Thus, a program that runs on one of the smaller family members will run successfully on all larger systems. However, the converse may not be true. The PDP-11 models currently available are the MICRO-11, PDP-11/04, 23, 23+, 24, 34, 44, 70, 73, and the MICRO-VAX, VAX-11/730, 750, 780, and 782 (and new models may have been introduced by the time you read this). The relationships between these models can be viewed as a set of concentric circles as shown in Figure 10-1.

The VAX-11 series of computers represents an architecture quite different from that of the PDP-11, and many people consider the VAX-11/730, 750, 780, and 782 to be an entirely different family of computers. However, the VAX-11 has a *com-*

FIGURE 10-1   The PDP-11, VAX-11 Family of Computers.

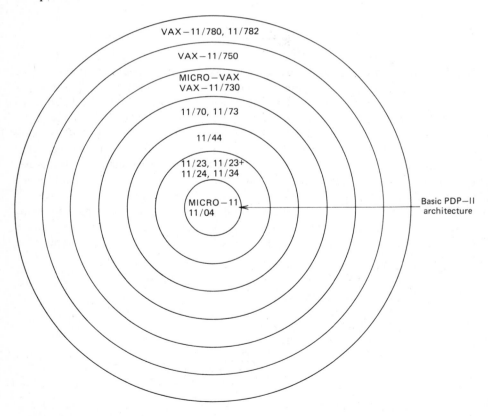

patibility mode that allows it to "look like" a PDP-11 and to execute all PDP-11 machine-language programs. Therefore, for the sake of this discussion, we consider the VAX series to be the "top of the line" of the PDP-11 family of computers.

Some of the features that distinguish different family members are:

1. *Memory capacity:* Smaller models use sixteen bits to store memory addresses, allowing an address space of 64K (65,536) bytes. Larger models use eighteen or twenty-four bits, providing 256K bytes or 16Mb (megabytes) of addressable memory.

2. *Additional hardware data types:* On smaller models, hardware floating point, extended integers, and BCD arithmetic may not be available. They are either standard or optional on larger systems.

3. *Bus structure:* The smaller members of the family have a single bus structure, similar to the one in Figure 7-9. This single bus, called a UNIBUS, carries all data transfers. Larger models have a second and third bus (called a MASSBUS) for handling high-speed I/O transfers.

4. *Number of registers:* Smaller models have eight general-purpose registers. The larger ones have sixteen.

5. *Number of operations:* The smallest PDP-11 has about ninety-five different operation codes. The largest VAX-11 has over three hundred.

These are only some of the technical differences among the models of the PDP-11 family. However, referring again Figure 10-1, you can see that most of the system capabilities lie within the innermost circle. This set of capabilities represents the features common to all family members, and this is the information that we describe here. Therefore, regardless of which family member is available at your location, whether it's a tiny PDP-11/04 or a giant VAX-11/782, everything we describe in Part III will apply to your computer, and every program listed should execute correctly on your system. This collection of fundamental capabilities is called the *basic PDP-11 architecture.*

10-3
Basic PDP-11 Architecture

The PDP-11 has, as a minimum, a 16-bit unsigned binary address. This allows an address space of 2^{16} (65,536) locations, with addresses ranging from 000000 to 177777 (octal). However, as we will see later, the highest numbered 8K addresses are reserved for special uses, so the available *user memory* is actually only 56K bytes, numbered from 000000 to 160000. Although many of the larger models of the PDP-11, VAX-11 family have memory capacities up to 16Mb, in the remainder of the text we assume a 64K address space to ensure compatibility with all models.

Each memory location is an 8-bit byte. The PDP-11 also allows memory to be accessed in terms of 16-bit *words*. A 16-bit word is defined as two consecutive 8-bit bytes, beginning with an even-numbered address. Thus, word 0 corresponds to bytes 0 and 1, and word 12 corresponds to bytes 12 and 13, with the even-numbered byte containing the low-order (i.e., least significant) eight bits, and the odd-numbered byte corresponding to the high-order (i.e., most significant) eight bits. An attempt to reference an odd-numbered word (e.g., word 5) will result in a fatal error, called an *odd-address error*.

Some of the larger members of the PDP-11, VAX-11 family have defined larger clusters of bytes to allow faster access to multiple cells. For example, as shown in Figure 6-3, the VAX-11/780 has defined clusters of four, eight, and sixteen bytes called longwords, quadwords, and octawords, respectively. Again, for the sake of compatibility with all family members, we limit ourselves to the memory units called the 8-bit *byte* and the 16-bit *word*.

The overall organization of memory in the basic PDP-11 architecture is shown in Figure 10-2. Notice the similarity between Figures 10-2 and 6-1. The PDP-11 memory structure follows quite closely the idealized Von Neumann architecture.

FIGURE 10-2   Organization of PDP-11 Memory.

Bytes		Word Address	
8 bits	8 bits		
1	0	0	⎫
3	2	2	
⋮	⋮	⋮	User memory
157777	157776	157776	
160001	160000	160000	⎫
·	·	·	
·	·	·	Reserved for special use
·	·	·	
177777	177776	177776	⎭

FIGURE 10-3   The Condition Codes.

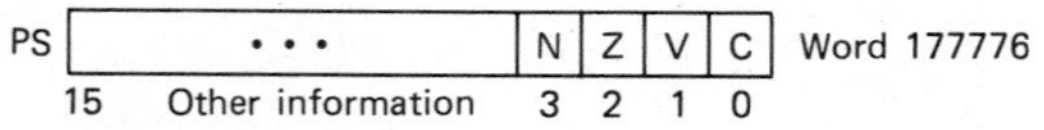

PS | ... | N | Z | V | C | Word 177776

15   Other information   3   2   1   0

The PDP-11 has eight 16-bit, general-purpose registers, called R0, R1, R2, ..., R6, and R7. (These eight registers can also be referred to as %0, %1, ..., %7, but the mnemonics R0, R1, R2, ..., are more commonly used.) Registers R6 and R7 are not really general purpose at all, but serve very special roles.

> *R6.* General register 6 is the *stack pointer register*. It points to the top of the system stack. The PDP-11 has a stack, and R6 serves the role of the value TOP described in Section 9.2.5 and shown in Figures 9-11 and 9-12. (In MACRO-11, general register R6 can also be referred to as SP, for *stack pointer*.)
>
> *R7.* General register 7 is the *program counter,* whose function was first introduced in Section 9.2.2. On the PDP-11, the program counter is available to the user, and as we will see shortly, this leads to some very interesting programming possibilities. (In MACRO-11, general register R7 can be referred to as PC.)

Because of the special functions of these two registers, only R0 to R5 can be considered to be true general-purpose registers. In the remainder of this text we adhere to the convention of using only these six registers for general computations, leaving R6 and R7 for the special purposes listed above.

There is one additional 16-bit register that we are immediately interested in: the *processor status word* (PS). This register, which occupies memory address 177776, describes the current state of the processor. Each of the sixteen bits of the PS is used to describe some aspect of the condition of the processor. Right now we are interested only in the low-order four bits of the PS. These four bits are called the *condition codes* (Figure 10-3).

The four bits are called the *C bit, V bit, Z bit,* and *N bit,* the correspond to the *carry bit, overflow bit, zero bit,* and *negative bit,* respectively. After each instruction is executed, these four bits are set by the system according to the outcome of the instruction. Figure 10-4 summarizes the rules for setting these four bits. (There are a few exceptions to these general rules; they will be discussed later.)

The data types supported by the basic PDP-11 architecture are:

> 8- and 16-bit unsigned binary
> 16-bit signed twos-complement integers
> 8-bit ASCII characters

FIGURE 10-4   Rules for Setting the Condition Codes.

Bit		Setting
N	1	If the instruction produced a negative result
	0	Otherwise
Z	1	If the instruction produced a zero result
	0	Otherwise
C	1	If the instruction generated a carry
	0	Otherwise
V	1	If the instruction generated an overflow
	0	Otherwise

Larger models of the PDP-11 and VAX-11 support 32-, 64- and 128-bit integer data types; 32-, 64-, and 128-bit floating-point data types; and a packed decimal BCD numeric type). However, since these data types are not available on all models we do not discuss them here. Descriptions of these additional capabilities are available in the PDP-11 Processor Handbook mentioned earlier.

Finally, the basic PDP-11 architecture includes about ninety-five instructions. These instructions are generally stored in 1-address or 2-address format (although there are a few specialized formats, noted later). Figure 10-5 describes these two standardized instruction formats.

From Figure 10-5 we can see that the op-code portion of an instruction is not a fixed size, but is either four or ten bits long, depending on the type of instruction.

FIGURE 10-5   Instruction Formats on the PDP-11.

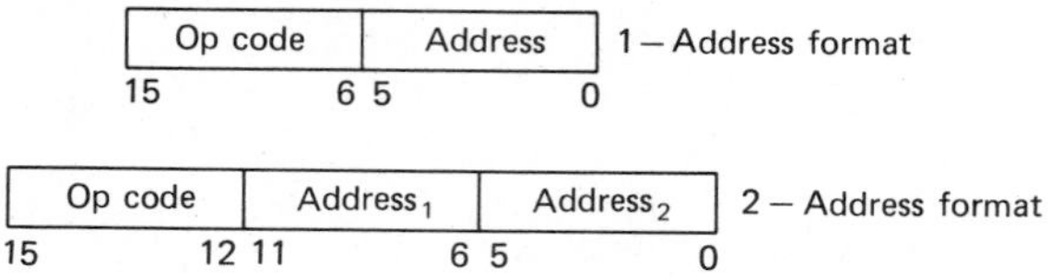

FIGURE 10-6   Format of the Address Field.

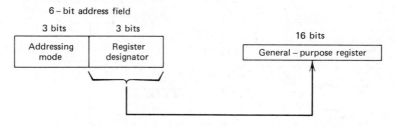

Figure 10-5 also shows that all the address fields are six bits long. This may initially seem impossible, since with six bits we can only address 2^6 (64) memory locations, and earlier we said that all PDP-11 computers have at least 2^{16} (64K) bytes. In fact, however, we can address 2^{16} bytes with only six bits by not storing the address itself in the address field of an instruction. Instead, we store only a *pointer* to a general-purpose register that contains the actual address.

Every 6-bit address field is divided into two 3-bit fields: a *mode field* and a *register designator*. The 3-bit mode field specifies the type of addressing that is being used. (The 8 [2^3] possible addressing modes are discussed in Chapter 11.) The register designator points to the general-purpose register that holds the actual address. With a 3-bit register designator field, we can reference any of the eight general-purpose registers, from R0 (register designator = 000) to R7 (register designator = 111).

Thus, an address field containing the 6-bit octal value 25 would mean that: (1) we are using addressing mode 2 (to be described), and (2) that the actual 16-bit address is contained in general register R5. The format of the address field on the PDP-11 is summarized in Figure 10-6.

The overall organization of the basic PDP-11 architecture is summarized in Figure 10-7. A few additional details will be added later, but for the most part, this is the computer system that we shall study. Again, notice the similarity between Figure 10-7 showing the basic PDP-11 architecture and Figure 9-18 describing our hypothetical PVM. The PDP-11 and VAX-11 families of computer systems are classic "Von Neumann-style" computers.

10.4
Assembly Language Versus Machine Language

Two terms that are occasionally (and incorrectly) used interchangeably are *machine language* and *assembly language*. The terms are not identical and should not be treated as such. Machine language is the instruction format that can be directly

FIGURE 10-7   Basic PDP-11 Architecture.

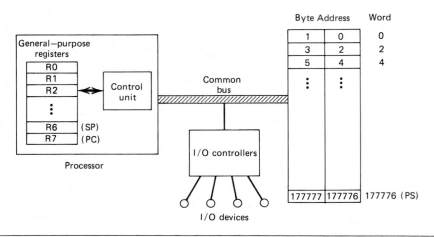

decoded and executed by a processor. It is composed of:

1. Binary operation codes.
2. Absolute binary memory addresses.

For example, the following is a machine-language instruction, meaning "Move the contents of register R4 to register R5" could be executed directly by a PDP-11:

0001000100000101

Obviously, programming directly in machine language would be extremely difficult and tedious, and it would be almost impossible to avoid making errors. To eliminate these problems when we want to program at the hardware level, we program instead in a variation of machine language called *assembly language*.

Assembly language is a mnemonic, user-oriented symbolic form of machine language, created to facilitate user programming at the machine-language level. Because it is a symbolic notation, like Pascal and BASIC, assembly-language instructions cannot be directly executed by the hardware. They must first be translated into machine language by a program called an *assembler*. This translation is much easier than the corresponding process of compilation—translating a high-level language into machine language—because assembly is typically a one-to-one process: One symbolic assembly-language command translates directly into one machine-language command. By contrast, with a high-level language, one statement (e.g., **while/do** or **if/then/else**) may ultimately produce dozens of machine-language instructions that are quite different in form from the original high-level statement.

FIGURE 10-8   The Relation Between Different Levels of
Language.

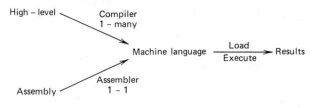

The intent of a high-level language is to create the "virtual programming environment," to which we have referred a number of times. An assembly language is not intended to create this type of artificial environment. It is simply a low-level language that offers limited symbolism and notational convenience for those who program at this level. (A few sophisticated assembly languages will offer arrays, loops, and user-oriented I/O—features typically found in higher level languages. Sometimes the distinction between low-level and high-level languages is not quite as clear as we may make it seem.) The relationship between machine language, asembly language, and high-level language is summarized in Figure 10-8.

An assembly language provides the programmer with six capabilities not available in machine language:

1. *Symbolic operation codes:*   Instead of having to use octal to specify an instruction, such as 01, we can write MOV, an abbreviation for MOVe data. Similarly, we can write ADD, SUB, CLR (for CLeaR), and JMP (for JuMP). These instruction mnemonics make a program easier to read and understand. Appendix A lists all symbolic operation codes in MACRO-11.

2. *More convenient representation of addressing techniques:*   The technique used for representing addresses on the PDP-11 is somewhat intricate, involving pointers to registers rather than addresses themselves. If we had to code this way directly, programming the PDP-11 would be very slow and tedious. Instead, assembly language allows us to write addresses in a more natural and convenient way, such as:

```
ADD     R0,R1     ;CON(R0) + CON(R1) → CON(R1)
JMP     LOOP      ;Jump to the address that we have
                  ;called LOOP.
```

The assembler will "fix up" these user-oriented symbolic addresses so they conform to the 6-bit address layout shown in Figure 10-6. It is important to remember that even though you may write addresses in the user-oriented formats shown above, they will be stored internally in a 6-bit field, exactly as shown in Figure 10-6. A summary of all MACRO-11 addressing modes is given in Appendix B.

3. *Assembler directives:* Assembler directives, also called *pseudo-ops,* are requests made by you to the assembler to perform a service on your behalf, rather than an instruction to be translated into machine language. About fifty of these assembler directives are available in MACRO-11. An example of a pseudo-operation is the following:

REGO = R0

This directive says that, for the remainder of the program, general register 0 can be referred to by the name REGO as well as by the built-in name R0. Appendix C lists all pseudo-ops in MACRO-11.

4. *More extensive error checking and control:* Appendix D lists error codes produced by the PDP-11 assembler during the assembly process.

5. *Independent program libraries:* In Pascal, we are accustomed to activating independent subprograms (e.g., sin, abs) from a library. The same feature can be provided by an assembler. The assembler on the PDP-11 has an extensive library of "canned" programs that can be included in your own program.

6. *Readable listings:* Finally, an assembler will print out your assembly-language program, its machine-language translation, error codes, diagnostics, and answers, all in a nice, readable, well-organized format.

The assembly language of the PDP-11 family of computers is called MACRO-11. In the following chapters, we describe it in detail and show the internal machine-language translation of MACRO-11 commands. In Part IV (Chapters 19 and 20) we show how the assembler itself can be constructed and how it carries out the translation operation.

10.5
Why Learn Assembly Language?

Before we delve into the details of MACRO-11, let's discuss why it (or, indeed, any assembly language) is worth studying. Not too many years ago, there were quite a few reasons to program in assembly language. First of all, it allowed you to optimize your program in terms of (minimal) running time and memory space. For example, to add the integer constant 3 to a value, in high-level languages you simply write:

A := A + 3;

without regard to how the command is accomplished. In assembly language, you may write either:

ADD #3,A ; Add the constant 3 to A

or

```
INC   A  ; Increment A by 1
INC   A  ; Increment A by 1
INC   A  ; Increment A by 1
```

Which sequence you chose depended on which was faster, one ADD or three INCrements.

Compilers used to be "dumb" and unable to make such decisions. They would mechanically produce code using a given set of rules without regard to whether or not there was a better or faster way to perform the operation. Typically, the code produced by a dumb compiler ran 30 to 50 percent slower than assembly-language code written by a professional programmer. This is no longer the case. Recent research in compiler design has resulted in "optimizing compilers" that make many passes over the source code to produce object code as good as, or better than, what can be produced directly by programmers. These compilers look for ways to structure the resulting machine-language code so that it runs as fast as possible with the least amount of memory space. An optimizing compiler would definitely know whether, in the last example, we should do one ADD or three INCrements.

However, there is an even more fundamental reason for the lack of concern with code optimization, and that is cost. If you are paying programmers $20 an hour (a realistic figure), it may not be economically feasible to have them work for days or weeks to get a program to run a few milliseconds faster or to use a few dozen fewer memory words. It might be cheaper in the long run to simply buy a faster (or an additional) processor or more memory. In general, assembly language is seldom used to optimize running time or memory utilization.

Another reason that is sometimes given for coding in assembly language is the convenience of being able to write programs that directly control some aspect of the computer system. These programs are typically called *systems programs;* examples include I/O device handlers, linkers, loaders, library managers, editors, compilers, and operating systems. Previously, these programs could not be coded in high-level language for the very reason we have been using to praise high-level langauges: they create a virtual environment that hides the computer system and its underlying components from the user. You can't very well write a systems program if you can't see the underlying system!

This situation is also changing. In the last few years, a class of languages called *systems implementation languages* (SILs) has been developed, and these languages are becoming increasingly popular. An SIL combines the user-oriented features of a high-level language (e.g., high-level control and data structures, scope rules, subprograms, and algebraic expressions) with the hardware-oriented capabilities of an assembler (e.g., bit-manipulation commands, register access, absolute addressing). There are many examples of SILs currently in use (BLISS, C, Ada, Concurrent Pascal, MODULA-2), and more and more systems programming is being done in an SIL rather than in assembly language.

Then why study assembly language? One reason remains valid. Studying assembly language helps you to understand the architecture of a specific computer system. Assembly language is a "window" into the design of a computer, and understanding the instruction set of a machine will provide insight into why the computer architect assembled the pieces in a particular way, and how the pieces fit together to form an integrated system.

You will be learning MACRO-11 not as a "production programming language" but as a way to understand and appreciate the structure of the PDP-11. Most of the programming assignments in this text do *not* involve balancing a checkbook, computing examination averages, or finding the root of an equation. Such applications-oriented assignments would never, or rarely ever, be done in MACRO-11. Problems like that are best done in higher level languages like Pascal. Instead, we concentrate on assignments that illustrate the low-level capabilities of assembly language and clarify some aspect of the PDP-11 architecture. (A typical assignment might involve normalizing the PDP-11 floating-point mantissa.) When you are faced with the task of understanding the internal structure of a new computer, one of the essential first steps will be to study and use its instruction set.

A study of assembly langauge will also help you to better understand the workings of high-level langauages. Many of the rules which exist in languages like FORTRAN or Pascal are simply accepted on faith, with no real understanding of why they exist (e.g., why won't the language allow me to use integers greater than 2,147,483,647). An understanding of assembly language can answer these and similar questions.

In the next chapter we begin our study of MACRO-11 by discussing its *addressing modes.*

Exercises for Chapter 10

1. What is wrong with the following commands?
    a.   Move the contents of word 4 to word 7.
    b.   Move the contents of word 12 to byte 76.

2.   If our PDP-11 model used twenty-two bits for addressing rather than sixteen as described in Section 10.3, what would be the range of valid memory addresses expressed in:
    a.   Octal?
    b.   Hexadecimal?
    c.   Decimal?

3.   Assume that our 22-bit memory (see Exercise 2) also reserved the highest numbered 8K addresses for special uses. What would be the range of valid user memory addresses expressed in:
    a.   Octal?

b. Hexadecimal?

c. Decimal?

4. Assume that the 64K memory shown in Figure 10-2 defined 4- and 8-byte clusters called longwords and quadwords, respectively. How many longwords and quadwords would there be in our memory? What would be the octal address of the last (i.e., the highest numbered) longword and quadword in our memory?

5. Given the memory organization described in Section 10.3 and diagrammed in Figure 10-2, how large would you expect the MAR and MBR registers to be?

6. Given the following twos-complement addition operation,

$$\begin{array}{r} 01101 \\ + \ \ 01110 \\ \hline \end{array}$$

show the setting of the C, V, Z, and N condition codes following the completion of the operation.

7. Given the following twos-complement subtraction operation,

$$\begin{array}{r} 11000 \\ - \ \ 00011 \\ \hline \end{array}$$

show the setting of the C, V, Z, and N condition codes following the completion of the operation.

8. With the 16-bit twos-complement integer representation on the PDP-11, what is the largest positive and negative decimal integer value that can be stored? What is the largest and smallest unsigned binary value that can be stored?

9. For the PDP-11 models that support a 32-bit integer data type, what is the largest positive integer than can be stored? For the PDP-11 models that support a 64- and 128-bit integer data type, approximately how many significant decimal digits are there in the largest positive integer that can be represented?

10. What is the advantage of having the address field of a PDP-11 instruction contain a pointer to a register rather than the address itself?

11. Assume that you decided (foolishly!) to write a program directly in PDP-11 machine language using absolute binary operation codes and addresses. Assume also that you are lucky enough to get the program working. Describe the problems that you are likely to encounter when you try to *change* the program.

12. Referring to Figure 10-5, what is the maximum number of 1-address and 2-address instructions that we can have on the PDP-11?

13. It is generally true that assembly language is seldom used to optimize running time. However, running time is absolutely critical for some programs, and for them we may have to resort to encoding in assembly language. Describe a program that would fall into this category.

14. Using any common high-level programming language (e.g., BASIC, COBOL, Pascal), is there any way to determine the following information about the underlying hardware?

a. The size of a minimally addressable memory unit.
b. The total amount of memory available.
c. The representational technique for signed integers.
d. The existence of a floating-point hardware unit.
e. The number of general-purpose registers.
f. The number of buses on the system.
g. The instruction set of the processor.
h. The addressing format of an instruction.

CHAPTER 11

ADDRESSING MODES

11.1
Introduction

A MACRO-11 program is made up of individual MACRO-11 *statements,* each in the format shown in Figure 11-1. The "label" and "comment" fields are optional; the "op-code" and "operand" fields are required. If you omit either the op-code or the operand field, the assembler will assume a default value for the missing item. Most MACRO-11 statements have either one or two operands, corresponding to the 1- and 2-address formats introduced in Chapter 9. (However, there are a few MACRO-11 operations do not require any operands. They are described later.) The statement layout in Figure 11-1 is totally free format and you may have any number of blanks between fields although no blanks are allowed *within* a field. There is one widely used convention for formatting MACRO-11 programs:

Label field :	Starts in column 1
Op code :	Starts in column 9
Operand(s):	Starts in column 17
Comment :	Starts in column 33

These guidelines are optional; if you choose another formatting convention, be sure that it produces readable program listings.

The *label field* is used to attach a symbolic name to a memory location or a constant. That name can then be used in place of the binary address or constant.

The *op-code field* contains the 3-, 4-, or 5-letter mnemonic abbreviation for the instruction to be carried out. The list of all MACRO-11 op codes is contained in Appendix A.

The *operand field* contains either the value or the address of the value upon which the instruction is to operate. Depending on the type of op code, there will be zero, one, or two operands. If there are two operands, they must be separated by a comma.

FIGURE 11-1   MACRO-11 Statement Format.

Label: Op Code   Operand(s)   ;   Comment

No blanks are allowed anywhere within the operand field. In fact, a blank terminates the entire operand field. There are eight different types of addressing mode that can be used to specify an operand address, and they are described in the upcoming sections.

A *comment* is any string of characters beginning with a semicolon (;). Comments are for explanatory purposes only. They are printed on the listing but are otherwise ignored by the assembler. Comments are especially important in a low-level assembly language because the intent of an individual statement is often not immediately apparent. Notice how helpful the comments are in the block of code shown in Figure 11-2. Without them, the effect of the four MACRO-11 instructions would be difficult to decipher. Get in the habit early of developing good commenting habits. Otherwise, when you look back at old programs, you probably won't be able to remember how or why they were written, and it will take hours of struggling with complex, low-level code to reconstruct your work.

As Figure 11-1 shows, learning MACRO-11 involves the study of two central concepts: the *op codes* and what they do, and the *operands* and how to specify them. (This can be viewed as being roughly analogous to learning the statements and data types of a high-level language.) In the next section we present the syntax of addresses in the operand field of a MACRO-11 instruction. In Chapter 12 we introduce the MACRO-11 instruction set.

FIGURE 11-2   Example of Good Use of Comments.

```
        ;
        ; This section of the program reads in
        ; one character from a VDT-type terminal device
        ; and moves it into the memory location called CH
        ;

        BIS    #1,TTYSR      ; Turn on the START bit
LOOP:   BIT    #200,TTYSR    ; Test if the DONE bit is ON yet
        BEQ    LOOP          ; No it isn't, keep waiting
        MOVB   TTYBUF, CH    ; Yes we are done. Move the
                             ; character into memory location CH
```

11.2
Addressing Techniques

An important concept in addressing is the *effective address,* which is the physical address that you arrive at after the manipulations specified by a particular addressing mode have been performed. The effective address represents the address upon which you will perform the operations indicated by the op code. The study of addressing techniques is really the study of how to determine the effective address from the information encoded in the address field of a MACRO-11 instruction. Remember that addresses in MACRO-11 are represented as 6-bit values—a 3-bit mode field and a 3-bit register designator (see Figure 10-6).

To illustrate the various addressing modes and their interpretation, we will use the two MACRO-11 instructions called clear and move. Clear, written CLR in MACRO-11, is a 1-address operation that clears (sets to 0) the contents of the effective address. Move, written MOV, is a 2-address operation that moves the contents of the effective source address to the contents of the effective destination address. The original contents of the source address are unchanged, but the original contents of the destination address are lost and replaced by the new value. Figure 11-3 summarizes the behavior of these two MACRO-11 instructions.

11.2.1 Register Mode (Mode 0)
In register mode addressing, the register specified in the address field is the effective address, and it contains the value upon which the instruction will operate. This is one of the simplest and most frequently used addressing modes in MACRO-11. The external syntax for register mode (mode 0) is simply:

$$External\ syntax: \%n \quad or \quad Rn \qquad n = 0, 1, \ldots, 7$$

FIGURE 11-3   Behavior of the Two MACRO-11
Instructions: Move, Clear.

Internal Octal Representation	*MACRO-11*	*Meaning*
0050aa	CLR addr	0→CON(eff. addr)
01ssdd	MOV addr$_1$,addr$_2$	CON(eff. addr$_1$)→CON(eff. addr$_2$)

where: aa   6-bit binary address in the format of Figure 10-6
      ss,dd   6-bit source, destination address in the format of Figure 10-6
      eff. addr   effective address
      CON(a)   contents of memory address a

When register mode addressing is used, the mode code is set to binary 000, and the register designator is set to a value between 000 and 111 corresponding to the general-purpose register being used.

EXAMPLES

(a)   **CLR   R1**   Internal representation: **005001**

R1 before: **123456**
R1 after: **000000**

General-purpose register R1 is the effective address. Its contents are cleared to 0.

(b)   **MOV   R3,R4**   Internal representation: **010304**

	Before	*After*
R3:	127777	127777
R4:	012345	127777

General-purpose register R3 is the effective source address. R4 is the effective destination address. The contents of R3 are copied into R4.

The major advantage of register mode addressing is *speed*. Accessing data stored in a general-purpose register is much faster than memory accessing. (We made this point when introducing registers in Section 7.3) For example, the CLR R1 instruction takes 2.65 μsec on a PDP-11/04. A CLR instruction that references a memory location takes 6.11 μsec. If you are trying to make your program run faster, move the operands into general purpose registers and make frequent use of mode 0.

Exercise 2 at the end of the chapter has some additional examples of register mode addressing.

11.2.2   Register Deferred Mode (Mode 1)

In register deferred mode, the register specified in the address field contains the address of the operands. In other words, the effective address is the *contents* of the specified register.

External syntax: (Rn)   or   @Rn $n = 0, 1, \ldots, 7$

When register deferred mode is specified, the mode code is set to binary 001 and the register designator is set to the register specified in the address field.

EXAMPLES

(a)   **CLR   (R1)**   Internal representation: **005011**

	Before	After
R1:	1234	1234
1234:	66	0

When we use register deferred mode, we go to the register specified in the instruction, R1 in this case, pick up its contents, the octal value 1234, and use that value as the effective address. Thus, memory address 1234 is cleared to 0.

(b)   MOV   R2,(R5)   Internal representation: **010215**

	Before	After
R2:	177777	177777
R5:	1000	1000
1000:	123321	177777

The first operand is using mode 0, so R2 is the effective address and its contents will be moved. The second operand is using mode 1, so register R5 contains the effective address, the memory location 1000. As a result, the contents of R2, the value 177777, are moved to memory address 1000.

On many computers, deferred addressing is called *indirect addressing,* and it is a very important technique. It is important because, in assembly language, you can perform arithmetic operations on *addresses* as well as on data. Assume that you have computed the address, A, of an item, I, and have stored the address A in register Rn, as shown in Figure 11-4. How do you now perform computations on data item I pointed to by A? Simple register mode addressing (mode 0) will only allow you to work on the address itself. Register deferred addressing, using register Rn in Figure 11-4, will allow you to go to register Rn, pick up its contents, address A, and use that address to access the desired item I. There are many examples of register deferred addressing in upcoming programs. Exercise 5 at the end of the chapter contains some additional examples of register deferred mode.

As you will see, for all of the eight addressing modes in MACRO-11, mode $i + 1, i = 0, 2, 4, 6$ is the deferred variant of mode i.

FIGURE 11-4   Need for Deferred, or Indirect, Addressing.

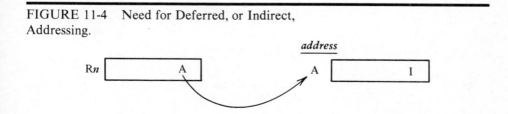

11.2.3 Autoincrement Mode (Mode 2)

Autoincrement mode (mode 2) behaves very much like register deferred mode, in that the register specified in the address field of the instruction contains the effective address. However, after the operation has been completed, the register is automatically incremented, by 1 if the operation code is a byte instruction, and by 2 if the operation code is a word instruction. As we learn in Chapter 12, all MACRO-11 operation codes are either byte or word instructions. CLR and MOV are both word instructions and will thus cause an increment by 2 when using autoincrement mode.

The external syntax for mode 2 is:

$$External\ syntax:\quad (Rn) +\qquad n = 0, 1, \ldots, 7$$

(Note: The + sign is placed after the register designator as a mnemonic reminder that the register is incremented after the operation is completed.)

EXAMPLES

(a) **CLR (R4) +**   Internal representation: **005024**

	Before	*After*
R4:	106	110	; Note: 106 + 2 = 110 (octal).
106:	177777	0

The effect of using autoincrement addressing is as follows:
(1) Go to register R4 and pick up its contents, 106. This is the effective address.
(2) Clear the effective address, 106, to 0.
(3) Increment register R4 by 2 (since CLR is a word instruction).

(b) **MOV R2, (R3) +**   Internal representation: **010223**

	Before	*After*
R2:	1	1
R3:	20	22
20:	177777	1

The contents of register R2 will be moved to the address contained in register R3, address 20. After the move is completed, register R3 will be incremented by 2 because MOV is a word instruction.

Autoincrement mode has a number of uses. One of the most important is stepping a register through a set of sequential addresses, such as a word-oriented array or table:

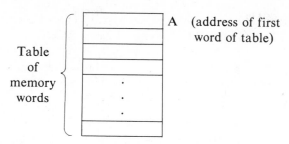

If we initialize a register to the value A, the address of the first word of the table, then we can easily clear the entire table to 0 using autoincrement mode as shown in Figure 11-5. Each time we go through the loop we will clear the address pointed to by R0 (which is some entry in the table) and then increment R0 by 2, which will point us to the next entry in the table. Without autoincrement mode, we would have to add two to the contents of R0 each time we went through the loop.

There are many more examples of autoincrement addressing in the following chapters. Exercise 8 contains additional examples of autoincrement mode.

11.2.4   Immediate Mode (Mode 2, Register 7)

This text treats a total of twelve different addressing techniques for the PDP-11. This initially seems impossible because the 3-bit mode field contains only enough room for 2^3 (8) types of addressing. In fact, there are only eight types of addressing that the hardware will recognize; however, the MACRO-11 assembler provides twelve addressing techniques. Four of them do not actually exist directly in hardware, but are translated by the assembler into one of the eight existing modes. However, as an assembly-language programmer, you can think and program in terms of twelve addressing modes. (The existence of these four additional addressing techniques can be viewed as a limited attempt by the assembler to create a more user-friendly, virtual programming environment). Immediate mode is the first of these four "pseudo-addressing" modes.

Immediate mode (frequently called *literal addressing*) is used in the following situation. If you wanted to move the integer constant 2 to register R0 and you wrote:

MOV   2,R0

FIGURE 11-5   Using Autoincrement Mode to Clear a Table.

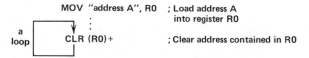

you would be wrong. All operands in the address field are interpreted as *addresses,* so the instruction would move the contents of memory word 2 (bytes 2 and 3) to register R0.

We would like to be able to refer directly to a constant and not have it interpreted as an address. Such a constant in the operand field of an instruction is called a *literal,* and in MACRO-11 it is specified in the following way.

> *External syntax:*   #constant or #expression

Thus, the symbol #2 in the operand field means the constant 2 rather than memory address 2, and our previous problem of loading register R0 with a 2 can be easily solved by writing:

> **MOV   #2,R0   ; Move the constant 2 into register R0**

Now, how is that literal constant stored internally? The answer is based on the fact that general register R7 is the program counter (PC), and the program counter always points to the word immediately following the instruction that we are currently executing. Because of this, immediate mode can be translated into autoincrement mode (mode 2) using the program counter (register 7) as the general-purpose register. The literal constant is assembled as a 16-bit quantity in the word *immediately following* the instruction. Thus, for any operation code, OP, if we write:

> **OP   #3**

the following two words will be produced internally:

address	mode register
A	op code 2 7
A + 2	0 0 0 0 0 3 ◄——— PC (after fetching instruction)

When the first word is fetched from memory, the PC will be pointing at the second word, address A + 2. The processor will evaluate the mode field and see that it is mode 2. Mode 2 says that the specified register, 7 in this case, contains the effective address. But register 7 contains the address A + 2. So A + 2 is the effective address, and it contains the literal constant 3. Thus, we will use the constant +3 in performing our operation. Finally, autoincrement mode says that when you have completed the operation, you increment the contents of the specified register. After we have incremented the PC by 2, it will contain the address A + 4, which is the address of the next instruction.

EXAMPLES

In these examples, assume that the instruction is in memory location 52 (octal).

(a)   **MOV   #5,R0**   Internal representation: **(52) 012700**
                                                    (54) 000005

	Before	*After*
R0:	4	5
PC:	54	56

Note: The PC will have the value 54 after the MOV instruction in location 52 has been fetched but before it has been executed. It will have the value 56 upon completion of the operation.

(b) MOV #100,(R1) Internal representation: **(52) 012711**
(54) 000100

	Before	*After*
R1:	40	40
40:	332	100
PC:	54	56

The constant 100 will be moved to the address contained in register R1, which is location 40.

When using literal mode, you must remember two things. First, each use of literal addressing mode will lengthen a MACRO-11 instruction by one word (sixteen bits). Thus, a MACRO-11 instruction can be either sixteen, thirty-two, or forty-eight bits long. Second, it must be possible to represent the literal constant being used in sixteen bits as a twos-complement quantity. Thus, while these two instructions are legal:

MOV #−1,R0
MOV #177777,R0

these two are not:

MOV #−432150,R0 ·This won't fit in 16 bits
MOV #777777,R0   ;This requires 18 bits

The last two examples would generate a T (truncation) error by the assembler, which means that you tried to use a literal quantity that was too large to fit in sixteen bits. See Appendix D for a list of all assembler error codes.

Exercise 10 contains additional examples of literal addressing made.

11.2.5 Autodecrement Mode (Mode 4)
Autodecrement mode is very similar to autoincrement mode (mode 2) with the following two exceptions.

1. The register is decremented rather than incremented.
2. The register is decremented *before*, rather than after, the effective address has been evaluated.

In autodecrement mode, we first decrement the specified register, either by 1 for a byte instruction, or by 2 for a word instruction. Then the register contains the effective address.

$$\textit{External syntax:} \quad -(\mathrm{R}n) \quad n = 0, 1, \ldots, 7$$

Note: The minus sign is placed *before* the register designator as a mnemonic to indicate that the decrementing is done *before* the operation is evaluated.

EXAMPLES

(a) **CLR**   **−(R5)**   Internal representation: **005045**

	Before	After
R5:	24	22
22:	30	0
24:	6	6

The effect of using autodecrement mode addressing is as follows:
(1) Go to register R5 and immediately decrement its contents by 2 (because CLR is a word instruction). This changes R5 to the value 22.
(2) R5 is now assumed to contain the effective address.
(3) Clear the contents of memory location 22. Address 24 is unaffected by this instruction.

(b) **MOV**   **(R0) +, −(R1)**   Internal representation: **012041**

	Before	After
R0:	50	52
50:	333	333
R1:	62	60
60:	1	333

The instruction will be executed in the following manner:
(1) Fetch the contents of R0, the value 50. This is the effective source address. The contents of memory cell 50 will be moved.
(2) Increment R0 by 2. The result is a 52.
(3) Decrement R1 by 2. The result is a 60. This is the effective destination address. Memory cell 60 will be the location to which the value is moved.
(4) Move the contents of address 50 (a 333) to address 60.

(c) MOV   #22, −(R3)   Internal representation: (52)   012743
                                                    (54)   000022

	Before	After
R3:	102	100
100:	0	22
PC:	54	56

First, register R3 is decremented by 2, giving the value 100. Then the integer constant 22, stored in the word immediately following the MOV instruction, is moved to the address contained in register R3, which is address 100. Finally, the program counter (register 7) is incremented by 2 to the value 56. It now points to the beginning of the next instruction.

Exercise 12 contains some additional examples of autodecrement addressing.

11.2.6 Index Mode (Mode 6)

Frequently in a program we want to refer to a memory location not by its own address, but by its relative distance from a fixed and known point. We use arrays and subscripts for this purpose in high-level languages. For example, the notation A[6] means the sixth element of an array counting from the beginning. We call the fixed reference point the *base address,* and the distance from the base is called the *offset.* This approach to addressing is diagrammed in Figure 11-6.

Index mode in MACRO-11 allows us to perform base and offset addressing like that shown in Figure 11-6. A *constant value* (the offset) in the word immediately following the instruction is added to the contents of the specified register that represents the base address. The constant is stored as a signed twos-complement value. The sum of these two quantities is the effective address. The program counter is then automatically incremented by 2 so that it correctly points to the beginning of the next instruction.

FIGURE 11-6   The Base and Offset in Indexed Addressing.

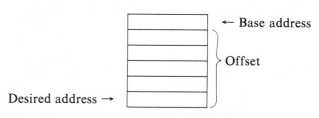

External syntax: $k(Rn)$ k = any 16-bit constant

$$n = 0, 1, \ldots, 7$$

The effective address of the above will be $[k + \text{CON}(Rn)]$.

EXAMPLES

(a)   CLR   55(R0)   Internal representation: **005060**

                                                    000055

	Before	*After*
R0:	1	1
56:	123321	0

The effect of using indexed addressing is:

(1)   The offset value 55 is added to the current contents of register R0. The result is 56. (R0 is not changed.)

(2)   56 is the effective address. Therefore, the contents of address 56 are cleared to 0. Notice that the effect was to clear the location fifty-five locations past the base address specified in register R0.

(b)   MOV   #1,50(R1)   Internal representation: **(52) 012761**

                                                    (54) 000001

                                                    (56) 000050

	Before	*After*
R1 :	22	22
72 :	777	1
PC :	54	60

The integer constant 1 is moved to the address 50 + CON(R1), which is 50 + 22 = 72. After the move operation has been performed, the program counter is advanced to the value 60 so that it points to the beginning of the next instruction.

As with immediate mode, the use of index mode will add one word (sixteen bits) to the length of a MACRO-11 instruction each time it is used. Thus, the length of a MACRO-11 instruction may be anywhere from one word (two bytes, sixteen bits) to three words (six bytes, forty-eight bits).

Example of one, two, and three word MACRO-11 instructions:

MACRO-11		Internal Representation
MOV	R0,R1	010001
(b) MOV	R0,50(R1)	010061
		000050
(c) MOV	#1,50(R1)	012761
		000001
		000050

In many ways, indexing is similar to subscripting an array. The base address corresponds to the array name, and the offset corresponds to the subscript. That is, the array reference A[5] may be considered to be roughly analogous to the address 5(R0) if we assume that register R0 contains the starting address of the array. However, you must understand the difference between subscripting and address offsets. If the first byte of a byte-oriented array is called A, then in a high-level language we would refer to that first element as A[1]. But in assembly language its address would be A + 0 (i.e., zero bytes from the beginning of the array). The second element of the array would be A[2] in high-level notation, but A + 1 in address notation (i.e., one byte past the beginning of the array). Figure 11-7 shows the difference between these two addressing modes.

The following chapters present many examples of indexed mode addressing being

FIGURE 11-7   Array Notation and Address Offset Notation.

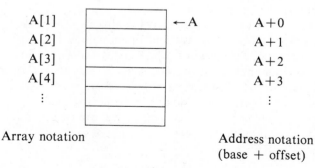

Byte-oriented array

Array notation

Address notation
(base + offset)

used to provide access into "array-like" data structures. Remember, though, that in assembly language there is no array data structure directly available; it must be simulated using consecutive blocks of memory and the appropriate type of addressing. Exercise 16 contains additional examples of indexed addressing.

11.2.7 Relative Addressing (Mode 6, Register 7)

The final addressing mode discussed in this chapter is *relative addressing*, also refered to as *symbolic addressing*, and like the immediate mode discussed in Section 11.2.4, it is also a "pseudo-addressing" technique provided by the assembler. It does not exist on the hardware as a separate and unique addressing mode.

In assembly language, we can equate a name (i.e., a symbol) with an address by using it in the label field of any MACRO-11 instruction.

label: MACRO-11 instruction

The assembler will take this to mean that the symbol in the label field is to be given the value of the address into which this MACRO-11 instruction is placed. A symbol can be any string of letters or digits that adheres to the following syntactic rules.

1. The first character must be alphabetic.
2. All succeeding characters must be alphabetic or numeric with no embedded spaces.
3. The name may be as long as desired, but the first six characters must form a unique string.

To determine the address associated with any particular MACRO-11 instruction, the assembler uses a value called the *location counter*. This is a counter that keeps track of the address of the word at which the next translated MACRO-11 instruction or data element is to be placed. After the instruction has been translated into machine language, the location counter will be updated by the assembler by two, four, or six bytes, depending on whether the instruction just translated took one, two, or three words. Figure 11-8 shows four MACRO-11 instructions and their internal translations and location counter values.

On most systems, the location counter is initialized to the value 0 and is incremented by the assembly during translation. In addition to this automatic updating of the location counter by the assembler, there are MACRO-11 directives that allow the user to directly manipulate the location counter. This effectively controls where in memory the MACRO-11 instructions are placed after they have been translated into machine code. We learn how to do this in the next section.

Now that we have defined a location counter, we can use the *rule of symbol definition* to explain exactly what happens when you use a symbol in the label field of an instruction.

> The value of any symbol used in the label field of an instruction is the value of the location counter at the time that the label is encountered.

FIGURE 11-8   Example of Location Counter Values.

(Assume that the value of the location counter was 100 when these statements are first encountered.)

Location Counter	Contents	MACRO-11		Statements
100	010001	L1:	MOV	R0,R1
102	012702		MOV	#1,R2
104	000001			
106	005063	L2:	CLR	100(R3)
110	000100			
112	005004	L3:	CLR	R4

Using this rule, the values of the three labels in Figure 11-8 are:

L1:   100
L2:   106
L3:   112

Using a symbol in the label field is equivalent to *defining* that symbol, because it becomes associated with an address. Once a symbol has been defined, it may then be *referenced,* or used in the address field of any MACRO-11 instruction. When a symbol is used in the address field of an instruction, the effective address is the address associated with that symbol. Thus the instruction:

MOV   L1,R0

will move the contents of the address associated with symbol L1 (address 100) to register R0. Using the values shown in Figure 11-8, the final contents of R0 after execution of the previous MOV instruction will be 010001.

In addition to using a single symbol in the address field, we can also write an *expression* of arbitrary complexity using the operators $+$, $-$, $*$, $/$. This expression is evaluated using the following rules.

1. The value of any symbol used in the expression will be its associated address value.

2. Evaluation of the expression is strictly left to right. The effective address will be the address that results from evaluation of the expression.

EXAMPLES

Use the values of L1, L2, and L3 from Figure 11-8.

			Effective Address
(a)	CLR	L1+2	102
(b)	CLR	L3−L1	12
(c)	CLR	L1+L2+2	210
(d)	CLR	L3*2	224
(e)	CLR	L1*3−6	272

Note that all arithmetic operations are on the address values of the labels, not their contents. Thus, in example a, we add two to the address value of L1 (i.e., 100 + 2), not to the contents of L1 (i.e., not 10001 + 2). Also remember that all values shown are octal, and all arithmetic is being done in base 8.

Now that we have seen how to define and use a label as an address, we need to know how to store that information internally in the 6-bit address notation of MACRO-11. Internal storage is accomplished when relative addressing is translated into indexed addressing (mode 6) using the program counter (register 7). As we have seen, the program counter will point to the word immediately following the instruction just fetched. This will be the base address. The assembler then computes an offset that will equal the "distance" (in bytes) between the current value of the PC and the symbolic address we are referencing. When we add the contents of the PC to the offset, we can locate the desired symbolic address.

For example, let's say that we have defined a label, COUNT, in our program, and later on refer to it in another instruction, as shown below.

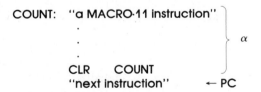

```
COUNT:   "a MACRO-11 instruction"
            .
            .                              α
            .
         CLR     COUNT
         "next instruction"      ← PC
```

We will assemble the CLR instruction into the following pair of 16-bit values.

005067
α

where α is an offset value such that $\alpha + CON(PC) = $ address of COUNT.

EXAMPLES

Assume COUNT = memory location 200.

(a)　What is the internal representation of:

CLR　　COUNT

(Assume the location counter is now 40.)

Address	Contents
(40)	005067
(42)	000134

The PC will have the value 42 after the CLR instruction has been fetched from memory. Since this instruction uses indexed addressing, we fetch the contents of the word pointed to by the PC, the constant 134, and the PC will be incremented to 44. We then add the offset value just fetched (134) to the current contents of the specified register (PC) to get the effective address:

$$44 + \quad 134 \quad = 200 \text{ (octal)}$$
$$\text{(Base)} \quad \text{(Offset)} = \text{Location of COUNT}$$

(b)　What is the internal representation of:

CLR　　COUNT

if we now assume that the location counter has the value 204 and that COUNT is still location 200?

Address	Contents	
(204)	005067	; the CLR instruction
(206)	177770	; the offset value

In this example, the offset is a negative value because we are referring to a memory location *before* the current instruction. After fetching the offset 177770, the program counter will contain the value 210. We then add the base and offset together using twos-complement arithmetic:

$$210 + 177770 \ = \ 200$$
$$\text{(Base)} \quad \text{(Offset)} \quad \text{(Location of COUNT)}$$

This example shows that the offset value in indexed addressing is a *signed* twos-complement integer value. (If you are unsure about the representation of negative quantities in twos complement, you may wish to go back and review Section 3.3.)

Don't worry if the computation of these offsets is confusing. The assembler will determine them for you whenever you use a symbolic address. The important thing is for you to be able to *interpret* the internal machine-language representation of your MACRO-11 commands. Exercise 21 contains some additional examples of relative or symbolic addressing.

There is one final point about symbolic addresses. It is critical to remember that the *value* of a symbol is its address, not the contents of that address. Thus, referring to Figure 11-8, the value of L1 is 100, not 010001. In all of the preceding addressing modes, wherever we said that you may use a constant, you may also use a symbolic address. The effective address computation will then be performed on the *value* of the symbol, that is, the address associated with that symbol.

EXAMPLES

Assume that the value of labels L1, L2, and L3 are as shown in Figure 11-8, and that CON(R0) = 500.

(a) MOV #L1,R5

Move the *value* of L1 directly to R5. The value of the symbol L1 is 100, so R5 will contain a 100 after completion of this instruction. This is how to get the memory address associated with a symbol into a register.

(b) MOV #L2+4,R5

The value of symbol L2 is 106. The computer will evaluate the expression 106 + 4 to get the address 112. The value 112 will then be moved directly into register R5. In a sense, this instruction says to load the *address* that is four bytes past the address of L2 into register R5.

(c) CLR L3(R0)

The offset is the value of the symbol L3. This is a 112. The base address is the contents of register R0, which is 500.

$$\text{effective address} = 500 + 112 = 612$$

The contents of memory location 612 will be cleared to 0.

(d) CLR L2+2(R0)

The offset is the value of the expression L2 + 2, which is 106 + 2 = 110. The base address is the contents of register R0, which is 500.

$$\text{effective address} = 500 + 110 = 610$$

The contents of memory location 610 will be cleared to 0.

(e) Looking back at Figure 11-5, we now see that we can translate the statement:

MOV "address A", R0

into MACRO-11 by writing:

MOV #A,R0

(f) CLR #L3(R0)

This is illegal because it mixes two completely different addressing techniques: immediate mode (mode 2) and indexing mode (mode 6). The instruction would cause a syntax error and would not assemble properly.

11.3
Summary

We have now introduced seven of the twelve addressing techniques available in MACRO-11. The external syntax of these seven modes is summarized in Figure 11-9.

In succeeding chapters we introduce five additional addressing techniques: modes 3, 3 (using register 7), 5, 7, and 7 (using register 7). However, the seven modes shown in Figure 11-9 represent the overwhelming majority of address references used in a typical program, and with them we can begin to write some interesting MACRO-11 programs.

You should have a solid understanding of these addressing techniques and be completely clear on the determination of the effective address for all methods before proceeding. The exercises at the end of the chapter contain examples of the first seven addressing modes. You should work a number of these problems to make sure that you are able to determine the effective address for each mode.

In the next chapter we introduce some of the most popular MACRO-11 instructions and write our first MACRO-11 program.

FIGURE 11-9   Summary of the First Seven Addressing Modes.

Notation*	Name	Mode
Rn	Register	0
(Rn) or @Rn	Register Deferred, Indirect	1
(Rn)+	Autoincrement	2
#expression	Immediate, Literal	2 (Reg 7)
−(Rn)	Autodecrement	4
expression(Rn)	Indexed	6
expression	Relative, Symbolic	6 (Reg 7)

*"Expression" can contain both integer constants and symbolic addresses combined with the binary operators +, −, *, and /.

Exercises for Chapter 11

1. Explain clearly the difference between the effective address and the address that appears in the operand field of a MACRO-11 instruction.

2. For the following examples of register mode addressing, show the internal representation of each instruction and the final contents of all registers referenced in the instruction. Assume the initial contents of the registers are: (All values are octal.)

$$R0 = 100 \quad R2 = 300$$
$$R1 = 200 \quad R3 = 400$$

    a.   CLR   R1
    b.   MOV R0,R3
    c.   MOV R2,R2
    d.   CLR   R2

3. Would the instruction shown in Exercise 2c have any effect on the general-purpose registers? Is it illegal?

4. What would be "dangerous" about writing the following instruction?

CLR   PC

What would happen immediately after this instruction was executed?

5. For the following examples of register deferred mode addressing, show the internal representation of each instruction and the before and after values for all registers and memory locations referenced by the instruction. Assume that the current contents of memory locations and registers are as follows. (All values are in octal.)

Registers		Memory	
R0:	100	100:	0
R1:	200	200:	123
R2:	300	300:	1777
R3:	400	400:	2

    a.   CLR   (R1)
    b.   MOV R2,(R3)
    c.   MOV R2,(R2)
    d.   CLR   (R2)
    e.   MOV (R1),(R2)

6. Would the instruction in Exercise 5c have any effect on the general-purpose registers or memory?

7. Assume that register R0 contained the value 1 and you issued the statement:

CLR   (R0)

What is wrong? What would happen if you tried to execute this instruction?

8. For the following examples of autoincrement mode addressing, show the internal representation for each instruction and the before and after values of all registers and memory locations referenced by the instruction. Assume that the current contents of the registers and memory are as follows.

Registers		Memory	
R0:	100	100:	0
R1:	200	200:	600
R2:	300	300:	444
R3:	400	400:	177600

a. CLR   (R0)+
b. MOV   (R0),(R1)+
c. MOV   R2,(R3)+
d. CLR   (R3)+

9. Explain exactly what would happen if you wrote the following instruction. Assume the initial value of R0 is 100.

MOV   (R0)+,(R0)+

Does this instruction have any effect on the general-purpose registers or memory? What is the final value contained in R0?

10. For the following examples of literal addressing, show the internal representation of each instruction and the before and after values of all registers and memory locations referenced by the instruction. Assume that the initial contents of the registers and memory are the same as those in Exercise 8.
a. MOV   #1,(R0)+
b. MOV   #174,(R1)
c. MOV   #16,(R2)+
d. MOV   #1776,R3

11. What, if anything, is wrong with the following MACRO-11 instructions?
a. MOV   R0,#100
b. CLR   #50
c. MOV   #1777777,R1

12. For the following examples of autodecrement addressing, show the internal representation of each instruction and the before and after values of all registers refer-

enced by the instruction. Assume that the initial contents of the registers and memory are as follows.

Registers		Memory	
R0:	102	100:	50
R1:	202	200:	777
R2:	300	300:	2
R3:	302	400:	66
R4:	400		

    a. MOV R2,−(R1)
    b. CLR   −(R0)
    c. MOV #100,−(R3)
    d. MOV −(R3),(R2)+
    e. MOV (R4),−(R0)

13.   Describe exactly what happens when the following instructions are executed. Assume the initial contents of R0 are 100.
    a. MOV −(R0),−(R0)
    b. MOV −(R0),(R0)+

14.   In Figure 11-7 we compared accessing a byte-oriented array using high-level language subscripting notation and indexed address notation. Do the same thing for a *word-oriented* array (i.e., an array in which each element is a 16-bit quantity). How would you refer to the seventh element (A[7]) of the array using indexed addressing?

15.   How long (in words) would each of the following MACRO-11 instructions be? For each, show the internal representation.
    a. MOV R0,R1
    b. MOV (R0),R1
    c. MOV #1,R1
    d. MOV 1(R0),R1
    e. MOV 1(R0),(R1)
    f. MOV 1(R0),2(R1)
    g. MOV #1,2(R1)

16.   For the following examples of indexed addressing mode, show the internal representation of each instruction and the before and after values of all registers and memory locations referenced by the instruction. Assume that the current contents of memory and registers are as follows. (All values are octal.)

Registers		Memory	
R0:	100	100:	6
R1:	200	120:	174

R2:	300	200:	44
R3:	402	300:	502
		340:	0
		400:	332
		502:	17676

a. MOV R0,40(R2)
b. MOV (R0),40(R2)
c. MOV (R0)+,40(R2)
d. MOV #5000,100(R3)
e. CLR 20(R0)
f. MOV −(R3),20(R0)
g. MOV 20(R0),−(R3)

17. What are the largest (positive and negative) offset values possible when using indexed addressing?

18. The instruction CLR 0(R0) is equivalent to which of the following?
   a. CLR R0
   b. CLR (R0)
   c. CLR (R0)+
   d. CLR −(R0)
   e. None of the above

19. State whether each of the following symbols is syntactically legal or illegal in MACRO-11. If the symbol is illegal, explain why.
   a. BEGIN
   b. 7UP
   c. MY NAME
   d. VERYVERYLONGNAME
   e. GROSS_SALES
   f. $PROFITS
   g. MACRO 11_

20. Assume that the current value of the location counter is 200. What address values will be assigned to the symbols X1, X2, and X3?

```
        MOV  R0,R1
X1: CLR  R0
        MOV  #1,R2
X2: CLR  R3
        MOV  5(R4),6(R5)
X3: MOV  R4,R3
```

21. Assume that the registers, memory, and symbols have the following values. (All values are octal.)

Registers		Memory		Symbols
R0:	100	100:	4	
R1:	200	104:	76	L1 is associated with address 100
R2:	300	106:	100	
		200:	176	L2 is associated with address 210
		210:	42	
		300:	1	

Also assume that the location counter currently has the value 50. Show the internal representation and before and after values for the following instructions.

- a.   MOV   L2,R0
- b.   MOV   (R1),L1+4
- c.   MOV   #L1,R2
- d.   MOV   #L1+6,(R2)
- e.   MOV   #L1+L2−10,(R0)

CHAPTER 12

SOME BASIC MACRO-11 COMMANDS

12.1
Introduction

In introducing the instructions available in MACRO-11, we will be describing only those that lie within the innermost circle of Figure 10-1 because they can be executed by all models of the PDP-11 family. There are a total of ninety-five such instructions and they are listed in Appendix A. With these instructions, any program presented in this book should run on your computer, regardless of the model number or the system configuration.

Instructions in MACRO-11 fall into two classifications: *word oriented* and *byte oriented*. A word-oriented instruction requires that its operands be 16-bit word quantities. Thus, the addresses of word-oriented instructions must always evaluate to even numbers, since all word addresses begin with even values (see Figure 10-2). A byte-oriented instruction operates on an 8-bit operand. These may be either odd or even addresses.

For many (but not all) of the operations in MACRO-11, there is both a word- and a byte-oriented format so that you may choose to operate on either an 8-bit or a 16-bit quantity. The byte instructions use the same mnemonic as the word instructions but with the letter B added at the end. For example:

Mnemonic	Meaning
CLR	Clear a word to all 0s
CLRB	Clear a byte to all 0s
MOV	Move a 16-bit word
MOVB	Move an 8-bit byte

You must be careful, however, because this rule does not apply to all instructions. For example, MACRO-11 has a word-oriented ADD instruction to add 16-bit twos-complement integers, but there is no corresponding ADDB instruction for 8-bit quantities.

Every instruction in MACRO-11 has two effects on the computer, one direct and one indirect (known as a *side effect*). The direct effect is the performance of the intended function. The side effect is the setting of the four condition codes (N, Z, C, and V) according to the outcome of the execution of the instruction. To completely describe a MACRO-11 instruction, we must specify all four of the following pieces of information:

1. The mnemonic name of the operation.
2. Its internal octal representation.
3. The meaning (i.e., direct effect) of the operation.
4. The indirect effect on the four condition codes.

To describe the effect of the operation on the condition codes, we use the following symbols.

Symbol	Meaning
0	The condition code is always cleared to 0, regardless of the outcome of the instruction.
1	The condition code is always set to 1, regardless of the outcome of the instruction.
*	The condition code is set conditionally, to either a 0 or a 1, depending on the outcome of the instruction and the rules given in Figure 10-4.
—	The condition code is not affected or changed by the instruction. It is left with the same value it had at the beginning of the instruction.

In introducing some of the more common MACRO-11 instructions, we have chosen to group them by function, so that all similar operations can be discussed as a unit, regardless of other minor distinctions (e.g., word instructions vs. byte instructions). The groups discussed in this chapter are the data transfer and arithmetic instructions.

12.2
Data Transfer Operations

The *data transfer instructions* move data either into a register or between registers. There are eight operation codes in this class: MOV, CLR, COM, and NEG, and their byte-oriented counterparts MOVB, CLRB, COMB, and NEGB.

12.2.1 Move, Move Byte

Mnemonic	Internal	Effect	N	Z	V	C
MOV s,d	01ssdd	CON(source addr.) → CON(dest. addr.)	*	*	0	—
MOVB s,d	11ssdd	CON(source addr.) → CON(dest. addr.)	*	*	0	—

The MOV instruction moves a 16-bit quantity from a source address (s in the above chart) to a destination address (d in the above chart). The original contents of the source address are left unchanged. The original contents of the destination address are lost and replaced by the new value. The N condition code is set to 1 if the contents of the source address are negative, that is, if the high-order bit has the value 1. The Z condition code is set to 1 if the original contents of the source address are 0.

The MOVB works in the same way except that it operates on an 8-bit operand. If you use MOVB to move an 8-bit quantity into a general-purpose register (which are sixteen bits long), the leftmost bit of the source address will be extended into the high-order eight bits of the destination register. This operation is called *sign extension*.

EXAMPLES

				Before	*After*
(a)	MOV	R0,R1	R0:	160000	160000
			R1:	000000	160000
			CC:		N = 1 Z = 0
					V = 0 C = unaffected
(b)	MOVB	A,B	A:	077	077
			B:	100	077
			CC:		N = 0 Z = 0
					V = 0 C = unaffected
(c)	MOVB	A,R0	A:	300	300
			R0:	000000	177700 (note the sign extension)
			CC:		N = 1 Z = 0
					V = 0 C = unaffected
(d)	MOV	(R0),R1	R0:	300	300
			R1:	444	0
			300:	0	0
			CC:		N = 0 Z = 1
					V = 0 C = unaffected

12.2.2   Clear, Clear Byte

Mnemonic	Internal	Effect	N	Z	V	C
CLR a	0050aa	0 → CON(addr)	0	1	0	0
CLRB a	1050aa	0 → CON(addr)	0	1	0	0

The clear instruction clears the contents of the effective address to 0. The clear byte operation, CLRB, works in the same way, but on an 8-bit quantity.

EXAMPLES

			Before	*After*
(a)	CLR R0	R0:	046100	000000
		CC:		N = 0 Z = 1
				V = 0 C = 0
(b)	CLRB A	A:	367	000
		CC:		N = 0 Z = 1
				V = 0 C = 0

12.2.3   Complement, Complement Byte

Mnemonic	Internal	Effect	N	Z	V	C
COM a	0051aa	¯CON(addr.) → CON(addr.)	*	*	0	1
COMB a	1051aa	¯CON(addr.) → CON(addr.)	*	*	0	1

The complement operation, COM, forms the ones complement of a value. Remember from Section 3.6 that the ones complement is formed by changing all 1 bits to 0 and all 0 bits to 1. Since the PDP-11 uses twos-complement arithmetic for storage of integer values, this operation is *not* the equivalent of an algebraic negate operation. This is a logical, bit-wise NOT operation. The N condition code bit is set to 1 if the high-order bit of the result is a 1. The Z bit is set to 1 if the result is all 0s (i.e., the value 177777 was complemented).

The complement byte operation, COMB works in the same way but on an 8-bit quantity.

EXAMPLES

			Before	*After*
(a)	COM	R0	R0: 012321	165456
			CC:	N = 1 Z = 0
				V = 0 C = 1

(b)	COM	(R0)+	R0: 100	102
			100: 100054	077723
			CC:	N = 0 Z = 0
				V = 0 C = 1

(c)	COMB	A	A: 377	000
			CC:	
				N = 0 Z = 1
				V = 0 C = 1

12.2.4 Negate, Negate Byte

Mnemonic	Internal	Effect	N	Z	V	C
NEG a	0054aa	$-$CON(addr.) $\rightarrow$ CON(addr.)	*	*	*	*
NEGB a	1054aa	$-$CON(addr.) $\rightarrow$ CON(addr.)	*	*	*	*

The negate operation, NEG, forms the twos complement of a 16-bit quantity. Recall from Section 3.3 that the twos complement is formed by changing all 0s to 1, all 1s to 0, and adding 1. Since the PDP-11 uses twos-complement integer arithmetic, this operation is numerically equivalent to forming the negative of a signed integer quantity.

The N bit is set to 1 if the result is a negative value (i.e., the high-order bit is a 1). The Z bit is set to 1 if the result is 0 (i.e., the value 00 . . . 0 was negated). The V bit is set to 1 if an attempt is made to negate the largest negative integer. Remember that in twos-complement representation, there is one more negative number than positive. If you try to form the twos complement of the octal value 100000, the largest negative value, you will get back the same result. This will cause the V bit to be set to 1. The C bit is cleared if the result is 0; otherwise, it is set. The negation of 0 will result in a carry bit and a result of 0. No other operands will produce a carry.

The negate byte operation, NEGB, works in the same way but on an 8-bit quantity.

EXAMPLES

				Before	*After*
(a)	NEG	R0	R0:	000067	177711
			CC:		N = 1 Z = 0
					V = 0 C = 1
(b)	NEG	R0	R0:	100000	100000
			CC:		N = 1 Z = 0
					V = 1 C = 1
(c)	NEG	R0	R0:	000000	000000
			CC:		N = 0 Z = 1
					V = 0 C = 0
(d)	NEGB	A	A:	304	074
			CC:		N = 0 Z = 0
					V = 0 C = 1

12.3
Arithmetic Instructions

There are eight arithmetic instructions. Four of them (ADD, SUB, MUL, DIV) work only on 16-bit quantities. The other four (INC, INCB, DEC, DECB) allow you to operate on either 8-bit or 16-bit values.

The multiply and divide operations are not standard on the smallest member of the PDP-11 family, the PDP-11/03, but are part of an option called the *extended instruction set* (EIS). Since EIS is standard on all other models and is almost invariably purchased for 11/03s, we include a description of MUL and DIV and assume that it is available on your system. However, if you have this model, check on the availability of the EIS option before using either the MUL or DIV instruction.

12.3.1   Increment, Increment Byte

Mnemonic	*Internal*	*Effect*	*N*	*Z*	*V*	*C*
INC a	0052aa	CON(addr.) + 1 → CON(addr.)	*	*	*	—
INCB a	1052aa	CON(addr.) + 1 → CON(addr.)	*	*	*	—

The increment instruction adds 1, using twos-complement arithmetic, to the contents of the effective address. The N bit is set if the result is negative, and the Z bit is set if the result is 0. The V bit is set if you try to increment the largest positive value (077777), since this will result in a negative quantity (100000). Otherwise it is cleared.

The increment operation is significantly faster than an ADD and is the preferred way to add 1 to a value. The increment byte instruction, INCB, works in exactly the same way but on an 8-bit quantity.

EXAMPLES

				Before	*After*
(a)	INC	R0	R0:	000001	000002
			CC:		N = 0 Z = 0
					V = 0 C = unaffected
(b)	INC	R0	R0:	177777	000000
			CC:		N = 0 Z = 1
					V = 0 C = unaffected
(c)	INC	50(R0)	R0:	20	R0: 20
			70:	4	70: 5
			CC:		N = 0 Z = 0
					V = 0 C = unaffected
(d)	INCB	A	A:	300	301
			CC:		N = 1 Z = 0
					V = 0 C = unaffected

12.3.2 Decrement, Decrement Byte

Mnemonic	Internal	Effect	N	Z	V	C
DEC a	0053aa	CON(addr.) − 1 → CON(addr.)	*	*	*	—
DECB a	1053aa	CON(addr.) − 1 → CON(addr.)	*	*	*	—

The decrement operation subtracts 1, in twos-complement arithmetic, from the contents of the effective address. The N bit is set if the result is negative, and the Z bit is set if the result is 0. The V bit is set if an attempt is made to decrement the largest negative value (100000), because the result will be positive (077777).

The decrement operation is significantly faster than a SUB and is the preferred way to subtract 1 from a value. The decrement byte instruction, DECB, works in exactly the same way but on an 8-bit quantity.

EXAMPLES

				Before	*After*
(a)	DEC	R0	R0:	000001	000000
			CC:		N = 0 Z = 1
					V = 0 C = unaffected
(b)	DEC	R0	R0:	177776	177775
			CC:		N = 1 Z = 0
					V = 0 C = unaffected
(c)	DEC	−(R0)	R0:	72	70
			70:	100000	077777
			CC:		N = 0 Z = 0
					V = 1 C = unaffected
(d)	DECB	A	A:	077	076
			CC:		N = 0 Z = 0
					V = 0 C = unaffected

12.3.3 Addition

Mnemonic	Internal	Effect	N	Z	V	C
ADD s,d	06ssdd	CON(source addr.) + CON(dest. addr.) → CON(dest. addr.)	*	*	*	*

The ADD instruction performs a twos-complement addition between the contents of the source address (s) and the contents of the destination address (d). The result is placed back into the destination address, destroying its previous contents. The original contents of the source address are not affected. In adding the quantity +1, it always is faster to use the INC instruction rather than the ADD.

The N bit and Z bit are set if the result is negative or 0. The V bit is set if the addition results in an overflow (i.e., if the addition of two positive numbers generates a negative result, or vice versa). The C bit is set if there is a carry bit generated beyond the high-order bit of the result.

As was mentioned in Section 3.4, an overflow is caused by an operation that results in a quantity that is too large to be represented in the number of available bits. In a high-level language like FORTRAN or Pascal, the system will check this condition for you. If it is detected, the program will typically be aborted with an error message similar to this one:

ERROR—INTEGER OVERFLOW

This "run-time support" does not exist in assembly language, and it is the programmer's responsibility to check for this condition to prevent the program from using an incorrect result. For example, on a 4-bit twos-complement machine:

$$7 + 7 = -2 \quad (0111 + 0111 = 1110)$$

Your only clue that something is wrong is that the V bit will be on after the addition operation is completed. If you do not check the V bit, you will be using an incorrect quantity (-2), which will invalidate your entire program. In the next section we discover how to check for and guard against this error.

EXAMPLES

				Before	*After*
(a)	ADD	R0,R1	R0:	001023	001023
			R1:	005106	006131
			CC:		N = 0 Z = 0
					V = 0 C = 0
(b)	ADD	R0,R1	R0:	077000	077000
			R1:	077710	176710
			CC:		N = 1 Z = 0
					V = 1 C = 0
(c)	ADD	R0,R1	R0:	077000	077000
			R1:	177000	076000
			CC:		N = 0 Z = 0
					V = 0 C = 1

12.3.4 Subtraction

Mnemonic	Internal	Effect	N	Z	V	C
SUB s,d	16ssdd	CON(dest. addr.) − CON(source addr.) → CON(dest. addr.)	*	*	*	*

The SUB instruction performs a twos-complement subtraction between the contents of the destination address (d) and the source address (s) using the destination address as the left operand. The result is placed back in the destination address, destroying its previous contents. That is, the operation performed is: d := d − s. The original contents of the source address are unchanged. In subtracting the quantity +1, it is always faster to use the DEC instruction rather than the SUB.

The N bit and the Z bit are set to 1 if the result is negative or 0; otherwise, they are cleared. The V bit is set if the subtraction results in an overflow (i.e., if the operands are of opposite signs and the sign of the result is the same as the sign of the source operand). The C bit is set if there was a "borrow" into the most significant bit of the result. For example, if A = −5 and B = +2, then B − A = 0010 − 1011. But subtracting 1011 from 0010 requires a "borrow" of a leading 1, so that we can subtract 10010 − 1011 (although the internal algorithm for subtraction does not use borrowing, as mentioned in Section 3.4). The existence of this hypothetical borrow from the high-order position is marked by setting the C bit to 1. Later on, we show how the C bit can be used to implement double-precision subtraction.

EXAMPLES

				Before	*After*	
(a)	SUB	R0,R1	R0:	000200	000200	
			R1:	000300	000100	
			CC:		N = 0	Z = 0
					V = 0	C = 0
(b)	SUB	R0,R1	R0:	000300	000300	
			R1:	000200	177700	
			CC:		N = 1	Z = 0
					V = 0	C = 1
(c)	SUB	R0,R1	R0:	100000	100000	
			R1:	000001	100001	
			CC:		N = 1	Z = 0
					V = 1	C = 1

12.3.5 Multiplication

Mnemonic	*Internal*	*Effect*	*N*	*Z*	*V*	*C*
MUL addr,reg	070raa	reg∗CON(address) → CON(reg,reg+1)	∗	∗	0	∗

The multiply operation, MUL, multiplies the contents of the specified general-purpose register by the contents of the effective address. The resulting 32-bit product is stored in two registers: the one specified in the instruction, and the next higher numbered register, if the register specified in the instruction is *even* (i.e., R0, R2, R4). If the register specified in the instruction is *odd* (i.e., R1, R3, R5), only the low-order sixteen bits of the product are stored in the named register. The high-order sixteen bits are discarded even if they contain something significant. Pictorially:

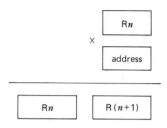

The condition codes are set on the basis of the full 32-bit result, even if only sixteen bits are stored. The N or Z bit is set if the product is negative or 0, respectively. The C bit is set if the product is too large to fit in sixteen bits. That is, C will be a 1 if there are any significant digits contained in the high-order sixteen bits of the product. The C bit can be used to determine whether any significant digits were discarded when only the low-order sixteen bits were stored.

EXAMPLES

			Before	*After*
(a)	MUL A,R0	A:	000050	000050
		R0:	000122	000000 (the high-order 16 bits)
		R1:	000000	006320 (the low-order 16 bits)
		CC:		N = 0 Z = 0
				V = 0 C = 0
(b)	MUL A,R1	A:	002422	002422
		R1:	100020	050440
		CC:		N = 1 Z = 0
				V = 0 C = 1

12.3.6 Division

Mnemonic	*Internal*	*Effect*	*N*	*Z*	*V*	*C*
DIV addr,reg	071raa	(CON(reg), CON(reg + 1)) ÷ CON(addr) Quotient → CON(reg) Remainder → CON(reg + 1)	*	*	*	*

The divide operation, DIV, divides the contents of the specified register (which *must* be even numbered) and the next sequentially numbered register. The two registers are treated as a single 32-bit integer quantity with the even-numbered register holding the high-order sixteen bits. This 32-bit quantity is then divided by the contents of the effective address. The 16-bit quotient of the division is placed in the specified register, while the 16-bit remainder goes into the next higher numbered register. Pictorially:

Quotient → Rn
Remainder → R(n + 1)

The N or Z bit is set if the quotient is negative or 0, respectively. The V bit is set if there is *divide overflow* (i.e., if the quotient is too large to be represented as a 16-bit twos-complement value). Finally, the C bit is set if the contents of the effective address are 0, and we illegally attempted a division by 0. If V or C or both are set, the contents of the specified register and the next higher numbered one are indeterminate, and the setting of the N and Z conditions codes is unspecified. These represent error conditions, and the results of the DIV should not be used.

EXAMPLES

			Before	*After*
(a)	DIV A,R0	A:	000004	000004
		R0:	000000	000005 (the quotient)
		R1:	000026	000002 (the remainder)
		CC:		N = 0 Z = 0
				V = 0 C = 0
(b)	DIV A,R0	A:	000004	000004
		R0:	177777	177740
		R1:	777600	000000
		CC:		N = 1 Z = 0
				V = 0 C = 0
(c)	DIV A,R0	A:	000000	000000 (division by zero)
		R0:	004000	? (indeterminate)
		R1:	012004	? (indeterminate)
		CC:		N = ? Z = ?
				V = 0 C = 1

12.4
The .WORD/.BYTE Pseudo-Operations

It's time to take a look at some examples of the usage of the MACRO-11 instructions thus far introduced. However, we need some data to work on, and to define the data we need to become familiar with *data-generation pseudo-ops.*

As mentioned earlier, pseudo-operations, or assembler directives, are commands to the MACRO-11 assembler to do something, rather than instructions to be translated. (A listing of all pseudo-ops in MACRO-11 is provided in Appendix C.) These pseudo-ops generally fall into the following two categories.

1. Pseudo-ops that provide a *service* to the user but generate no information inside the machine. Examples include pseudo-ops for listing control or for marking the end of a program.
2. Pseudo-ops that generate *data* or reserve *space* for data structures. These generate data inside the machine and advance the location counter.

The .WORD and .BYTE pseudo-ops are of the latter type. All pseudo-operation names, except one, begin with a period to distinguish them from regular operations. The one exception is the direct-assignment pseudo-op described in Section 13.4.1.

The .WORD pseudo-op generates one or more 16-bit twos-complement signed values at the current position of the location counter. If there is a label on the .WORD directive, the symbol will be associated with the value of the location counter at the time the pseudo-operation is first encountered.

The syntax of the .WORD directive is:

label: .WORD   expr,expr,expr, . . .

The quantities in the address field may be either constants or expressions of arbitrary complexity as long as they evaluate to a quantity that can be stored in sixteen bits. If a symbol is used in the address field, the assembler will use its value (i.e., the *address* with which it is associated) when evaluating the expression. Any constant in the address field is interpreted as an octal value unless it is followed by a period, in which case it is interpreted as a decimal constant.

EXAMPLES

Assume that the location counter has the value 100 at the beginning of each example.

(a)

			Generated Internally	Address
COUNT:	.WORD	0	000000	(100)
X:	.WORD	5	000005	(102)

(b)

			Generated Internally	Address
DATA:	.WORD	1,−1,0	000001	(100)
			177777	(102)
			000000	(104)

The value of DATA will be the value of the location counter when the pseudo-op was first encountered, namely, 100.

(c)

			Generated Internally	Address
Z:	.WORD	DATA	000100	(100)
	.WORD	COUNT+X,5	000202	(102)
			000005	(104)

If the symbols DATA, COUNT, and X have the values given in Examples a and b, the pseudo-ops in Example c would generate the data shown.

(d)

		Generated Internally	Address
.WORD	20	000020	(100)
.WORD	20.	000024	(102)

Notice that the quantity 20. is interpreted as a decimal value because of the period immediately following it. Therefore, we have stored an octal 24, because 24 (octal) = 20 (decimal).

The .BYTE directive works in exactly the same way as does the .WORD directive, but it generates an 8-bit unit of data rather than a 16-bit unit. The address fields must evaluate to a quantity that can be represented in eight bits.

EXAMPLES

Assume that the location counter has the value 100 at the beginning of each example.

(a)

			Generated Internally	Address
A:	.BYTE	100.	144	(100)

Remember: A period after a number indicates a decimal value.

(b)

			Generated Internally	Address
B:	.BYTE	5, 10, 15, − 1	005	(100)
			010	(101)
			015	(102)
			377	(103)

The value of the symbol B is 100.

(c)

			Generated Internally	Address
C:	.BYTE	B + 3,0	103	(100)
			000	(101)

(d)

D:	.BYTE	500.	000	(100)

This will generate a syntax error because the decimal value 500 cannot fit into an 8-bit byte. The assembler will place a 0 into memory when this condition occurs.

There is one very important point to remember when using *any* data-generation pseudo-op such as .WORD or .BYTE. The value generated internally represents a piece of data, not an instruction, and it must not appear in a section of your program where it could accidentally be executed, as if it were an instruction. If you fail to heed this warning, you will begin to execute your data with unpredictable and potentially disastrous results, as demonstrated in Exercise 16.

There is no required way to structure a MACRO-11 program, but one possibility is to place all data-generation pseudo-ops at the front of the program followed by the executable code, as shown in Figure 12-1.

This is similar to the structure of a Pascal program in which the declaration section is first, followed by the executable statements. This organization, or something similar, should reduce the likelihood of confusing instructions with data.

If you incorrectly place data in among instructions, unpredictable results will occur and you will create an error that may be very difficult to locate and correct.

FIGURE 12-1   Suggested Structure for a MACRO-11 Program.

Data-generation pseudo-ops

First statement →
to be executed

Program

For example:

MACRO-11		*Internal Code*
MOV	R0,R1	010001
.WORD	5200	005200

After executing the MOV instruction, the processor will attempt to execute the "next instruction," the octal constant 5200. Unfortunately, executing data will not be treated as an error, because, as we mentioned in Chapter 9, on a Von Neumann machine, data and instructions are indistinguishable. As it turns out, the octal pattern 5200 corresponds exactly to the internal representation of the command:

INC   R0

So the contents of R0 will be accidentally incremented, and you will not know that you have a serious error in your program until much later when you see an improper value in R0. To avoid such errors, make sure that you place data where they cannot be executed. We discuss this point again in the next chapter when we present some complete MACRO-11 programs.

12.5
Examples of MACRO-11 Code

Assume that we have made the following declarations at the beginning of our MACRO-11 program.

A:	.WORD	0
B:	.WORD	0

```
          C:      .WORD   0
          K:      .WORD   0
      THREE:      .WORD   3
       DISC:      .WORD   0
```

(a)   A := B + C

```
        MOV  C,TEMP    ; Load the right operand C into TEMP
        ADD  B,TEMP    ; TEMP now contains B + C
        MOV  TEMP,A    ; Put the result into A
```
   or

```
        MOV  C,R1      ; Load the right operand C into R1
        ADD  B,R1      ; R1 now contains B + C
        MOV  R1,A      ; Put the result into A
```

(b)   C := C − 3

```
        MOV  #3,R0     ; R0 contains the constant 3
        SUB  R0,C      ; Subtract 3 from C, and put the
                       ; result back into C
```
   or

```
        MOV  THREE,R0  ; THREE is a location containing a 3
        SUB  R0,C      ; Subtract 3 from C, and put the
                       ; result back into C
```
   or

```
        MOV  C,R0      ; Put C into R0
        DEC  R0        ; Do three decrements instead of a
                       ; subtract
        DEC  R0
        DEC  R0
        MOV  R0,C      ; Put the result into C
```

(c)   discriminant := $b^2 - 4ac$ (using only 16-bit multiplication)

```
        MOV  B,R1      ; R1 contains B
        MUL  B,R1      ; R1 contains B² to 16-bit accuracy
        MOV  #4,R3     ; Put constant 4 into R3
        MUL  A,R3
        MUL  C,R3      ; R3 now contains 4AC to 16-bit
                       ; accuracy
        SUB  R3,R1     ; R1 now contains B² − 4AC
        MOV  R1,DISC   ; Put the result into DISC
```

(d) $k := -\left(\dfrac{a}{b} + \dfrac{b}{c} + 1\right)$ (assume integer division)

```
EXD:  CLR   R0    ; Necessary for the divide operation
      MOV   A,R1  ; Put A in the lower part of the
                  ; numerator
      DIV   B,R0  ; The quotient A/B is now in R0
      CLR   R2
      MOV   B,R3
      DIV   C,R2  ; The quotient B/C is now in R2
      ADD   R0,R2 ; R2 now contains (A/B) + (B/C)
      INC   R2    : Add one to R2
      NEG   R2    ; R2 now contains the desired value
      MOV   R2,K  ; Put the result into K
```

(e) This time, assume that A, B, and C are byte quantities defined as:

```
A:   .BYTE 0
B:   .BYTE 0
C:   .BYTE 0
```

Evaluate:

$$A := -(B + 2)$$

```
INCB   B
INCB   B    ; 2 has now been added to B
NEGB   B    ; This forms the negative of B + 2
MOVB   B,A  ; This puts the 8-bit result into A
```

Exercise 17 contains some additional examples to give you practice with the MACRO-11 data transfer and arithmetic operations.

In the next chapter, we add the MACRO-11 control statements (conditional, branching, and looping) to our repertoire, so that we may write interesting and complete MACRO-11 programs, rather than just fragments.

Exercises for Chapter 12

1. For each of the following data transfer instructions, show:

   • The internal representation

   • The before and after values of any register or memory location referenced by the instruction

- The value of the four condition codes following completion of the instruction

Assume the following initial values:

Registers		Memory		Symbols
R0:	000100	100:	000122	X is location 120
R1:	000200	120:	000050	
R2:	000300	200:	177776	
R3:	000000	240:	000002	
		300:	001442	

a. MOV   R0,R1
b. MOV   (R0),R1
c. MOVB R0,R1
d. CLR   R2
e. CLR   (R2)+
f. CLRB 121
g. COM   R2
h. COM   40(R1)
i. COMB (R1)
j. NEG   R3
k. NEG   X
l. NEGB 40(R1)

2.   Explain exactly how the NEG and COM operations differ by showing exactly what happens when you execute each of the following instructions.

NEG   X

and

COM   X

where X contains the octal value 000001.

3.   What, if anything, is the difference between writing:

MOV   #0,X

and

CLR   X

4.   Describe what will be in the 16-bit general-purpose register R0 if the 8-bit value contained in X is 234 and we execute the following instruction.

MOVB   X,R0

5. For each of the following arithmetic instructions, show:

- The internal representation
- The before and after values of any register or memory location referenced by the instruction
- The value of the four condition codes following completion of the instruction

Assume the following initial octal values:

Registers		Memory		Symbols
R0:	000100	100:	000122	X is location 120
R1:	000200	120:	000050	
R2:	000300	200:	177776	
R3:	000000	240:	000002	
		300:	001442	

a. ADD   R0,R1
b. ADD   (R0),R1
c. ADD   (R0),(R1)
d. SUB   R0,R1
e. SUB   R1,R0
f. SUB   R0,(R1)
g. MUL   X,R1
h. MUL   (R1),R2

i. MUL   40(R1),R1
   For the next three instructions, assume
   R4 = 000000 and R5 = 000201.
j. DIV   #4,R4
k. DIV   R1,R4
l. DIV   X,R4

6. What is the problem with the following instruction?

MUL   A,R6

7. What is the problem with the following instruction?

DIV   A,R3

8. If the contents of memory cells A and B are as follows:

A: 077777
B: 000001

which of the following operations will cause an *overflow?*

a. ADD   A,B
b. ADD   B,A
c. SUB   A,B
d. SUB   B,A

9. Using the values for A and B from Exercise 8, which of the following operations would cause the C bit to be set to 1?

    a.   ADD   A,B
    b.   ADD   B,A
    c.   SUB   A,B
    d.   SUB   B,A

10. If the C bit was 0 after the following operation, what would that indicate?

MUL X,R1

11. If the contents of R1 were 0 after the following operation, what would that indicate?

DIV X,R0

12. Using the DIV instruction from Exercise 11, what would be indicated if the V bit was on following completion of the operation? What will be in R0?

13. Assuming that the initial value of the location counter is 0, show what would be generated by the following pseudo-operations.

```
X:    .WORD   0, 5, 0, 177020
      .WORD   300.
Y:    .BYTE   10, 18.
      .WORD   − 1
```

What are the values of symbols X and Y?

14. In Exercise 13, how could you reference the second integer constant (5)? Show two ways to reference the integer constant −1.

15. What is wrong with each of the following pseudo-operations?

    a.   .BYTE   400
    b.   .WORD 777777
    c.   .WORD 1
         .BYTE   0
         .WORD 20
    d.   .BYTE
    e.   .WORD   R0

16. What would happen if you incorrectly wrote the following intermixed sequence of operations and pseudo-operations?

```
MOV     #100,R0    :Put 100 into R0
.WORD   5300       :The octal constant 5300
ADD     #1,R0      :Add 1 to R0
```

How could this be corrected?

17. Show the MACRO-11 fragments that correctly translate the following expressions. Assume that the symbols A, B, C, and so on, have been properly defined using .WORD pseudo-operations. In the arithmetic expressions, all constants are *decimal* values.)

    a. A := (B * C) − (D * E) Use 16-bit multiplication

    b. A := B + C + 19

    c. A := (B + 1)/(C − 1)   Use integer division

    d. A := −1/(B + C + D)

    e. A := [(B * C)/(D − E + 2)] / (B − 1)

    f. A := −(B + C + D + 100)

    g. A := (B^2 * C^4) + D

CHAPTER 13

COMPARE AND BRANCH INSTRUCTIONS

13.1
Introduction

Control structures are the statements in a language that alter the normal sequential flow of control. We need them in order to write complete programs. In higher level languages like Pascal, these control structures take the form of conditionals (**if/then/else** or **case**) and loops (**repeat, while, for**). However, in assembly language, such higher level constructs do not exist directly; they must be synthesized from more primitive elements. These powerful user-oriented control structures are yet another aspect of the user-friendly virtual environment created by high-level languages.

The two primitive instruction types in MACRO-11 that are used to create the necessary control structures are the *compare* and *branch* instructions. In assembly language, alteration of the flow of control is handled in two stages.

1. Set the condition codes (N, Z, V, and C), by means of a compare instruction, to reflect the relationship between two quantities.

2. Branch to a location (address) in the program, by means of a branch instruction, based on the current value of one or more of the condition codes.

In the next two sections we describe these two types of instruction and give numerous examples of their usage in constructing the standard control structures of programming.

13.2
The Compare Instructions

There are four compare instructions in MACRO-11: The one-address TST and TSTB, and the two-address CMP and CMPB.

13.2.1 Test, Test Byte

Mnemonic	Internal	Effect	N	Z	V	C
TST addr	0057aa	Setting of the N and Z condition codes	*	*	0	0
TSTB addr	1057aa	Setting of the N and Z condition codes	*	*	0	0

The TST instruction examines the contents of the effective address, which must be a 16-bit word, and sets the N or Z bit according to whether the contents of the effective address are negative or zero, respectively. The V and C bits are cleared. There is no other effect, and neither the contents of the effective address nor the registers are changed. The TSTB instruction works in the same way but on an 8-bit quantity.

The test instructions only set the condition codes; they do not cause any branching. They will typically be followed immediately by a branch instruction, of the type described in the next section, which will cause the actual branch.

EXAMPLES

Assume:

$$R0 = 000001$$
$$R1 = 177770$$
$$CON(location\ 1) = 000$$

(a)   TST R0 Condition codes: N = 0 Z = 0
The value in register R0 is a +1, so the N and Z bits are cleared.

(b)   TSTB (R0) Condition codes: N = 0 Z = 1
The contents of R0 are the effective address, so this instruction will test the 8-bit quantity in location 1, which is 0. The Z bit is set, and the N bit is cleared.

(c)   TST R1 Condition codes: N = 1 Z = 0
The N bit is set because the high-order bit of register R1 is a 1, indicating that the value is negative. (In twos-complement representation, this value is a −8.)

13.2.2 Compare, Compare Byte

Mnemonic	Internal	Effect	N	Z	V	C
CMP s,d	02ssdd	CON(source) − CON(dest) and set condition codes	*	*	*	*
CMPB s,d	12ssdd	CON(source) − CON(dest) and set condition codes	*	*	*	*

The compare instruction, CMP, performs an arithmetic subtraction between the contents of the 16-bit effective source address and the contents of the 16-bit effective destination address. (Note: The order of operands in a compare is the *reverse* of their order in a subtraction. In a compare, the source address is the left operand; in a subtract, it is the right operand. Be sure to write the two addresses in the proper sequence.) The result of the subtraction is not saved in a register, but is used only to set the four condition codes.

The N or Z bit is set to 1 if the result of the subtraction is negative or zero, respectively. The V bit is set if an arithmetic overflow occurs during the subtract operation. The C bit is set if there is a borrow into the most significant bit. (See the discussion of the SUB instruction in Section 12.3.4. for an explanation of the setting of the C bit.) The CMPB instruction works in exactly the same way but on 8-bit quantities.

The compare instructions only set the condition codes; they do not themselves cause any branching to take place. They will typically be followed by a branch instruction, of the type described in the upcoming section, which will cause the actual branch.

EXAMPLES

Assume:

$$R0 = 000000$$
$$R1 = 000100$$
$$R2 = 177000$$
$$R3 = 077777$$
$$CON(word\ 100) = 177001$$
$$CON(byte\ 0) = 123$$

		N	Z	V	C
(a)	CMP R1,R0	0	0	0	0

This instruction will subtract the contents of register R0 from the contents of register R1. That is, it will form the difference R1 − R0. Since the quantity 100 − 0 is positive and causes neither a carry nor an overflow, all four condition codes are cleared.

		N	Z	V	C
(b)	CMP R0,R1	1	0	0	1

Since the quantity 0 − 100 is negative and also causes a borrow into the most significant bit, the N and C bits are set to 1.

		N	Z	V	C
(c)	CMP #100,R1	0	1	0	0

The quantity 100 − 100 is zero, so the Z bit is set.

		N	Z	V	C
(d)	CMP (R1),R0	1	0	0	0

The quantity 177001 − 0 is negative, since the high-order bit of the result is a 1. In addition, there is no borrow or overflow, so only the N bit is set.

(e) CMP R3,R2

N	Z	V	C
1	0	1	1

Both a carry and an arithmetic overflow are caused by the subtraction 077777 − 177000. The final result, 100777, is negative. Therefore, the N, V, and C bits are set to 1.

(f) CMPB #0,(R0)

N	Z	V	C
1	0	0	1

The quantity 0−123 is negative. This instruction is identical to the instruction TSTB (R0) except for the side effect of setting the V and C bits.

13.2.3 Direct Setting and Clearing of the Condition Codes

MACRO-11 contains 10 special "zero address" instructions for unconditionally clearing or setting the four condition codes. When setting or clearing any one specific bit, the other three are unaffected and do not change. None of the following 10 operation codes requires an address field. In fact, using an address field will produce a syntax error.

Mnemonic	Internal	Operation
CLN	000250	Clear the N bit to 0
CLZ	000244	Clear the Z bit to 0
CLV	000242	Clear the V bit to 0
CLC	000241	Clear the C bit to 0
CCC	000257	Clear all 4 condition codes to 0
SEN	000270	Set the N bit to 1
SEZ	000264	Set the Z bit to 1
SEV	000262	Set the V bit to 1
SEC	000261	Set the C bit to 1
SCC	000277	Set all 4 condition codes to 1

EXAMPLES

		Before	After
(a)	CLZ	N = 1, Z = 1	N = 1, Z = 0
		V = 1, C = 0	V = 1, C = 0
(b)	SCC	N = 1, Z = 0	N = 1, Z = 1
		V = 0, C = 0	V = 1, C = 1

13.3
The Branch Instructions

The branch instructions (whose mnemonics are always of the form B*xx*, except for the JMP) cause a branch to a specified location in the program based on the current

FIGURE 13-1   Internal Layout of All MACRO-11
Branch Instructions.

8 bits	8 bits
Op code	Offset

setting of one or more of the condition codes. These instructions will usually come immediately after a CMP, CMPB, TST, TSTB. However, they may follow *any* instruction in MACRO-11 that sets one or more of the condition codes.

The internal representation of a branch instruction is different from the instruction formats we have studied so far. The branch instructions do *not* use a 6-bit address field of the type shown in Figure 10-6. Instead they use a relative 8-bit *offset field*. The format of all branching instructions, except the JMP, is shown in Figure 13-1.

The offset field represents the number of *words* between your current location (i.e., the value of the PC) and the point to which you wish to branch. Since this offset field is a signed twos-complement quantity, the maximum distance you may branch is limited by the 8-bit field to:

$$(-2^7) \quad -128 \text{ words} \leq \text{branching distance} \leq +127 \text{ words} \quad (2^7 - 1)$$

An attempt to branch a greater distance using a branch instruction will result in an addressing error and a message from the assembler. Branches of greater length require the use of the JMP instruction, as discussed shortly.

The only type of addressing mode allowed with branching instructions is relative

FIGURE 13-2   Example of Offset Addressing.

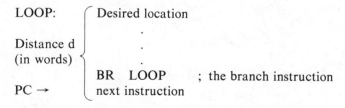

LOOP: Desired location

Distance d   .
(in words)   .
                          .
              BR   LOOP   ; the branch instruction
PC →   next instruction

Offset address in the BR instruction = d

BR	d

op code   offset

mode (i.e., a label or expression). The assembler converts this relative address into the proper word offset, so that when the quantity (2 × offset value) is added to the current value of the PC, the program will arrive at the proper location. This is depicted in Figure 13-2. It is not critical for you to be able to compute these offsets because the assembler will do that. However, it *is* necessary for you to be able to interpret them.

None of the branching instructions that follow has any effect on the four condition codes, and they remain unchanged. This allows a sequence of two or more branching instructions to follow a single compare or test instruction.

13.3.1 The Simple Branches

Mnemonic	Name	Op Code (+ offset)	Condition Causing Branch
BR addr	Unconditional Branch	000400	Always branches
BNE addr	Branch If Not Equal to Zero	001000	$Z = 0$
BEQ addr	Branch If Equal to Zero	001400	$Z = 1$
BPL addr	Branch If Plus or Zero	100000	$N = 0$
BMI addr	Branch If Minus	100400	$N = 1$
BVC addr	Branch If Overflow Clear	102000	$V = 0$
BVS addr	Branch If Overflow Set	102400	$V = 1$
BCC addr	Branch If Carry Clear	103000	$C = 0$
BCS addr	Branch If Carry Set	103400	$C = 1$

The nine simple branches allow you to test the four condition codes individually for each of their two possible settings. They are called simple branches because they test only one condition code at a time. However, some conditions can be determined only by simultaneously checking pairs of codes. We have more to say about this point in the next two sections.

EXAMPLES

(a) Branch to VERN if A is exactly equal to B.

```
            CMP   A,B
            BEQ   VERN   ; Branch if A = B
```

(b) Branch to NTKAY if the sum of A and B is nonzero.

```
            ADD   A,B      ; B ← A + B
            BNE   NTKAY   ; Branch if sum is nonzero
```

(c) Branch to RAY if A is greater than or equal to B.

```
CMP   A,B   ; (A) − (B)
BPL   RAY   ; Branch if A > = B
```

or

```
CMP   B,A   ; (B) − (A)
BMI   RAY   ; Branch if A > B
BEQ   RAY   ; Branch if A = B
```

(d) Branch if the addition of A and B causes an overflow condition.

```
ADD   A,B    ; B ← A + B
BVS   ERROR  ; Branch if overflow
```

This is an important sequence because if you do not check for overflow, you might incorrectly use the value placed in B. The system will not perform this checking for you.

(e) See if A is greater than or equal to 0. If it is, branch to label POSITIVE.

```
TST   A          ; Test A
BPL   POSITIVE ; Branch if A > 0 or A = 0
```

(f) Compute $b^2 - 4ac$. If the result is less than 0, branch to COMPLEX. If the result is exactly 0, branch to DOUBLE. If the result is positive, branch to REAL.

```
      MOV   B,R1
      MUL   B,R1      ; R1 now contains b²
  ;
      MOV   #4,R3
      MUL   A,R3
      MUL   C,R3      ; R3 now contains 4ac
  ;
      SUB   R3,R1     ; R1 now contains b² − 4ac
      TST   R1        ; Check its value
  ;
      BMI   COMPLEX   ; Branch if b² − 4ac < 0
      BEQ   DOUBLE    ; Branch if b² − 4ac = 0
      BR    REAL      ; Otherwise branch to REAL
```

13.3.2   Signed Conditional Branches

Mnemonic	Name	Op Code (+ offset)	Condition Causing Branch
BGT addr	Branch If Greater Than	003000	Will always cause a branch if it follows a compare in which the source was strictly greater than the destination. That is, $[(N = 0, V = 0)$ or $(N = 1, V = 1)]$ and $Z = 0$
BGE addr	Branch If Greater Than or Equal To	002000	Same as BGT but will also cause a branch if the Z bit is set. $(N = 0, V = 0)$ or $(N = 1, V = 1)$
BLT addr	Branch If Less Than	002400	Will always cause a branch if it follows a compare in which the source was strictly less than the destination. $(N = 0, V = 1)$ or $(N = 1, V = 0)$
BLE addr	Branch If Less Than or Equal To	003400	Same as BLT but will also cause a branch if the Z bit is set. $(N = 0, V = 1)$ or $(N = 1, V = 0)$ or $Z = 1$

The signed conditional branches are used to test the result of comparing operands that are signed twos-complement integer values. Specifically, they are designed to ensure that the branching works properly, even if an overflow occurs when the two operands in the compare instruction are subtracted from each other—something that the simple branches do not do.

Let's assume that A and B are signed twos-complement integer values, and $A > B$. When we execute the instruction:

$$\text{CMP} \quad \text{A,B} \quad ; \quad (A) - (B)$$

there are two possible results.

Case 1:   No overflow occurs during the subtraction. Then $(A) - (B)$ will be positive and $N = 0, V = 0$.

Case 2:   Overflow occurs. Then, even though $A > B$, $(A) - (B)$ will be negative and $N = 1, V = 1$. (Remember that when overflow occurs, the result has an incorrect sign bit.)

Therefore, to make sure that we can properly detect the condition $A > B$, even in the presence of overflow, we must check the two cases above: namely $(N = 0, V = 0)$ and $(N = 1, V = 1)$. This is the function of the BGT and BGE instructions.

Similarly, if A and B are signed twos-complement integers, and A < B, then when we execute:

$$\text{CMP} \quad \text{A,B} \quad ; \quad (A) - (B)$$

the following two possibilities exist.

Case 1: No overflow occurs during the subtraction. (A) − (B) will be negative, since A < B, and N = 1, V = 0.

Case 2: Overflow occurs. (A) − (B) will be positive, and N = 0, V = 1.

Therefore, to make sure that we can properly detect the condition A < B, even in the presence of overflow, we must check both of the above cases, namely (N = 1, V = 0) and (N = 0, V = 1). This is the function of the BLT and BLE instructions.

Whenever you compare signed twos-complement quantities using a CMP or CMPB instruction, you should always use the signed branches introduced in this section. Using the simple branches described in Section 13.3.1 will work correctly only if there is no overflow. Thus, looking back at some examples in the previous section, we see that if overflow is possible, the methods used might not be the best for encoding the specified tests. The following examples perform the same kinds of tests using the signed branches instead.

EXAMPLES

(a) Branch to WEISS if A is greater than or equal to B.

```
CMP   A,B    ; (A) − (B)
BGE   WEISS  ; Branch if A > = B
```

(b) Branch to OK if A is less than B, or A is exactly equal to 5.

```
CMP   A,B    ; Compare A to B
BLT   OK     ; Branch if A < B
CMP   A,#5   ; Compare A to the constant 5
BEQ   OK     ; Branch if A = 5
```

(c) Evaluate C := (A * B) + 138 and branch to NEXT if C is positive and the expression is correctly evaluated (i.e., there is no overflow, and the result fits into sixteen bits). Otherwise, branch to ERROR.

```
        MOV   A,R1        ; (A) → R1
        MUL   B,R1        ; A * B → R1
        BCS   ERROR       ; A * B too big for 16 bits
        ADD   #138.,R1    ; (A * B) + 138 → R1
        BVS   ERROR       ; The ADD caused an overflow
        MOV   R1,C        ; Save result in C
        TST   R1          ; Test if the result is positive
        BGT   NEXT
```

(d)   Translate the following Pascal statement into MACRO-11.

$$\textbf{if } (a = 0) \textbf{ and } (b > 11) \textbf{ then}$$
$$c := 1$$
$$\textbf{else}$$
$$c := -(d/e);$$

```
        TST   A           ; Test the value of A
        BNE   ELSE        ; a is nonzero, so jump to else clause
        CMP   B,#11.      ; Now check if b > 11
        BLE   ELSE        ; It is not, so jump to else clause
;
THEN:   MOV   #1,C        ; Set c to 1
        BR    DONE
;
ELSE:   CLR   R0
        MOV   D,R1
        DIV   E,R0        ; R0 contains the quotient (d/e)
        NEG   R0          ; R0 now contains -(d/e)
        MOV   R0,C        ; Store R0 in C
DONE:
```

13.3.3   Unsigned Conditional Branches

Mnemonic	Name	Op Code	Condition
BHI addr	Branch If Higher	101000	Causes a branch if it follows a compare in which the source is higher than the destination when both are treated as unsigned binary quantities. (C = 0, Z = 0)
BHIS addr	Branch If Higher or the Same	103000	Same as BHI, but will also cause a branch if the source and destination are exactly the same. (C = 0)

Mnemonic	Name	Op Code	Condition
BLO addr	Branch If Lower	103400	Causes a branch if it follows a compare in which the source address is less than the destination address when both are treated as unsigned binary quantities. (C = 1)
BLOS addr	Branch If Lower or the Same	101400	Same as BLO but will also cause a branch if the source and the destination are identical. (C = 1 or Z = 1)

The unsigned conditional branches allow you to branch based on a comparison of unsigned binary quantities in the range 000000 to 177777 (sixteen bits) or 000 to 377 (eight bits). These branches follow the same test and compare instructions we have been using all along. (Exercise 12 at the end of the chapter asks you to show why these instructions check the particular combination of condition codes that they do.) These unsigned branches should always be used after memory addresses or other unsigned quantities have been compared. The branches will treat the two operands being compared as unsigned quantities of the type described in Chapter 2.

EXAMPLES

Assume:

$$R0 = 000000$$
$$R1 = 077777$$
$$R2 = 100000$$
$$R3 = 177777$$

(a)   CMP R1,R0   CMP R2,R1   CMP R3,R2
       BHI   OK   BHI   OK   BHI   OK

All three sequences will cause a branch to the instruction labeled OK. In an unsigned compare, R3 > R2 > R1 > R0.

Notice what would happen if we improperly used a signed branch:

          CMP R2,R1
          BGT   OK

This sequence will *not* cause a branch to OK. In twos complement, the value in register R2 (100000) is a very large negative number (in fact, it is the largest negative integer in terms of absolute value). The value in R1 is a large positive value (again, the largest). Therefore, the test R2 > R1 is *false* in twos complement, and we will not branch to OK.

(b)   See if the address A is beyond or before the address B.

```
            CMP   A,B
            BHI   BEYOND   ; A > B
            BLO   BEFORE   ; A < B
    SAME:                  ; A = B
```

(c)   Translate the following Pascal program fragment. Assume that all quantities are unsigned binary.

```
        sum := 0;
        i := 0;
        while sum < 20000 do
            begin
            sum := sum + i;
            i := i + 1
            end;
```

```
        CLR     SUM             ; Set SUM to 0
        CLR     I               ; Set I to 0
;
LOOP:   CMP     SUM,#20000.     ; Test if SUM > = 20000
        BHIS    DONE            ; We are done
        ADD     I,SUM           ; SUM := SUM + I
        INC     I               ; I := I + 1
        BR      LOOP            ; Let's do it again
DONE:
```

13.3.4   The Jump Instruction

Mnemonic	Meaning	Op Code	Condition
JMP addr	Unconditional Branch	0001aa	Will always branch

The jump instruction is an unconditional branch much like the BR instruction described in Section 13.3.1. It differs from the BR command in that it uses the normal 6-bit addressing technique shown in Figure 10-6, and therefore can use any of the eight addressing modes available in MACRO-11 except mode 0.

JMP allows you to branch anywhere in memory without the $+127$ or -128 word limitation placed on all other branching instructions. You may use any addressing mode with a JMP except mode 0. It is illegal to try to branch to a register rather than to a memory address. Writing an instruction like

JMP   R0   ;   This is ILLEGAL

will result in an error message from the assembler. Because instructions always begin on a word boundary (i.e., an even address), the effective address of a JMP command is always an even number. Failure to guarantee this will result in a run-time error.

EXAMPLES

Assume:

R0 = 100
R1 = 200

(a)	JMP	(R0)	Will cause a branch to address 100.
(b)	JMP	(R1)+	Will cause a branch to address 200, and R1 will be incremented to 202.
(c)	JMP	MOLNAR	Will cause a branch to the instruction labeled MOLNAR.
(d)	JMP	R0	This is ILLEGAL.
(e)	JMP	4(R0)	Will cause a branch to location 104.
(f)	JMP	1(R0)	This will result in an error because the effective address is 101 (1 + 100), an odd number. The program will terminate with an "odd address" error message if you attempt to execute this instruction.

13.3.5   The Halt Instruction

Mnemonic	Internal Representation	Effect
HALT	000000	Halts execution of your program

The halt instruction terminates execution of your program and halts the processor. In this sense, it is similar to the STOP statement in FORTRAN, or the "end." line in a Pascal program. The condition codes are unaffected by the halt instruction.

On multiuser systems, you do not want to halt the processor (in fact, you may not be allowed to) because there might be other users on the system. It is better to terminate your program using the special system service called .EXIT, which will stop execution of only your program, while the processor continues working on other jobs. To terminate your program in this way, use the following pair of commands.

```
.MCALL   .EXIT    ;   Put this line anywhere before the .EXIT
    .                    command (usually at the very beginning)
    .
    .
    .
.EXIT                ;   Use this command to stop your program
```

These two statements are examples of special routines called *system macros*. They will be explained in detail in Chapter 17. For now, simply use this statement pair exactly as shown above.

13.4
Some Additional Pseudo-Operations

We are now ready to write some complete and interesting MACRO-11 programs. We only need to add a few more pseudo-operations (like the .WORD and .BYTE pseudo-ops) to complete the basic set of MACRO-11 directives.

13.4.1   Direct Assignment
The direct-assignment pseudo-operation allows you to directly assign a value to a symbol. (And it is the only pseudo-op in MACRO-11 that does not begin with a period.) Previously, the only way to assign a value to a symbol was to use the symbol in the label field of an instruction. The syntax of the direct-assignment pseudo-op is:

$$symbol = expression$$

The expression on the right-hand side is evaluated and its value becomes the value of the symbol on the left-hand side.

EXAMPLES

(a)   SPECIAL = 100
      The value of SPECIAL is 100, and any further reference to the symbol SPECIAL will use that value. For example:

```
MOV  SPECIAL,R0  ;  Will move the contents of cell 100
                 ;  into R0
```

```
MOV   #SPECIAL,R0   ;   Will move the contents of cell 100
                    ;   into R0
```

The effect of the statement SPECIAL = 100 is exactly the same as if the name SPECIAL had appeared in the label field of an instruction when the location counter had the value 100.

(b)   ENDLOOP = SPECIAL + 20

The value of ENDLOOP will be 120 (if SPECIAL is defined as in Example a).

The direct-assignment pseudo-op can be used to give symbolic names to constants, enhancing the readability of the resulting program. For example, instead of writing:

```
MUL   #4,R0
```

we could write:

```
PAYPERIODS = 4
        .
        .
        .
MUL   #PAYPERIODS,R0
```

In this sense, the direct assignment is being used in exactly the same way that a **const** declaration is used in Pascal: namely, to increase the use of mnemonic names within the program.

It is very important to understand the difference between the direct assignment and the .WORD directives introduced in Chapter 12. For example, consider the following pair of directives:

```
A = 10
```

and

```
A:  .WORD   10
```

In the first statement, the *value* of the symbol A is 10. In the second, the value of A is whatever the value of the location counter is when this pseudo-op is encountered. The *contents* of that location is the octal constant 10. Failure to recognize this difference can result in errors caused by confusing addresses and their contents. For example, the instruction:

```
MOV   A,R0
```

will move the contents of memory cell 10 into R0 if A was defined by saying A = 10. The octal constant 10 will be moved into R0 if, instead, we defined A as:

$$A: \quad .WORD \quad 10$$

Always be careful to distinguish between an address and its contents.

There is one other highly useful form of the direct assignment. Whenever the character "." appears as a distinct symbol in a MACRO-11 instruction, it means "the current value of the location counter." By combining the symbol "." with the direct-assignment pseudo-op, you can control and manipulate the location counter, thus affecting where your program is placed in memory.

EXAMPLES

(a) . = 100

Set the location counter to the octal value 100. The next instruction will be assembled into location 100.

(b) . = . + 100

Increase the location counter value by one hundred (octal) bytes. The next one hundred locations will be skipped, and the next instruction will be assembled one hundred bytes beyond the previous one. Nothing can be assumed about what has been placed in these locations.

(c) A = .

The symbol A will be given the value of the current value of the location counter.

13.4.2 The .BLKB and .BLKW Directives

The two "block reservation" directives allocate a block of memory, in units of bytes or words, by advancing the location counter a specified amount. This causes a block of memory to be skipped over, and that block can then be used for any purpose. The syntax for these two block reservation commands is

```
label:  .BLKB   expression  ; Reserve a block of bytes
label:  .BLKW   expression  ; Reserve a block of words
```

In both of these commands, if there is a label in the label field, it is given the value of the location counter *before* it is updated. The expression in the address field is evaluated and, if the operation is a .BLKB, the location counter is advanced by the value of the expression. If the command is a .BLKW, the location counter is advanced by *twice* the value of the expression, to reserve that number of words. In a sense, the .BLKx commands are similar to the high-level language declarations that reserve contiguous memory locations for array storage, such as:

DIMENSION A(100)
var A : **array**(1..100) **of** integer:

However, unlike those declarations, the label on a .BLKB or .BLKW directive is associated not with the entire block of memory (i.e., it is not the "name of the array"), but only with the address of the first element.

A: .BLKB 5

will produce:

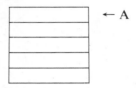

We have reserved five bytes of memory. The address of the first byte is known by the symbol A. The remaining memory locations must be referenced by offsets relative to location A as shown in Figure 11-7.

EXAMPLES

Assume that the location counter is initially 200 in all examples.

(a) A: .BLKB 10
A will be given the value 200, and the location counter will be reset to 210. Locations 200-207 will be skipped over. The effect is identical to writing:

A = .
. = . + 10

This statement can be thought of as creating a 10-byte array.

(b) B: .BLKW 10
B will be given the value 200, and the location counter will be reset to 220. The eight words in locations 200–217 will be skipped over.

(c)

	MACRO-11	Location	Contents
	JMP (R0)	200	000110
C:	.BLKW 20		
START:	CLR R1	242	005001

(d)   Clear the array A created in Example a above to all zeros.

```
        MOV   #A,R0   ; Put address A in register R0
        MOV   #10,R1  ; Put length of array in R1
NEXT:   CLRB  (R0)+   ; Clear next element
        DEC   R1      ; Count one more element done
        BNE   NEXT    ; See if we are done yet
```

13.4.3   The .TITLE and .END Directives

In most languages, there are special statements used to mark the beginning and end of a complete program. For example, in Pascal:

program name (input, output);
.
.
.
end.

In MACRO-11, the (optional) directive .TITLE is used to introduce a program, and the required directive .END is used to end it. The syntax of these two directives is as follows:

```
.TITLE   string of one to thirty-two characters
.END     address
```

The .TITLE directive, if used, assigns the 1- to 32-character name in the address field to the resulting object program. It is also printed on the top of each page of the listing. There can be only one .TITLE directive per program, and it may appear anywhere in the program. However, we will adopt the convention that, if we choose to use it, we will always make it the first line of the program.

The .END directive is required in every MACRO-11 program and it must be the last line in the program. The .END directive tells the assembler where to stop the assembly process. Nothing that appears after the .END directive will be assembled into PDP-11 machine language.

The .END directive in the main unit of the program also specifies the address at which to begin execution of the program. The value appearing in the address field will be loaded into the PC when the program is about to be executed. Thus, the first instruction fetched will be the instruction whose address was specified in the .END directive. A common error is to forget to put an address in the .END directive. Blank address fields are assembled as 000000, so the program will begin execution at location 0, regardless of whether it is supposed to. Only the .END directive of the *main*

FIGURE 13-3   General Structure of a MACRO-11
Program.

```
         .TITLE    name
         .MCALL    .EXIT
            .              ; Here will be the .WORD,
            .              ; .BYTE, .BLKW, .BLKB
            .              ; Pseudo-operations
START:                     ; First instruction to be executed
            .              ; The rest of the MACRO-11 program

            .
            .
         .EXIT             ; Where we will stop execution
         .END      START   ; The end of the main program
```

program should contain this starting address. The .END directive at the end of
MACRO-11 subroutines (discussed in Chapter 16) does not contain address values
in the address field.

Figure 13-3 shows the general structure of most MACRO-11 programs.

13.5
Example MACRO-11 Programs

In this section we have included three complete and nontrivial MACRO-11 programs that use most of the capabilities described in the past three chapters. The
programs do not include I/O because we have not yet discussed it.

EXAMPLES

(a)   A program to add up a series of nonzero numbers in a LIST. The end of the
      list is identified by the value 0. When finished, the program should compute
      the average of the values in the list and leave the result in a memory location
      called AVERAGE. (Assume that there will not be arithmetic overflow.)

```
            .Title        Sample1
            .MCALL        .EXIT

List:       .Word    5,13,−8.,70,−100,9.,0 ; The values to be added
Count:      .Word    0     ; This will be a count of the values
Average:    .Word    0     ; The average will go here when we are
                           ; done
```

```
Start:   CLR   R0              ; Necessary for the divide operation
         CLR   R1              ; R1 will accumulate the running sum
         CLR   Count           ; Set the count to zero
         MOV   #List,R2        ; The address of the beginning of the list

Loop:    ADD   (R2)+,R1        ; Add in this value, then move pointer to
                               ; next value
         INC   Count           ; Increment count of values
         TST   (R2)            ; Check to see if this value is zero
         BNE   Loop            ; If not, go back to add in this value

         DIV   Count,R0        ; Find R0 = Sum / Count, R1 is remainder
         MOV   R0,Average      ; Move result to Average

;    Here we would output the results.
;    We will show how to do this in the next section

         .Exit
         .END  Start
```

(b) A program to move a 100-word block of memory labeled Source to another 100-word block labeled Dest. As the move is performed, the program counts how many positive numbers, negative numbers, and zeros were moved.

```
         .Title        Sample2
         .MCALL        .EXIT

PosCount:    .Word    0
NegCount:    .Word    0
ZeroCount:   .Word    0

MoveCount    =        100. ; The number of words to be moved
Source:      .BlkW    MoveCount
Dest:        .BlkW    MoveCount

Start:   CLR   R0                        ; R0 is the offset into the data
                                         ; blocks
Again:   MOV   Source(R0),Dest(R0)       ; Move this word
         TST   Dest(R0)                  ; Test its sign
         BEQ   Zero                      ; If it is zero, go to increment
                                         ; ZeroCount
         BMI   Minus                     ; If it's negative, go to increment
                                         ; NegCount
Plus:    INC   PosCount                  ; The number must be positive
         BR    Next

Zero:    INC   ZeroCount                 ; The number is zero
         BR    Next
```

```
Minus:    INC    NegCount    ; The number is negative

Next:     ADD    #2,R0       ; Point to the next number in the block
          CMP    #MoveCount·2,R0   ; See if we have moved
                             ; MoveCount ·2 bytes
                             ; MoveCount is given in words
          BGT    Again       ; Not done, move the next word
```

; Here we could output the results.
; Again, let's postpone that until the next
; section.

```
          .EXIT
          .END   Start
```

(c) Write a program to go through a block of memory, fifty bytes long, containing ASCII characters, and make the following changes.

(1) Change all lowercase characters (ASCII codes 141-172) to uppercase characters (ASCII codes 101-132).

(2) Change all nonprinting ASCII characters (codes 0-37, 177) to the printing character "?" (ASCII code 077).

(3) At the end of the text, marked by the character "!" (ASCII code 041), insert blanks (ASCII code 040) into remaining positions in the 50-byte block.

You may assume that the high-order (i.e., parity) bit bit in all of the characters is zero.

```
          .Title       Sample3
          .MCALL       .EXIT

BlockSize        =   50.      ; The length of the block of
                              ; characters

Text:     .BlkB   BlockSize   ; The block of characters
          .Even               ; To make sure the program starts on
                              ; an even address. This directive will
                              : be described in the next chapter.

Start:
                              ; Assume that here we input char·
                              ; acters to the block of memory called
                              ; Text. We will show how to do
                              ; that in the next section.


          CLR    R0           ; R0 will be offset into text
NextCH:   MOVB   Text(R0),R1  ; Move the char to R1 to examine it
          CMPB   R1,#141      ; The lowercase letter 'a'
```

```
              BLT      NotLC          ; Smaller than all the lowercase
                                      ; letters
              CMPB     R1,#172        ; The lowercase letter 'z'
              BGT      NotLC          ; Larger than all the lowercase
                                      ; letters

              SUB      #40,R1         ; Change character to uppercase
                                      ; using the ASCII code set
              BR       Next           ; now we must check for end of text

NotLC:        CMPB     R1,#37         ; Check for nonprinting characters
                                      ; less than or equal to 37
              BLOS     NoGood         ; Yes, change to a question mark
              CMPB     R1,#177        ; Is this character a DELETE?
              BNE      Next           ; No, check end of text

NoGood:       MOVB     #077,R1        ; Make the character a question
                                      ; mark (?)

Next:         MOVB     R1,Text(R0)    ; Move the character back into the
                                      ; buffer
              CMPB     #041,R1        ; Is this an exclamation mark (!)?
              BEQ      Pad            ; Yes, End of text; now fill rest
                                      ; with spaces
              INC      R0             ; Move pointer to next character
              CMP      R0,#BlockSize  ; See if we are done
              BNE      NextCH         ; No, check next character
              BR       Done           ; Yes, exit

Pad:          INC      R0             ; Move pointer to next character
              MOVB     #40,Text(R0)   ; Put a space into the text buffer
              CMP      R0,#BlockSize — 1  ; Are we done putting spaces
                                         ; into the buffer?
              BNE      Pad            ; No, put another space

;   Now we should output the final text buffer.

Done:    .EXIT
         .END    Start
```

13.6
Running MACRO-11 Programs

You have seen a number of complete MACRO-11 programs and you should be ready to write and run some on your own. To complete the MACRO-11 programming exercises at the end of the chapter, you will need two things. We provide one, and the other will have to come from your instructor or your local computer center.

The first thing you will need is an interim mechanism for performing input/output. We will not be discussing MACRO-11 input/output until Chapter 15. To allow you to write interesting programs before that, we have provided (in Appendix E) four subroutines called INCHAR, OUTCHAR, IN and OUT, whose functions are described below.

> *INCHAR:* Inputs one character from the terminal and places it in the rightmost 8 bits of register R0.
>
> *OUTCHAR:* Prints on the user's terminal the one character contained in the rightmost 8 bits of register R0.
>
> *IN:* Prints out the single character ">" on the terminal and then waits for you to enter from one to six octal digits followed by a carriage return. These characters are converted to an integer representation and placed in general-purpose register R0. The subroutine then returns and the input value is in R0.
>
> *OUT:* Takes the octal value placed in register R0, converts it to characters, and prints out those octal characters on your terminal. The subroutine then returns.

To use these subroutines, you must follow these steps.

1. Insert the subroutines from Appendix E into your program exactly as they appear. You may place them anywhere in your program.

2. Whenever you want to input a single octal value from the terminal, execute the following statement:

```
        JSR   PC,IN
```

After this statement has been executed, the number will be in register R0 and you may move it wherever you wish.

3. Whenever you want to output a single octal value (e.g., NUMBER), execute the following pair of statements:

```
        MOV   NUMBER,R0
        JSR   PC,OUT
```

After executing these instructions, NUMBER will have been printed on the terminal.

4. Whenever you wish to read in a single ASCII character, execute the following statement:

```
        JSR   PC,INCHAR
```

Following the execution of this instruction, the character will be in the rightmost 8 bits of R0.

5. Whenever you wish to print a single ASCII character, (e.g., CH), execute the following pair of statements:

```
MOVB   CH,R0
JSR    PC,OUTCHAR
```

Following the execution of this pair of instructions, the character will have been printed on the terminal.

This is a very rudimentary I/O facility, but it should serve until we have discussed the topic more fully. It will allow you to complete the programming assignments in the next few chapters. (Your instructor or computer center may choose to provide a more extensive interim I/O capability than the one shown in Appendix E.)

The second thing you will need to know is the specific job control statements for executing MACRO-11 on your computer system. To execute your MACRO-11 program, you will have to enter the source program into a file and then provide a series of commands that specify to the computer that you want to assemble, link, and execute the contents of the file as a MACRO-11 source program. The exact syntax of these commands will depend on which operating system you are using: RT-11, RSTS, RSX-11, or UNIX. It may also depend on other special considerations or limitations that are specific to your installation. You will need to find out from your instructor or local computer center the following information:

1. How to obtain an account number and password for your system and how to log on and off.

2. How to use the editor to create MACRO-11 source files.

3. The specific commands needed to execute MACRO-11 programs.

This information should allow you to complete the programming exercises at the end of this chapter.

When you have written and assembled your program, you will get a *program listing*. Figure 13-4 shows a typical listing for the first sample program in Section 13.5, with one intentional error included. The listing format may differ slightly at your installation, but it should contain basically the same information.

The listing contains several columns of information, and it is important to understand the meaning of each of these pieces of information. (1) The first column is just a sequential, decimal *line number*. It numbers the original source statements but has no effect on the assembly; it is for informational purposes only. (2) The second column contains the value of the *location counter*. It specifies the octal address where the instruction on that line will be placed in memory. All MACRO-11 machine-language instructions take one, two, or three words of memory. The address in the listing is the address of the *first* of these words used for the instruction. Pseudo-ops that change the value of the location counter (e.g., . = 100, .BLKW 100) will cause the value in this column to change accordingly. (3) The third, fourth, and fifth columns contain the internal octal *machine code*. This is the instruction as it was originally assembled and placed in memory. Depending on the type of operation and addressing modes used, there may be one, two, or three columns of machine code. Also, remember that assembly-language instructions can be modified during execu-

FIGURE 13-4   Sample MACRO-11 Listing.

```
 1                                      .TITLE Sample1
 2                                      .MCALL .EXIT
 3
 4 000000 000005 000013 177770  List:              .Word  5,13,−8.,70,−100,9.,0
   000006 000070 177700 000011
   000014 000000
 5 000016 000000                Count:             .Word  0
 6 000020 000000                Average:           .Word  0
 7
 8 000022 005000                Start:     CLR  R0
 9 000024 005001                           CLR  R1
10 000026 005067 177764                    CLR  Count
11 000032 012702 000000    :               MOV #List,R2
12
13 000036 062201                Loop:      ADD  (R2)+,R1
14
U 15 000040 005000 000000                  INC  Coumt
16 000044 005712                           TST  (R2)
17 000046 001373                           BNE  Loop
18
19 000050 071067 177742                    DIV  Count,R0
20 000054 010067 177740                    MOV R0,Average
21
22                             ; Here we would output the results
23
24 000060 000000                           HALT
25        000022                            .END Start
```

tion. Therefore, what ultimately gets executed may not be the instruction that you see in the listing. (4) The remainder of the line contains an exact copy of the original MACRO-11 *source statement,* including any and all comments. (Although the comments were not included on this example because it would be too wide to print on these pages. Your listings will include all comments.)

There may (unfortunately!) be some additional information in the listing. If the MACRO-11 source statement contains any errors, an *error code* will be printed either under the line that contains the error or in the left-hand margin. The error code letter will give you a clue about the nature of the error. For example, line 15 in Figure 13-4 contains the error code "U." This is the code for an undefined symbol. Notice that we misspelled the operand, writing it as Coumt instead of Count. Of course, the assembler could not find any definition for the symbol Coumt, and so it was marked as an error. A complete listing of MACRO-11 error codes is provided in Appendix D.

In the next chapter, we have much more to say about debugging assembly-language programs.

Exercises for Chapter 13

1. What is the difference between the following operations?

```
TST     R0
CMP     #0,R0
```

2. Is it possible to get an overflow when comparing (using CMP) operands of the same sign? Of opposite signs?

3. Is it possible in twos complement to have both the N and Z bits set to 1 by a single operation? In ones complement?

4. Given that MACRO-11 instructions can occupy two, four, or six bytes, depending on the addressing mode, what is the maximum number of MACRO-11 *instructions* thay you could branch around using any of the branch (B*xx*) instructions?

5. Assume that you want to branch to POS if X ≥ Y. What is wrong with the following sequence?

```
CMP     X,Y
BPL     POS
```

6. Assume that you want to branch to NEXT if A > B, and you write the following sequence:

```
CMP     A,B
BPL     NEXT
```

What *two* problems are associated with this sequence?

7. Assume that you want to evaluate the assignment operation:

$$C := A + B$$

and you also want to make sure that no overflow occurred during the addition. You write the sequence:

```
MOV     A,R0
ADD     B,R0
MOV     R0,C
BVS     ERROR ; Branch if there was an overflow
```

What is wrong with this sequence?

8.   Assuming that A, B, C, and D are signed twos-complement integers, write the MACRO-11 fragment that is equivalent to the following:

$$c := (a * b) - (a + b);$$
$$\text{if } c <= 15 \text{ then}$$
$$d := 1$$

You may disregard the problem of overflow, and perform the multiplication using only sixteen bits. All integer constants above are given in decimal.

9.   Write a MACRO-11 fragment which first tries to perform the following twos-complement multiplication in sixteen bits:

$$X := Y * Z$$

If the result cannot be stored in sixteen bits, the program will redo the operation using full thirty-two bit multiplication.

10.   Translate the following fragment into MACRO-11 code. Assume that a, b, and d are twos-complement integer values, and that all are given in decimal.

$$\text{if } (a + b) < 15 \text{ then}$$
$$d := 1$$
$$\textbf{else}$$
$$\text{if } (a + b) < 30 \text{ then}$$
$$d := 2$$
$$\textbf{else}$$
$$d := 3;$$

11.   Translate the following logical expressions into MACRO-11 code.

   a.   Branch to REBECCA if A equals 0 or A equals 5 or A equals 11.
   b.   Branch to DICKR if B = 100 and C is strictly greater than 5.
   c.   Branch to BENJY if it is *not* the case that both A and B are 0.

12.   Show why the unsigned branches introduced in Section 13.3.3 use the setting of the C bit to determine the relationship between unsigned quantities.

13.   If you accidentally use the unsigned branches after comparing twos-complement values, will an error always result? Under what conditions will the unsigned branches act correctly?

14.   Assume that you have defined A and B in the following way:

```
A = 2
B :  .WORD    2
```

Explain the difference in the behavior of the following sequences:

```
MOV   #A,R0      MOV   #B,R0
MOV   (R0) ,R1   MOV   (R0) ,R1
```

15.   Assume the value of the location counter is initially 0. Show its value following the completion of each of the following MACRO-11 operations or pseudo-operations.

```
          .TITLE        SAMPLE
          . = 100
          MOV           R0 ,R1
          MOV           #1,R2
          . = . + 10
LOOP:     .WORD         1,2,3
LOOP2:    .BLKB         4
```

16.   Are the following pairs of statements equivalent? If not, why?

```
          . = . + 10
          .BLKW      10
```

Exercises 17-20 contain four complete MACRO-11 programming assignments. In writing these programs, you may use the I/O routines in Appendix E. If these are inappropriate for your system, use any other I/O routines provided by your instructor or computer center.

17.   Write a complete MACRO-11 program to read in a sequence of octal values one at a time. Keep separate running sums and counts of the positive values and the negative values. Stop inputting values when you read in a zero value. Then output the following four values and stop.

   a.   The sum of all the positive numbers.
   b.   The total number of positive numbers.
   c.   The sum of all the negative numbers.
   d.   The total number of negative numbers.

18.   Read in two values, called MEM_LOW and MEM_HIGH, that represent two even-numbered memory addresses, where MEM_HIGH ≥ MEM_LOW. Then read in a sequence of 16-bit octal values and store them in memory locations MEM_LOW, MEM_LOW +2, MEM_LOW + 4, . . . , MEM_HIGH. When you have stored a value into the last memory location, print out the contents of all memory cells from MEM_LOW to MEM_HIGH inclusive.

19.   Read in two values, called MEM_LOW and MEM_HIGH, that represent two

odd or even numbered memory addresses MEM_HIGH ≥ MEM_LOW. Switch the contents of these memory cells in the following way:

$$
\begin{array}{rcl}
\text{MEM\_LOW} & \Leftrightarrow & \text{MEM\_HIGH} \\
\text{MEM\_LOW} + 1 & \Leftrightarrow & \text{MEM\_HIGH} - 1 \\
\text{MEM\_LOW} + 2 & \Leftrightarrow & \text{MEM\_HIGH} - 2
\end{array}
$$

.
.
.

When you are finished, print out the contents of all memory cells from MEM_LOW to MEM_HIGH inclusive.

20.   Read in an octal value N, $N \leq 20$. Then proceed to read in N octal values and store them in memory. Then *sort* the N values into descending order using any well known sorting algorithm. Assume the N octal values that were read in are *unsigned quantities*. This, if the input is:

```
        5     (N = 5)
  000017  ⎤
  100000  ⎥
  177770  ⎬  The five input values
  077770  ⎥
  177777  ⎦
```

The output would be:

```
  177777
  177770
  100000
  077770
  000017
```

which is the correct unsigned binary ordering of the input data. When you are done sorting, print out the sorted list.

CHAPTER 14

LOGICAL AND SHIFT COMMANDS

14.1
Introduction

The MACRO-11 instructions for performing arithmetic operations and for implementing control structures are groups of instruction types that appear (albeit in different forms) in high-level languages, and their function should be quite obvious to any programmer.

In this chapter we introduce the *bit-wise logical instructions* and the *shift instructions*. These types of instruction are quite different from any high-level language facility, and allow you to perform operations that are difficult or impossible in languages like COBOL or Pascal. (However, these facilities typically do appear in high-level Systems Implementation Languages [SILs]. Refer to Section 10.5 for a discussion of this class of language.)

14.2
Logical Instructions

Logical instructions allow you to perform the boolean operations AND and OR either on the contents of registers or on bytes or words of memory. (In MACRO-11, the boolean function NOT is performed by the COM and COMB instructions discussed in Section 12.2.3) The exclusive-OR operation, XOR, an option that is discussed in Exercise 1, is not available on all systems; therefore, it is not described here.

Logical instructions allow you to access and manipulate the individual bits of the general-purpose registers, memory bytes, and words. This is quite difficult in higher level languages. In a language like Pascal, when you write:

ch := 'x';

269

you are generally unaware of the underlying implementation of these characters and you would have no reason to manipulate the individual 8 bits of the internal representation of the character 'x'. Similarly, when you write:

$$i := 100;$$

you are also ignorant of the internal representation technique. You treat the integer variable i as a single indivisible quantity rather than as a collection of 16 or 32 distinct bits.

However, Parts I and II have presented numerous situations in which you may want to be aware of and actually manipulate the individual bits or fields of a piece of data. For example:

1. To set or check the parity bit of a character.
2. To check the sign bit of an integer.
3. To extract the exponent field of a real number.
4. To look at one bit of a processor register.

The logical operations of MACRO-11 allow you to access and manipulate the individual bits of any register or memory cell. This capability does not usually exist in higher level languages.

The execution of all logical instructions is carried out *bit by bit*. That is, bit i of the source address operates on bit i of the destination address to produce bit i of the result, for $i = 0, \ldots, 7$ if it is a byte instruction, or $i = 0, \ldots, 15$ if it is a word instruction. Thus, the logical operations always treat the operands as quantities that are simply strings of unrelated 0s and 1s. This bit-wise style of operation is shown in Figure 14-1.

FIGURE 14-1   The Bit-Wise Nature of the Logical Operations.

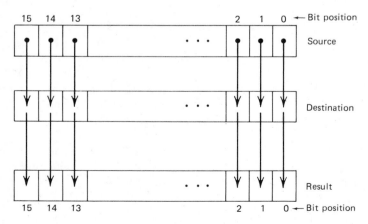

In most cases, the source address contains a special "dummy" value, set up by the programmer with 0s and 1s in just the right places so that when the bit-wise logical operation is performed, the desired effect is achieved. This special 0 and 1 "template" is called a *mask;* the next few sections give numerous examples of masks.

14.2.1   Bit Set, Bit Set Byte

Mnemonic	Name	Internal	Effect	N	Z	V	C
BIS s,d	Bit Set	05ssdd	CON(source) .OR. CON(dest)→CON(dest)	*	*	0	—
BISB s,d	Bit Set Byte	15ssdd	CON(source) .OR. CON(dest)→CON(dest)	*	*	0	—

The BIS instruction performs a bit-wise logical OR between the contents of the effective source address and the contents of the effective destination address, and places the result into the destination. The source address is unchanged. The original contents of the destination address are lost and replaced by the result of the operation.

Since anything ORed with a 1 is a 1, and anything ORed with a 0 is just itself (i.e., 0 .OR. 0 = 0, 1 .OR. 0 = 1), the result of the BIS instruction can be summarized as follows.

1. Wherever there is a 0 in the source address, the corresponding bit position of the destination address is left unchanged.

2. Wherever there is a 1 in the source address, the corresponding bit position of the destination address is set to 1, regardless of its original value.

Therefore, to use the BIS instruction, we design a source operand that contains the proper configuration of 0s and 1s, with 0s in the positions where we want to leave the value unchanged, and 1s in the positions we want set to 1. The BISB works in the same way, but on an 8-bit quantity.

EXAMPLES

(a) Set bits 5 and 12 to 1 in register R3. (Remember that bit positions are numbered right to left beginning with 0.)

The proper mask would have 1s in bit positions 5 and 12, and 0s elsewhere:

$$0001000000100000_2 = 010040_8$$

The proper instruction would be:

BIS   #010040,R3   ; Set bits 5 and 12

The N or Z bit will be set if the result of this operation results in either a negative or 0 value, respectively. The V bit is cleared, and the C bit is unaffected by this instruction.

(b)   Assume that you have a 16-bit word, called TWOCH, containing two ASCII characters. Set the parity (i.e., high-order) bit of each character to 1.

The layout of the word is:

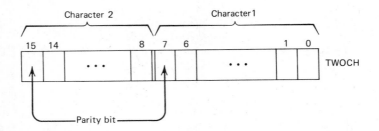

The high-order bits are in postions 7 and 15. The proper mask is:

$$1000000010000000_2 = 100200_8$$

    BIS   #100200,TWOCH   ;   Set high-order bit of both
                            ;   characters to 1

(c)   Set to 1 every bit position except the sign bit in the byte address labeled BYTE.

The correct mask would have a 0 in the sign bit (bit 7) and 1s in all other positions:

$$01111111_2 = 177_8$$

The correct instruction would be:

    BISB   #177,BYTE   ; Set every bit except the sign

14.2.2   Bit Clear, Bit Clear Byte

Mnemonic	Name	Internal	Effect	N	Z	V	C
BIC s,d	Bit Clear	04ssdd	⁻CON(source) .AND. CON(dest)→CON(dest)	*	*	0	—
BICB s,d	Bit Clear Byte	14ssdd	⁻CON(source) .AND. CON(dest)→CON(dest)	*	*	0	—

The BIC instruction performs a bit-wise logical AND between the complement of the contents of the source address and the contents of the destination address. The results are placed back into the destination. The original contents of the source address are unchanged. The original contents of the destination are lost and are replaced by the result of the BIC operation.

Complementing the source changes all 0s to 1s and all 1s to 0s. Since anything ANDed with a 0 is a 0, and anything ANDed with a 1 is just itself (i.e., 0 .AND. 1 = 0, 1 .AND. 1 = 1), the results of the BIC instruction can be summarized as follows.

1. Wherever there is a 0 in the source address, the corresponding bit position of the destination address is left unchanged.

2. Wherever there is a 1 in the source address, the corresponding bit position of the destination address is cleared to 0.

Therefore, to use the BIC instruction, we design a source address that contains the proper configuration of 0s and 1s, with 0s in the positions where we want to leave the value unchanged and 1s in the positions we want cleared to 0. The BICB works in the same way but on an 8-bit quantity.

EXAMPLES

(a) Clear bits 3, 4, 9, and 11 in the word whose address is currently located in register R1.

The proper mask has 1s in bit positions 3, 4, 9, and 11.

$$0000101000011000_2 = 005030_8$$

The correct instruction is:

BIC   #005030,(R1)   ;   Clear bits 3, 4, 9, 11

The N or Z bit will be set if the result of this operation is negative or 0, respectively. The V bit is cleared, and the C bit is unaffected by this operation.

(b) Assume a 16-bit floating-point value, FP, in the following format:

FP	s	Exponent	Mantissa
	15 14	10 9	0

Clear the mantissa field and the sign bit to 0. If the entire word is now all 0s, branch to ALLZERO. Otherwise, branch to PROCESS.

The correct mask is:

$$1000001111111111_2 = 101777_8$$

```
BIC   #101777,FP  ; Clear the mantissa and the sign
BEQ   ALLZERO     ; If word is all zeros
BR    PROCESS     ; If word is not all zeros
```

(c)   Clear bit position 3 of the byte whose address is contained in register R5.

The proper mask has a 1 in bit position 3, and 0s elsewhere.

$$00001000_2 = 010_8$$

The correct instruction is:

```
BICB  #010,(R5)  ; Clear bit position 3
```

14.2.3   Bit Test, Bit Test Byte

Mnemonic	Name	Internal	Effect	N	Z	V	C
BIT s,d	Bit Test	03ssdd	CON(source) .AND. CON(dest)	*	*	0	—
BITB s,d	Bit Test Byte	13ssdd	CON(source) .AND. CON(dest)	*	*	0	—

The BIT instruction performs a bit-wise logical AND operation between the contents of the source address and the contents of the destination address. Unlike the BIS or the BIC, however, the result of the BIT operation is not saved anywhere. This operation is used only for its effect on the N and Z condition codes. In this sense it is very much like the CMP and TST operations described in Section 13.2 and, like them, it typically is followed by a branch instruction that branches according to the setting of the condition codes.

Since the only way to obtain a 1 when using an AND operation is by having a 1 in *both* the source and the destination, the BIT operation is used to test whether any bits set in the source are also set in the destination. If any are set, there will be at least one 1 bit in the result, and the Z bit will be 0. If none are set, the result will be all 0s, and the Z bit will be 1. The BITB works in the same way on an 8-bit quantity.

EXAMPLES

(a) Test if either bit 13 or bit 14 of the word whose address is in R4 is set to a 1. If either one is set, branch to SET. If both bits are clear, branch to NOTSET.

The correct mask is:

$$0110000000000000_2 = 060000_8$$

```
BIT   #060000,(R4)   ; Test bits 13, 14
BNE   SET            ; If Z = 0, at least one of the
                     ; two bits was set
BEQ   NOTSET         ; If Z = 1, both were zeros
```

(b) Test whether *both* bits 13 and 14 are set in the word whose address is in R4.

We cannot use a single BIT to accomplish this operation because that will tell us only if *either* bit is set. To see whether *both* are set, we must check each bit individually.

```
BIT   #040000,(R4)   ; Test bit 14
BEQ   NOTSET         ; Bit 14 was off
BIT   #020000,(R4)   ; Test bit 13
BEQ   NOTSET         ; Bit 13 was off
JMP   SET            ; Both were on
```

(c) Test whether *any* bit in the byte labeled BYTE is set to 1. If every bit is a 0, branch to ALLCLEAR.

The correct mask would have 1s in every bit position:

$$11111111_2 = 377_8$$

The correct instruction:

```
BITB  #377,BYTE     Test if the byte is all zeroes
BEQ   ALLCLEAR
```

Of course, a more straightforward way of doing that same operation would be to write:

```
TSTB  BYTE          ; Test if the byte is all zeroes
BEQ   ALLCLEAR
```

14.3
Shift Instructions

14.3.1 Arithmetic Shifts

Mnemonic	Name	Internal	Effect	N	Z	V	C
ASR addr	Arithmetic Shift Right	0062aa	See Figure 14-2	*	*	*	*
ASRB addr	Arithmetic Shift Right Byte	1062aa	See Figure 14-2	*	*	*	*
ASL addr	Arithmetic Shift Left	0063aa	See Figure 14-2	*	*	*	*
ASLB addr	Arithmetic Shift Left Byte	1063aa	See Figure 14-2	*	*	*	*

The arithmetic shift instructions treat the quantity to be shifted as a signed 8- or 16-bit quantity. They shift the quantity one bit position to the left (ASL, ASLB) or to the right (ASR, ASRB), while maintaining the same sign in the result (unless there was an overflow). This left or right shift by one bit is equivalent to multiplying or dividing the contents of the effective address by 2. Figure 14-2 summarizes the effect of each of the four arithmetic shift instructions.

FIGURE 14-2 Behavior of the Four Arithmetic Shift Instructions.

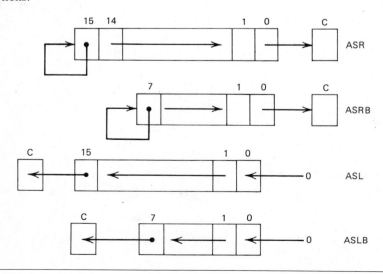

Notice that the right shifts, ASR and ASRB, copy the old sign bit into the new sign bit, so that a negative operand will remain negative and a positive operand will remain positive at the completion of the operation. The low-order bit is shifted into the C bit.

The left shifts, ASL and ASLB, shift 0s into the low-order positions and move the sign bit into the C bit. This can result in an overflow if you try to double a large positive or negative value. You could obtain a result of the opposite sign. This condition will be reflected by the state of the V bit.

EXAMPLES

Assume:

$$RO = 177776$$
$$R1 = 000004$$
$$R2 = 077700$$
$$CON(XYZ) = 077$$

			Final Contents	*Condition Codes*
(a)	ASL	R1	000010	N = 0 Z = 0 V = 0 C = 0
(b)	ASL	RO	177774	N = 1 Z = 0 V = 0 C = 1
(c)	ASL	R2	177600	N = 1 Z = 0 V = 1 C = 0

This left shift resulted in an overflow. We began with a positive quantity and ended with a negative result.

			Final Contents	*Condition Codes*
(d)	ASRB	XYZ	037	N = 0 Z = 0 V = 0 C = 1
(e)	ASR	R1	000002	N = 0 Z = 0 V = 0 C = 0
(f)	ASR	RO	177777	N = 1 Z = 0 V = 0 C = 0
(g)	ASRB	XYZ	037	N = 0 Z = 0 V = 0 C = 1

(h)   Shift the contents of the word pointed at by R1 six bit positions to the right.

```
            MOV   #6,R0   ; Shift count
     AGAIN: ASR   (R1)    ; Shift one place
            DEC   R0      ; Count down by 1
            BNE   AGAIN   ; Keep going until you reach 0
```

Note that the arithmetic shift operations shift a value only one bit position. To implement a shift of n positions, $n > 1$, you must incorporate the shift within a looping control structure. Another alternative is to use the extended shift instructions described in Section 14.2.3.

14.3.2 Logical Shifts

Mnemonic	Name	Internal	Effect	N	Z	V	C
ROL addr	Rotate Left	0061aa	See Figure 14-3	*	*	*	*
ROLB addr	Rotate Left Byte	1061aa	See Figure 14-3	*	*	*	*
ROR addr	Rotate Right	0060aa	See Figure 14-3	*	*	*	*
RORB addr	Rotate Right Byte	1060aa	See Figure 14-3	*	*	*	*

These instructions cicularly rotate an 8- or 16-bit quantity left or right one bit position. The rotate instructions are also called the *logical shifts* because they do not treat the quantity being shifted as a signed 8- or 16-bit value. Instead, it is simply treated as eight or sixteen individual bits. An ROL or ROR does not always correspond to a multiplication or division by 2 because the sign bit may not be set properly. Figure 14-3 summarizes the behavior of the four rotate instructions.

Notice that on both word-oriented rotates, ROL and ROR, the shift effectively

FIGURE 14-3   Behavior of the Four Rotate Instructions.

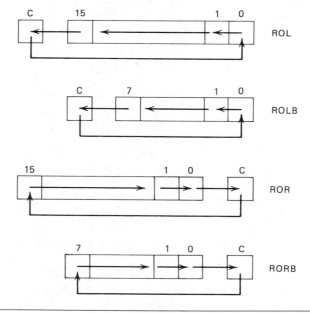

involves seventeen bits: the 16-bit word itself plus the C bit. Similarly, in both byte-oriented rotates, ROLB and RORB, the shift involves nine bits: the 8-bit byte plus the C bit.

The N or Z bit is set if the result is negative or 0, respectively. Even though the rotate operations treat the operand as an unsigned logical quantity, the N bit is set as if the number were signed, by examining the leftmost bit of the result. The V bit is set to the result of the exclusive-OR of the C bit and the N bit at the completion of the rotate, that is, $V = (C .XOR. N)$. The V bit is not very useful in rotate instructions because the operand is not considered to be a numeric value.

EXAMPLES

Assume:

$$
\begin{aligned}
R0 &= 077777 \\
R1 &= 000000 \\
R2 &= 100004 \\
C \ bit &= 1
\end{aligned}
$$

Operation		Final Result	N	Z	V	C
(a)	ROR R0	137777	1	0	0	1
(b)	ROR R1	100000	1	0	1	0
(c)	ROR R2	140002	1	0	1	0
(d)	ROL R0	177777	1	0	1	0
(e)	ROL R1	000001	0	0	1	0
(f)	ROL R2	000011	0	0	0	1

(g) Count the number of bits that are set to 1 in a 16-bit word, called W. Leave the word itself unchanged when you are finished and place the count in a variable called COUNT.

```
                CLR    R0           ; Here we will accumulate the count
                MOV    #17.,R1      ; We will rotate seventeen times
                                    ; This will leave the number unchanged
        AGAIN:  ROL    W            ; Shift high-order bit into C bit
                BCC    NOTSET       ; Test the C bit, branch if clear
                INC    R0           ; Count one more 1 bit
        NOTSET: DEC    R1           ; Decrement shift count
                BNE    AGAIN        ; Keep doing seventeen times
                MOV    R0, COUNT    ; Done, move the count into COUNT
                ROL    W            ; Do this last shift to restore
                                    ; W to its original condition
```

14.3.3 Extended Shifts

Mnemonic	Name	Internal	Effect	N	Z	V	C
ASH addr,reg	Arithmetic Shift	027rss	See Fig. 14-4	*	*	*	*
ASHC addr,reg	Arithmetic Shift Combined	073rss	See Fig. 14-4	*	*	*	*
SWAB addr	Swap Bytes	0003aa	See Fig. 14-4	*	*	0	0

All eight shift instructions introduced in Sections 14.3.1 and 14.3.2 shifted the contents of the effective address one bit position. To shift more than one place, we had to construct a loop and repeat the shift instruction. The extended shifts described in this section allow you to use a single instruction to shift a byte or word N positions right or left, where $N \geq 1$. Figure 14-4 summarizes the behavior of these three extended shift instructions.

The ASH and ASHC allow you to provide a *shift count* in the low-order six bits of the specified source address. The remaining higher order bits of the source address are disregarded. This shift count is treated as a signed twos-complement value, so with six bits, the range of possible shift count values is:

$$-32 \leq \text{shift count} \leq +31$$

A negative shift count results in a rightward shift. A positive shift count results in a leftward shift. In all other respects the ASH behaves like the arithmetic shifts described in Section 14.3.1. The ASH and ASHC instructions, like the MUL and DIV, are part of the option called the extended instruction set, first introduced in Section 12.3. Therefore, these two instructions almost surely will be available on your computer. Before attempting to use them, though, be sure they are available at your installation.

The ASHC instruction performs an arithmetic shift on a 32-bit quantity. The high-order 16 bits are the contents of the specified register, which must be even-numbered. The low-order sixteen bits are the contents of the next higher numbered register. The shift count is handled in the same way as with the ASH instruction. The four condition codes are set in the same way as for the ASR and ASL instructions described in Section 14.3.1.

Finally, the SWAB instruction, Swap Byte, allows you to interchange (swap) the high- and low-order bytes of a word. The effective address of the SWAB must be a word-oriented quantity (i.e., a register or even-numbered address). The effect of the following:

SWAB   WORD

FIGURE 14-4   Behavior of the Three Extended Shifts.

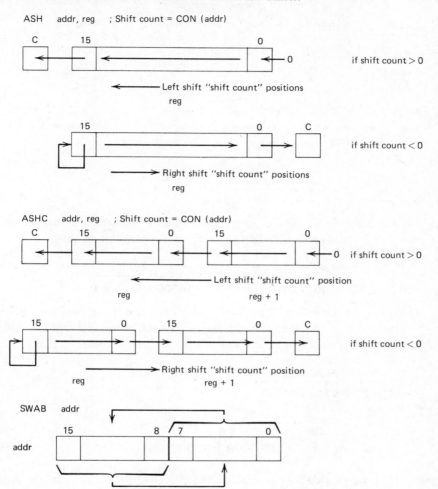

is identical to:

```
MOVB   WORD,TEMP        ; Temp is a temporary location
MOVB   WORD+1,WORD
MOVB   TEMP,WORD
```

EXAMPLES

Assume:

$$R0 = 077770$$
$$R1 = 000001$$

$$R2 = 100001$$
$$X = 000005$$
$$Y = 000076$$
$$Z = 000072$$
$$C \text{ bit} = 0$$

Final Contents

(a) ASH X,R0   R0 = 177400   C = 1

The low-order six bits of the source address are a +5. This corresponds to a left shift of five bit positions.

Final Contents

(b) ASH Y,R0   R0 = 017776   C = 0

The low-order six bits of the source address are a 76_8, which, in twos complement, corresponds to a −2. This is a right shift of two bit positions.

Final Contents

(c) ASHC Z,R0   R0 = 000777   R1 = 160000   C = 0

The low-order six bits of Z are a 72_8, which corresponds in twos complement to a −6. This is a right shift of six places. The thirty-two bits that are shifted are the thirty-two bits in registers (R0,R1).

Final Contents

(d) SWAB R2   R2 = 000600   C = 0

14.4
Example Programs

In this section, we provide four examples of MACRO-11 programs. Like the examples at the end of Chapter 13, they do not include I/O instructions (except for example d). To run these programs you could use the interim I/O routines shown in Appendix E. In other respects they are logically complete.

EXAMPLES

(a) Assume that you have a 16-bit unnormalized floating-point value in register R0, in the following format:

R0	S	Mantissa	Exponent
	1	10	5	← Field size

The base of the biased exponent is $B = 2$, and the mantissa is in sign/magnitude notation. Normalize the floating-point value (if possible) and put the normalized result back into R0. A mantissa will be considered normalized if its value is in the range: $\frac{1}{2} \le |M| < 1$.

```
Normal:     TST    R0            ; Is the number Zero?
            BEQ    Done          ; Yes, it is already normalized

            MOV    R0,R1         ; R1 holds the mantissa
            BIC    #100037,R1    ; Clear the sign and exponent bits
            MOV    R0,R2         ; R2 holds the exponent
            BIC    #177740,R2    ; Clear the mantissa bits and the
                                 ; sign bit

            BIC    #077777,R0    ; R0 holds the sign bit
Again:      BIT    #040000,R1    ; Is it normalized?
            BNE    Combine       ; Yes, put the number back together

            ASL    R1            ; Multiply the mantissa by 2
            DEC    R2            ; Decrease the exponent
            TST    R2            ; Is the exponent too small?
            BGE    Again         ; If not, check if normalized again
            MOV    #0,R0         ; Exponent underflow: set number to
                                 ; 0 and

.           BR     Done          ; Exit
Combine:    BIS    R1,R0         ; Combine mantissa and sign
            BIS    R2,R0         ; Add exponent to the rest
Done:
```

(b)   Generate Parity Check

Assume that you have a 7-bit ASCII character in the memory location pointed to by register R0. Generate and store the correct setting for the eighth bit so that the character will be stored in *odd* parity (i.e., an odd number of 1 bits). See Section 4.2. for a discussion of the purpose and use of this parity bit.

```
Count:   .Word  0          ; Used to count number of 1 bits

Mask:    .Byte  0          ; Used to determine which bit we
         .Even             ; are currently examining

Start:   MOV    #7,R1      ; Check seven bits of the character
         CLR    Count      ; Zero the number of set hits found
         MOVB   #1,Mask    ; Set the least significant bit in
                           ; Mask to a 1

NxtBit:  BITB   Mask,(R0)  ; Is this bit on?
         BEQ    NotSet     ; No, check the next bit
```

```
            INC    Count         ; Yes, increment the number of bits
                                 ; found

NotSet: ASLB   Mask          ; Move the set bit to the next
                                 ; position
            DEC    R1            ; Are we done checking the seven
                                 ; bits?
            BNE    NxtBit        ; No, check the next bit
```

```
;   Count now contains the total number of bits in the character.
;   Check if it is odd or even.
```

```
            BIT    #1,Count      ; Test the least significant bit
            BEQ    Even          ; If it is 0, the number is even

Odd:    BICB   #200,(R0)     ; Clear the eighth bit to get odd
                                 ; parity

            BR     Done

Even:   BISB   #200,(R0)     ; Set the eighth bit to get odd
                                 ; parity
Done:
```

(c) Triple-Precision Arithmetic

Assume that we have two 48-bit (3-word) integer values. The address of the
first of the three sequential words holding the first number is in R0, while the
address of the first of the three sequential words holding the second number is
in R1. Write the MACRO-11 code to add these two numbers together, using
R1 to point to the first of the three words containing the result.
Diagrammatically:

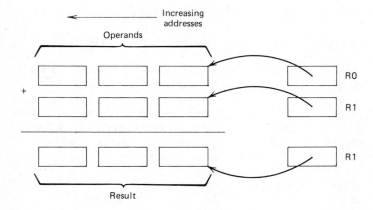

We do this by adding two numbers at a time, using the regular ADD instruction. If there is a carry, we must add 1 to the next pair of words being added.

```
NumWords  =  3                      ; Number of words in each operand

          MOV  #NumWords,R2         ; R2 will count the number of
                                    ; additions that must be done
Again:    ADD  (R0)+,(R1)+          ; Add the next two words together
          BVC  NoOvfl               ; Overflow didn't occur
          CMP  #1,R2                ; Overflow is only important on
                                    ; the last word pair added
          BEQ  Error                : This is the last add, so jump
                                    ; to Error (Not included here.)

NoOvfl:   BCC  Next                 ; No carry, so add next pair
          INC  (R0)                 ; Add the carry into one of the
                                    ; next words

Next:     DEC  R2                   ; Are we done yet?
          BGE  Again                ; No, add the next two words

          SUB  #NumWords·2,R1       ; Set R1 back to the beginning of
                                    ; the block
```

The last example is quite complex, involving four branch instructions and some intricate logic. Because the operation of adding the carry bit into another word is so common (it is used for any extended precision mode), MACRO-11 provides a separate instruction for it, called Add Carry.

Mnemonic	Name	Internal	Effect	N	Z	V	C
ADC addr	Add Carry	0055aa	CON(addr)+C →CON(addr)	*	*	*	*
ADCB addr	Add Carry Byte	1055aa	CON(addr)+C →CON(addr)	*	*	*	*

Using this new instruction, an alternative solution would be:

```
ADD (R0)+,(R1)+
ADC (R0)
ADD (R0)+,(R1)+
ADC (R0)
ADD (R0)+, (R1)+
SUB #NumWords·2,R1
BVS ERROR
```

Notice how simple this solution is compared to the previous code.

(d) Bubble Sort

This program implements the well-known algorithm called the bubble sort. It reads in a series of numbers ending with a 0 and sorts them into ascending order. It is a complete program, including input/output. The program uses the I/O routines contained in Appendix E.

```
.Title Bubble Sort Program
.MCALL .EXIT
MaxSize = 50              ; The maximum number of words in
                         ; the list
    List:   .BlkW   MaxSize   ; The list of the values to be
                              ; sorted
    Switch: .Word  0          ; A flag to tell us if we have to
                              ; go through the list again while
                              ; sorting
    Temp:   .Word  0          ; A temporary for switching the
                              ; values while sorting
    Size:   .Word  0          ; The actual number of values in
                              ; the list times 2

;     Here we could place subroutines IN and OUT from Appendix E.

Start:    CLR   R1           ; Set the pointer into List to the
                             ; beginning

Again:    JSR   PC,In        ; Get a value and place it in R0
          TST   R0           ; Is it Zero?
          BEQ   InDone        ; Yes, sort the list
          MOV   R0,List(R1)  ; Move the value into the list
          ADD   #2,R1        ; Increment the pointer to the next
                             ; list element
          CMP   R1,#MaxSize·2 ; Have we filled the whole list?
          BLT   Again        ; No, get another value

InDone:   SUB   #2,R1        ; Don't count the zero as part of
                             ; the list
          MOV   R1,Size      ; Save the size of the list

Anothr:   CLR   Switch       ; Clear the flag that will tell us if
                             ; any values were out of order in
                             ; the list
          CLR   R1           ; Point to the beginning of the
                             ; list

Loop:     CMP   List(R1),List+2(R1)   ; Are these two elements in
                                      ; order?
```

```
        BLE    Ok                    ; Yes, skip the swapping

        MOV    List(R1),Temp         ; Swap the two values. Move one
                                     ; into Temp
        MOV    List + 2(R1),List(R1)  ; Switch one of them
        MOV    Temp,List + 2(R1)     ; Move the first one to the other
        MOV    #1,Switch             ; Set the switch flag because we
                                     ; swapped

Ok:     ADD    #2,R1                 ; Move R1 to point to the next word
        CMP    R1,Size               ; Have we checked the whole list
                                     ; yet?
        BLT    Loop                  ; No, keep checking

        TST    Switch                ; Did we switch any this time
                                     ; through?
        BNE    Anothr                ; Yes, check through the list again

        CLR    R1                    ; Set the pointer back to the
                                     ; beginning
OutLp:  MOV    List(R1),R0           ; Put this value into R0
        JSR    PC,Out                ; Print the value of R0
        ADD    #2,R1                 ; Point to the next value
        CMP    R1,Size               ; Have we printed them all?
        BLE    OutLp                 ; No, keep printing them

        .EXIT                        ; This will terminate the program

        .End   Start
```

14.5
Some Additional Pseudo-Operations

In this section we add to the basic set of pseudo-ops introduced in Sections 12.4 and
13.4. There are many more assembler directives that we do not mention. Refer to
Appendix C for a complete listing of all assembler directives.

14.5.1   The .ASCII and .ASCIZ Directives
We have studied data-generation pseudo-ops (.BYTE, .WORD) for generating 8- or
16-bit integer quantities. We now turn to the pseudo-ops for generating character
data: the .ASCII and .ASCIZ directives. The syntax for these pseudo-ops is:

```
        label:  .ASCII   / . . . any string of characters . . ./
        label:  .ASCIZ   / . . . any string of characters . . ./
```

If there is a label, it will be given the current value of the location counter. Each of
the individual characters between the delimiters (the "/" characters) will be stored

consecutively in bytes according to the ASCII character code listed in Chapter 4. The difference between the two pseudo-ops is that the .ASCIZ will append to the end of the string one extra byte containing all 0s.

EXAMPLES

Assume that the location counter has the value 100.

(a) **STRING: .ASCII   /Hello/**

Internally:	Address	Contents
	100	110 (H)
	101	145 (e)
	102	154 (l)
	103	154 (l)
	104	157 (o)

and the identifier STRING has the value 100.

(b) **DIRTY: .ASCIZ   /!#@'?/**

Internally:	Address	Contents
	100	041 (!)
	101	043 (#)
	102	100 (@)
	103	042 (')
	104	077 (?)
	105	000

and the label DIRTY has the value 100. Notice the extra byte containing 000, which is automatically added to the end of the string. Because 000 is *not* a printing ASCII character, this extra byte can be used as a "signal" or a *flag* to mark the end of the string.

(c) **MYWIFE: .ASCII   /RUTH/**

Internally:	Address	Contents
	100	122 (R)
	101	125 (U)
	102	124 (T)
	103	110 (H)

(d) **.ASCII !C = A/B!**

will generate:	Address	Contents
	100	103 (C)
	101	040 (blank)

Address	Contents
102	075 (=)
103	040 (blank)
104	101 (A)
105	057 (/)
106	102 (B)

The choice of the "/" as the delimiting character is strictly arbitrary; *any* printing character can be used to bracket the beginning and end of the string. Whatever character is used to mark the beginning of the string is also used to mark the end of the string.

Note that in this example, the character '!' is used to mark the beginning and end of the string, because the '/' character is being used within the string itself.

We should mention that the .ASCII and .ASCIZ directives can be used to generate only the *printable* ASCII characters, whose codes are 040 to 176 octal. Should you wish to generate the internal representation of any of the control characters (codes 00 to 37, and 177), you will need to use the .BYTE directive and generate their internal binary code directly.

(e)   Generate a string containing the characters "Kimberly" followed by a carriage return and line feed.

```
.ASCII   /Kimberly/
.BYTE    015        ; Carriage return is an octal 15
.BYTE    012        ; Line feed is an octal 12
```

(f)   Assume that a string has been created by means of the .ASCIZ directive, and the address of the first character is contained in R0. Count the number of characters in the string, *excluding* the signal marker 000 appearing at the end of the string.

```
        CLR COUNT    ; Clear the count field to 0
LOOP:   TSTB (R0)+   ; Test if we have come to the end
                     ; marker
        BEQ DONE     ; Yes we have
        INC COUNT    ; No, count one more character
        BR  LOOP     ; and loop
        ;
DONE:
```

14.5.2   The .EVEN Directive

There is one potential problem with both of the directives introduced in the previous sections. Because their length may be either an even or an odd value, errors could occur during assembly. Take a look at the following sequence:

```
STR:   .ASCII   / ... some string .../
  X:   .WORD  0
```

If the last byte in the string is located at an odd address, there is no problem. The location counter will have an even value, and the next directive will be correctly assembled on a word boundary. However, if the last byte filled is on an even address, the location counter will have an odd value and therefore will not be on a word boundary. Any attempt to load a word-oriented quantity (e.g., .BLKW, .WORD, or any instruction) at an odd address will result in an error, specifically a 'B' (as in Boundary) error.

MACRO-11 has a pseudo-op to handle this situation. The .EVEN directive forces the location counter to an even-numbered value. If it is already even, nothing happens. If it is odd, 1 is added to the value of LC. You should use the .EVEN pseudo-op whenever there is a possibility of obtaining an odd address. For example:

```
.BYTE   0
.BYTE   0

  .       .
  .       .
  .       .
.BYTE   0        .BLKB   "n"        .ASCII  / ... /
.EVEN            .EVEN              .EVEN

  (a)              (b)                (c)
```

Even if you know that in this particular circumstance the value will be even, it is a good idea to include an .EVEN directive to make the program easier to maintain. For example, in sample c, if we do not use the .EVEN, the program may be properly assembled now, but if the message within the .ASCII directive is ever changed, it could generate assembly error messages caused by odd-address errors. Similarly, in sample a, if we add one more .BYTE directive, we could end up with a boundary error. The use of the .EVEN directive will prevent that from happening.

14.5.3 Listing and Function Control

The .LIST and .NLIST directives turn on or off a total of fifteen binary flags that control the format and the content of the output listing. The syntax of these two directives is:

```
.LIST    arg,arg, . . .
.NLIST   arg,arg, . . .
```

where "arg" is one of the fifteen symbolic arguments recognized by the .LIST and .NLIST directives. The .LIST directive turns the flag ON, while .NLIST turns it OFF. These fifteen arguments are listed in Figure 14-5. Some of them may not yet make sense because we have not discussed the statements to which they relate. We will be discussing these statements later.

FIGURE 14-5   Arguments for the .LIST and .NLIST
Directives.

Argument	Default	Meaning
SEQ	ON	Controls printing of source line sequence numbers
LOC	ON	Controls printing of the location counter field
BIN	ON	Controls printing of the internal machine code
BEX	ON	Controls printing of the binary extensions
SRC	ON	Controls printing of the MACRO-11 source code
COM	ON	Controls printing of comments
MD	ON	Controls listing of macro definitions (discussed in Chapter 17)
MC	ON	Controls listing of macro calls
ME	OFF	Controls listing of macro expansion
MEB	OFF	Controls listing of macro expansion binary code
CND	ON	Controls listing of unsatisfied conditional assembly directives (discussed in Chapter 17)
LD	OFF	Controls listing of all listing directives
TOC	ON	Controls listing of table of contents
SYM	ON	Controls listing of the symbol table
TTM	ON	Controls the overall listing output format; default set by local installation

EXAMPLE

Assume that we are concerned about the amount of paper being generated by our listings (all those trees!). We could reduce the amount of paper generation by writing:

.NLIST   COM,TOC,SYM

which would eliminate the printing of comments within the program and the table of contents and symbol table after the program. This declaration should appear at the beginning of the program, immediately below the .TITLE directive.

The .ENABL and .DSABL directives control a wide range of functions having to do with the assembly process itself. These two directives allow you to invoke or suppress certain MACRO-11 functions directly within your program. The syntax of these two directives is:

.ENABL   arg,arg, . . .
.DSABL   arg,arg, . . .

where "arg" is any symbolic argument that is recognized by the .ENABL and .DSABL pseudo-ops. The .ENABL directive turns that option ON, and the .DSABL turns it OFF. Some of these assembly options are listed in Figure 14-6. For a complete list, refer to Section 6.2 of the MACRO-11 Language Reference Manual.

EXAMPLE

Let's sat that you are working on a system that has full upper- and lowercase capabilities, and you would like to enter input data in upper- and lowercase without having all characters converted to uppercase. You could do this using the following .ENABL pseudo-op:

.ENABL   LC

This directive should appear at the beginning of your program, immediately below the .TITLE directive.

14.6
Summary

We have completed a discussion of "elementary MACRO-11," representing the parts of the language that are the most important, the most essential, and the most frequently used. This basic set includes:

1. The seven addressing techniques summarized in Figure 11-9.
2. The data transfer, arithmetic, compare, branch, logical, and shift operations introduced in Chapters 12, 13, and 14.

FIGURE 14-6   Some Arguments to the .ENABL and .DSABL Directives.

Argument	Default	Function
AMA	OFF	Assembles all relative addresses (mode 6, reg 7) as absolute addresses (mode 3, reg 7) instead
CDR	OFF	Treats source columns 73 and beyond as comments
FPT	OFF	If ON, causes floating-point truncation; otherwise, floating-point rounding
LC	OFF	If ON, accepts lowercase input without converting to uppercase
REG	ON	Allows you to use the symbols R0, R1, . . . , R5, SP, PC for the general-purpose registers, without defining them yourself

3. The assembler directives .WORD, .BYTE, .ASCII, .ASCIZ, .BLKW, .BLKB, .EVEN, .TITLE, .END, listing control, function control, and direct assignment (=).

In the following chapters, we introduce a number of advanced features of the language, including I/O, subroutines, stacks, macros, additional addressing techniques, new assembler directives, and advanced programming and debugging techniques for assembly language. Before reading on, be sure that you understand the concepts and language facilities presented so far.

Exercises for Chapter 14

1. Implement a word-oriented bit-wise exclusive-OR operation, as defined by the following truth table.

Destination bit

XOR	0	1
0	0	1
Source bit 1	1	0

$\left.\right\}$ Result bit

Use the logical operations introduced in Section 14.2 to implement a 16-bit, bit-wise exclusive-OR. The operation should perform the bit-wise XOR operation between a source address called S and a destination address called D. The result should be placed back into D.

2. Implement a word-oriented, bit-wise, logical implication operation, which is defined by the following truth table.

Destination bit

LIMPL	0	1
0	1	1
Source bit 1	0	1

$\left.\right\}$ Result bit

Use the logical operations introduced in Section 14.2 to implement a 16-bit, bit-wise, logical implication operation. The operation should use as its source address the word labeled S, and as its destination address the word labeled D. The result should be placed back into D.

3. Assume that the registers currently have the following contents: (All values are octal.)

```
R0 = 104607
R1 = 067420
R2 = 107070
```

Show the final contents of the referenced registers after performing the following logical operations.

    a.   BIS   #006517,R0
    b.   BIS   #067000,R1
    c.   BIS   #070706,R2
    d.   BIS   R0,R1
    e.   BIC   #103401,R0
    f.   BIC   #062007,R1
    g.   BIC   #107060,R2
    h.   BIC   R0,R1

4.   Assume that general-purpose register R0 contains the octal value 004077. State whether a branch will take place in each of the following cases, and if so, to what label.

    a.   BIT   #1,R0
          BEQ   X
          BMI   Y
    b.   BIT   #3700,R0
          BEQ   X
          BMI   Y
    c.   BIT   #4100,R0
          BNE   X
          BEQ   Y

5.   Write a MACRO-11 fragment that branches to label L1 if *either* of the following conditions is true:

    a.   Both bit positions 2 and 7 of register R4 are 1, or
    b.   Both bit positions 3 and 8 of register R4 are 0.

If neither of these conditions is met, branch to label L2.

6.   Assume that the contents of byte address 100 is 217, and that general register R1 contains the value 100. Show the final contents of address 100 after each of these logical operations has been completed.

    a.   BISB   #240,(R1)
    b.   BISB   #10,(R1)
    c.   BICB   #200,(R1)
    d.   BICB   #207,(R1)

7.   For each of the following logical operations, state whether they could possibly do anything meaningful, or whether they are worthless "no operations."

    a.   BIS   #177777,R0
    b.   BIS   #0,R0
    c.   BIC   #177777,R0
    d.   BIC   #0,R0
    e.   BIT   #177777,R0
    f.   BIT   #0,R0

8. Assume that the general registers and the C bit initially contain the following octal values.

$$RO = 107400$$
$$R1 = 077001$$
$$C = 1$$

Show the final contents of the referenced register and the four condition codes after each of the shift operations has been completed.
- a. ASL R0
- b. ASL R1
- c. ASR R0
- d. ASR R1
- e. ROL R0
- f. ROR R1

9. Assume that the initial values of the registers and the C bit are the same as given in Exercise 8. Furthermore, assume that the variables A and B have the following octal values.

$$A = 000011$$
$$B = 177774$$

Show the final contents of the referenced registers and the four condition codes after each of the extended shifts has been completed.
- a. ASH A,R0
- b. ASH B,R1
- c. ASHC B,R0

10. Assume that you do not have a Swap Byte command on your computer. Write a MACRO-11 fragment that uses the other shift commands to implement a Swap Byte Operation (instead of using the MOVB commands as shown in Section 14.3.3).

11. What would be the advantage in writing:

```
MOV   X,R1
ASL   R1
ASL   R1
MOV   R1,X
```

rather than:

```
MOV   X,R1
MUL   #4,R1
MOV   R1,X
```

Would there be any disadvantages?

12. Use an .ASCIZ directive to create the following string:

•• ERROR ••

Show the internal contents of memory produced by this pseudo-operation.

13. Use the .ASCII directive to create the following output string:

X (TAB) SIN(X)

where (TAB) indicates the horizontal tab character. Make sure the message ends on an even address boundary.

14. Referring to the sample MACRO-11 listing in Figure 13-4, show how you would suppress the printing of the line sequence numbers in column 1.

Exercises 15–18 ask you to write complete MACRO-11 programs. To complete these projects, you should use the interim I/O facility given in Appendix E.

15. Read in a value, N, N > 0. Then proceed to read in a sequence of N 6-digit octal numbers. Add up the total number of 1 bits in all N numbers. When you have finished reading in all N numbers, output the total number of 1 bits, and stop.

16. Assume that register R0 contains four BCD digits. (See Section 3.7 for a review of BCD representations.) Write a MACRO-11 program that takes the contents of R0, converts the digits to characters, and stores the characters in a block of memory labeled CHOUT. Your routine should also handle the following two special cases.
   a. If the number is greater than 999, insert the character "," into the output array.
   b. Suppress leading zeros. Replace them with blank characters in the output array.

For example,

Input:	1000	0011	0111	0000	(This is in R0.)
	8	3	7	0	

Output:	CHOUT:	070	'8'
		054	','
		063	'3'
		067	'7'
		060	'0'

Input:	0000	0000	1001	0001	(This is in R0.)
	0	0	9	1	

Output:	CHOUT:	040	blank
		040	blank
		071	'9'
		061	'1'

17. Write a MACRO-11 program that clears (i.e., sets to 0) all memory locations *following* the memory used by the program itself. That is, if the program occupies memory locations 0–1462 then clear memory locations 1463–177777. Assume that the highest address in memory is 177777.

18. Write a MACRO-11 program that reads in a sequence of 6-digit octal numbers and stores them in a sequential block of memory called ARRAY, which is defined via:

ARRAY: .BLKW   100.   ; 100 decimal

The input is terminated by the occurrence of the octal pattern 177777 or by reading in 100 (decimal) words, whichever comes first.

After you have read in the array, write the MACRO-11 code that finds the largest and smallest values in the array. Assume that the values are signed twos-complement quantities. When you are finished, output the following four values:

    a. The largest value.
    b. The byte offset from ARRAY where the largest value occurred.
    c. The smallest value.
    d. The byte offset from ARRAY where the smallest value occurred.

CHAPTER 15

INPUT/OUTPUT IN
MACRO·11

15.1
Introduction

In most ways, the PDP-11 and VAX-11 are typical of modern computer systems. However, in one area they differ significantly from other computers: namely, in the way that they perform input and output operations. On the PDP-11 and the VAX-11, there are no separate and unique machine-language instructions for performing I/O. On many other machines, there are distinct I/O commands that look something like this:

```
IN    addr(channel)    ; Start an input operation
OUT   addr(channel)    ; Start an output operation
```

These commands might be to input or output to the device connected to the specified "channel" a physical record of information beginning at the memory address called "addr."

But there are no such commands on the PDP-11. Instead, an input or output device is treated as if it were a *memory location*. The process of "storing" a value into the address associated with an output device causes it to be written to the output unit. The process of "fetching" a value from the address associated with an input device causes a byte or word to be read in from that device. Thus, we can use the regular data transfer operations introduced in Section 12.2 to perform all I/O operations on the PDP-11 and VAX-11 computers. This I/O architecture is referred to as *memory-mapped I/O* and is diagrammed in Figure 15-1.

On the PDP-11, the special addresses for I/O are in the highest 4K (4,096) words of memory (see Figure 10-2). On a 64K system (16-bit addresses), this would correspond to addresses 160000 to 177776. On a 256K system (18-bit addresses), these

FIGURE 15-1   Examples of Memory-Mapped Input/
Output.

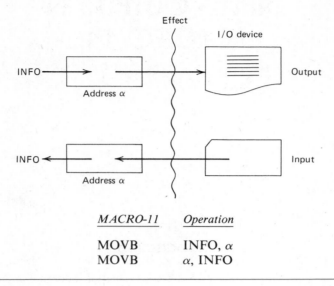

$$\begin{array}{cc} \underline{MACRO\text{-}11} & \underline{Operation} \\ MOVB & INFO, \alpha \\ MOVB & \alpha, INFO \end{array}$$

addresses would correspond to 760000 to 777776. These memory locations are *not* available to the user and are reserved strictly for I/O operations. For a list of addresses and their corresponding I/O devices, refer to the PDP-11 Processor Handbook, "UNIBUS Addresses."

15.2
Character-Oriented Input/Output

Character-oriented I/O devices transfer one character at a time to or from the processor. Examples of character-oriented devices are:

1.   VDT screen and keyboard.
2.   Slow character printer.
3.   Paper tape reader, punch.

In this section, we discuss character-at-a-time I/O. Higher speed "block-oriented" I/O devices—including tapes, disks, and drums—are discussed in Section 15.4. (You should be sure that you are familiar with the general concepts of I/O presented in Chapter 8 before proceeding).

15.2.1 Input

On the PDP-11, every input device has associated with it two special memory addresses:

> *Receive Buffer (RB):* The RB holds the 8-bit character that has just been received from the input device.
>
> *Status Register (SR):* The SR contains a set of flags that describe the status of the current input operation.

The exact bit-by-bit layouts of the RB and SR depend on the specific I/O device. However, for most character-oriented input devices, the RB and SR are quite similar, and their general layout is shown in Figure 15-2.

The received character is always placed in the low-order eight bits of the receive buffer. The high-order eight bits are not used.

The four bits of the status register shown in Figure 15-2 are in the same location and serve the same purpose for all character-oriented I/O devices. These are the only four status bits that we refer to in this chapter. Bits 1–5 and 8–14 may contain additional status information unique to a specific input device. The location of these two registers for some common input devices is shown in Figure 15-3.

The bits in the status register have the following meanings, regardless of the input device.

> *Device Enable Bit (Bit 0):* When set to 1, enables the device and allows it to begin inputting a character. In a sense, this bit can be considered the "ON button" that initiates the input operation.

FIGURE 15-2 Layout of the Receive Buffer and Status Register.

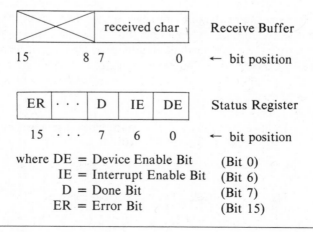

where DE = Device Enable Bit   (Bit 0)
      IE = Interrupt Enable Bit   (Bit 6)
       D = Done Bit   (Bit 7)
      ER = Error Bit   (Bit 15)

FIGURE 15-3   Addresses of Some Common Input
Devices.

```
Keyboard status register   = 177560
Keyboard receive buffer    = 177562
Paper tape status register = 177550
Paper tape receive buffer  = 177552
```

Interrupt Enable (Bit 6):   If set to 1, will generate an interrupt when the
input operation is complete. (Interrupts are discussed in the next section.)

Done Bit (Bit 7):   When set by the input device to 1, indicates that the
input operation is complete and the character is in the receive buffer. This
bit is read-only and cannot be set by the user. It may be tested by the
user to see whether input is finished.

Error Bit (Bit 15):   When set by the input device to 1, indicates that an
error occurred during input. The bit is read-only and cannot be set by
the user. It may be tested by the user to see whether an error occurred.
The exact nature of any error will be specified by other bits in the status
register unique to each device.

Now, using these two registers, we can begin to describe the general model of input
for all PDP-11 character-oriented input devices, as summarized in the flowchart in
Figure 15-4.

We initially set the device enable bit to 1, telling the input device to begin an input
operation. On some devices, it is not necessary to set this bit because the device is
always ready to produce an input character. On these devices the enable bit is simply
ignored. Since setting the enable bit can never hurt, let us adopt the convention of
always setting it to 1 to initiate an input operation. To set this bit, we must reference
the status register for the corresponding input device. This will be an address in high
memory, above 160000 (or above 760000 on a model with 18-bit addresses). We can
do this in one of two ways. One way is to use *relative addressing mode* (mode 6, reg
7) introduced in Section 11.2.7.

```
        RCSR = 177560  ; Console terminal status register
        RBUF = 177562  ; Buffer register
             .
             .
             .
        BIS     #1,RCSR ; Set the enable bit to 1

  (or INC     RCSR    ; This will also work)
```

FIGURE 15-4   Flowchart of Character-Oriented Input on the PDP-11.

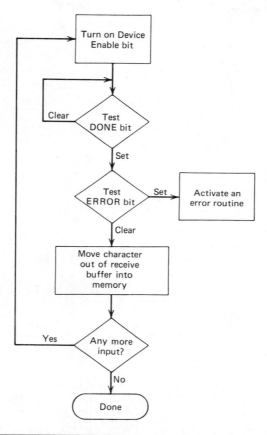

The BIS operation above will be translated into indexed addressing using the PC. Internally it will be assembled into three words:

$$052767$$
$$000001$$
$$nnnnnn$$

where "nnnnnn" is an octal value such that, when it is added to the current contents of the PC, will result in the address 177560.

A second way to reference the address 177560 involves an addressing mode that has not yet been introduced. It is called *absolute addressing,* and the syntax is:

@#address

The effective address is the absolute octal address given in the address field. The above address is translated into mode 3, register 7, and the absolute address is stored in the word immediately following the instruction. Therefore, to set the status register enable bit to 1 using absolute addressing, we could also say:

```
        BIS   #1,@#177560
or
        RCSR = 177560
            .
            .
            .
        BIS   #1,@#RCSR

(or INC   @#RCSR   ; This will also work)
```

Internally, the BIS instruction will be assembled into the following three words:

```
        052737
        000001
        177560
```

The only real difference between these two techniques is the addressing mode used to internally encode the instruction. Both will lead to the same result: setting bit 0 in the status register to 1, and beginning an input operation. In fact, if the AMA directive has been enabled with the .ENABL directive (see Section 14.5.3), all relative addresses (mode 6, reg 7) will be automatically assembled as absolute addresses (mode 3, reg 7) by the MACRO-11 assembler.

Once the enable bit has been set, the input device begins the process of moving a character into the receive buffer. How this is accomplished will depend on the particular device (e.g., keys making electrical contact, cards passing over contact brushes). When the character has arrived and is available, the DONE bit of the receive buffer will be set to 1 by the input controller. (The DONE bit is *read-only* and can only be tested, not set, by your program.) You cannot use the character in the input buffer until the DONE bit has been turned on, so you must test it repeatedly to see when it becomes a 1. The following is an example of how this test may be done.

```
AGAIN:  BIT   #200,@#RCSR   ; Test bit 7 of the status register
        BEQ   AGAIN         ; Not ready, keep waiting
```

This sequence of code is called a *wait loop,* or an *idle loop,* and represents the simplest form of input processing. Essentially, we do nothing until the character is ready. This can be extremely inefficient because character-based I/O is an inherently slow operation, and 99.9 percent of the time within a program can be spent waiting for an input operation to be completed. We have much more to say about improving the efficiency of I/O processing in Section 15.3. For now, we simply use idle loops to wait until input is finished. We can worry about inefficiency later.

When the character is in the receive buffer, we can process it as necessary and then move it to a permanent location in memory. We can't leave it in the receive buffer because the next character would overwrite it, causing a *data overrun error.* One particularly important piece of processing is to make sure that the character has arrived correctly. To do this, we interrogate the error bit (bit 15) of the status register. If bit 15 is a 1, it means that an error has occurred. Possibilities include:

1. Parity error (see Section 4.2).
2. Data overrun.
3. Device not turned on.
4. Device not properly loaded (with paper, cards, tape, etc.).
5. Physical malfunction (jam, overheating, etc.).

The exact cause of the error will be specified by other bits in the status register, which are specific to that particular I/O device.

```
        BIT     #100000,@#RCSR   ; Check if an error occurred
        BNE     ERROR            ; Jump to error routine
        MOVB    @#RBUF,LOC       ; Put character into LOC
          .
          .
          .
ERROR:                           ; The error-processing routine
```

This is the general model of input for all character-oriented devices. Figure 15-5 shows a MACRO-11 program fragment for reading characters from a console VDT into a memory buffer called LINE. The routine will continue until it has read a maximum of eighty characters or until it has encountered a carriage return (octal code 15). If an error occurs on input, the bad character will be discarded and not stored. Finally, the delete character, DEL (octal code 177), is interpreted as a 1-character rubout that erases the last character just read as long as there is a character to delete. Exercises 3 and 4 at the end of this chapter include some additional problems based on character-oriented input.

Once the program in Figure 15-5 has been executed, you should be aware that the information contained in the 80-character buffer called LINE will be a sequence of ASCII characters. If the sequence of characters is to be used as an integer or floating-point value, you will need to write the routines that convert them from their current character-based representation to the proper integer or floating-point representation used on your system (e.g., sign/magnitude, twos-complement). For example, if you had entered the four characters '1', '2', '3', and 'CR', the memory buffer called LINE would contain the following:

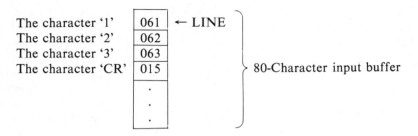

The character '1'	061 ← LINE
The character '2'	062
The character '3'	063
The character 'CR'	015

80-Character input buffer

and *not* the value:

0000000001111011

which is the twos-complement or sign/magnitude representation of the integer value +123.

Appendix E contains a routine called IN for converting characters to unsigned integers, and you should look closely at the program to be sure that you understand the manipulations being performed. The need for these conversion routines earlier in the text should now be apparent. Without them, we would not be able to input or output integer or real values, only characters. Exercises 5 and 6 ask you to write some additional character-conversion routines for integer input in other number bases.

15.2.2 Output

The technique for performing output on the PDP-11 and VAX-11 is similar to that for input. There are two registers associated with each output device: the *transmit buffer* (TB) and the *transmit status register* (TSR). Their layouts are shown in Figure 15-6.

The character to be output is written to the transmit buffer, automatically starting the process of output. Notice that we do not need an enable bit in the transmit status register. The output operation starts as soon as the character is loaded into the transmit buffer. As before, we must wait until the output operation is completed before initiating another one. We must repeatedly check the DONE bit (bit 7). When that bit is set to 1 by the output controller, the output device has handled that character and is ready for the next. The DONE bit is ready-only and cannot be set by the user. It can only be tested. Upon completion of an output operation, we also should check bit 15 (the ERROR bit) to ensure that the last character was processed correctly. Like the DONE bit, the ERROR bit is read-only and cannot be set by the user. The

FIGURE 15-5   Example of Character-Oriented Input.

```
              RCSR  =  177560
              RBUF  =  177562
      LINE:  .BLKB    80.                ; The input buffer
                .
                .
                .
              CLR      R0                ; R0 is the index into LINE
    NEWCH:  BIS      #1,@#RCSR           ; Turn on the enable bit
  NOTDONE:  BIT      #200,@#RCSR         ; Wait until done
            BEQ      NOTDONE
;
            BIT      #100000,@#RCSR      ; Test if error
            BNE      NEWCH               ; If error, get a new char
;
            CMPB     #177,@#RBUF         ; Was this a delete?
            BNE      GOODCHAR            ; No
            TST      R0                  ; See if there is a character
                                         ; to delete
            BEQ      NEWCH               ; This was the first char
            DEC      R0                  ; Delete previous char
            JMP      NEWCH               ; Get next character
;
  GOODCHAR: MOVB     @#RBUF,LINE(R0)     ; Store character
            CMPB     LINE(R0),#15        ; Was it a CR?
            BEQ      DONE                ; Yes
            INC      R0
            CMP      R0,#80.             ; Have we processed 80
                                         ; characters?
            BGE      DONE                ; Yes
            JMP      NEWCH               ; Get next character
;
      DONE:
```

general model for character-oriented output is summarized in the flowchart in Figure 15-7.

Figure 15-8 shows a program for outputting the five characters "hello" on a line printer, followed by a carriage return. If a character is not printed correctly, it is printed again. (This could lead to a disastrous infinite loop, and Exercise 8 asks you to rewrite this example to eliminate that problem.)

When performing output, you must be careful to remember two points that were made in Chapter 8. First, all output is character-oriented. You cannot directly print

FIGURE 15-6   Layout of the Transmit Buffer and Status
Register.

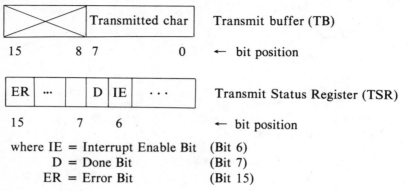

Transmit buffer (TB)

15   8 7   0   ← bit position

Transmit Status Register (TSR)

15   7   6   ← bit position

where IE = Interrupt Enable Bit   (Bit 6)
      D = Done Bit   (Bit 7)
     ER = Error Bit   (Bit 15)

FIGURE 15-7   Flowchart of Character-Oriented Output
on the PDP-11.

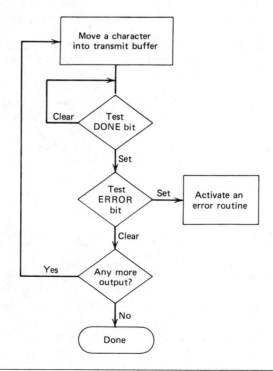

FIGURE 15-8   Example of Character-Oriented Output.

```
              CR   =  15          ; The carriage return character
              TCSR =  177564      ; The status register
              TBUF =  177566      ; The transmit buffer
MESSAGE:      .ASCII  /hello/      ; The message to be printed
              .BYTE   CR           ; Carriage return
              .EVEN
                 .

                 .

              CLR     R0           ; R0 is the index
                                   ; into message
TRYAGAIN: MOVB    MESSAGE(R0),@#TBUF ; Print the next char
NOTDONE:  TSTB    @#TCSR           ; Wait until it's done
          BEQ     NOTDONE
          BIT     #100000,@#TCSR   ; Check if error
          BNE     TRYAGAIN         ; Yes
;
          INC     R0
          CMP     #6,R0            ; See if all six
                                   ; chars were printed
          BNE     TRYAGAIN         ; Loop to get next char
;
```

values that are stored internally as integer or real values. If you try, they will be erroneously interpreted as ASCII characters. For example, if we use the technique shown in Figure 15-8 to print the integer value 12,667, which would be stored internally as:

$$0011000101111011$$

the system will print instead the character pair:

$$1\{$$

because the binary digits will be incorrectly interpreted as the two ASCII characters 061_8 ('1') and 173_2 ('{'):

00110001	01111011
061	173
'1'	'{'

We must first convert all integers to their proper character sequence before printing. Appendix E shows a routine called OUT for converting integer values to characters prior to output, and you should take a close look at that program to make sure you understand the manipulations being carried out. Exercise 9 at the end of the chapter contains some additional exercises concerning the conversion of numeric values to characters.

The second point to remember about output is that all devices have a maximum line length. You cannot transmit characters in an unbroken stream because at some point you will fill up the line and possibly lose information. Some output devices automatically move to column 1 of the next line. This feature is called *wrap-around.* Others simply overstrike the last character on the line. To avoid this problem, be sure to transmit the carriage return character (octal code 015) and/or the line feed character (octal code 012) before the maximum number of characters has been sent. This will move the output device to the next line and prevent the loss of information.

Figure 15-9 shows a complete MACRO-11 program that reads in lines containing from one to eighty ASCII characters and then searches the text for the exact sequence of five characters "MACRO"; each time it finds the sequence, it outputs the following message:

> **Sequence found at position nnn**

where "nnn" is the character position on that line, beginning with $n = 1$. For example, if the current line of input is:

> **MAKAMACROQXYMACROZ**

the output would be:

> **Sequence found at position 5**
> **Sequence found at position 13**

The end of input is marked by a "!" character in column 1.

15.3
Interrupt-Driven Input/Output

15.3.1 Interrupt Processing
All of the I/O examples in the previous section used *idle loops,* which required us to simply wait and do nothing until the I/O operation was completed. This is a *very* inefficient way to perform I/O because of the potentially great difference between internal processing speed and the speed of I/O. For example, in the following sequence:

```
            BIS    #1,@#RCSR
    LOOP: BIT    #200,@#RCSR
            BEQ    LOOP
```

FIGURE 15-9   Complete MACRO-11 Program for Text
Processing.

```
            .Title   Search
            .MCALL .EXIT
Key:                    .Ascii    /MACRO/
KeyLen                  =         5
Message:                .Ascii    /Sequence found at position/
                        .Byte     0           ; The end of the message
                        .Even
ExpPt                   =         41          ; The exclamation point denotes
                                              ; the end of input
CR                      =         15          ; The carriage return denotes an
                                              ; end of line

LineLen                 =         80.         ; This is the maximum line length

Loop0:      CLR         R1                    ; R1 is the pointer through the
                                              ; search string
            CLR         R2                    ; R2 counts chars as they come
                                              ; in
            JSR         PC,InChar             ; Get the first character, put in R0
            CMPB        R0,#ExpPt             ; Is it the end of input?
            BEQ         Done                  ; Yes, Exit
            BNE         Check                 ; No, see if the first character
                                              ; is part of the key

Next:       INC         R2                    ; Add 1 to the number of chars
                                              ; on this line
            CMP         R2,#LineLen           ; Have we read the maximum
                                              ; number of characters?
            BGT         Loop0                 ; Go back and put next char on
                                              ; next line

            JSR         PC,InChar             ; Get this character
            CMPB        R0,#CR                ; Is this an end-of-line char?
            BEQ         Loop0                 ; Yes, put the next character on
                                              ; next line

Check:      CMPB        R0,Key(R1)            ; Does this character match the
                                              ; key
            BEQ         FoundC                ; Yes, we found one of the chars

            TST         R1                    ; No, did we check the first char
                                              ; of the key?
```

FIGURE 15-9   Complete MACRO-11 Program for Text
Processing. (*Continued*)

```
              BEQ   Next           ; Yes, check the next char in
                                   ; the input
              CLR   R1             ; No, but it still might match the
              BR    Check          ; first char in the key, so check

FoundC:       INC   R1             ; Move pointer to next char in key
              CMP   R1,#KeyLen     ; Have we found the whole key yet?
              BLO   Next           ; No, keep checking

              CLR   R3             ; Yes, print the message
MsgLp:        MOVB Message(R3),R0  ; Put one char of the message into
                                   ; R0
              BEQ   MsgDne         ; If we found the end of the
                                   ; message, we're done
              JSR   PC,OutChar     ; Print that character
              INC   R3             ; Move pointer to the next char in
                                   ; the message
              BR    MsgLp          ; Print the next character

MsgDne:       MOV   R2,R0          ; Subtract the length of the key
                                   ; less 2 from the position past the
              SUB   #KeyLen−2,R0   ; end of the key to
              JSR   PC,Out         ; find and print the position of
                                   ; the start of the key
              MOV   #CR,R0         ; Print a carriage return
              JSR   PC,OutChar
              BR    Next           ; Continue searching the strings

Done:         .EXIT

              .End  Loop0
```

each of the three MACRO-11 instructions—BIS, BIT, and BEQ—takes approximately 1 μsec (10^{-6} sec) to complete. However, if the terminal is a typical 30 characters/second input device, it will take 33 msec ($33 * 10^{-3}$ sec) for the character to arrive. We will go around the loop about 16,500 times, and 99.999 percent of our time will be spent waiting!

Interrupt processing, first described in Chapter 8, provides a way to overcome this problem. (You may wish to review the discussion on interrupt processing in Section 8.5 before reading on.) It allows us to initiate an I/O operation and then go off and do some other useful processing, which will be interrupted when the I/O operation is completed. In this way, the computer system does not need to sit in an idle loop, wasting valuable processing capability.

Associated with each I/O device on the PDP-11 is a special pair of words called an *interrupt vector*. These interrupt vectors are located in lower memory, typically at addresses 0–376$_8$. The first word of this pair contains the address of a special program called the *interrupt service routine,* which should be activated when input or output on that device has been completed. The second word of the pair contains the processor status word value that should be loaded into the PS register before executing the interrupt service routine. The PS register contains the N, Z, V, and C condition codes described earlier. It also contains, in bits 4–6, the *priority level* of the interrupt. There are eight priority levels, from 000 to 111. The following fragment shows the loading of the interrupt vector for the console terminal, which is located in words 60 and 62. The code fragment loads the address of a program called INTRTN into the first word and sets the priority level to 5 in the second word of the vector.

```
INTVECT =   060
  .
  .
  .

MOV     #INTRTN,@#INTVECT
MOV     #120,@#INTVECT+2   ; 120 = priority level 5
```

To take advantage of the interrupt facility, we must (1) load the interrupt vector, and (2) enable the interrupts via bit 6 of the appropriate status register. If bit 6 is off, the entire interrupt facility for that I/O device is disabled and none of the interrupt signals will be processed.

```
BIS   #100,@#RCSR ; Enable the interrupt system
```

Once these two steps have been followed, we can initiate an I/O operation and go off and do something useful while the interrupt system monitors the progress of the I/O operation.

```
BIS   #1,@#RCSR   ; Start the I/O operation
  .               ; Do other processing instead
  .               ; of waiting in an idle loop
  .
```

When the I/O operation is complete, the following sequence of events will occur automatically, if the interrupt is enabled.

1. The user's program is interrupted.
2. The current state of the machine (i.e., the PC and the PS registers) is saved.
3. The PS is loaded with the second word of the interrupt vector for that device.

4. The PC is loaded with the address of the interrupt service routine for that device.

5. The interrupt service routine is executed.

6. When the interrupt service routine is completed, the machine is restored to the state it was in before the interrupt (i.e., the PC and PS are reset).

7. Execution of the user's program is resumed exactly as if it had not been interrupted.

The interrupt service routine will perform operations that we had previously handled in our main program. For example, Figure 15-10 shows the identical output operation of Figure 15-8 handled via interrupt-driven I/O. The program sets a switch called LINE to 1 when all the characters are printed. Presumably, this switch will be checked somewhere in the main program.

The main program of Figure 15-10 initializes the interrupt vector and status register, initiates the first I/O operation, and then is free to continue with other processing. When that first character has been printed, the program will be interrupted and control will be passed to location INTRTN, the interrupt service routine. This routine processes the newly input character, and if there are more characters to be printed, begins the next output operation and returns to the user program. If all six characters have been transferred, no more I/O transfers are initiated, and variable LINE is set to 1, which is a signal to the main program that the entire message has been completed. The main program may check this flag at any time. It does *not* need to sit in an idle loop continually checking this variable.

Notice that the last line of the interrupt handler is a special MACRO-11 instruction called RTI (return from interrupt). All interrupt service routines must end with this instruction. The RTI will correctly restore the previous state of the system by reloading the PS and PC registers to their original contents. You cannot end an interrupt service routine by branching or jumping back to the main program. Figure 15-11 shows an interrupt-driven solution to the input example in Figure 15-5.

The PDP-11 has a *priority interrupt system* with eight levels of priority. (There are actually four levels of hardware priority and eight levels of software priority. We refer here to the software priorities only.) In a priority interrupt system, an interrupt service routine can interrupt only a program with a lower priority level than its own. If the processor is currently executing a program of higher priority (as indicated by bits 4–6 of the PS), then the interrupt routine must wait until the current program is completed (by an RTI, HALT, or .EXIT). An interrupt that is waiting to be executed is said to be *pending*.

We must assign priorities to our interrupt routines so that the most time-critical operations have the highest priority. Otherwise, they might remain in the pending state for an unacceptably long time. For example, suppose that we have two input operations going on, one from a 30-character-per-second terminal, and one from a high-speed terminal (2,400 characters/sec). With the former, we have 33 msec between characters and there is quite a bit of time before we encounter data overrun condition (i.e., a new character overwrites a previous character). But with the latter, we have only about 400 μsec between characters. If the interrupt service routine for

FIGURE 15-10   Interrupt-Driven Output.

```
             CR       =    15               ; Carriage return
             TTYVECT =     60               ; The interrupt vector
             TCSR     =    177564           ; The status register
             TBUF     =    177566           ; The transmit buffer
MESSAGE: .ASCII       /hello/               ; The message to be
                                            ; printed
             .BYTE        CR
             .EVEN
LINE:    .WORD         0                    ; A switch set to
                                            ; indicate we are done
                 .

                 .
                 .
             CLR          R0                ; R0 is the index into
                                            ; message
             MOV          #INTRTN,@#TTYVECT ; Set the interrupt
                                            ; routine address
             MOV          #120,@#TTYVECT+2  ; Set priority to 5
             BIS          #200,@#TCSR       ; Enable the interrupt
                                            ; system
             MOVB         MESSAGE(R0),@#TBUF ; Start an output
                                            ; operation
                 .
                 .      Go off and do other useful work until the output
                 .      operation has been completed. At that time, the
                 .      interrupt system will stop us and cause a branch
                 .      to INTRTN, the interrupt service routine. We know
                 .      that we are all done when the variable LINE = 1.

INTRTN:   BIT           #100000,@#TBUF      ; See if there was an
                                            ; error
          BNE           DOAGAIN             ; Yes, don't keep this
          INC           R0
          CMP           #6,R0               ; Are we all done?
          BEQ           SETLINE             ; Yes
DOAGAIN:MOVB            MESSAGE(R0),@#TBUF  ; Start the next out-
                                            ; put operation
          BR            DONE
SETLINE:  INC           LINE                ; LINE=1 indicates we
                                            ; are all done
DONE:     RTI                               ; Return from interrupt
```

FIGURE 15-11   Example of Interrupt-Driven Input.

```
                INTVECT = 60        ; The interrupt vector
                RCSR    = 177560    ; The status register
                RBUF    = 177562    ; The receive buffer
FINISHED:       .WORD    0
LINE:           .BLKB    80.
                  .
                  .
                  .

                CLR      R0                   ; R0 is the index
                                              ; into LINE
                MOV      #RDRINT, @ #INTVECT
                MOV      #160, @ #INTVECT + 2 ; Set priority to 7
                BIS      #101, @ #RCSR        ; Set device and
                                              ; interrupt enable

                  ·  Go off and do something useful until
                  ·  the variable called FINISHED is set
                  ·    to 1

RDRINT:         BIT      #100000, @ #RCSR ; Check for error
                BNE      NEWCH            ; If error, get new character
    ;
                CMPB     #177, @ #RBUF    ; See if it was a delete
                BNE      GOODCHAR         ; No, so keep the char
                TST      R0               ; Is there a character
                                          ; to delete
                BEQ      NEWCH            ; No
                DEC      R0               ; Yes, decrement R0
                JMP      NEWCH            ; and get next char
    ;
GOODCHAR:       MOVB     @ #RBUF,LINE(R0) ; Store this character
                CMPB     LINE(R0),#15     ; Was it a CR?
                BEQ      DONE             ; Yes, we are all done
                INC      R0
                CMP      R0,#80.          ; Have we read all 80
                                          ; characters?
                BGE      DONE             ; Yes, we are all done
    ;
NEWCH:          BIS      #1, @ #RCSR      ; Start next input
                RTI
    ;
DONE:           INC      FINISHED         ; Set FINISHED switch
                RTI
```

the high-speed terminal cannot get the processor and process the input within 400 μsec of the occurrence of the interrupt signal, another character will come in and overwrite the current one. Obviously the higher speed device should have a higher priority to try to eliminate this problem. (We have more to say about interrupt priorities in our discussion of traps in Section 18.4.)

15.3.2 Multibuffering

In Figures 15-10 and 15-11, we wrote the phrase "do some useful work" to indicate that a program should perform some meaningful processing during I/O rather than sit in an idle loop. What is the nature of "useful work" and how is it handled? One trivial possibility is not to do any useful work, and to simply wait for the interrupt signal. To do this, we could use a MACRO-11 instruction called WAIT. WAIT is a "no-operation" command that does nothing.

```
BIS     #101,@#RCSR  ; Set interrupt and device enable
WAIT                 ; Wait for interrupt signal
```

When the interrupt signal occurs, the WAIT instruction will terminate. We will execute the interrupt service routine and return to the instruction *following* the WAIT. The advantage of using a WAIT instead of an idle loop to "kill time" is that the WAIT does not use precious memory accesses to fetch instructions or data, and therefore will not interfere with the I/O controller as it fetches characters and stores them in memory. Obviously, I/O with interrupts and WAITs is no more efficient than idle loops.

Another possible and extremely useful piece of work that can be done in connection with an I/O operation is called *multibuffering,* that is, working on one buffer while the other one is being filled up. Then you switch, and work on the second buffer while the first one is filled. Diagrammatically:

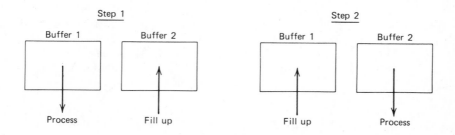

If the rate of processing a buffer is comparable to the rate of filling a buffer, our program will never have to wait after the first buffer has been filled. We will always have a full buffer's worth of information to process.

Figure 15-12 shows a program that uses multibuffering. There are two 80-char-

FIGURE 15-12   Example of a Multibuffering Program
Using Interrupts.

```
        .Title   Multibuffering
        .MCALL   .EXIT

;       InBuf points to the start of the buffer being filled.
;       R0 points into the buffer being filled.
;       OutBuf points to the start of the buffer being processed.
;       R1 points into the buffer being processed.

LineLen           =        80.      ; 80-character buffers
Filled:           .Word    0        ; Switch indicating if all buffers
                                    ; are filled
BufA:             .BlkB    LineLen  ; These are the two 80-
BufB:             .BlkB    LineLen  ; character buffers
                  .Even

InBuf:            .Word    0        ; These are pointers telling
OutBuf:           .Word    0        ; which buffer is being filled
                                    ; and processed

TTYIAdr           =        50       ; Interrupt vector handler address
TTYIpsw           =        52       ; Interrupt processor status word
RCSR              =        177560   ; Read status register
RBUF              =        177562   ; Read buffer
Start:  CLR   R0                    ; Move fill pointer to
                                    ; beginning of the buffer
        CLR   R1                    ; Move process pointer to beginning
                                    ; of the buffer
        CLR   R4                    ; Done flag
        MOV   #Int,@#TTYIAdr        ; Initialize interrupt vector
        MOV   #200,@#TTYIpsw        ; Set priority to 4 and clear all
                                    ; condition codes when interrupt
                                    ; occurs
        MOV   #BufA,InBuf           ; Get ready to fill up BufA
        MOV   #BufA,OutBuf          ; Get ready to process BufA when
                                    ; read is done
        CLR   Filled                ; All buffers aren't full

Loop1:  MOV   #101,@#RCSR           ; Interrupt enable + initial read
                                    ; request
Loop0:  CMP   InBuf,OutBuf          ; Are we trying to process the same
                                    ; buffer as the one we are filling?
        BEQ   Loop0                 ; Yes, wait until buffer is filled
```

FIGURE 15-12   Example of a Multibuffering Program
Using Interrupts. (*Continued*)

```
; Here we process the buffer pointed at by OutBuf. When
; ending the program is desired, R4 should be set to a
; nonzero value.

          TST    R4              ; Has all processing been
                                 ; completed?
          BNE    Fin             ; Yes, end the program

; Increment the buffer we are filling.

          CMP    #BufA,OutBuf    ; Have we just processed BufA?
          BNE    NotA            ; No, set process buffer to A
          MOV    #BufB,OutBuf    ; Yes, set process buffer to B
          BR     Ok

NotA:     MOV    #BufA,OutBuf    ; Process buffer B

Ok:       CLR    R1              ; Set pointer to beginning of
                                 ; process buffer
          TST    Filled          ; Are all buffers full?
          BEQ    Loop0           ; No, process the next buffer

          CLR    Filled          ; Yes, clear filled up and issue a
          BR     Loop1           ; command to fill the buffer I have
                                 ; just completed processing

Fin:      .EXIT

InBufR0:         .Word   0       ; This temporary is used to compute
                                 ; the correct position for the byte
                                 ; in the buffer

; This is the interrupt routine that is executed as each
; character is read from the input device.

Int:      MOV    InBuf,InBufR0      ; Calculate the address of InBuf
          ADD    R0,InBufR0         ; offset by R0
          MOVB   @#RBuf,@InBufR0    ; Move the char into the buffer
          INC    R0                 ; Increment the pointer into the
                                    ; buffer
          CMP    R0,#LineLen        ; Have we finished filling this
                                    ; buffer?
          BLT    IntOk              ; No, return from this interrupt
```

FIGURE 15-12   Example of a Multibuffering Program
Using Interrupts. (*Continued*)

```
              CMP    #BufA,InBuf      ; Have we just filled BufA?
              BNE    IntSetA          ; No, set fill buffer to A
              MOV    #BufB,InBuf      ; Yes, set fill buffer to B
              BR     IntCheck         ; Branch always
IntSetA:      MOV    #BufA,InBuf      ; Set fill buffer to A
IntCheck:
              CLR    R0               ; Set pointer to beginning of fill
                                      ; buffer
              CMP    InBuf,OutBuf     ; Have we filled up both buffers?
              BEQ    IntAllFilled     ; Yes, don't start filling the next
                                      ; buffer!
IntOk:        MOV    #101,@#RCSR      ; Start filling the next buffer
              RTI                     ; Return from interrupt
IntAllFilled:
              MOV    #1,Filled        ; Set filled flag
              RTI                     ; Return from interrupt
              .End Start
```

acter buffers, called BufA and BufB, which are alternately filled and processed. The interrupt routine, INT, fills up one buffer and then begins working on the other. Register R0 contains the address of the buffer currently being filled, and R1 contains the address of the buffer currently being processed. The program will WAIT only when there is no buffer to process (i.e., the processing has caught up to the input) or when we cannot begin filling the other buffer because processing is not complete (i.e., input has caught up to processing).

The overlapping of processing and I/O could allow our program to be speeded up by a factor of 2. Instead of the sequential approach taken in earlier sections:

$$\text{Input} \, . \, \text{Process} \, . \, \text{Input} \, . \, \text{Process} \, . \, . \, . \, .$$

we now overlap operations:

$$\begin{array}{l}
\text{Input} \, . \, \text{Process} \, . \\
\qquad \text{Input} \quad . \, \text{Process} \, . \\
\qquad \qquad . \, \text{Input} \quad .
\end{array}$$

. . . .

This is consistent with the philosophy described in Chapter 9: if you can't do something twice as fast, do two things at once! Exercise 13 asks you to generalize the two buffer schemes shown in Figure 15-12 to a program that works for any arbitrary number, N, $N \geq 2$, of buffers.

15.4
Block Transfer Devices

One of the problems with the interrupt technique discussed in Section 15.3 is that an interrupt will be generated upon the transfer of *every* character. This is fine for slow- or medium-speed devices, but for high-speed transfers the characters may be coming in so fast that the processor will be interrupted constantly and will have little or no time to spend on processing user programs. Figure 15-13 shows typical transfer rates for some well-known high-speed storage devices.

At the rate of 50,000 bytes/sec, there will be an interrupt generated every 20 μsec. Even if the interrupt service routine were only four or five instructions long, it would take on the order of 10 μsec to complete, and the processor would be spending at least half of its time servicing interrupts. Obviously, having a separate interrupt for each character is an extremely inefficient approach. What is needed for these higher speed devices was discussed in Chapter 8: an I/O controller that can store characters directly into memory and issue an interrupt only when the *entire* physical record has been transmitted. Such an I/O controller is called a *direct memory access channel (DMA)* and is diagrammed in Figure 8-11.

The operation of a DMA channel on the PDP-11 is extremely complex, and we cannot describe the exact workings of DMA-based I/O as we did character-oriented I/O. (As an example of this complexity, the DMA controller for the RM02 disk drive for the PDP-11 includes 22 separate registers, and the technical description runs to 40 pages.) If you will be writing MACRO-11 programs to control DMA-type devices, refer to the document entitled "Peripherals and Interfacing Handbook." This reference contains a detailed description of the various I/O registers, the interpretation of each bit in these registers, and the mechanical characteristics of the device. In this section, we give only a general idea of how to program DMA devices.

On the PDP-11 DMA controllers, there are numerous registers typically 10-20, but three of them are especially critical to the operation and programming of DMA-type devices.

1.   *Control and status register (CSR):* The CSR serves much the same general role as the status register in character-oriented transfers, namely, to initiate the I/O

FIGURE 15-13   Typical Transfer Rates.

Device	Transfer Rate (bytes/sec)
9-channel magnetic tape	10,000–100,000
5¼-in. Winchester disk	500,000
5¼-in. floppy diskette	50,000

transfer and describe the status of the current I/O operation. The general layout of a CSR is shown below:

E	...	R	IE	...	F	G	Control and status register

  15   7   6   3   1 0 ← Bit position

where: G Sometimes called the Go bit. Initiates the I/O function described in bits 1–3. When set to a 1, begins the specified operation.

      F Function code. Describes exactly which function the hardware should perform (e.g., move read/write arm, locate a sector address, read a sector). The use of three bits for the function code allows up to eight unique operations for each I/O device.

   IE Interrupt enable bit.

    R Ready bit. When set (by the system) to a 1, indicates that the function described in bits 1–3 has been completed.

    E Error bit.

The layout of the CSR is generally the same as that of the receive status register shown in Figure 15-2, with the addition of a 3-bit *function code*. Typically, the more complex higher speed I/O devices are capable of performing a number of different operations. The function code is used to select and specify exactly what operation we want to perform. Here are eight typical function codes from an RK-11 disk drive:

000	Control Reset
001	Write a Sector
010	Read a Sector
011	Write Check
100	Seek
101	Read Check
110	Drive Reset
111	Write Lock

By setting bits 1–3 to the appropriate octal code, we can select any of these eight operations.

To perform the I/O operation, we must do the following.

    a. Set the function code (bits 1–3) to the proper bit configuration for the desired operation.

    b. Set the interrupt enable bit (bit 6) to 1.

    c. Set the Go bit (bit 0) to 1 to begin the I/O operation specified in bits 1–3.

    d. Wait for the READY bit (bit 7) to come on and the interrupt to occur. (This assumes that you have properly loaded the correct values into the interrupt vector.)

    e. In the interrupt routine, process the information and check the error bit

(bit 15) to see whether any errors were encountered during the I/O transfer.

If the function code selected in bits 1–3 was an actual data transfer (as opposed to a mechanical operation like starting up a tape or seeking a sector address), then two additional registers will be needed.

2. *Word count register (WC):* This register is loaded with the 16-bit value representing the negative of the physical record size in words for this I/O device. The register will be incremented by 1 as each word is transferred, and the I/O operation will terminate either when the word count register reaches 0 or when the physical end of the block is reached. Most DMA devices transfer 16-bit word quantities rather than 8-bit bytes to increase speed and throughput. In our examples in this chapter, we always assume *word-oriented* DMA controllers that transfer 16-bit units of information.

3. *Buffer address register (BA):* This register contains the starting memory address of the buffer that will hold the data being transferred. The buffer must begin on a word boundary and be at least as large as the word count value loaded into the WC. As each word is transferred, it is automatically stored into the memory address contained in BA, and BA is incremented by 2.

FIGURE 15-14   General Operation of DMA Input.

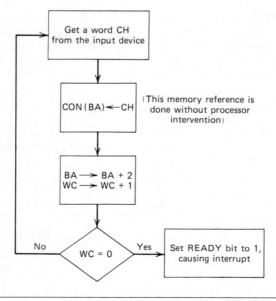

The CSR, WC, and BA registers are the three crucial registers in the operation of a DMA device. To initiate a DMA data transfer, we must load both the WC and the BA with the proper values *before* we perform the five steps (a–e) listed above.

a. $WC \leftarrow -(N)$
b. $BA \leftarrow$ address of an N-word buffer
c. Initiate the DMA data transfer

Now the transfer will take place under the control of the DMA controller and without interruption to the processor. The general sequence of operations carried out by the DMA controller is summarized in the flowchart in Figure 15-14. The flowchart summarizes the behavior of an input operation. The steps for output are similar.

The program fragment in Figure 15-15 shows how DMA input is typically coded in MACRO-11. It shows the input of an 80-column punched card using DMA techniques. The program transfers forty words (eighty characters) from the card reader to memory. When the entire card has been read, an interrupt occurs. The program is interrupted and control transfers to the location labeled INT. At that point the eighty characters on the card will have been stored in memory locations CARDBUF to CARDBUF+79.

FIGURE 15-15   MACRO-11 Code for DMA Card
Reader Input.

```
            CDIV  =    230       ; The interrupt vector address
            CDBA  =    177164     ; The buffer address register
            CDWC=     177162      ; The word count register
            CDST  =    177160     ; The status register
CARDBUF:    .BLKB     80.         ; The input buffer
            .
            .
            .

            MOV     #INT,@#CDIV      ; Load the address of the
                                     ; interrupt routine
            CLR     @#CDIV+2         ; Set interrupt priority to 0
            MOV     #-40.,@#CDWC     ; Set word count to 40,
                                     ; which is 80 bytes
            MOV     #CARDBUF,@#CDBA  ; Set buffer address
            MOV     #101,@#CDST      ; Start reading. Function
            WAIT                     ; code for read is 000.
            .
            .
            .
INT:                                 ;Arrive here when entire card has been read
```

We must emphasize that our discussion has been quite general and is insufficient for writing actual programs. You will need additional detailed information on other DMA registers, function codes, and the mechanical characteristics of these high-speed devices. This information is available from the handbook mentioned earlier.

15.5
Debugging in MACRO-11

An introductory programming class using a high-level language should stress that output statements are useful not only for printing final answers, but also for printing out intermediate results, status information, and data values that can help in the process of debugging. The same is true in MACRO-11. The proper use of output is critical for locating and debugging errors in your assembly-language program. Debugging MACRO-11 or, indeed, any assembly language is especially difficult because many types of error are not detected by either the compiler or the run-time support environment. Instead, these errors lead to strange or anomalous behavior. For example, if you wrote the following sequence in Pascal:

> **var**   x :   **array (1 . . 10) of** integer;
> .
> .
> .
> **for   i: = 1 to 11 do** x(i) := 0;

you would get either a syntax error from the compiler or a run-time error message that says:

> ·· **Array bounds exceeded. Program terminated.** ··

and your job of debugging would be relatively easy. However, if you made the same type of mistake in MACRO-11:

```
        X:    .BLKB   10.
        START: CLR    R0
        LOOP:  CMP    R0,#11. ; This is an error
               BGE    DONE ; We should check if R0 = 10
               CLR    X(R0)
               INC    R0
               BR     LOOP
        DONE:
```

the error would not be detected at run time. The code would simply clear the 10-byte array X *and* the byte immediately following the array (X the clear instruction labeled START.) If you ever tried to reexecute this sequence by performing a JMP

START, the program would halt, because the instruction 000000, which is what was improperly stored in this location, corresponds to a HALT instruction. Looking only at the listing above, you would be totally baffled when the program halted at address START. The run-time support provided for error detection is yet another example of the advantages of programming in a high-level language.

Since the hardware provides no support for us, we must provide our own. To assist us in this type of debugging, we will need a good deal of supporting output, and two kinds are particularly helpful—*traces* and *memory dumps*. A trace is a snapshot of the state of the machine at any instant in time. Naturally, the exact contents of a trace depends on exactly what you are doing in your program, but it usually includes the contents of the eight general-purpose registers and the processor status word.

Figure 15-16 shows part of the code for a trace that prints out the values in R0–R2 and PS along with some identifying output. The code sequence uses the routine called OUT, which appears in Appendix E. The code would be much more efficient if we had written it using a subroutine to print out the contents of a single register,

FIGURE 15-16   Sample Trace Program.

```
M1:     .ASCII    /R0 = /
M2:     .ASCII    /R1 = /
M3:     .ASCII    /R2 = /
M4:     .ASCII    /PS = /
        .EVEN
          .
          .
          .
        CLR       R3                   ; R3 is the index into M1
NEXT:   MOVB      M1(R3),@#OUTBUF      ; Load the next character
LOOP:   BIT       #200,@#OUTSCR        ; Wait until it's printed
        BEQ       LOOP
        INC       R3
        CMP       R3,#5                ; Have we printed the 5-
                                       ; character header?
        BLT       NEXT                 ; No, so print next char
        JSR       PC,OUT               ; Now print the contents of
                                       ; register R0
          .
          .        Repeat the 8 lines above for registers
          .        R1, R2, and PS and then generate a
          .        carriage return and line feed.
          .        The only difference is that you will first need to move the
                   values in R1, R2, and PC into R0 before printing them.
```

passed as a parameter. Then we could call it once for each register we want traced instead of repeating the code. We learn how to do this in the next chapter.

Now whenever we want to see what is happening in our program, we can trace the activity by inserting the above code directly into our program or, better yet, making the code in Figure 15-16 a subroutine and calling it whenever we need to. We will now get the following output.

```
RO = nnnnnn    R1 = nnnnnn    R2 = nnnnnn    PS = nnnnnn
RO = nnnnnn    R1 = nnnnnn    R2 = nnnnnn    PS = nnnnnn
```

Comparing the values printed with what was expected will help lead you to the source of the error.

Another useful type of debugging output is called a *memory dump*. This is simply the contents of all memory locations from address A to address B, where $0 \leq A < B \leq$ largest memory address. This information can be useful for checking the current values of various data items as well as ensuring that the instructions in the program have not been corrupted and changed. The dump is either byte or word oriented and may be presented in any one of numerous formats. Figure 15-17 shows a program fragment to dump the contents of all memory addresses from the location called FIRST to the location called LAST, where LAST $\geq$ FIRST. The dump will ·first print the address of an 8-word memory block to be dumped, followed by the contents of those eight addresses. It will keep dumping 8-word memory blocks until it reaches the address called LAST. The program uses the routines OUT and OUT-CHAR listed in Appendix E.

Now whenever we wish to dump all or part of the contents of memory, we merely load the variables FIRST and LAST with the starting and ending address of the dump, respectively, and then insert the code from Figure 15-17 into our program. Better yet, we can make the code a subroutine and simply call it whenever we need to.

On many versions of MACRO-11, the debugging capabilities are provided as *system macros* in a system macro library. When we introduce macros in Chapter 17, we describe these debugging services and how they can be activated.

However, regardless of whether you must write these routines yourself, or whether they are provided for you by the system, it is important to produce adequate debugging output to assist you in correcting your assembly-language program. Debugging output typically includes the contents of key registers and selected memory locations. You must carefully compare, instruction by instruction, the expected results with the actual values printed by the trace or dump. This slow and tedious process is the only sure-fire way to debug in assembly language because of the extreme freedom to access and modify both instructions and data.

Some PDP-11 and VAX-11 systems provide a sophisticated programming support tool called an ODT—*on-line debugging tool*—for use in debugging MACRO-11 programs. An ODT is almost a miniature operating system that controls the execution

FIGURE 15-17   Sample Memory Dump Program.

```
LF              =       12    ; This is a line feed
CR              =       15    ; This is a carriage return
Colon           =       72    ; This is a colon
Space           =       40    ; This is a space
Count:          .Word   0
First:          .Word   0     ; Address of the first location to print out.
                              ; This must be filled in before you execute
                              ; Dump
Last:           .Word   0     ; Address of the last location to print out
                              ; This must be filled in before you execute
                              ; Dump

                .
                .
                .


Dump:   MOV     First,R0      ; Print the starting address
        JSR     PC,Out
        MOV     #Colon,R0     ; Print a colon
        JSR     PC,OutChar
        CLR     Count

Dloop1: CMP     First,Last    ; Are we done yet?
        BGT     DDone         ; Yes, Exit
        MOV     #Space,R0     ; Print a space
        JSR     PC,OutChar
        MOV     @First,R0     ; Get a word to dump
        JSR     PC,Out        ; Print it
        INC     First         ; Point to the next word
        INC     First
        INC     Count
        CMP     Count,#8.     ; Have we printed 8 words on this line?
        BNE     Dloop1        ; No, get the next word

        MOV     #CR,R0        ; Print a carriage return
        JSR     PC,OutChar
        MOV     #LF,R0        ; Print a line feed
        JSR     PC,OutChar
        BR      Dump          ; Do another line

DDone:  MOV     #CR,R0        ; Print another return
        JSR     PC,OutChar
                .
                .
                .
```

of your program and allows it to be run in what is called *debug mode*. In debug mode, you can examine memory and registers, single step through your program, and set *breakpoints*—interruption points in your program where control will return to the ODT. If your installation has an ODT, learn how to use it. It can be very helpful and may save you hours of frustration.

Exercises for Chapter 15

1. Explain what is wrong with the following code segment:

```
OVER:  BIT    #200,@#RCSR   ; Test the DONE bit
       BEQ    OVER          ; Not DONE
       BIC    #200,@#RCSR   ; DONE. Now clear the DONE bit
```

2. Assume that a BIT and BEQ instruction each takes 1.2 μsec to execute, and that you are transferring characters at the rate of 9,600 bits per second (8 bits/character). Exactly how many times will you go around the following idle loop waiting for the DONE bit to go on?

```
LOOP:  BIT    #200,@#RCSR
       BEQ    LOOP
```

3. Write a MACRO-11 fragment that reads a line of up to eighty characters from a character-oriented input device and echoes them back according to the following rules.
   a. Lowercase characters are echoed as uppercase characters.
   b. All nonprinting characters (0–37, 177) are echoed as a '?'
   c. The '<' character is not printed.
   Read a line until you have read eighty characters or encountered a carriage return, and echo print the characters according to the above rules.

4. Write a MACRO-11 program fragment that reads in lines from a character-oriented input device. The lines are composed of exactly eighty ASCII characters. The fragment should input a line and store the characters in EBCDIC code in a memory buffer called NEWCODE, defined as:

```
NEWCODE:   .BLKB   80.
```

Assume (for simplicity's sake) that the only characters that are input are the capital letters A to Z and the digits 0 to 9.

5a.   Assume that you have an input buffer called LINE, which contains a base-10 integer value stored as a sequence of ASCII characters. The syntax of the integer value is:

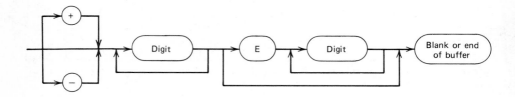

The letter E stands for "times 10 to the power of". The exponent value can only be positive to insure that the number was an integer. Assuming that the character string in the buffer is syntactically valid, and that the resulting integer will fit in a single 16-bit memory location, write a MACRO-11 program that converts the character string in LINE to a single twos-complement integer value.

5b.   Perform the same operation, but assume that there is a possibility for overflow. If the resulting integer will not fit in sixteen bits, set a flag called OVERFLOW to 1 and set the integer value being evaluated to 0.

6.   Generalize the integer conversion problem in Exercise 5 so that it will work for any base. Assume that you have a location called BASE, defined as:

BASE: .WORD 0

The *contents* of BASE are an integer value ≥ 2. This value is the base of the number that is stored in LINE. Convert the character string in LINE into an integer value assuming that the digits are in the given base. For example, if the contents of BASE were 5, and LINE contained the following character string:

'+'	'1'	'2'	'3'	'b'

then your program should produce the integer value 38_{10}, which is 123_5. If, instead, BASE contained a 9, your program should produce the value 102_{10}, which is 123_9. If you encounter a digit that is illegal for a given base, such as a '6' in a base 5 number, set an ERRORFLAG to 1.

7.   What is incorrect about the following procedure for outputting two characters located in locations L1 and L2?

```
MOVB   L1,@#TBUF   ; TBUF is the transmit buffer
MOVB   L2,@#TBUF   ; Now print the second character
```

8.   Rewrite the program in Figure 15-8 so that you only reprint a character three times. If it is not printed correctly after three attempts, set an ERRORFLAG to 1 and stop the program.

9a.   Assume that you have a signed twos-complement integer value stored in a memory location called I:

I: .WORD   0   ; Contains a signed integer

Write a MACRO-11 fragment that converts the integer value stored in I to a character string and prints the character string on a typical character-oriented output device. The syntax of the character string to be produced is:

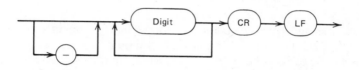

If the number is positive, do not proceed it with a '+' character. After all of the digits have been printed, print a carriage return and a line feed character.

9b.   Assume that you have a 1-byte memory location called BOOLEAN that contains either a 0 or a 1. Write a MACRO-11 fragment that writes out the characters 'FALSE' if the contents of boolean are a 0, and 'TRUE' if the contents are a 1. If the value is anything else, set ERRORFLAG to a 1 and don't write out anything.

10.   Write the commands to load an interrupt vector at locations 40 and 42 with the following values:
   a.   The interrupt service routine is called ISROUT.
   b.   The priority of the interrupt routine is 1.

11.   Given the interrupt vector values in Exercise 10, describe exactly what would happen if an interrupt signal corresponding to that interrupt vector occurred between the execution of the following two instructions in your program:

```
INC   R0
                ← Interrupt occurs here
MOV   R0,R1
```

12.   Which of the following conditions do you think should be given the *highest* priority as it relates to interrupt processing? Which should be given the *lowest*?
   a.   power failure.
   b.   a real-time clock.
   c.   a character has been read and is in the receive buffer.

13. Generalize the 2-buffer scheme shown in Figure 15-12 to an arbitrary multi-buffering program for N buffers, N ≥ 2. Assume that the buffers are "circular" in the sense that after buffer (N − 1), you start again with buffer 0.

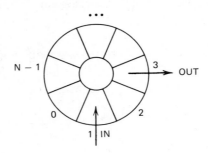

Your program should have two pointers: IN, the buffer number you are currently filing, and OUT, the buffer number you are currently processing. Your program will have to handle the two special cases of IN catching up to OUT (all buffers are full), or OUT catching up to IN (all buffers are empty). This type of multibuffering scheme is called *circular buffers*.

14. In a number of examples in this chapter, we used the idea of an "error handler"—a program which is activated if the ERROR bit is on following an I/O operation. Discuss what kinds of error recovery are possible and what "error handler" could do for each of the following I/O errors.
- a. A parity error on input.
- b. Paper jam on a printer.
- c. Device not turned ON.
- d. Data overrun on a disk unit.

15. Assume that you have an RK-11 disk drive with 256 (decimal) byte sectors. Show how you would load the WC, BA, and CSR registers to read one sector from the disk into memory locations SECT to SECT + 255, using a DMA channel. Assume that the seek operation has already been performed and you are positioned on the correct track. (The "Read Sector" function code is 010_2.)

16. Write the interrupt routine INT referred to in Figure 15-15. The interrupt routine should do one thing: go through the input buffer and determine whether the card just read had any information on it. That is, was it just eighty blanks? If a nonblank character is located anywhere on the card, then set the variable NONBLANK to 1; otherwise, set NONBLANK to 0. In either case, after performing that operation, return from the interrupt.

17. Find out about the availability of an on-line debugging package on your own system, and do a report for presentation about the types of operations that are possible. Discuss how these operations can help eliminate some of the assembly-language debugging problems discussed in Section 15.5.

CHAPTER 16

SUBROUTINES

16.1
Introduction

In this chapter we begin to investigate how the PDP-11 and MACRO-11 implement *subprograms,* or subroutines, as they are referred to in MACRO-11. You should already be very familiar, from introductory or advanced programming courses, with the important contributions of subroutines to program development, and you should be aware of the advantages of techniques like modularization, stepwise refinement, abstraction, and unit testing. The same advantages are useful for assembly-language, and the subroutine is an important programming tool in MACRO-11. It is assumed that you are familiar with these software design issues and we concentrate only on how subroutines are implemented in MACRO-11.

The subroutine facility in MACRO-11 makes extensive use of the *system stack,* and to understand subroutines fully you must be completely familiar with the stack data structure and the push and pop operations introduced in Section 9.2.5. You may wish to review that section before proceeding.

16.2
Stacks

The system stack is a built-in data structure provided for you by the PDP-11 hardware. It is used by the system in a number of ways, including subroutine linkage, parameter passing, and interrupt processing. You may also use the system stack for your own purposes as long as you are careful not to rearrange or destroy information placed there by the system. Altering the information on the stack will almost invariably lead to a fatal error.

The TOP pointer into the system stack is general register R6. (R6 is also abbreviated SP, for stack pointer, and that is the notation we use in this chapter.) The SP register always points to the top item currently on the stack. If the stack is empty, SP contains the address of the word immediately "below" the stack, that is, the next higher address. (See Figure 16-1a.)

The stack itself is located in main memory, the exact location depending on which operating system you are using. For example, the operating system called RT-11 uses memory locations 400–1000 (octal) for the system stack. Other operating systems utilize different locations. Regardless of the actual physical addresses used, the proper initial address will be automatically loaded into SP before your program is executed. Therefore, when your program begins execution, SP will correctly point to the location of the stack on your system. This operation is performed for you by the operating system of the computer. On a "naked computer" (one without an operating system), you must allocate space for the system stack and initialize SP yourself.

On the PDP-11, the system stack grows *downward*. That is, as new items are placed on the stack, they are loaded into lower numbered addresses. As items are removed, the address of the top item on the stack gets larger. Figure 16-1 illustrates the operation of the PDP-11 system stack (assuming the stack begins at octal location 1000).

The system stack is *word oriented,* and only 16-bit quantities can be stored in it. An attempt to store an 8-bit byte in the stack will result in an error. The SP must always be incremented or decremented in steps of 2, corresponding to a word-oriented value.

Although there is only one system stack, MACRO-11 programmers can set up other stacks for their own purposes. To create your own "private stack" you must:

1. Allocate a register to be the stack pointer (not SP or PC!).

2. Allocate space for the stack in main memory.

3. Initialize the stack pointer register to the value A + 2, where A is the highest address in the memory space allocated for the stack.

FIGURE 16-1   The PDP-11 System Stack: (a) Initial State (b) After Storing Three Items (c) After Removing Two Items.

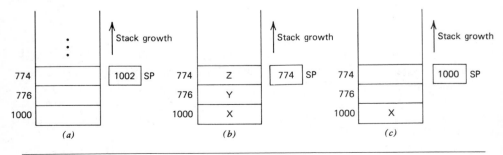

FIGURE 16-2 Setting up a Private Stack Using Register 5.

```
        STACKSIZE   = 200.        ; The stack will be 200 words
STACK:  .BLKW         STACKSIZE   ; Here is the stack
        ENDOFSTACK = ·            ; This address is the end of
                ·                 ; the stack
                ·
                ·
        MOV         #ENDOFSTACK,R5   ; Initialize TOP to the
                                     ; end of stack
```

You will then be in the same situation shown in Figure 16-1a, except that you will be using one of the general-purpose registers, R0, . . . , R5, instead of SP. The code in Figure 16-2 shows one way to set up such a private stack using register R5 as the TOP pointer.

To add items to a stack (i.e., to perform a push operation) we must do the following.

Push(X) 1. Decrement the stack pointer register by 2.
         2. Store the item, X, at the location currently pointed at by the stack pointer register.

Reexamining the addressing mode called autodecrement discussed in Section 11.2.5, we note that these two steps correspond exactly to the process of computing the effective address in autodecrement mode. Thus, on the PDP-11, a push operation is always accomplished by means of autodecrement mode on the stack pointer:

Push(X) on the system stack: MOV X, −(SP)
Push(Y) onto my private stack: MOV Y, −(R5)

The first example indicates that SP will be decremented by 2 (since MOV is a word operation), and then the contents of X will be stored at the address pointed at by SP, that is, the top of the stack.

To remove items from the stack (i.e., to perform a pop operation) we must do the following.

Pop(Y) 1. Remove the top item from the stack and store it in memory location Y.
        2. Increment the stack pointer by 2.

This is identical to computing the effective address for autoincrement mode, introduced in Section 11.2.3. Thus, on the PDP-11, a pop operation is always accomplished with autoincrement addressing on the stack pointer.

Pop(Q) off the system stack: MOV   (SP),Q
Pop(R) off my private stack: MOV   (R5),R

Looking at the first example, you can see that the value pointed at by SP, the top of the stack, will be stored in the location designated by Q. Then SP will be incremented by 2 (since MOV is a word operation), effectively removing that item from the stack. (The item is not actually discarded, and it still remains in its original memory location. However, it cannot be accessed because the register SP no longer points to it. Since it is inaccessible, we may think of it as having been "removed" from the stack.)

There are two error conditions associated with stacks: *stack overflow* and *stack underflow*. *Stack overflow* occurs if you attempt to add items to the stack when there is no more room. For example, under the RT-11 operating system, the system stack will occupy locations 400–1000, as shown in Figure 16-3.

If the stack is full and you execute a push operation:

MOV   DATA,−(SP)

you will begin to wipe out the interrupt vectors in memory locations 0–376. Similarly, *stack underflow* occurs if you try to remove an item from an empty stack. Referring to Figure 16-3, you can see that if the stack is empty and you execute a pop operation:

MOV   (SP)+,LOC

you will begin to store your own program!

In both cases, most (but not all) of PDP-11 operating systems (e.g., RT-11, RSTS, RSX-11) treat these two conditions as fatal errors and terminate the execution of your program with an appropriate error message. Some operating systems check for stack overflow but not underflow. In any case, however, this error-checking service

FIGURE 16-3   Layout of Low Core in RT-11.

interrupt vectors	0
	376
	400
system stack	
	1000
	1002
user program	⋮

applies only to the system stack, not to any private stack that you have set up. For these private stacks, you must perform your own overflow and underflow checking and write your own error-handling routine. In the next section we write such a routine.

16.3
Subroutine Linkage

As with a high-level language, we need special instructions to handle the linkage between a calling program and a subroutine. We cannot use a simple unconditional branch (e.g., goto, JMP) to get to a subroutine because that will not save the return address within the calling program, specifying where we should return. Similarly, we need a special command to return us to the proper location, namely, the return address saved when the subroutine was activated.

In MACRO-11, these two functions are performed by the two operations called JSR (Jump to Subroutine) and RTS (Return from Subroutine). The syntax of these two instructions is:

       JSR   link register,address of subroutine
       RTS   link register

where "link register" is any one of the eight general-purpose registers except SP. The link register used in the address field of the RTS instruction must be the same one that was used in the JSR instruction in the initial branch to the subroutine.

The simplest case, and the one we describe first, uses the program counter, PC, as the link register. When you execute the following instruction:

       JSR   PC,SUB

two things happen.

1. The current contents of the PC are pushed on top of the system stack: Push(PC).
2. The address SUB (which should be the address of the first instruction of the subroutine) is loaded into the program counter: PC ← SUB.

After fetching the JSR instruction above, the PC will be pointing to the next word in memory. Putting this value on top of the stack is, in effect, saving the return address. Then loading the address SUB into PC will cause the actual branch to the subroutine. Thus, the JSR command handles both aspects of subroutine linkage—jumping to the subroutine, and saving the location to which we must return. Figure 16-4 shows the condition of the system stack before and after the execution of the above JSR command assuming the JSR instruction is in location 1100, and the subroutine SUB begins in location 1500.

Within a MACRO-11 subroutine you may use *any* instruction that we have dis-

FIGURE 16-4   Example of Subroutine Linkage in
MACRO-11: (a) Before executing the JSR (b) After
executing the JSR

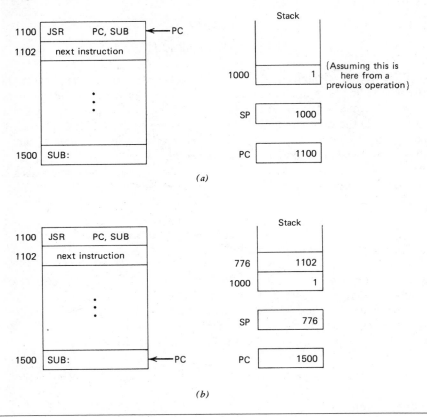

(a)

(b)

cussed so far, including another JSR. Nested subroutine calls are perfectly acceptable. At the end of each subroutine we use the statement:

RTS PC

to return. The RTS command pops the top item off the system stack and puts it into
PC. Since the top item will be the return address stored by the JSR (as long as you
have not put anything else on top), the return address will go into the program
counter, and it will be the next statement executed. The return linkage will be
completed.

Figure 16-5 shows MACRO-11 subroutines for push and pop operations that
check for stack overflow and underflow. These routines assume that the stack occu-

FIGURE 16-5 Subroutines for Push and Pop Operations
with Error Checking.

```
       PUSH:    CMP   SP,#MEMLOW      ; See if we are at the top
                                      ; of the stack
                BEQ   OVERFLOW        ; Yes, this is an overflow
                CLR   ERRFLAG         ; Clear the error flag
                MOV   R0,-(SP)        ; Push the item on the stack
                RTS   PC              ; and return
   OVERFLOW:    INC   ERRFLAG         ; Set the error flag
                RTS   PC              ; and return

        POP:    CMP   SP,#MEMHIGH+2   ; See if we are at the
                                      ; bottom of the stack
                BEQ   UNDERFLOW       ; Yes, this is an underflow
                CLR   ERRFLAG         ; Clear the error flag
                MOV   (SP)+,(R0)      ; Pop this item off the stack
                RTS   PC              ; and return
  UNDERFLOW:    INC   ERRFLAG         ; Set the error flag
                RTS   PC              ; and return
```

pies memory addresses MEMLOW to MEMHIGH, and that the value to be pushed onto the stack, or the address in which to store the top item, is in register R0. The program counter, PC, is used as the link register.

To use these two subroutines, we simply call them with the JSR operation code. Of course, we must first perform any operations needed by the subroutine, such as loading R0 and defining MEMLOW, MEMHIGH, and ERRFLAG. The following fragment shows an example of the usage of these two subroutines.

```
              MEMLOW  = 400      ; Stack runs from 400
              MEMHIGH = 1000     ; to 1000 octal
  ERRFLAG:    .WORD     0        ; Error information goes here
        X:    .WORD     0
                        .
                        .
                        .
              MOV       X,R0     ; Value to be pushed is in R0
              JSR       PC,PUSH  ; This does the push
              TST       ERRFLAG  ; See if we had overflow
              BNE       ERROR    ; Yes, go to the error routine
                        .
                        .
                        .
```

```
MOV        #X,R0      ; Address of where to store the
                      ; top item is put in R0
JSR        PC,POP     ; This does the pop
TST        ERRFLAG    ; See if we had underflow
BNE        ERROR      ; Yes, go to the error routine
```

Notice that when we used the push operation we loaded the *contents* of X into R0, because the push subroutine uses register mode addressing to refer to R0 (line 4 of the push routine). However, we loaded the *address* of X into R0 when using the pop operation because pop uses register deferred addressing (line 4 of the pop routine), and it expects to see an address in R0. This is just one more example of the importance of remembering the distinction between an address and its contents. Also notice that we used the labels PUSH and POP in our JSR command. This is because these labels were attached to the first instruction in the subroutine, and that is where execution of the subroutines should begin.

We can now generalize our use of the PC as the link register and show what happens when you use any of the other general-purpose registers (R0, ... , R5) for linkage. When you execute:

$$\text{JSR} \quad \text{Rn,SUB} \quad n = 0, 1, \dots , 5$$

three things happen.

1. The current contents of Rn are pushed on top of the system stack: Push(Rn).

2. The current contents of the program counter are stored in Rn: R$n \leftarrow$ PC.

3. The address of the subroutine is stored in the program counter: PC $\leftarrow$ SUB.

As a result of all this, Rn (not PC) now points to the return address. As we see in the next section, the block of memory immediately after the JSR command frequently is used for holding the parameters of the subroutine. Thus, the register Rn can be used to fetch these parameters without having to access and change the value on top of the system stack. Figure 16-6 shows the situation just before and after executing a JSR R0,SUB.

To return from a subroutine called in this way, we must write:

$$\text{RTS} \quad \text{R}n$$

where Rn is the same general-purpose register used in the JSR command. The effect of this RTS is as follows.

1. The current contents of Rn are copied into the program counter: PC $\leftarrow$ CON(Rn).

2. The top of the stack is put into Rn: Pop(Rn).

Thus, Rn is left unchanged by the overall operation, since its value is saved on top of the stack by the JSR and restored from the top of the stack by the RTS.

FIGURE 16-6   Using General-Purpose Registers for
Linkage: (a) Before execution of the JSR (b) After
execution of the JSR

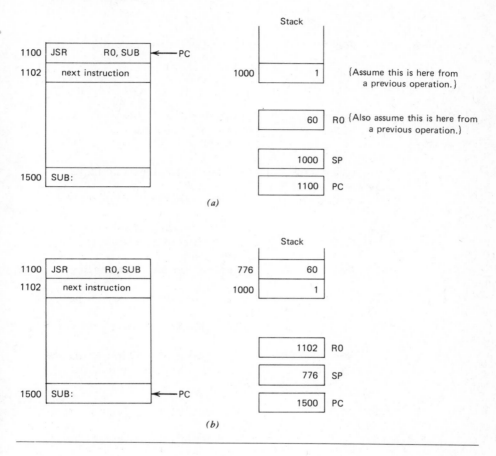

(a)

(b)

Figure 16-7 shows a complete MACRO-11 subroutine for converting a 32-bit
unsigned binary value, corresponding to the number of elapsed milliseconds, into the
corresponding equivalent number of days, hours, minutes, and seconds, rounded to
the nearest second. The value to be converted is stored in the 32-bit global variable
called MILLISEC. The program is an example of subroutine linkage in MACRO-
11.

Ideally, for the subroutine CONVERT in Figure 16-7, we would like to make the
variable MILLISEC a parameter so that it may take on different values. This would
make the subroutine much more general and more widely applicable to a range of
problems. This is the topic of the next section.

FIGURE 16-7   Subroutine for Conversion of Time Units.

```
Millisec:  .WORD  0,0          ; The value to be converted
           .
           .
           .
   Start:  JSR    PC,Convert    ; Here is how the subroutine is called
           .
           .
           .

SecInMin          =   60.      ; 60 seconds in a minute
MinInHr           =   60.      ; 60 minutes in an hour
HrInDay           =   24.      ; 24 hours in a day

Convert:  MOV  Millisec,R2     ; Move the 32-bit value into R2,R3
          MOV  Millisec+2,R3   ; R3 is low half
          DIV  #1000.,R2       ; This puts the number of seconds in
                               ; R2
          CMP  R3,#500.        ; Round the number of seconds
          BLT  NoRound         ; Less than half of a second, so
                               ; round down
          INC  R2              ; Round the number of seconds up

NoRound:  Mov  R2,R3           ; Move seconds to low half for next
                               ; divide
          CLR  R2              ; Clear high half for next divide

          DIV  #SecInMin,R2    ; Divide seconds by 60 to get minutes
          MOV  R3,Seconds      ; The remainder R3 is the number of
                               ; seconds

          MOV  R2,R3           ; Move quotient to low half for next
                               ; divide
          CLR  R2              ; Zero high half of number for next
                               ; divide
          DIV  #MinInHr,R2     ; Divide minutes by 60 to get hours
          MOV  R3,Minutes      ; The remainder is the number of
                               ; minutes

          MOV  R2,R3
          CLR  R2
          DIV  #HrInDay,R2     ; Divide hours by 24 to get days
          MOV  R3,Hours        ; The remainder is the number of hours
          MOV  R2,Days         ; The quotient is the number of days

          RTS  PC
```

16.4
Parameters

In this section, we discuss four different techniques for passing parameters to and from subroutines. These techniques utilize global variables, registers, in-line code, and the system stack.

16.4.1 Parameter Passing with Global Variables

Assembly-language program units do not generally have the powerful scope rules available in higher level languages like Pascal or PL-1. There are no begin/end blocks or hierarchical procedure structures to delineate the scope of local variables. Instead, the scope rule of MACRO-11 is much simpler:

Any symbol defined in a label field or direct assignment pseudo-op (=)
is global to the entire program unit in which it is contained.

Therefore, a very simple way to pass information into or out of a subroutine within the same program unit is to use a global variable. Simply refer to the address by the name it was defined with. This is exactly what was done in the conversion subroutine in Figure 16-7. The variable MILLISEC is global to, and therefore accessible by, the subroutine called CONVERT.

Figure 16-8 shows a simple subroutine for saving the contents of general registers R0–R5. The address of the block of memory where they should be saved is called TEMP, and is referred to globally within the subroutine.

When using global variables, we encounter the same limitation caused by using

FIGURE 16-8   Using Global Variables for Parameter Passing.

```
TEMP:     .BLKW  6            ; Here is where we will
              .                ; save the registers
              .
              .
          JSR    PC,SAVEREG   ; Activate the subroutine
              .
              .
              .
SAVEREG:  MOV    R0,TEMP      ; TEMP is a global
          MOV    R1,TEMP+2    ; variable
          MOV    R2,TEMP+4
          MOV    R3,TEMP+6
          MOV    R4,TEMP+10
          MOV    R5,TEMP+12
          RTS    PC
```

global objects in any language, namely, inflexibility. The subroutine in Figure 16-8 is *bound* to the name TEMP. We cannot change the address of the memory block where the data are to be stored without changing the program and recompiling it.

In general, the use of global variables is the least desirable method of passing parameters and is probably inappropriate for most applications. Global variables also make program maintenance more difficult. If you change the definition of the variable TEMP in the main unit, the subroutine may fail even though nothing within the subroutine itself has been changed. For these reasons, we will minimize the use of this parameter-passing technique in our examples.

16.4.2 Parameter Passing with Registers

Parameter passing using registers is not really a different technique, but simply a generalization of the global variable method described in the previous section. The register designators R0, . . . , PC are global to every program unit in MACRO-11. Therefore, to pass information between program units all we need to do is put the parameters into the appropriate registers and call the subroutine, which can then access them directly. For this method to work properly, the calling program and the subroutine must agree on two things:

1. Which register will hold which items.
2. Whether the register will hold the address of a value or the value itself.

This latter point is extremely important, because the two cases lead to two very different parameter-passing mechanisms available in most newer high-level languages (e.g., Pascal, Ada). If we put the values themselves in the registers, as in the following fragment:

```
X:   .WORD   0   ; These are the two values
Y:   .WORD   0   ; to be passed to SUB
         .
         .
         .
     MOV   X,R0
     MOV   Y,R1
     JSR   PC,SUB
```

then the subroutine will have access only to the values of X and Y, but not their addresses. Therefore, it is impossible for SUB to access, change, or destroy the original contents of X and Y. This is analogous to the *call-by-value* parameter-passing technique in Pascal.

If instead we pass the addresses of the parameters, as in the following:

```
X:   .WORD   0      ; These are the parameters
Y:   .WORD   0      ; to the subroutine
         .
         .
         .
```

```
MOV    #X,R0   ; This loads the addresses
MOV    #Y,R1   ; of X and Y into R0 and R1
JSR    PC,SUB
```

then the subroutine can access the original data items by using register deferred addressing mode. For example, the following instructions perform the operations $X := X + 1; Y := Y + 1$, changing the original values of X and Y:

```
INC   (R0)
INC   (R1)
```

By passing addresses rather than values, we have allowed the subroutine SUB to access and possibly change the original values. This parameter-passing technique is equivalent to the *call-by-reference* parameter-passing method in Pascal, Ada, PL-1, and FORTRAN.

Figure 16-5 showed subroutines for push and pop operations on a stack that used register R0 for passing the one parameter. Figure 16-9 shows another subroutine for performing a floating-point ADD on two 32-bit floating-point numbers in the following format:

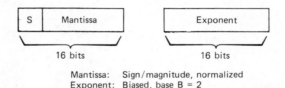

Mantissa: Sign/magnitude, normalized
Exponent: Biased, base B = 2

The four parameters are:

R0: The address of the first of the two words containing the left operand.

R1: The address of the first of the two words containing the right operand.

R2: The address of the first of the two words containing the result.

R3: The error flag. If R3 returns with a 0, everything was computed correctly. If R3 returns with a nonzero value, there was an error. Here is the meaning of the error codes:

> If bit 0 is a 1 it indicates floating-point overflow
> If bit 1 is a 1 it indicates floating-point underflow
> If bit 2 is a 1 it indicates loss of all significant digits

Register passing is a very popular method for transferring parameters and it works quite well. Its only limitation is that there may not be enough registers available for

FIGURE 16-9   Floating-Point ADD Subroutine.

```
           .Title Floating Point Add

A:         .Word    140000,100003    ; First word holds the mantissa and
                                     ; sign.
B:         .Word    040000,100002    ; Second word holds the exponent.
C:         .Word    0,0              ; Result goes here

Start:     MOV      #A,R0            ; Here is the main program
           MOV      #B,R1
           MOV      #C,R2
           JSR      PC,FAdd          ; Activate the subprogram
             .
             .
             .
AMant:     .Word    0
ASign:     .Word    0
AExp:      .Word    0

BMant:     .Word    0
BSign:     .Word    0
BExp:      .Word    0

MantMask        =        077777
SignMask        =        100000
;
; The subroutine begins here
;
;

FAdd:      CLR      R3
           CMP      2(R0),2(R1)      ; Does the first number have
                                     ; the smaller exponent?
           BLE      Move             ; Yes, move the numbers into the
                                     ; local variables

; Swap the pointers to the two numbers so R0 always points to the
; one with the smaller exponent.

Swap:      MOV      R0,-(SP)         ; Put R0 on the stack
           MOV      R1,R0            ; Switch the vaue of R0
           MOV      (SP)+,R1         ; Switch the vaue of R1 from the
                                     ; stack

; Move the input parameters to the local variables.
```

FIGURE 16-9   Floating-Point ADD Subroutine.
(*continued*)

```
Move:    MOV     (R0) ,AMant       ; Move sign and mantissa into AMant
         MOV     (R0) ,ASign       ; Move sign and mantissa to ASign
         MOV     2(R0) ,AExp       ; Move the exponent into AExp
         BIC     #SignMask,Amant   ; Clear the sign bit leaving just the
                                   ;   mantissa

         BIC     #MantMask,ASign   ; Clear the mantissa leaving just the
                                   ; sign

         MOV     (R1) ,BMant       ; Move sign and mantissa into BMant
         MOV     (R1) ,BSign       ; Move sign and mantissa to BSign
         MOV     2(R1) ,BExp       ; Move the exponent into BExp
         BIC     #SignMask,BMant   ; Clear the sign bit leaving just the
                                   ; mantissa
         BIC     #MantMask,BSign   ; Clear the mantissa leaving just the
                                   ; sign

; Now shift the mantissa of A and increase the exponent
; until the two exponents are the same.

Scale:   CMP     AExp,BExp         ; Have we finished scaling?
         BGE     AddMant           ; Yes, now add the mantissa

         INC     AExp              ; Increase the exponent of the
                                   ; number
         BEQ     OverFlow          ; Exponent is too big, return
                                   ; exponent overflow error
         ASR     AMant             ; Shift the mantissa right to
                                   ; maintain the number

         BNE     Scale             ; Did we lose all of the mantissa?

         BIS     #4,R3             ; Turn on NoMant error flag
         BR      Combine           ; Since A is zero, we just have
                                   ; to move B to the result

; Compare the signs of the two numbers, add the mantissas,
; and pick the correct sign.

AddMant;
         CMP     ASign,BSign       ; Are the signs the same?
         BEQ     SameSign          ; Yes, Add the mantissas

; The signs are opposite. Subtract mantissas and pick the sign
; of the larger one.
```

FIGURE 16-9   Floating-Point ADD Subroutine.
(*continued*)

```
          SUB     AMant,BMant      ; Subtract mantissa of A from B.
                                   ; Is the result positive?
          BPL     ReNormalize      ; Yes, use sign of B for result
          MOV     ASign,BSign      ; No, use sign of A for result,
          NEG     BMant            ; and negate the mantissa
          BR      ReNormalize      ; Now normalize the result

; The signs are the same. Add the mantissas.

SameSign:
          ADD     AMant,BMant      ; Add the mantissas. Did the
                                   ; result overflow the mantissa?
          BPL     ReNormalize      ; No, ReNormalize the number

          INC     BExp             ; Yes, Increment the Exponent of
                                   ; the result,
          BEQ     OverFlow         ; check for Exponent overflow,
          CLC
          ROR     BMant            ; and shift the mantissa right

; The two numbers have been added, and are stored in B.
; Now shift the mantissa left and decrease the exponent until
; the most significant bit of the mantissa is a one.

ReNormalize:
          BIT     #040000,BMant    ; Is the mantissa normalized?
          BNE     Combine          ; Yes, combine the result and
                                   ; return

          ASL     BMant            ; Shift the mantissa left
          TST     BExp             ; Is the exponent too small?
          BEQ     UnderFlow        ; Yes, return with a Zero and
                                   ; underflow error
          DEC     BExp             ; Decrement the exponent
          BR      ReNormalize      ; Check to see if it is normal-
                                   ; ized yet

; Now put the result in B into the return value.

Combine:
          MOV     BMant,(R2)       ; Move Mantissa into the result
          BIS     BSign,(R2)       ; Add the sign bit
          MOV     BExp,2(R2)       ; Move the exponent into result
          RTS     PC
```

FIGURE 16-9   Floating-Point ADD Subroutine.
(*continued*)

; The exponent is too large. Return the exponent overflow flag.

```
Overflow:
        BIS     #1,R3           ; Set on the overflow flag
        RTS     PC
```

; The exponent is too small. Return a zero as the result, and
; the exponent underflow flag.

```
Underflow:
        BIS     #2,R3           ; Set on the underflow flag
        CLR     (R2)            ; Zero the number
        CLR     2(R2)
        RTS     PC


        .END    Start
```

all of the parameters we want to pass. For example, the following Pascal procedure call:

optimize (xcoor, ycoor, stepsize, h, slope, fmax,
        gmax, result, errorflag);

would be difficult to implement using registers, since there are nine parameters and only eight registers. For this situation, we would have to use one of the techniques described in the next two sections.

16.4.3   Parameter Passing with In-Line Code

Instead of using a separate register for each parameter, we can use only one register, regardless of how many parameters we have. We do this by placing all of the parameters in a block of contiguous memory locations, and then passing a single register that contains the address of the beginning of this *parameter block*. This approach is shown in Figure 16-10.

To successfully implement this type of parameter passing, the calling program and the subroutine must agree on three conventions:

1.   Which register to use for passing the address of the parameter block.

2.   The order of the parameters in the parameter block.

3.   The type of each parameter in the parameter block (a value or the address of a value).

FIGURE 16-10   Parameter Passing Using Parameter Blocks.

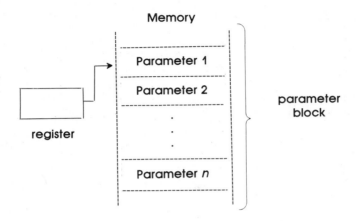

You can use any memory block and any register to implement this method. However, one of the most popular techniques is to use the memory block immediately following the JSR instruction itself. This approach, called parameter passing using *in-line code,* is popular because the register that points to the parameter block is simply PC, which always points to the word immediately following the current instruction. Thus, the procedure call $P(x,y)$ might be translated using in-line code as shown in Figure 16-11.

FIGURE 16-11   Example of In-Line Parameter Passing.

Address

```
500    X:    .WORD 0   ; These are the two
502    Y:    .WORD 0   ; parameters to be passed
         .
         .
         .
1000   JSR   PC,P
1002   .WORD   X        ; Address currently on top of the stack
1004   .WORD   Y
1006   next instruction
```

Now in the subroutine, we must pick up these two parameters. How we do it, and exactly what we store again depend on whether we want to use a call-by-value or a call-by-reference parameter-passing mechanism. For example, the following sequence picks up the two parameter *addresses* stored in locations 1002 and 1004 of Figure 16-11 and stores them in local variables called P1 and P2. This approach is equivalent to call-by-reference. As you look through this fragment, remember that the return address (1002) is currently on top of the system stack.

```
P:  MOV    (SP),RO    ;  RO now holds the address 1002
    MOV    (RO)+,P1   ;  P1 now holds the address of X
    MOV    (RO)+,P2   ;  P2 now holds the address of Y
    MOV    RO,(SP)    ;  Fix up the return address

         .
         . Rest of the subroutine
         .

    RTS            PC
```

Exercise 17 at the end of the chapter asks you to implement call-by-value for this example.

The preceding example demonstrates one very important operation that must always be carried out for in-line code. The return address must be correctly recomputed and stored on top of the stack. For example, when we first arrive at the subroutine, label P in the code fragment, the top of the stack points to the address of the first parameter (1002 in this example). If we do not correctly update that return address, then we will return to location 1002 and incorrectly execute our data when we execute the RTS instruction at the end of subroutine P. The return address on top of the stack must always be reset according to the formula:

return address := (value on top of stack) + 2 * (number of parameters)

which is exactly what was done in the example.

There is one other point about this last example. In the subroutine P shown above, when we pick up the parameters, we use, and thus destroy register RO. This would be a very undesirable *side effect* of this routine. Every time we wrote JSR PC,P we would wipe out RO. Any important value that RO held would be lost to us. To avoid this, every routine that you write should save and restore the registers RO, . . . , R5 that it uses for its own private purposes. Then you can be sure that calling a subroutine will not have any undesirable or unexpected side effects on the overall program behavior. For example, the subroutine P could have been written:

```
P:     MOV    RO,TEMP    ; Save RO before using it
       MOV    (SP),RO
       MOV    (RO)+,P1
       MOV    (RO)+,P2
```

```
            MOV    R0,(SP)
              .
              .
              .
            MOV    TEMP,R0 ; Restore R0 to its original value
            RTS    PC
    TEMP:   .WORD  0
```

You should always follow the rule that every subroutine you write leaves registers R0, . . . , R5 unchanged, unless the specifications of the subroutine indicate that they are to be changed.

Figure 16-12 shows a subroutine for performing a *table look-up*. The table contains pairs of words. The first word of the entry contains an integer value, and the second word contains the address of a subroutine. You will be given an integer key and you are to look that key up in the table. When you have matched the key against the first word of an entry, set a variable called FOUND to the address in the table where the key was found, and branch to the subroutine in the second word of the entry. This is a very common data structure called a *jump table*. For example, in the following diagram:

you will find the key at address 1004. You should set FOUND to 1004 and then branch to the subroutine located in memory location 4010. When that subroutine is finished executing, it should return to the table look-up routine, which will in turn return to the program that called it. The subroutine uses in-line code to pass its four parameters: the table, the table size, the key, and the found flag.

16.4.4 Parameter Passing with Stacks

Our final parameter-passing technique relies on the system stack. We have already used this stack for storing the return address. Now we also use it for passing the addresses or the values of the parameters themselves.

Before we call the subroutine, we must push the parameters onto the stack (whether we push addresses or values depends, as always, on whether we are using call-by-value or call-by-reference). The following sequence pushes three values (X, Y, and Z) onto the stack before activating the subroutine SUB.

```
            MOV   X,−(SP)
            MOV   Y,−(SP)
            MOV   Z,−(SP)
            JSR   PC,SUB
```

FIGURE 16-12   Table Look-up Subroutine.

```
            .Title   Table Lookup
xTable:     .BlkW    100.              ; This is the table of keys and
                                       ; jump addresses. It is 100 words long.

xFound:     .Word    0                 ; Address in table of key if found,
                                       ; or zero if not found

Start:      .
            .
            .
            JSR      PC,Lookup         ; Here we activate the subroutine
            .Word    xTable            ; The address of the table
            .Word    200.              ; The value of the table size: 200 bytes
            .Word    5                 ; The value of the key
            .Word    xFound            ; The address of the found switch
            .
            .
            .


;
; The subroutine starts here
;
Lookup:     MOV      R0,Temp           ; Save R0 in Temp for later
            MOV      (SP),R0           ; Get return address off stack
            MOV      (R0)+,Table       ; Get address of Table
            MOV      (R0)+,Size        ; Get size of table
            MOV      (R0)+,Key         ; Get value of key to search for
            MOV      (R0)+,Found       ; Get address of found variable
            MOV      R0,(SP)           ; Put updated return address back
                                       ; on stack

            CLR      R0                ; Start at beginning of table
Loop:       CMP      R0,Size           ; Have we looked through the whole
                                       ; table?
            BGE      NotFound          ; Yes, return a 0 in found
            MOV      Table,Loc         ; Add R0 to Table to get location
            ADD      R0,Loc            ; of the next key in the table
            CMP      Key,@Loc          ; Have we found key in the table?
            BEQ      GoThere           ; Yes, set found, and JSR to the
                                       ; correct routine

            ADD      #4,R0             ; Point R0 at the next key in the
                                       ; table
            BR       Loop              ; Check again
```

FIGURE 16-12   Table Look-up Subroutine (*Continued*)

```
GoThere:    MOV    Table,@Found    ; Add Table to R0 to get position
                                   ; in table
            ADD    R0,@Found
            INC    R0              ; Point R0 at address of correct
                                   ; routine in table
            INC    R0
            MOV    Table,Loc       ; Add R0 to Table to get the
            ADD    R0,Loc          ; location of the jump address
            MOV    @Loc,Loc        ; Get the jump address
            JSR    PC,@Loc         ; Jump indirectly using Table
                                   ; offset by table
            MOV    Temp,R0         ; Restore the value in R0
            RTS    PC              ; Return to main program

NotFound:   CLR    @Found          ; Return a zero in Found
            MOV    Temp,R0         ; Restore the value of R0
            RTS    PC              ; Return to main program

;
;   Local variables used by the subroutine
;
Table:      .Word  0              ; Address of beginning of xTable
Size:       .Word  0              ; Length of table in bytes
Key:        .Word  0              ; Value of key to search for
Found:      .Word  0              ; Address of xFound
Temp:       .Word  0              ; Temporary to hold R0
Loc:        .Word  0              ; Temporary location for computing
                                  ; table addresses

            .End   Start
```

When we arrive at subroutine SUB, the condition of the system stack will be:

To access the three parameters X, Y, and Z, we must first remove the return address, since it is on top, and then remove the parameters one by one from the stack and store them in local variables. Any result computed by the subroutine that is to be returned to the calling program must be put back on the stack *before* the return address is finally placed back on top. The return address must always be the last item placed on the stack.

The following code fragment shows one possible sequence for accessing the parameters from the stack.

```
SUB:  MOV    (SP)+,TEMP  ; Pop the return address
      MOV    (SP)+,P3    ; Pop the parameters
      MOV    (SP)+,P2
      MOV    (SP)+,P1

         .
         .   The subroutine now computes a
         .   RESULT using parameters P1, P2,
         .   and P3
         .

      MOV    RESULT,-(SP); Push result on stack
      MOV    TEMP,-(SP)  ; Push return address
      RTS    PC
```

This fragment first removes the return address and stores it in the temporary variable TEMP. It then removes the three parameters X, Y, and Z and stores them in P1, P2, and P3. In this case, P1, P2, and P3 will contain the values of X, Y, and Z because values were originally placed in the stack. If we had instead wished to pass addresses, we would have placed the addresses of X, Y, and Z on the stack as follows:

```
MOV  #X,-(SP)   ; Place addresses on the stack
MOV  #Y,-(SP)
MOV  #Z,-(SP)
JSR  PC,SUB     ; And activate the subroutine
```

Notice that when we remove the parameters from the stack, they come off in the *reverse* order from which they were put on. The first parameter removed (P3) is equivalent to the last one pushed on (Z). Also notice that we put the final RESULT on the stack *before* the return address. If we had incorrectly written:

```
MOV  TEMP,-(SP)    ; Store return address
MOV  RESULT,-(SP)  ; Store the result
RTS  PC
```

then the variable called RESULT would be on top of the stack and would be incorrectly interpreted as the return address. The program would try to branch to a totally unpredictable location.

16.5
Case Study: Two-Dimensional Arrays

We are now going to do a reasonably long and complex case study concerning data structures in assembly language. We developed a subroutine that allows us to mimic in assembly language the behavior of 2-dimensional arrays from high-level languages. As we have stressed many times, such complex data structures as multidimensional arrays or records do not exist directly in assembly languages. We must create them from the only structures available: sequential blocks of addressable memory. Our case study shows how these structures can be simulated in assembly language. Compiler writers use these operations to provide high-level languages with a rich and powerful set of data structures.

A 2-dimensional array can be stored either by row (called *row major ordering*) or by column *(column major ordering)*. The storage of an $M \times N$ array in row major order is shown in Figure 16-13.

In a high-level language, we create a 2-dimensional array by writing:

DIMENSION   A(M,N)

FIGURE 16-13   Row Major Storage of a Two-Dimensional Array.

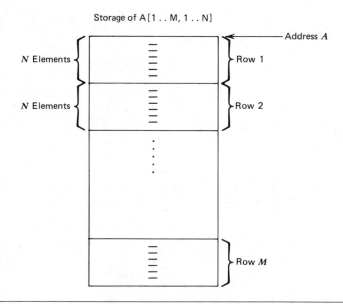

Storage of A [1 .. M, 1 .. N]

or

Var A: array(1 . . M, 1 . . N) of "element"

where M and N are either constants or symbolic constants. In MACRO-11, we perform the corresponding operation by allocating the necessary amount of memory space with a .BLKB or .BLKW directive.

A: .BLKB   M * N * B

or

A: .BLKW   M * N * W

where B is the number of bytes or W is the number of words it takes to store one array element. On the PDP-11, W = 1 for integer values, and W = 2 or 4 for floating point.

Once the memory space has been allocated, how do we map from high-level language subscript references, like $A[i,j]$, into the correct memory address for the memory block shown in Figure 16-13? This figure indicates that the elements of row i have all of the elements of rows 1, 2, . . . , $i - 1$ stored ahead of them. Thus the location of the beginning of row i will be at address:

$$start + N * B * (i - 1)$$

where:

start = starting address of the entire block
N = number of elements per row (i.e., number of columns)
B = number of bytes of storage per array element

Once we have located the beginning of row i, we want to access the element in column j. This element has items 1, 2 . . . , $j - 1$ stored ahead of it. So, to locate the $[i,j]$th item of an $M \times N$ array stored in row major order, we must evaluate the following expression, assuming that all subscripts begin at 1.

(16.1)   address of the $[i,j$th] item = start + $N * B * (i - 1) + B * (j - 1)$

Every time we wish to access element $A[i,j]$ of the 2-dimensional array, we must evaluate expression 16.1 to obtain an address and use that address to fetch the proper element.

Figure 16-14 shows a subroutine called ACCESS that computes the correct location of the $[i,j]$th item of a 2-dimensional array stored in row major order. The subroutine takes two input parameters—the row and column subscripts i and j—and returns a single value called addr, which is the memory address of that element. If the subscript i or j falls outside the boundaries of the array, then addr is set to the value 177777. The subroutine uses the system stack for transmitting parameters and returning the result.

FIGURE 16-14   Subroutine to Describe and Access a
Two-Dimensional Array.

```
          A:           .BLKB      50     ; This allocates the actual space

;
DopeVec:               .WORD      A      ; Starting address (start)
                       .WORD      5      ; 5 rows (M)
                       .WORD      10     ; 10 columns (N)
                       .WORD      1      ; 1 byte per array element (B)
                         .
                         .
                         .
Start:    MOV    #DopeVec, -(SP)         ; Put address of dope vector on the
                                         ; stack
          MOV    #2, -(SP)               ; Put row number on the stack
          MOV    #3, -(SP)               ; Then put column number on stack
          JSR    PC,Access               ; Call the subroutine
          MOV    (SP) +,R0               ; Get the correct address for A(2,3)
                                         ; off of the stack
                    .
                    .
                    .
i:                     .Word      0      ; The row requested
j:                     .Word      0      ; The column requested
Location:              .Word      0      ; The return value we are finding

Temp0:                 .Word      0      ; A storage place for R0
Temp1:                 .Word      0      ; A storage place for R1
RetAdr:                .Word      0      ; A storage place for the return
                                         ; address

Access:   MOV    R0,Temp0                ; Save R0
          MOV    (SP) +,RetAdr           ; Save the return address
          MOV    (SP) +,j                ; Pull requested column from stack
          MOV    (SP) +,i                ; Pull requested row from stack
          MOV    (SP) +,R0               ; Pull dope vector address from stack

          CMP    i,#1                    ; Is i > = 1?
          BLT    NoGood                  ; No, return illegal value
          CMP    j,#1                    ; Is j > = 1?
          BLT    NoGood                  ; No, return illegal value

          CMP    i,2(R0)                 ; Is i < = m?
          BGT    NoGood                  ; No, return illegal value
          CMP    j,4(R0)                 ; Is j < = n?
          BGT    NoGood                  ; No, return illegal value
```

FIGURE 16-14   Subroutine to Describe and Access a
Two-Dimensional Array. (*continued*)

```
        MOV   R1,Temp1          ; Save register R1
        MOV   (R0),Location     ; Move the base of the array to
                                ; Location

        MOV   i,R1              ; The row
        DEC   R1               ; (i − 1)
        MUL   6(R0),R1          ; B*(i − 1)
        MUL   4(R0),R1          ; n*B*(i − 1)
        ADD   R1,Location       ; Add n*B*(i − 1) (the row offset)
                                ; to the base

        MOV   j,R1              ; The column
        DEC   R1               ; (j − 1)
        MUL   6(R0),R1          ; B*(j − 1)
        ADD   R1,Location       ; Add B*(j − 1) to the base and the
                                ; row offset
        MOV   Location,−(SP)    ; Put Base + n*B*(i − 1) + B*(j − 1)
                                ; on the stack
        MOV   Temp1,R1          ; Restore the value of R1

        MOV   Temp0,R0          ; Restore R0
        MOV   RetAdr,−(SP)      ; Put the return address back on
                                ; the stack
        RTS   PC               ; Return to the caller with Location
                                ; on the stack

NoGood: MOV   #177777,−(SP)     ; Put the illegal value on the stack
        MOV   Temp0,R0          ; Restore R0
        MOV   RetAdr,−(SP)      ; Put the return address back on
                                ; the stack
        RTS   PC               ; Return with the illegal value

        .End  Start
```

The four characteristics that describe the array—start, M (the number of rows), N (the number of columns), and B (the number of bytes of storage per array element)—are not built into the subroutine itself but are kept in a separate 4-word block of memory called DOPEVEC and are accessed by the subroutine. Placing data structure parameters in a separate table is a very common technique, and such a *data structure descriptor block* is frequently called a *dope vector*. Putting all of the parameters of the 2-dimensional array into this dope vector makes the subroutine in Figure 16-14 general for *any* arbitrary 2-dimensional array whose subscripts begin at 1. To use this routine, we must pass the parameters i and j, and one additional parameter as well: the address of the dope vector describing the characteristics of the array. The subroutine will now use the values in the dope vector provided.

Now, to use the subroutine in Figure 16-14, we merely pass it two subscripts, i and j, and the address of the dope vector of the array. For example, the following statement in Pascal:

$$A(2,3) := 0;$$

would be translated into MACRO-11 as follows:

```
MOV    #DOPEVEC,-(SP)    ; Descriptor of A
MOV    #2,-(SP)          ; We want row 2
MOV    #3,-(SP)          ; And column 3
JSR    PC,ACCESS         ; Call subroutine
MOV    (SP)+,R0          ; This is the location
                         ; of element A (2,3)
CLR    (R0)              ; This clears it
```

The assignment statement:

$$A(x,y+1) := c + d$$

would be:

```
MOV    c,R0
ADD    d,R0              ; R0 holds the answer
MOV    #DOPEVEC,-(SP)
MOV    x,-(SP)           ; We want row x
MOV    y,-(SP)
INC    (SP)              ; And column y + 1
JSR    PC,ACCESS         ; Call subroutine
MOV    (SP)+,R1          ; Here is the location
                         ; of A(x,y + 1)
MOV    R0,(R1)           ; Store the answer
```

16.6
Recursion

In some high level languages (e.g., BASIC, FORTRAN, and COBOL) recursion is not allowed. In other high-level languages (Pascal, PL/1, Algol, Ada), it is used as a powerful problem-solving tool. In MACRO-11, recursion is perfectly legal, since we are, in a sense, "in charge of" the placement of subroutine addresses on the system stack. When we write:

```
JSR    PC,SUB
```

FIGURE 16-15   Recursive Routine for Computing
Factorials.

```
        .Title    Factorial

Retadr: .Word  0                ; A place to save the return address

Fact:   MOV    (SP)+,Retadr     ; Get return address off stack
        MOV    (SP)+,R1         ; Get N
        CMP    R1,#1            ; Is this a trivial case (N <= 1)?
        BLE    FDone            ; Yes, return 1 for 1!
        MOV    R1,-(SP)         ; Put N on the stack
        MOV    Retadr,-(SP)     ; Followed by the return address
        DEC    R1               ; Find the factorial of N - 1
        MOV    R1,-(SP)         ; Push N - 1 onto the stack
        JSR    PC,Fact          ; Call factorial
        MOV    (SP)+,R1         ; Pull (N - 1) ! from the stack
        MOV    (SP)+,Retadr     ; Pull the return address
        MUL    (SP)+,R1         ; Multiply N*(N - 1)! to get N!

FDone:  MOV    R1,-(SP)         ; Push N! onto the stack
        MOV    Retadr,-(SP)     ; Push the return address
        RTS    PC               ; Return to the caller

N       =      5                ; This will compute 5!

        ;
        ; Here is the main program
        ;
Start:  .
        .
        .
        MOV    #N,-(SP)         ; Put N on the stack
        JSR    PC,Fact          ; Call the factorial routine
        MOV    (SP)+,R2         ; Put N! in R2
        .
        .
        .
        .End    Start
```

there is no checking to see whether the address "SUB" is the same address as the subroutine in which we are currently executing, hence a recursive call.

The well-known recursive definition of n factorial ($n!$), which is:

$$n! = n * (n - 1)! \qquad n \geq 2$$
$$1! = 1$$
$$0! = 1$$

FIGURE 16-16   A Binary Tree.

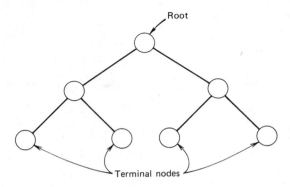

can be implemented as a recursive MACRO-11 subroutine, called FACT. This routine is shown in Figure 16-15. The parameter to FACT is stored on the system stack before the subroutine is called. The result is left on the system stack when the routine completes.

Searching a binary tree is a somewhat more realistic example of a recursive MACRO-11 subroutine. A binary tree is a linked-list data structure in which each node has at most two pointers, and no node is pointed at twice. A model of a binary tree is shown in Figure 16-16.

Because of its recursive nature, a binary tree is best manipulated via recursive algorithms: whenever you follow a pointer from a node in a binary tree, you are left with a binary tree.

FIGURE 16-17   Representation of a Binary Tree.

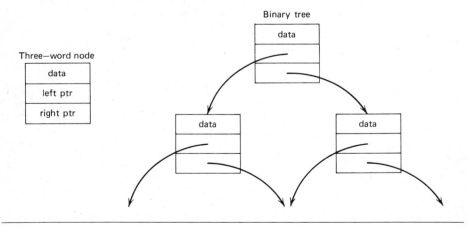

A node in a binary tree can be implemented in MACRO-11 by using a 3-word memory block for each node. The first word can contain the 16-bit data value associated with the node, while the next two words contain the left pointer and right pointer, respectively. These are simply addresses to the first word of other nodes in the structure. A special bit pattern (e.g., all 1s) indicates that the pointer field is not pointing to anything but instead is a terminal node. This structure is diagrammed in Figure 16-17.

Figure 16-18 shows a recursive MACRO-11 subroutine for searching a binary tree and counting the total number of nodes in the tree. The single input parameter to the routine is a pointer to the root of the tree. The single output parameter is the number of nodes in the tree.

When you write recursive routines, you must have some way to terminate the recursion. In the factorial case it occurs when you reach 1! In the binary tree example, it occurs when you reach a terminal node. In any case, there must always be a terminating condition. If you simply keep making recursive calls:

```
SUB:    .

           .

           .

        JSR   PC,SUB
```

you will eventually cause a stack overflow. This is a fatal error and will terminate execution of your program.

16.7
External Subroutines

All of the examples so far have been of subroutines that are part of the same program as the calling program and are assembled as a single unit. Therefore, when we write:

```
JSR   PC,SUB
```

the assembler will always be able to find, somewhere in our program, a statement of the form:

```
SUB:   -----
```

Thus, the assembler will always be able to determine the address of the beginning of the subroutine and correctly assemble the JSR instruction.

However, often we want to use subroutines that are not part of our own program but have been separately written, assembled, and placed in a *subroutine library*. We have used library subroutines many times in higher level languages (e.g., the routines abs, sqr, sin, or round from the Pascal library) and they are equally useful in assembly language. For example, the routine called ACCESS in Figure 16-14 would be an excellent candidate for inclusion in a MACRO-11 subroutine library. A subrou-

FIGURE 16-18   Recursive Subroutine to Search a Binary
Tree.

```
                    .Title    CountNodes

Retadr:             .Word 0          ; This holds the return address
                                     ; from the stack
Num:                .Word 0          ; This is the number of nodes

; This is a recursive routine for counting the
; number of nodes in a binary tree

CountNodes:
            MOV     (SP)+,Retadr     ; Save return address for later
            MOV     (SP)+,R0         ; R0 holds location of root
            CLR     Num              ; Set number of nodes to 0 to
                                     ; start
            CMP     #177777,R0       ; Are we looking at an empty node?
            BEQ     CNDone           ; Yes, Return with number of
                                     ; nodes = 0
            MOV     Retadr,-(SP)     ; Put return address back on stack
            MOV     2(R0),-(SP)      ; Save the values of the left and
            MOV     4(R0),-(SP)      ; right pointers on the stack
            JSR     PC,CountNodes    ; Find out how many nodes are in
                                     ; the right subtree
            MOV     (SP)+,Num        ; Switch the positions of Num and
                                     ; Left pointer
            MOV     (SP)+,R0         ; This is really 2(R0) from above
            MOV     Num,-(SP)        ; Put them back on
            MOV     R0,-(SP)
            JSR     PC,CountNodes    ; How many in the left subtree?
            MOV     (SP)+,Num        ; Move this value to Num
            ADD     (SP)+,Num        ; Add in the number in the right
                                     ; subtree
            ADD     #1,Num           ; Add in one more for this node
            MOV     (SP)+,Retadr     ; Pull return address off stack
CNDone:     MOV     Num,-(SP)        ; Put total number in this tree on
                                     ; the stack
            MOV     Retadr,-(SP)     ; Then put the return address on
            RTS     PC               ; and return to the caller
;
;       Here is the main program
;
Start:          .
                .
                .
```

FIGURE 16-18   Recursive Subroutine to Search a Binary
Tree. (*continued*)

```
        MOV     #List,−(SP)        ; Put address of root on stack
        JSR     PC,CountNodes      ; Call routine to count nodes
        MOV     (SP)+,R1           ; Move the number of nodes to R1
        .
        .
        .
        .End    Start
```

tine that is not part of the program unit being assembled, but instead comes from a separate library, is called an *external routine.*

We will need some new MACRO-11 directives to allow us to use external routines. Without them, the assembler will think we have made an error. For if we write:

JSR   PC,SUB

but nowhere in the program do we define the label SUB (since it is located in another program unit), the assembler will consider it to be an "undefined symbol" and mark it as a fatal error.

To prevent this, we use the assembler directive called "global," whose syntax is:

.GLOBL   symbol,symbol, . . .

This declaration, called an *external reference,* states that all the symbols in the address field of the .GLOBL directive are *external symbols.* Their definition will not be found in this program unit, but somewhere else, and this condition is not to be flagged as an error. Instead, the assembler will save information about the references to these external symbols, and when this program unit is *linked* in with the other libraries, we will be able to satisfy all address references.

The .GLOBL directive must also be used in the external routine itself. This is called an *external definition,* and it states that the symbols listed in the address field will be referenced externally by other programs and that this is the routine in which they are defined. It is the job of a program called the *linker* to match the external references in one routine with the proper external definitions in another routine. We describe the operation of the linker in detail in Chapter 20.

Figure 16-19 shows an example of an external reference and an external definition using the .GLOBL assembler directive.

When the assembler assembles the unit called "MAINPROG" in Figure 16-19a, it will save information about the references to the as-yet unknown symbols called SUB and DATA. It will not complete the assembly of either the JSR or MOV command, since we do not yet know the correct addresses for the symbols in the address field. Later, when the assembler assembles the unit called "EXTERNAL", it will

FIGURE 16-19 Examples of External References and
Definitions.

```
        .TITLE     MAINPROG            .TITLE     EXTERNAL
        .GLOBL     SUB,DATA            .GLOBL     SUB,DATA
          .                    SUB:
          .
          .
        JSR        PC,SUB
          .
          .
          .
        MOV        DATA,R0
          .
          .                    DATA:  .WORD   0
        .END       START              .END
```

(a) External References   **(b) External Definitions**

make a note that any other program unit referencing the external symbol SUB or DATA will find the definition given in this program unit.

The linker now takes these two pieces of information and, during the linking process, completes the assembly of the JSR and MOV instructions in MAINPROG by inserting the proper addresses for SUB and DATA specified in the routine called EXTERNAL.

Notice that even though a single directive called .GLOBL is being used for two purposes, it is not possible to confuse the two functions. If the symbol in the .GLOBL directive is being referenced (i.e., used in the address field), then it is an external reference, and we must look for the matching definition in another routine. If the symbol in the .GLOBL directive is being defined in this unit (i.e., used in the label field or in a direct-assignment pseudo-op), then it is an external definition, and some other program unit will be referencing this symbol.

Finally, notice that we did *not* put an address on the .END directive of the subroutine called EXTERNAL. There can only be one start address in a program, and this START address is on the .END directive at the end of the main program unit. The .END directive of each separately compiled subroutine should not contain a start address, and if one is included it will simply be ignored. Having two starting addresses would be equivalent to having two main program units. We wouldn't know where to begin.

In addition to using the .GLOBL directive within the program, you may need to use some special operating system commands to correctly utilize external routines. These commands tell the linker the names of the libraries that must be searched to satisfy all external references. For example, the command to the RT-11 linker to build an executable program unit from the main program (MYPROG), the file called MYFILE, and the MACRO-11 library LIB would be:

```
LINK
*PROG = MYPROG,MYFILE,LIB
```

You should check into the necessary linker commands needed for your particular operating system and hardware. This information should be available from your instructor or local computer center.

Exercises for Chapter 16

1. Referring to the condition of the stack as shown in Figure 16-1b, which of the following shows the correct order in which the three items X, Y, and Z were pushed onto the stack:

push X		push Z
push Y	or	push Y
push Z		push X

2. Using the discussion in Chapter 15 on errors and assembly-language programming (Section 15.5), what do you think would happen if the system stack were in the empty state shown in Figure 16-1(a) and you tried to perform a "pop x" operation which tries to remove something from the stack and store it in memory location x?

3. Referring to Figure 16-2, why couldn't the last line be written as follows:

```
MOV   #STACK,R5  ;  Initialize the TOP pointer
```

What would happen if you initialized R5 in this way?
What would be wrong with initializing R5 by saying:

```
MOV   ENDOFSTACK,R5  ;  Initialize the TOP Pointer
```

4. Create your own personal 500-word stack called MYSTACK that uses register R0 as the TOP pointer. Allocate all necessary space and initialize R0 to the correct value.

5. Assume that you have stored a value into the word called I defined via:

```
I:  .WORD  0  ;  Holds a value
```

Push the contents of I onto the stack defined in Exercise 4.

6. Remove the item on top of the stack defined in Exercise 4 and place it in the memory location whose address is currently contained in register R1.

7. Show the JSR command that would be used to jump to this 4-line subroutine:

```
EX7: MOV  A,R0
     ADD   #7,R0
     MOV   R0,A
     RTS   PC
```

Can you use any link register or are you required to use a specific one? How would the subroutine jump command change if the last line had been RTS R2?

8. Assume that you have nested subroutine calls to subroutines A, B, and C in the following way:

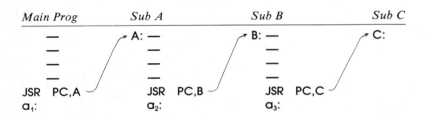

Main Prog	Sub A	Sub B	Sub C
—	A: —	B: —	C:
—	—	—	
—	—	—	
—	—	—	
JSR PC,A	JSR PC,B	JSR PC,C	
a_1:	a_2:	a_3:	

Show what the values are on the system stack as you execute subroutine C. Assume that a_1, a_2, and a_3 are the addresses of the memory locations immediately following the JSR.

9. Assume that at the end of subroutine C in Exercise 8 you want to return directly to the main program rather than to subroutine B. How could you accomplish this in a way that does not jeopardize the integrity of the system stack (i.e., that does not leave unintended values on the stack that could cause future errors)?

10. Assume that you want to evaluate the expression:

$$A := B * C + D$$

and put it in the following prefix notation:

$$:= + * B C D A$$

Use the system stack and the push and pop operations in Figure 16-5 to evaluate this expression in prefix notation.

11. What would happen if you wanted to use the pop subroutine shown in Figure 16-5, but you improperly put the contents of X, rather than the address of X, in R0?

```
X:    .WORD   0
        .
        .
        .
      MOV     X,R0      ; This should be #X,R0;
      JSR     PC,POP    ; What does this do?
```

12. Write a MACRO-11 subroutine that clears to 0 a block of memory from MEMLOW to MEMHIGH. Assume that MEMLOW and MEMHIGH are global variables and MEMHIGH $\geq$ MEMLOW.

13. Take the clearing subroutine from Exercise 12 and generalize it so that MEM-LOW and MEMHIGH are parameters passed to the subroutine using general registers R0 and R1. Assume registers R0 and R1 contain the *value* of MEMLOW and MEMHIGH. Furthermore, assume that register R2 is set to 1 if the error condition MEMLOW > MEMHIGH or if either MEMLOW or MEMHIGH exceeds the octal value 160000. Otherwise, R2 will contain a 0.

14. Does the following subroutine activation pass the value or the address of its one parameter, X? Is this equivalent to call-by-value or call-by-reference?

```
      X = 100       ; X is location 100
        .
        .
        .
      MOV   @X,R0   ; Put parameter in R0
      JSR   PC,SUB  ; Activate the subroutine
```

15. Write a subroutine called NPOP that takes a single integer value N as a parameter, $N \geq 1$. The subroutine will pop N items off the system stack and then return. Use in-line code to pass the parameter, and pass N by value. Assume that there are at least N items on the stack.

16. Generalize the subroutine in Exercise 15 so that it takes two parameters—the value N as before, and a second parameter called STACKBGN, which is the address of the bottom element of the stack. NPOP should now attempt to pop N items off the system stack, but it should also check to make sure that there are at least N items available. If there are not N items on the stack, pop as many off as you can and leave the stack empty. Use in-line code to pass both parameters.

17. Implement subroutine P from Figure 16-11 so that you create local variables P1 and P2, which hold the *value* of the parameters X and Y. That is, P1 and P2 would hold the contents of memory locations 500 and 502, respectively. This would be equivalent to call-by-value.

18. Write a subroutine called ADDUP that adds up all values in a block of memory. The parameters to the subroutine are:

STARTADR: The starting address of the memory block to be summed up.

N: The length, in words, of the memory block starting with STARTADR.

SUM: The sum of all values contained in the memory block.

OVFLW: A parameter that specifies whether an overflow occurred during the operation. If OVFLW is a 1, there was an overflow, and the value in SUM is incorrect. Otherwise, OVFLW is a 0.

Use an in-line parameter-passing technique to pass the parameters to ADDUP.

19. Write a subroutine called BITCHECK that checks any arbitrary bit (from 0 to 15) of any arbitrary word in memory. The four parameters to the subroutine are:

ADDR: The address of the 16-bit word in memory to be checked.

POS: The bit position whose value you will be checking (bits are numbered right to left from 0 to 15).

VAL: The value returned by the subroutine. If bit position POS of word ADDR has the value 1, then VAL will be a 1. Otherwise, VAL will be a 0.

ERROR: ERROR is set to 1 if POS is outside the range 0 to 15. Otherwise, ERROR is set to 0.

Use the system stack to pass parameters to the subroutine BITCHECK.

20a. Why is expression 16.1, for the location of element $A[i,j]$ in a row major array, not dependent on the value M, the total number of rows?

20b. Develop a corresponding formula for the location of element $A[i,j]$ when A is stored in column major order.

CHAPTER 17

MACROS AND CONDITIONAL ASSEMBLY

17.1
Introduction

In this section we introduce a new class of subprogram quite different from the type discussed in Chapter 16. This type of subprogram, called a *macro*, does not exist in higher level languages. (A macro-like capability was included in the ALGOL dialect called "Burrough's extended-ALGOL." However, this facility does not appear in any of the more widely used high-level languages such as BASIC, FORTRAN, COBOL, or Pascal.)

A *macro* is a named body of text that can be referenced and activated by its name. Superficially, this sounds like the definition of a subroutine, which is also a named body of text, but there are important conceptual differences. For example, a "regular" subroutine of the type described in Chapter 16 is statement oriented, but a macro is character-string oriented. A subroutine must be composed of legal MACRO-11 instructions, but the body of text associated with a macro name can be any arbitrary string of characters, regardless of whether it makes sense in the MACRO-11 language. A macro called JUNK defined as follows:

$$@\#!( )\{ \}''+/-\bullet$$

would be perfectly legal. If we defined this 12-character string to be a subroutine called JUNK, it would not assemble correctly and would generate a stream of error messages.

Even though it is perfectly legal to create a macro containing any arbitrary sequence of characters, if we were to attempt to use that macro as if it were composed of meaningful MACRO-11 instructions, it would also create a stream of error

FIGURE 17-1a   Macro Processing.

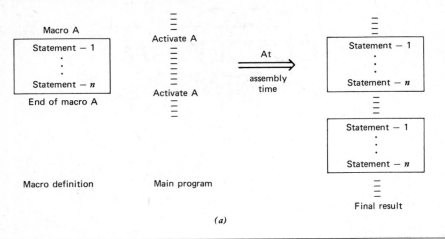

(a)

messages. But these errors would result because of an incorrect or improper use of the macro, not because the macro was syntactically invalid.

Another major difference between subroutines and macros is that a macro is completely processed at assembly time either by the assembler or by a special program called a *macro preprocessor,* which is executed just before the assembler. A "regular" subroutine is compiled, but it is not activated until execution time, when the procedure call (the JSR) is encountered.

During assembly, when a macro call is encountered, the entire body of the macro is copied directly into the program in place of the macro call. Each call is replaced by a full copy of the macro text. When the program is executed, there are no more

FIGURE 17-1b   Subroutine Processing.

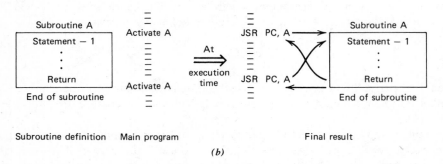

(b)

"subprogram names" or "subprogram calls"; there is only a single expanded program that can be assembled and executed. This situation is summarized in Figure 17-1(a). This organization differs sharply from a subroutine; of course there is only one copy of a subroutine, and the program branches and returns to it as many times as needed (Figure 17-1(b)).

Figure 17-1(a) reveals how the macro gets its other common name: *in-line subroutine*. The code of the macro is copied directly into the lines of the main calling program.

Summarizing the characteristics just discussed, we can say that a macro is used to give a name to a string of characters, and activating a macro copies that string of characters into the main text. Instead of viewing a macro as an alternative type of subroutine facility, we should think of it as a very powerful and quite sophisticated *string processor*. The unique features of macros allow us to perform a number of programming operations that are not possible with regular subroutines.

17.2
Macro Processing

Macro processing is typically handled before the regular assembly of a program. Sometimes this is accomplished by a special "Pass 0" of the assembler or by a totally separate package called a macro preprocessor. In either case, the result of this preprocessing is a regular MACRO-11 program with all references to macros replaced by the body of the text itself. This new program is called the *expanded source program,* which can be translated to object code by the assembler and executed by the hardware. This sequence of translations is shown in Figure 17-2.

Macro processing itself is divided into two separate steps: *macro definitions* and *macro calls.*

17.2.1 Macro Definitions

To *define* a macro is to associate a macro *name* with a sequence of characters. A macro must be defined before it can be referenced (used). The syntax of a macro definition in MACRO-11 is shown in Figure 17-3.

The macro "name" can be any legal MACRO-11 symbol. The "parameter list" is a list of formal parameters to the macro separated by commas. The macro name and the parameter list may be separated by either a comma or a blank. In this chap-

FIGURE 17-2 Sequence of Program Translations.

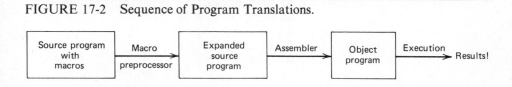

FIGURE 17-3   Syntax of a Macro Definition.

```
.MACRO    name   parameter-list
          .
          .
          .   ; Any sequence of characters. This is
          .   ; the macro body.
          .
          .
.ENDM
```

---

ter, we use a blank. Each formal parameter of the macro must be a legal MACRO-11 identifier and, once declared as a parameter, it can be used anywhere within the body of the macro. Formal parameters are replaced by actual parameters when the macro is expanded. This replacement process is described in the upcoming section on referencing macros.

Figure 17-4 shows the definition of a macro called SAVEJ (for SAVE and Jump) that saves the contents of registers R0 to R5 and then jumps to a location called ADDR. The location of the memory block where the registers will be saved (SAVELOC) and the jump address (ADDR) are parameters of the macro.

When a macro definition like the one in Figure 17-4 is encountered, either during assembly or by the macro preprocessor, two very important operations are performed. First, the name of the macro is added to a data structure called the *macro name table* (MNT). Second, the body of the macro (including information about the formal parameters) is copied, character by character, to the *macro definition table* (MDT). When the characters are copied to the MDT, no processing is done and no attempt is made either to translate the statements or to validate them as meaningful instructions. Instead, it is simply a "raw" character-by-character transfer. Figure

---

FIGURE 17-4   Sample Macro Definition.

```
.MACRO    SAVEJ   SAVELOC,ADDR
MOV       R0,SAVELOC
MOV       R1,SAVELOC+2
MOV       R2,SAVELOC+4
MOV       R3,SAVELOC+6
MOV       R4,SAVELOC+10
MOV       R5,SAVELOC+12
JMP       ADDR
.ENDM
```

FIGURE 17-5 Effect of a Macro Definition on the MNT and MDT.

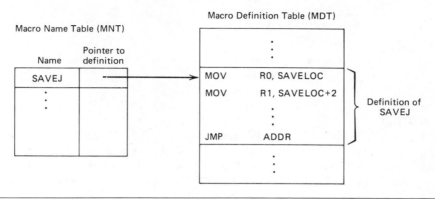

17-5 shows the effect of encountering the definition of the macro called SAVEJ from Figure 17-4.

The process of putting a name into the MNT and putting its corresponding definition into the MDT is called making a macro *known*. Once a macro is known, it may be used anywhere within the remainder of the program. An attempt to use a macro before it is known will result in either an error or unexpected behavior. Exactly what will happen depends on the name you reference. If, for example, you incorrectly reference a macro called XYZ before it is defined, the result will be an undefined name and a fatal error. If you refer to a macro called MOV before you have defined it, the system will assume that you meant the MACRO-11 move operation and will assemble that instruction. Since this is not what you meant, unpredictable behavior will follow. If you select a macro name that is the same as a valid MACRO-11 op code (e.g., MOV or CLR), any future use of that op code will refer to your macro rather than to the system-defined meaning. The renaming of op codes is legal, but it is not recommended.

We must stress again that the characters contained in the body of a macro do not need to correspond to meaningful MACRO-11 statements when the macro is first defined. For example, the character " ' " (apostrophe) means *concatenation* whenever it appears within the body of a macro. If the identifier B is a formal parameter of a macro, then the character string:

X'B

appearing within that macro means the letter X concatenated with whatever actual parameter is substituted for the formal parameter B when the macro is referenced. However, at the time the macro is defined, the macro processor will simply store the

FIGURE 17-6   Macro Definition for TEST.

```
.MACRO   TEST   REG1,REG2,COND,LOC
CMP      REG1,REG2
B'COND   LOC
.ENDM
```

three characters "X'B" into the MDT regardless of whether they make sense in MACRO-11.

As a more concrete example, look at Figure 17-6, a macro called TEST, which compares the values in two registers, REG1 and REG2, and branches to location LOC based on the result of the test. The operation code B'COND has no meaning yet and would be considered illegal in MACRO-11. However, if the formal parameter COND takes on the 2-character value "EQ" when the macro is used, we will concatenate the letter 'B' with the string 'EQ' and generate the valid MACRO-11 op code BEQ. If COND takes on the value "LT", we will generate the valid op code BLT. We can use the string-processing capabilities of macros to generate the instruction we want at the time the macro is used. This is something that we cannot do with ordinary subroutines because all statements in a subroutine must compile correctly at the time they are encountered.

In Figure 17-7, the macro GENMESS allows you to generate any arbitrary message, with any arbitrary name, using the .ASCII or .ASCIZ directive. The parameter "NAME" will be used in the label field to name the message. The parameter "TYPE" will be either "I" or "Z" and will be used to build the proper directive, either .ASCII or .ASCIZ. Finally, the parameter "TEXT" will be placed between the two "/" characters and will become the actual message itself. In this macro, the text may not contain the "/" character. (See Exercise 2 for a more generalized version of this macro.)

As this last example clearly demonstrates, the formal parameters of a macro may appear anywhere in the instruction: in the label field, the op-code field, or the address field.

Macro definitions may also be *nested*. That is, a macro definition may appear completely inside another definition. For example, let's assume that we have in our subroutine library three trigonometric subroutines called SIN, COS, and TAN. They

FIGURE 17-7   Macro Definition for GENMESS.

```
        .MACRO     GENMESS  NAME,TYPE,TEXT
NAME:   .ASCI'TYPE  /TEXT/
        .EVEN
        .ENDM
```

all take one parameter, X, and in the absence of macro capabilities, are activated as follows:

```
        JSR     PC,SIN    JSR     PC,COS    JSR     PC,TAN
        .WORD   X         .WORD   X         .WORD   X
```

Because these 2-line calling sequences are somewhat confusing and cryptic, we would like to create three macros—called SIN, COS, and TAN—to simplify these subroutine calls. To do this, we could write the following three macros:

```
.MACRO   SIN VALUE        .MACRO   COS VALUE        .MACRO   TAN VALUE
JSR      PC,SIN           JSR      PC,COS           JSR      PC,TAN
.WORD    VALUE            .WORD    VALUE            .WORD    VALUE
.ENDM                     .ENDM                     .ENDM
```

but this is unnecessarily repetitive. Instead, we could write one macro whose purpose is to generate the above macro definitions: in a sense, a macro that creates macros! Such a macro, called DEFINE, appears in Figure 17-8.

When the definition in Figure 17-8 is encountered, the outer macro called DEFINE will be made known. The characters making up the body of DEFINE, from the .MACRO on line 2 to the first .ENDM on line 5, are copied into the MDT. It is not important at this time that there happens to be another macro inside. Remember that during macro definition, the body of a macro is stored but is not processed in any way. The inner macro becomes known only when the outer macro is referenced. We see an example of this in Section 17.2.2, where we learn to reference the macros SAVEJ, TEST, GENMESS, and DEFINE in a program.

17.2.2   Macro Expansions

The process of using or referencing a known macro is called *macro expansion.* To expand a macro, we use the name of the macro in the op-code field. The syntax of a macro call is:

(label:)   macro-name   argument list

FIGURE 17-8   Example of a Nested Macro Definition.

```
.MACRO   DEFINE   NAME,VALUE
        .MACRO    NAME VALUE    ⎤
        JSR       PC,NAME       ⎥
        .WORD     VALUE         ⎬  The body of the macro called DEFINE
        .ENDM                   ⎥
.ENDM                           ⎦
```

If there is a label attached to the macro call, it will be appended to the first line of code generated by the call. The macro name appearing in the op-code field must be known before it can be used. In this section we assume that whenever we reference a macro, it has already been defined. Finally, the "argument list" is the list of actual arguments separated by commas.

During the assembly process, the assembler takes any identifier found in the op-code field and searches for its meaning in two places, and in the order given below.

1. The macro name table.
2. The list of all legal MACRO-11 mnemonics (Appendix A).

The order of the search implies that if you define a macro to have the same name as a MACRO-11 instruction (e.g., MOV), your definition will be used in place of the standard built-in meaning, and you will lose that intrinsic meaning for the remainder of the program.

If the symbol in the op-code field is a known macro name, some interesting things begin to happen. First, the characters in the body of the macro (from the MDT) are copied directly into the body of the text, in place of the macro call. The actual arguments replace the formal parameters in a strict positional ordering. That is, the first actual parameter is copied in place of the first formal parameter, and so on. The replacement is accomplished on a straight, *string replacement* basis. The characters making up the actual parameter replace the characters making up the formal parameter. Thus, the following MACRO-11 instruction:

SAVEJ   TEMP,LOOP   ; The macro defined in Figure 17-4

will be recognized as a macro and will produce the sequence of instructions shown in Figure 17-9.

Notice that the expressions in the address field (e.g., TEMP + 2, . . .) have not been evaluated. All we did was replace the formal parameter characters "ADDR" with the actual parameter characters "TEMP."

Whether the expanded code is included in the program listing depends on the setting of the ME (macro expansion) option on the .LIST directive. If it is ON, all code produced during macro expansion will be included in the listing. If it is OFF, only

---

FIGURE 17-9   Sample Macro Expansion.

```
MOV     R0,TEMP
MOV     R1,TEMP+2
MOV     R2,TEMP+4
MOV     R3,TEMP+6
MOV     R4,TEMP+10
MOV     R5,TEMP+12
JMP     LOOP
```

call itself will be included, without the code generated by the call (i.e., not the seven lines shown in Figure 17-9). See Section 14.5.3 for a discussion of how to use the .LIST directive.

The macro call:

```
TEST   R0,R1,GT,BIG   ; The macro of Figure 17-6
```

will be expanded into:

```
        CMP     R0,R1
        BGT     BIG
```

Again, notice the string concatenation to form the op code BGT. If we had accidentally mistyped the parameters and called the macro in the following way:

```
TEST   R0,R1,TG,BIG   ; TG instead of GT
```

we would produce the following two lines of code:

```
        CMP     R0,R1
        BTG     BIG
```

The macro has been properly expanded, but because macro expansion is only a string-processing operation and not assembly, it has produced the meaningless instruction BTG. When that instruction is assembled, it will produce the "O" error code—illegal operation code. You must be extremely careful when expanding macros that the expansion leads to code that makes sense. Because the macro processor is just a glorified string handler, it will not do that for you. It will expand whatever you provide.

As one final example, let's expand the macro in Figure 17-7 called GENMESS to generate the code for the message: "Hello, my name is Mike!" If we erroneously try to write:

```
GENMESS   M,I,"Hello, my name is Mike!"
```

we will get an error message stating that we have too many actual parameters. In a macro call, commas are used to separate parameters, and the comma in the message itself is being incorrectly interpreted. To indicate that a string of characters is to be treated as a single parameter, even if it contains a comma, we must enclose the entire parameter in angle brackets: ⟨ ⟩. Thus, the proper call to the macro GENMESS would be:

```
GENMESS   M,I,⟨"Hello, my name is Mike!"⟩
```

This call would correctly expand into the following code:

```
M:    .ASCII /"Hello, my name is Mike!"/
      .EVEN
```

The macro expansion:

```
GENMESS    VOWELS,Z,AEIOU
```

would produce the two lines:

```
VOWELS:    .ASCIZ /AEIOU/
           .EVEN
```

During macro expansion, any macro definitions encountered are added to the macro name table and the macro definition table, and are thus made known. As we know, a macro defined within another macro is called a nested macro definition. A nested macro can be made known only by expanding the outer macro. For example, the following macro call:

```
DEFINE    COS,X
```

where DEFINE is the macro definition in Figure 17-8, will result in the following four lines of code:

```
.MACRO    COS X
JSR       PC,COS
.WORD     X
.ENDM
```

This is not code for the assembler, but will simply result in the creation of a new macro called COS with a single parameter called X. The name COS will be placed in the MNT, and its definition, the JSR instruction and .WORD directive will go into the MDT. Similarly, the statements:

```
DEFINE    SIN,X
DEFINE    TAN,X
```

will create and make known macros called SIN and TAN, respectively. Once COS, SIN, and TAN are known, they may be referenced within the program.

During the expansion of a macro, we may encounter another macro call. This is called *nested macro expansion*. For example, given the following sequence:

```
.MACRO  A
        .
        .
        .
```

```
.ENDM

.MACRO   B
         .
         .
         .
A            ; This is an expansion of macro A
         .
         .
         .
.ENDM
         .
         .
         .
B            ; This is an expansion of macro B
```

the expansion of macro B at this point will result in an encounter with the expansion of macro A.

When we encounter a nested expansion, we always complete the expansion of the *inner* call before continuing the expansion of the outer one. In this sense, the order of processing is identical to the order in which nested for loops or do loops are handled in BASIC, FORTRAN, or Pascal, with the inner loop always being completed first. In this example, we begin expanding macro B. When we encounter the expansion of A, the *entire* body of macro A will be copied into the input text before we continue the expansion of B.

Let's define a new macro called TRIG that uses the macros called SIN, COS, and TAN defined earlier. TRIG will have two parameters: an angle, X and a label (ERROR) to handle the condition that the value of X is illegal.

```
.MACRO   TRIG X,ERROR
     TST  X
     BLT  ERROR          ; ERROR is a global label
     SIN  X              ; not part of the macro
     COS  X
     TAN  X
.ENDM
```

Now let's assume that the following three operations have been completed.

1. The macro called DEFINE in Figure 17-8 has been created and made known.
2. DEFINE has been expanded three times to create macros called SIN, COS, and TAN.
3. The macro called TRIG has been created and made known.

Then the following macro call:

```
TRIG   Z53,BADVAL
```

will result in the expansion of the macro called TRIG. This will first generate the following two lines of code:

```
TST  Z53
BLT  BADVAL
     .
     .
     .
```

Neither of these first two lines is itself a macro call, so the expansion process continues. At this point, we encounter an operation code called "SIN", which is recognized as another macro call. We will push on a stack (not the system stack, but some stack mechanism local to the macro processor) the message, "We are expanding the macro called TRIG and are currently at line 4." With that informatin saved, we can then begin the expansion of the inner macro called SIN, resulting in the following two lines of code:

```
JSR      PC,SIN
.WORD    Z53
```

With the inner macro SIN now completed, we pop the top item off the stack to see what we should do next. In this case, we continue expanding TRIG at line 4. The same process of saving information about what we are doing and then working on the inner macro is used with the nested calls to both COS and TAN. The final result of the expansion of the call on the TRIG macro is the following eight lines:

```
TST    Z53
BLT    BADVAL
JSR    PC,SIN
.WORD  Z53
JSR    PC,COS
.WORD  Z53
JSR    PC,TAN
.WORD  Z53
```

As this example has clearly demonstrated, macro processing is a highly recursive operation. A macro expansion can initiate either another expansion, via a nested call, or a macro definition, via a nested definition. For this reason a stack is an absolutely essential data structure to support macro processing. If we encounter either a nested call or a nested definition, we push information (name, parameters, location) about the current macro onto the stack and begin processing the new definition or call. When we complete a definition or call, we pop the stack to see exactly where we left off. Processing of the current macro is finished when the stack is empty.

17.2.2   Labels in Macros

You must be careful to avoid one potential pitfall with macro processing, namely, the problem of using a local label within a macro definition. For example, the macro

FIGURE 17-10 A Divide Macro.

```
        .MACRO  DIVIDE    X,Y,QUOT,REMAIN    ; X/Y
        CLR     QUOT
        CLR     REMAIN
        TST     Y         ; See if the denominator is zero
        BEQ     ZERODIV   ; If yes, branch to the end of
                          ; the macro
        CLR     R0        ; If no, carry out the division
        MOV     X,R1
        DIV     Y,R0
        MOV     R0,QUOT   ; This is the quotient
        MOV     R1,REMAIN ; This is the remainder
ZERODIV: .ENDM
```

shown in Figure 17-10 divides two 16-bit quantities, X and Y, to produce a Quotient and a Remainder. The division is not performed if $Y = 0$. In that case, we simply skip the operation and continue.

The first time we expand DIVIDE by writing something like:

$$\text{DIVIDE} \quad \text{A,B,Q,R} \quad ; \text{Divide A/B giving Q and R}$$

we will produce nine lines of code *and* the label called ZERODIV attached to the first instruction that follows the macro call. The second time we expand DIVIDE by writing:

$$\text{DIVIDE} \quad \text{I,J,Q,R} \quad ; \text{Divide I/J giving Q and R}$$

we will produce nine more lines of code and *another* occurrence of the same label ZERODIV. This is illegal and will cause the assembler to produce an "M" error flag: a multiply defined label. Unless you take precautions, you cannot include a label in any macro that will be expanded more than once.

There are several ways to solve this problem, and which one you choose depends on the operations you are performing.

1. *Make the label a parameter to the macro:*

```
        .MACRO  SAMPLE X,Y,LABEL
                .
                .
                .
LABEL:
        .ENDM
```

Now each time you expand the macro you provide your own unique name for the label.

```
SAMPLE   A,B,LAB1   ; The label will be LAB1
SAMPLE   I,J,LAB2   ; The label will be LAB2
```

This was the approach taken with the GENMESS macro in Figure 17-7.

2. *Use concatenation to build unique labels:* We can use the concatenation operator (') to create a new label each time the macro is expanded. We concatenate a user-supplied string to a fixed string to create unique labels. For example:

```
.MACRO   SAMPLE,X,Y,N
         .
         .
         .
LABEL N
         .ENDM
```

Now each time we expand SAMPLE we use a unique character for N, such as 0, 1, 2, ... This will result in a unique sequence of labels, LABEL0, LABEL1, ...

```
SAMPLE   A,B,0
SAMPLE   I,J,1
```

3. *Use only location counter addressing:* Instead of using labels to indicate where to branch, we can refer to the relative position of the desired destination via the location counter. For example:

```
         BEQ   AROUND
         MOV   #1,R0
AROUND:
```

The move instruction occupies two words, or four bytes, of memory. Therefore, to branch around it we must advance the location counter by four. This will put the proper offset value into the offset field of the BEQ instruction. Remembering that the period character in the address field refers to the current value of the location counter, the previous sequence can be rewritten without labels as:

```
BEQ   .+4      ; Branch around the MOV instruction
MOV   #1,R0
```

This type of addressing is called *location counter addressing* and allows you to refer to a location not by its address by but its relative distance from the current instruction. The use of location counter addressing can be dangerous and requires great care. It is very easy to miscount the distance to another instruction, since MACRO-11 instructions can be two, four, or six bytes long, depending on the operation code and the addressing mode. If you do miscount, the assembler cannot detect it, and your program will contain an error that is difficult to locate and correct. Also, if you make any changes to the program between the branch and its ultimate destination, you may inadvertently change the count and introduce an error into the program. For example, in the following program fragment:

the distance between the branch and move instructions must always remain exactly thirty (octal) bytes. Otherwise, the branch will not refer to the correct location. Any change (either to an instruction or to a piece of data located between these two points) that changes this distance will result in an error. If this distance is large, it is easy to make a change without realizing the effect that it will have on other instructions.

In general, location counter addressing is used only for very short branches, such as branching two, three, or four words in either direction. It is not recommended for longer branches, because errors are likely to be introduced at some future point, and because the program becomes difficult to maintain.

4. *Use the MACRO-11 feature called "generated labels":* MACRO-11 can generate unique labels for you during expansion. You request this feature by prefacing the label name with a question mark in the macro definition formal parameter list:

```
        .MACRO  SAMPLE X,Y,?LABEL
                .
                .
                .
LABEL:
        .ENDM
```

In the macro call, if you omit the parameter preceded by the ?, the macro processor will generate a unique label each time the macro is expanded, placing it in the correct location. (The unique labels generated are of the form 64$, 65$, 66$, etc.) Macro calls that omit the third parameter:

```
        SAMPLE  A,B
        SAMPLE  I,J
```

will cause the macro processor to replace the parameter LABEL with 64$ the first time, and 65$ the second time. If you do not omit the parameter preceded by the question mark, as in:

SAMPLE   M,N,LOOP

the parameter replacement will proceed in the normal way, with the actual parameter LOOP replacing the formal parameter LABEL.

Regardless of which technique you use, you must ensure that the same label cannot be generated more than once during macro expansion. Failure in this regard will always result in an error caused by a multiply defined symbol.

17.3
Uses of Macros

We have spent a great deal of time describing the mechanics of macro processing without explaining how we can best use them. Now we describe some of the advantages to be gained from macro processing.

17.3.1   Elimination of Repetitive Code Segments

With macros, we can avoid writing out segments of code that appear over and over again in MACRO-11 programs. This is one very simple but quite handy reason for using them. For example, at the beginning of each MACRO-11 subroutine, you will typically find code to save registers R0 to R5 and, at the end, code to restore their initial value. If the program has many subroutines, this will become tedious. If instead you define two macros called SAVE and RESTORE as follows:

```
.MACRO SAVE
     MOV    R0,-(SP)
     MOV    R1,-(SP)
     MOV    R2,-(SP)
     MOV    R3,-(SP)
     MOV    R4,-(SP)
     MOV    R5,-(SP)
     .ENDM
```

```
.MACRO RESTORE
     MOV    (SP)+,R5
     MOV    (SP)+,R4
     MOV    (SP)+,R3
     MOV    (SP)+,R2
     MOV    (SP)+,R1
     MOV    (SP)+,R0
     .ENDM
```

then you can write all of your subroutines as follows:

```
SUB:   SAVE
              .
              .
              .
       RESTORE
       RTS        PC
```

The code to save and restore the registers will now be inserted into the program automatically.

Similarly, you could simplify the following 3-line allocation of space for a user stack:

```
.EVEN
.BLKW      50
STACK = .
```

to one line by defining the macro SPACE:

```
.MACRO   SPACE   NAME,SIZE
.EVEN
.BLKW    SIZE
NAME =   .
.ENDM
```

Now, to allocate a 50-word (octal) stack called STACK you simply write:

```
SPACE   STACK,50
```

The macro called DIVIDE in Figure 17-10 shortened the overall procedure for division from nine lines to one. A program with a great number of integer divisions would be significantly easier to write because of the existence of this macro.

Finally, the very common I/O sequence:

```
         INC    @#CRTSR       ; Initiate the input operation
LOOP:    BIT    #200,@#CRTSR  ; Test if it's done
         BEQ    LOOP          ; If not, keep waiting
         MOVB   @#CRTBUF,X    ; Move the character to memory
```

could easily be made a macro, permitting a character to be input from the CRT keyboard with one line instead of four. The following READ macro assumes that the status and buffer register symbolic names have already been defined and are of the form dddSR and dddBUF, where "ddd" is a 3-letter abbreviation for the device name.

```
        .MACRO  READ  DEVICE,LOC,?LABEL
        INC     @#DEVICE'SR
LABEL:  BIT     #200,@#DEVICE'SR
        BEQ     LABEL
        MOVB    @#DEVICE'BUF,LOC
        .ENDM
```

Now, to read one character from the CRT into memory location CH, we simply write:

```
        READ    CRT,CH
```

This macro call will generate the following four lines:

```
        INC     @#CRTSR
64$:    BIT     #200,@#CRTSR
        BEQ     64$
        MOVB    @#CRTBUF,CH
```

When we shorten the writing of the code, we often also make it more "mnemonic" and easier to understand. It is much easier to think of input/output in terms of a READ macro than as an INC, BIT, BEQ, and MOVB sequence.

The program listings that result from the judicious and clever use of macros are usually clearer and much more understandable and, as a result, much easier to maintain. In addition, these listings begin to resemble higher level languages, rather than the often cryptic notation of assembly language. For example, the Pascal fragment:

```
        Read (A,B);
        C := A/B
```

might resemble the following, using our own macros READ and DIVIDE:

```
        READ    CRT,A
        READ    CRT,B
        DIVIDE  A,B,C,REMAINDER
```

This is certainly more lucid than the code that would result from using MACRO-11 directly.

17.3.2 Extending a Language

MACRO-11 has over two hundred unique operation codes in its repertoire. But no matter how many it had, there would always be operations for particular programs that could not be performed directly. A macro processor provides a way to build new operation codes into the language and then program with these new codes exactly as if they were part of the language. As a result, we can create a "customized" extended

FIGURE 17-11 Language Extensibility Using Macros.

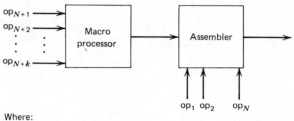

Where:

op$_1$, · · ·, op$_N$ are the operation codes of the language
op$_{N+1}$, · · ·, op$_{N+k}$ are the operation codes created using the
macro preprocessor

assembly language with exactly the operations we want to include. This is diagrammed in Figure 17-11.

As Figure 17-11 shows, instead of thinking only in terms of the N operations provided directly by the assembler itself, we can think of the language as containing the
$N + k$ operations provided by the assembler *and* the macro processor.

Let's say that before we began programming on the PDP-11 we had worked extensively on a stack-oriented zero-address computer of the type described in Section
9.2.5, and that we were accustomed to the power and convenience of zero-address
instructions. We could, if desired, add "stacklike" zero-address instructions to the
MACRO-11 language as follows:

```
.MACRO   PUSH X
MOV      X,−(SP)
.ENDM

.MACRO   POP X
MOV      (SP)+,X
.ENDM

.MACRO   ADDST
ADD      (SP)+,(SP)
.ENDM
```

Once these definitions have been made, we can program using these newly developed
stack instructions. The evaluation of the expression $W = X + Y + Z$ would be
coded as:

```
PUSH    Z
PUSH    Y
PUSH    X
ADDST
```

```
ADDST
POP     W
```

exactly as if we were using our old zero-address, stack-oriented computer. The code
that would be produced by the expansion of the preceeding macros is:

```
MOV   Z,−(SP)
MOV   Y,−(SP)
MOV   X,−(SP)
ADD   (SP)+,(SP)
ADD   (SP)+,(SP)
MOV   (SP)+,W
```

MACRO-11 does not support an "Add Byte" instruction that adds two 8-bit quantities in the following way:

$$ADDB \quad addr_1, addr_2 \quad ; \quad CON(addr_1) + CON(addr_2) \rightarrow CON(addr_2)$$

If we needed such an instruction, we could add it to the language with the macro
definition facility. An add byte macro called ADDB is shown in Figure 17-12.

We could also begin to add some of the features of high-level languages that we
have repeatedly said are missing in assembly languages. For example, the following
macro adds a very limited if/then/else construct that compares two variables and
branches to one of two locations based on the outcome.

```
.MACRO   IF,X,Y,OP,THEN,ELSE
CMP      X,Y
B'OP     THEN
JMP      ELSE
.ENDM
```

Thus, the following macro expansion:

```
IF   A,B,GT,BIG,SMALL
```

will expand into the following three lines of code:

```
CMP   A,B
BGT   BIG
JMP   SMALL
```

which will result in a branch to BIG if $A > B$, and SMALL otherwise. The following
macro expansion:

```
IF   C,D,EQ,L1,L2
```

will branch to L1 if $C = D$, and L2 otherwise.

FIGURE 17-12   An Add Byte Macro.

```
         .Title   AddByte
TmpFlg   =        0              ; Flag to indicate that this is the first
                                 ; time the macro has been expanded
         ;
         ; Here is the macro definition
         ;
.Macro   AddB     Arg1,Arg2;?ChA2,?Ovr,?NoOvr,?NoCarry,?ClrV,?Done
.If      DIF      ⟨TmpFlg⟩,1   ; Is this the first time this macro has been
                                 ; used? The .IF will be described in the
                                 ; next section
         JMP      AB1            ; Yes, Make sure the program jumps
                                 ; over the data

ABT1:    .Word    0              ; Temporary to hold first argument
ABT2:    .Word    0              ; Temporary to hold second argument
OvrFl:   .Byte    0              ; Temporary to hold overflow bit
         .Even
TmpFlg   =        1              ; Set temp flag so compiler knows that
                                 ; the temporary words have been
                                 ; defined
AB1:
         .EndC                   ; End of the If. This psuedo-op will
                                 ; also be described in the next section

         CLR      ABT1           ; Clear the first temporary
         CLR      ABT2           ; Clear the second temporary

         MOVB     Arg1,ABT1      ; Move the first argument to word 1
         MOVB     Arg2,ABT2      ; Move the second argument to word 2

         CLRB     OvrFl          ; Assume no overflow will occur
         ADD      ABT1,ABT2      ; Add the two words

         TSTB     Arg1           ; Is the first argument positive?
         BPL      ChA2           ; Yes, Check the second argument
         TSTB     Arg2           ; The first is negative, Is the second
                                 ; positive?
         BPL      NoOvr          ; Yes, Overflow cannot have occurred
         TSTB     ABT2           ; Both are negative, Is the result
                                 ; negative?
         BMI      NoOvr          ; Yes, all is well
         BR       Ovr            ; No, Overflow occurred

ChA2:    TSTB     Arg2           ; The first is positive, Is the second
                                 ; positive?
```

FIGURE 17-12   An Add Byte Macro. (*continued*)

```
            BMI   NoOvr      ; No, Overflow cannot have occurred
            TSTB  ABT2       ; Both are positive, Is the result
                            ; positive?
            BPL   NoOvr      ; Yes, all is well
Ovr:        MOVB  #1,OvrFl   ; No, Set the overflow flag

NoOvr:      TSTB  ABT2+1     ; The high byte of the result holds the
                            ; carry, Is there a carry?
                            ; (TSTB clears the carry bit)
            BEQ   NoCarry    ; No, the C bit is already clear
            SEC              ; Yes, Set the C bit

NoCarry:
            DECB  OvrFl      ; (Luckily this leaves C alone) Is
                            ; overflow set?
            BNE   ClrV       ; No, jump to ClrV

            MOVB  ABT2,Arg2  ; Move result back into second argument
                            ; (MOVB conditionally sets N and Z,
                            ; clears V, and leaves C alone)
            SEV              ; Overflow occurred, turn on the V bit
            BR    Done       ; All condition codes are set, Jump to
                            ; the end of the macro

ClrV:       MOVB  ABT2,Arg2  ; Move result back into second argument
                            ; (MOVB conditionally sets N and Z,
                            ; clears V, and leaves C alone)
                            ; V is clear
Done:       .EndM            ; End of the macro


a :         .Byte 0          ; The left operand goes here
b :         .Byte 0          ; The right operand and the result go here
Start:
              .

              .

              .
            AddB  a,b        ; Here is the macro expansion

              .

              .
            .End  Start
```

There are many other areas for which you probably can imagine new and interesting operation codes:

1. String-processing capabilities.

2. Looping structures.

3. Array operations.

4. Higher level I/O operations (e.g., read an integer).

The inclusion of macros for these and other operations greatly expands the capabilities of MACRO-11 and begins to give the language many of the characteristics of higher level languages. Exercises 16 and 17 ask you to design and code such macros.

17.3.3   Simulating an Entire Language

Let's say that you have a "Whiz Bang 100" computer system with many important programs written in Whiz Bang Assembly Language (WHALE?). WHALE is a 1-address language similar to the instructions shown in Figure 9-10. You have decided to purchase a new VAX-11/782 computer and are wondering how to run your WHALE programs when the new VAX arrives in about two or three weeks. The VAX cannot execute programs written in WHALE. Initially, it seems that you have only two choices.

1. Rewrite the WHALE programs in MACRO-11 or a high-level language that executes on the VAX.

2. Write a WHALE *cross assembler* and *simulator* for the VAX. The cross assembler on the VAX would produce WHALE object code while the WHALE simulator would execute the instructions.

Both of these options involve long and expensive software development projects and, in the latter case, fail to use the increased capabilities of the new system. There is a third approach that may offer the quickest and least costly interim solution during the changeover period. This third approach utilizes the macro capabilities of MACRO-11.

You will need to write one MACRO-11 macro for each of the legal operation codes and assembler directives in WHALE. The name of the macro will be the same as the mnemonic WHALE op code, and the body of the macro will implement the exact meaning of that WHALE instruction using the allowable MACRO-11 instructions and addressing modes. For example, the LOAD, STORE, and OUT instructions in WHALE whose behavior is identical to those of Figure 9-10, might be implemented as follows:

```
.MACRO  LOAD X   ; CON(X) → CON(accumulator)
MOV     X,R0     ; We will use R0 for the accumulator
.ENDM

.MACRO  STORE X  ; CON(accumulator) → CON(X)
MOV     R0,X
.ENDM
```

```
            .MACRO   OUT X,?LOOP
            MOVB     X,@#177562
   LOOP:    BIT      #200,@#177560
            BEQ      LOOP
            .ENDM
```

Now, with these and all of the other macros in place, you can take your WHALE assembly-language programs and submit them directly to the new VAX. For example, in the following WHALE instruction sequence:

```
   LOAD   X
   STORE  Y   ; Y: = X
```

each of the operation codes (LOAD, STORE) will be recognized as a macro and will result in the expansion of that macro to produce the proper MACRO-11 sequence:

```
   MOV   X,R0
   MOV   R0,Y
```

The macro processor handles the translation of WHALE to MACRO-11 through your macro definitions.

When you use this approach, you may notice that the resulting code tends to be quite inefficient, since each line is translated independently of what comes before or after. For example, the preceding code would be better written as:

```
   MOV   X,Y
```

taking one instruction instead of two.

Although code efficiency is a problem, and there are other problems that we have not discussed, the use of macros is a quick way to execute the assembly language of one computer on another machine. It is usually an excellent interim solution until the software for the new system is completed.

17.4 System Macros

Most computer systems, including the PDP-11 and the VAX-11, provide extensive *libraries* of macros that can be accessed by users within their own MACRO-11 programs. Unlike the standardized libraries of higher level languages, no fixed list of services is provided with MACRO-11 implementations. Each installation is free to develop and include whatever macros would be helpful to its users. In this text, we have referred to some of the possible *system macros* that you may encounter on your system; they are summarized in Figure 17-13. However, this list is illustrative only. You must check with your own computer center to see exactly which library routines exist on your computer and exactly how they work. Notice that all system macros

FIGURE 17-13   Examples of System Macros.

Name	Purpose
.EXIT	To handle program termination
.TTYIN	To input one character from a CRT
.TTYOUT	To output one character to a CRT
.SNAP	To produce a snapshot dump
.TRACEON	To turn the trace mechanism on
.TRACEOFF	To turn the trace mechanism off
.PMD	To produce a post-morten dump and halt
.DUMP	To produce a memory dump and continue program execution

begin with the character ".". Therefore, when choosing names for your own local macros, do *not* select a name beginning with a period. This will avoid any possible conflict with the names of system macros.

Before a system macro can be used, its name must first appear in an .MCALL (Macro Call) directive.

.MCALL   name,name, . . .

The names in the address field are the names of all system macros referenced in the program. The .MCALL directive must appear *before* the first reference to any of these macros. Typically, it is placed at or near the beginning of the program, as in Figure 17-14.

Another example of the .MCALL directive is given in the subroutines IN and OUT listed in Appendix E.

In addition to the .MCALL directive, you may have to provide one or more special

FIGURE 17-14   Use of the .MCALL Directive.

```
            .TITLE    Sample Use of .MCALL
            .MCALL    .EXIT,.SNAP
    START:    .
              .
              .          ;  Your program
              .
              .

            .SNAP
            .EXIT
            .END      START
```

commands to the operating system to indicate that you will be using library macros. Check on this with your instructor or with your local computer center.

Macro processing in MACRO-11 is an extremely powerful and highly complex tool. For more information on this subject, refer to the PDP-11 MACRO-11 Language Reference Manual, Chapter 7, "MACRO Directives."

17.5
Conditional Assembly

In higher level languages, decisions are implemented by writing out two complete sequences of instructions and then, at execution time, selecting which sequence you want to execute:

If B then
S_1
else
S_2

At execution time, if B has the value TRUE, instruction sequence S_1 will be executed; otherwise, instruction sequence S_2 will be executed. The same idea is supported in assembly language by the compare and branch instructions:

```
              TST   B
              Bxx   ELSE   ; Where xx is a 2-letter mnemonic
       THEN:  .
              .
              .
              S₁
              .
              .
              JMP   DONE
       ELSE:  S₂
              .
              .
       DONE:  .
```

Regardless of which sequence is actually executed, however, both S_1 and S_2 must be included as part of the program and will occupy valuable memory space. If the sequences are quite long, this might result in a great deal of memory being occupied, even though only one sequence may ever be used.

If the criterion for deciding which sequence to select will not be known until the program is executed, there is nothing we can do. However, if the selection criterion is known when the program is assembled, there is a very attractive alternative. Instead of translating and storing both sequences of instructions and then choosing

FIGURE 17-15   General Structure of a Conditional
Assembly Block.

```
      .IF        condition,argument(s)
                 .
                 .
                 .
                 .    ; Any sequence of MACRO-11 instructions
                 .
      .ENDC
```

which one to execute, we can choose which sequence to translate and store, and assemble only that code. The other code will be skipped over, and neither assembled nor stored in memory. This process, called *conditional assembly,* allows us to produce programs that contain only the instructions that are needed for our particular environment and conditions. The resulting programs occupy considerably less memory space.

The general form of a conditional assembly block is shown in Figure 17-15. The conditions that can be tested for are:

Condition	Arguments	Assemble Block If:
EQ	An expression	The expression evaluates to 0
NE	An expression	The expression does not evaluate to 0
GT	An expression	The expression is greater than 0
LT	An expression	The expression is less than 0
GE	An expression	The expression is greater than or equal to 0
LE	An expression	The expression is less than or equal to 0
DF	A symbol	The symbol has been defined
NDF	A symbol	The symbol has not been defined
IDN	Two expressions	The two expressions are identical
DIF	Two expressions	The two expressions are different

If the condition specified in the .IF directive is satisfied, then all instructions within the condition block are assembled in the normal way. However, if the condition is *not* met, the assembler will skip over and not assemble all instructions between the .IF and the occurrence of the matching .ENDC directive. These instructions will not appear in the program and will not occupy memory space.

For example, let's say that we are writing a program to input a block of characters from either a card reader (an 80-character physical record) or a disk (with 256 char-

FIGURE 17-16   Example of Conditional Assembly for I/O Devices.

```
          .IF         EQ,DEVICE   ; See which device is being used
          RECSIZE = 80 .          ; Here are the card reader
                                  ; declarations
     BUF: .BLKB       RECSIZE
          STREG    = 177160
          WC       = 177162
          BA       = 177164
          .ENDC

          .IF         NE,DEVICE
          RECSIZE = 256 .         ; Here are the disk declarations
     BUF: .BLKB       RECSIZE
          STREG    = 174400
          WC       = 174402
          BA       = 174404
          .ENDC
```

acters per sector). We will know which device will be used when the program is being assembled. Instead of allocating buffer space for the largest buffer we would require and then using only what is actually required, we can conditionally assemble the code for the proper-sized buffer allocation based on a flag specifying whether we are using the disk or the card reader.

Assume a flag called DEVICE that is set to 0 if we are using the card reader, and 1 if we are using the disk. The code in Figure 17-16 will correctly assemble the buffer allocation directives for the proper device while skipping over those for the device not being used.

One of the most popular uses of conditional assembly is for the inclusion or exclusion of debugging statements during program development, as shown in Figure 17-17.

FIGURE 17-17   Example of Conditional Assembly in Debugging.

```
          .IF       NE,DEBUG
          .SNAP
          .DUMP     START,END
          .ENDC
```

If the debugging flag DEBUG has a nonzero value at assembly time, then both the snapshot and memory dump macro calls will be expanded. Otherwise, they will not. Since both of these macros typically expand into dozens of lines of code, the use of conditional assembly is far superior to writing something like:

```
            TST     DEBUG
            BEQ     NODUMP
            .SNAP
            .DUMP   START,END
NODUMP:
```

In this example, even though the two macros will not be executed if DEBUG contains a 0, they will always be expanded at assembly time, occupying large amounts of memory. By using conditional assembly, we avoid this waste entirely.

In conditional assembly, it is very important to remember that the arguments of an .IF directive are tested at assembly time, and the value of a symbol at assembly time is a value of the location counter when the symbol is encountered in the address field. When you write:

```
FLAG :   .WORD   0
```

the value of FLAG *at assembly time* is *not* 0 (except by the coincidence of having this word be assembled into location 0). It is the *address* of the word into which the constant 0 has been assembled. Thus, if you write the following conditional assembly block:

```
        .IF       EQ,FLAG
                    .
                    .
                    .
        ; Block
                    .
                    .
        .ENDC
```

and you want to set FLAG to 0 to assemble the block, you must *not* do it using the technique shown above. (There is only one chance in 65,536 that FLAG will be assembled into location 0!) Instead, you must use the direct-assignment pseudo-op (=), which assigns a value to a symbol at assembly time. The correct way to set FLAG to the value 0 at assembly time is:

```
        FLAG = 0
```

This directive specifies to the assembler that FLAG has the value 0. The EQ condition on the .IF directive will now be satisfied. Similarly, to indicate that we are using the disk for input in Figure 17-16, we would insert the following line in our program:

$$DEVICE = 1$$

And, finally, to exclude all debugging calls in the code of Figure 17-17, we would write:

$$DEBUG = 0$$

Exercises 18 and 19 contain other examples of the use of conditional assembly directives. For more information, refer to the MACRO-11 Language Reference Manual, Section 6.10, "Conditional Assembly Directives."

Exercises for Chapter 17

1. Consider the differences in implementation for macros and subroutines (Figure 17-1), and discuss how they might differ in terms of:
    a. The total execution time of a program.
    b. The total memory space needed to hold the program.

2. Rewrite the definition of the GENMESS macro in Figure 17-7 to eliminate the restriction that the text of the message cannot contain the "/" character.

3. Assume that you want to write a DEFINE macro to create calls to subroutines with three parameters. That is, given values for p, x, y, and z, DEFINE would correctly generate the call:

p(x,y,z)   ; Call procedure p with parameters x, y, z

Write a nested macro definition, similar to the one in Figure 17-8, that would accomplish this.

4. Show what is produced by each of the following macro expansions. The macros referred to are those defined in Section 17.2.1.
    a.   SAVEJ   X,A
    b.   L: SAVEJ   X+2,LOC
    c.   L2:   TEST   R3,R5,HI,LOOP
    d.   L3:   TEST   R1,R1,EQ,L3
    e.   GENMESS GREETING,Z,⟨HI,THERE HARRY!⟩
    f.   L4: GENMESS DATE,Z,THE DATE IS 1/1/86

5.   Show exactly what would happen if you expanded the DEFINE macro from Exercise 3 by writing the following:

DEFINE   RANDOM   SEED,X,R

6.   Given the following sequence of macro definitions:

```
.MACRO  A
   line 1
   line 2
   line 3
.ENDM
.MACRO  B
   line 4
   line 5
      A
   line 6
   line 7
.ENDM
```

exactly what sequence of statements will be expanded if you now expand macro B?

7.   Given the following sequence of macro definitions:

```
.MACRO  A
   line 1
   line 2
   line 3
    .MACRO  B
    line 4
    line 5
       A
    line 6
    line 7
    .ENDM
   line 8
.ENDM
```

exactly what sequence of statements will be generated by:
   a.   An expansion of macro A?
   b.   An expansion of macro B?
   c.   An expansion of macro A and then macro B?

8.   Show exactly what the macro expansion stack would contain as it expanded the macro call:

TRIG   VAL, LAB

where TRIG is the macro defined in Section 17.2.2.

9. Replace all local labels in the following fragment with location counter addressing.

```
LOOP:   CMP   X,Y
        BGT   BIG
        ADD   #10,R0
        BR    LOOP
BIG:    MOV   #2,R1
```

Do you think using location counter addressing in place of labels is a good programming technique?

10. Rewrite the code fragment in Exercise 9 as a macro. The parameters of the macro are the values X and Y. For the two local labels LOOP and BIG, use the "generated labels" feature of MACRO-11 described in Section 17.2.3.

11. Write a macro called DUMP that takes two parameters LOW and HIGH which are byte addresses. The macro should check if HIGH $\geq$ LOW. If it is, the macro should dump all bytes from memory location LOW to memory location HIGH in ASCII format. That is, it should print the character corresponding to the contents of each byte. The output should look like the following:

Address	Contents	
xxx	c	← This is address LOW
xxx	c	
.		
.		
.		
xxx	c	← This is address HIGH

If LOW $>$ HIGH, the macro should do nothing. If the value stored in a byte corresponds to a nonprinting character, then print a blank. For output, use the routine OUT shown in Appendix E.

12. Write a macro called BITVAL that takes an address and a bit position (0–7) and returns the binary value of that bit position. If the bit position parameter is not in the range 0–7, the macro should set an error parameter called ERROR to 1.

13. Write a macro called BIGSHIFT that takes two parameters—a 16-bit address and an unsigned shift count. The macro will shift the indicated address to the right the number of times indicated in the shift count parameter.

14. Write a macro called MULTIPLY that shortens the sequence of operations needed to do a multiply operation. The macro should perform the multiplication, check whether the quotient does or does not fit into sixteen bits, and store either one or two words depending on the size of the result.

15. Modify the PUSH and POP macros of Section 17.3.2 so that they correctly handle the problems of stack overflow and stack underflow. Also, add macros for other stack-oriented operations such as:

```
DISCARD   ; Discard the top item on the stack
SUB       ; Subtract the top two items on the stack
COMPARE   ; Compare the top two items on the stack
          ; and set the condition codes accordingly
```

16. Write a pair of macros called FOR and ENDFOR that allow you to implement a primitive for-like "counted loop." The macro should allow you to provide an initial value, a final value, and a step size, and should correctly terminate when the loop count has been reached.

17. Write a macro called DIMENSION that correctly mimics the BASIC or FORTRAN dimension statement. That is, it allows you to create arrays by writing:

```
DIMENSION   A,50.
```

rather than:

```
A:   .BLKW   50.
```

The macro can assume that all constants provided will be decimal quantities.

18. Given the following conditional assembly block:

```
.IF     GT,X
MOV     X,R0
INC     R0
.ENDC
```

exactly what will be produced if X is defined in each of the following ways?
   a. X = 0
   b. X: .WORD 0

19. Write a conditional assembly block of code that uses the ASH command to perform a multiple position shift, if your system has the EIS option. If it does not, perform the shift using the regular 1-bit ASL and ASR commands. Assemble the proper shift sequence only and omit the unneeded one. Assume that a variable called EIS has the value 1 if your system has the EIS option and has the value 0 otherwise.

20.   What would happen if we created a zero-address ADD instruction in the following way:

```
.MACRO  ADD
ADD     (SP)+,(SP)
.ENDM
```

Would this macro work correctly? If not, rewrite it so that it will.

CHAPTER 18

OTHER TOPICS IN MACRO-11

This is the last chapter in which we discuss MACRO-11 directly. Here we introduce some important, but not necessarily related, issues concerning the language, to complete our treatment of operation codes, addressing modes, and programming in assembly language.

18.1
Floating-Point Instructions in MACRO-11

Floating-point hardware is an option available on all members of the PDP-11 family except the LSI-11 and the PDP-11/20. (The option called the FIS, Floating Instruction Set, provides a limited floating-point capability for the LSI-11 and LSI-11/2. Refer to the Microcomputer Handbook for a description of this option.) The floating-point hardware includes a totally separate floating-point processor (FPP) that can execute instructions in parallel with the CPU. The FPP includes six special-purpose 64-bit registers called *floating-point accumulators* (AC0, AC1, . . . , AC5), and a *floating-point status register* (FPSR), which contains four condition codes, FN, FZ, FC, and FV. These codes are set by each floating-point instruction executed by the FPP. The FPP also includes a number of other status registers, error registers, and working registers that will not be described here. The architecture of the FPP is summarized in Figure 18-1.

The PDP-11 floating-point hardware provides two floating point formats, called *single precision* (or *floating*) *mode* and *double precision* (or simply *double*) *mode*. The VAX, as described earlier in Figure 5-2, contains two additional floating-point formats called G and H format. These two latter modes are not described here. The characteristics of floating and double modes are summarized in Figure 18-2. (You may wish to review the discussion of floating-point representations in Section 5.1 before continuing.)

FIGURE 18-1   Floating-Point Processor Architecture.

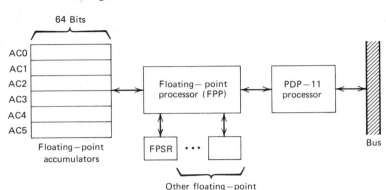

The floating-point processor provides a powerful range of instructions to manipulate the 32- and 64-bit formats shown in Figure 18-2. This includes not only arithmetic operations, but register transfer, compare, and conversion instructions as well. A total of forty-six instructions are recognized and executed by the FPP. Figure 18-3 lists some of the more important ones. For a complete listing of all forty-six instructions and their exact behavior, including their effect on the floating condition codes, refer to the PDP-11 Processor Handbook, Chapter 11, "Floating Point."

When specifying an effective address in a floating-point instruction (the "addr" field in Figure 18-3), you may use any of the eight addressing modes we have discussed in this text. However, when using mode 0 (register mode), you must specify an FP accumulator AC0, . . . , AC5 rather than a general-purpose register R0, . . . , R7. When you use autoincrement or autodecrement addressing modes, the hardware will automatically add or subtract 4_8 for single-precision instructions and 10_8 for double-precision instructions. In all other respects, the addressing for floating-point instructions is identical to other MACRO-11 instructions.

The "reg" field of a floating-point instruction in Figure 18-3 refers to a floating-point accumulator. However, this field is only two bits wide in the instruction itself (see Figure 18-4), allowing us to directly reference only four registers. Thus, the "reg" field can only refer to AC0, AC1, AC2, or AC3. The result is that there cannot be direct communication and transfer between main memory and floating-point accumulators AC4 and AC5.

The floating-point accumulators are all sixty-four bits long. If you refer to one of these registers using a single-precision 32-bit instruction, the hardware will automatically use only the leftmost thirty-two bits of the register and will disregard the other thirty-two bits. In double-precision mode, the entire 64-bit register is used.

FIGURE 18-2   Summary of PDP-11 Floating-Point Representation

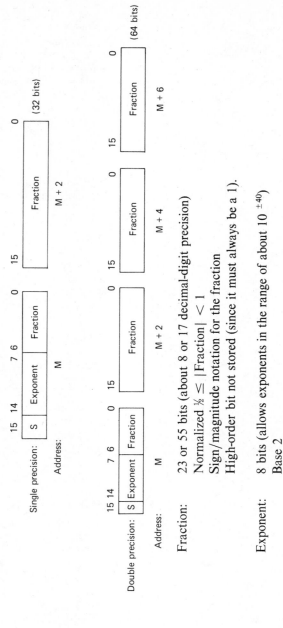

Fraction: 23 or 55 bits (about 8 or 17 decimal-digit precision)
             Normalized ½ ≤ |Fraction| < 1
             Sign/magnitude notation for the fraction
             High-order bit not stored (since it must always be a 1).

Exponent: 8 bits (allows exponents in the range of about $10^{\pm 40}$)
             Base 2
             Excess-200 notation

FIGURE 18-3   Some of the More Important Floating-Point Instructions.

Operation	Meaning	Effect
ADDF addr,reg	32-bit floating add	CON(addr, addr + 2) + CON(reg) → CON(reg)
ADDD addr,reg	64-bit floating add	CON(addr, addr + 2, addr + 4, addr + 6) + CON(reg) → CON(reg)
CFCC	Copy floating condition codes	C ← FC, F ← FV, Z ← FZ, N ← FN
CLRF addr	32-bit floating clear	0 → CON(addr, addr + 2)
CLRD addr	64-bit floating clear	0 → CON(addr, . . . , addr + 6)
CMPF addr, reg	32-bit floating compare	Compare CON(addr, addr + 2) with CON(reg). Set floating condition codes
CMPD addr, reg	64-bit floating compare	Compare CON(addr, . . . , addr + 6) with CON(reg). Set floating condition codes.
DIVF addr,reg	32-bit floating divide	CON(reg) ÷ CON(addr, addr + 2) → CON(reg)
DIVD addr,reg	64-bit floating divide	CON(reg) ÷ CON(addr, . . . , addr + 6) → CON(reg)
LDF addr,reg	32-bit floating load	CON(addr, addr + 2) → CON(reg)
LDD addr,reg	64-bit floating load	CON(addr, . . . , addr + 6) → CON(reg)
MULF addr,reg	32-bit floating multiply	CON(reg)∗CON(addr, addr + 2) → CON(reg)
MULD addr,reg	64-bit floating multiply	CON(reg)∗CON(addr, . . . , addr + 6) → CON(reg)
NEGF addr	32-bit floating negate	−CON(addr, addr + 2) → CON(addr,addr+2)
NEGD addr	64-bit floating negate	−CON(addr, . . . , addr + 6) → CON(addr, . . . , addr + 6)
STF reg,addr	32-bit floating store	CON(reg) → CON(addr, addr + 2)
STD reg,addr	64-bit floating store	CON(reg) → CON(addr, . . . , addr + 6)
SUBF addr,reg	32-bit floating subtract	CON(reg) − CON(addr, addr + 2) → CON(reg)
SUBD addr,reg	64-bit floating subtract	CON(reg) − CON(addr, . . . , addr + 6) → CON(reg)
TSTF addr	32-bit floating test	Set condition codes based on the contents of addr
TSTD addr	64-bit floating test	Set condition codes based on the contents of addr

where: addr is a regular memory reference using addressing modes 0–7
reg is one of the first four general-purpose floating-point accumulators, AC0-AC3. (You cannot use AC4 and AC5 in this field).

FIGURE 18-4   Format of Floating-Point Instructions.

```
Float—op        addr, reg        ; Two—address floating point instruction
```

op--code	reg	source address

```
15       8 7 6 5                0
```

```
Float—op        addr            ; One—address floating point instruction
```

op—code	source address

```
15              6 5             0
```

Finally, there are two assembler directives for creating floating-point constants:

```
(label:)   .FLT2   List of decimal values separated by commas
(label:)   .FLT4   List of decimal values separated by commas
```

The .FLT2 directive will store each decimal quantity in the 32-bit single-precision format shown in Figure 18-2. The .FLT4 directive will store it in the 64-bit double-precision format. The quantities in the address field are signed or unsigned real quantities. They may be written out in either decimal notations ($\pm nn.nn$) or scientific notation ($\pm nn.nnE \pm nn$).

EXAMPLES

(a)   Generate the constants 53, 8.1, $-1,872$, 135,000, and -0.00001 as 32-bit floating-point values:

```
EXAMPLE1:   .FLT2   53,8.1,−1872,1.35E5,−0.1E−4
```

(b)   Evalute the expression X = (Y*Z) + 1.5 in single-precision floating-point mode.

```
CONST:  .FLT2   1.5
    X:  .FLT2   0.0
    Y:  .FLT2   0.0
    Z:  .FLT2   0.0
```

```
LDF    Y,AC0
MULF   Z,AC0       ; AC0 holds Y·Z
ADF    CONST,AC0   ; AC0 holds (Y·Z) +1.5
STF    AC0,X       ; Store it in X
```

(c) Given a table of fifty double-precision (i.e., 64-bit) floating-point numbers, pointed at by R0, add them up and put the total in SUM.

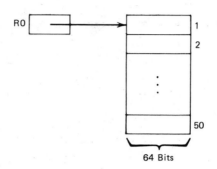

```
SUM:   .FLT4   0.0
        .
        .
        .
        CLRD    AC1         ; AC1 will accumulate the sum
        CLR     R1          ; R1 will be the loop count
NEXT:   ADDD    (R0) +,AC1  ; Add in next table entry
        INC     R1
        CMP     R1,#50.     ; Are we all done?
        BLT     NEXT        ; No
        STD     AC1,SUM     ; Yes, store result in SUM
```

(d) Evaluate the expression $(X^2/Y - 125/Z)$.

```
X:    .FLT4   0.0
Y:    .FLT4   0.0
Z:    .FLT4   0.0
K:    .FLT4   +.125E3
       .
       .
      LDD    X,AC2
      MULD   AC2,AC2   ; AC2 holds X**2
      DIVD   Y,AC2     ; AC2 holds X**2/Y
      LDD    K,AC3
```

```
        DIVD   Z,AC3      ; AC3 holds 125/Z
        SUBD   AC3,AC2    ; Subtract them, put result in AC2
```

(e)   Write a subroutine called CMUL that takes two complex numbers $(a + bi)$, $(c + di)$ and multiplies them according to the formula:

$$(a + bi) * (c + di) = (ac - bd) + (ad + bc)i$$

```
        .Title   MultiplyComplex

A:              .Flt2   0.0      ; Real part of number 1
B:              .Flt2   0.0      ; Imaginary part of number 1
C:              .Flt2   0.0      ; Real part of number 2
D:              .Flt2   0.0      ; Imaginary part of number 2
RealPart:       .Flt2   0.0      ; Real part of the result
ImagPart:       .Flt2   0.0      ; Imaginary part of the result
Start:    .
          .
          .
        JSR    PC,CMul           ; Call the complex multiply routine
        .Word A                  ; Pass the addresses of A, B, C, D
        .Word B
        .Word C
        .Word D
        .Word RealPart           ; Pass the addresses of where to place
        .Word ImagPart           ; the two answers, RealPart and ImagPart
          .
          .
          .

; These are local variables used by the subroutine
AAdr:           .Word  0         ; These locations hold the addresses
BAdr:           .Word  0         ; of all the passed parameters: A,
CAdr:           .Word  0         ; B, C, D
DAdr:           .Word  0
RPAdr:          .Word  0         ; RealPart and ImagPart
IMAdr:          .Word  0
Temp:           .Word  0         ; This temporary holds value of R0

; The code for the subroutine CMul begins here
CMul:   MOV  R0,Temp             ; Save R0 in Temp for later
        MOV  (SP)+,R0            ; Pull return address off the stack
        MOV  (R0)+,AAdr          ; Get the address of A using the
                                 ; return address
        MOV  (R0)+,BAdr          ; Get the address of B using the
                                 ; return address
        MOV  (R0)+,CAdr          ; Etc. . . . .
```

```
         MOV  (R0)+,DAdr
         MOV  (R0)+,RPAdr      ; Get the address of the real part
                               ; using R0
         MOV  (R0)+,IPAdr      ; Get address of the imaginary part
         MOV  R0,-(SP)         ; Put the updated return address back
                               ; on the stack

         LDF   @AAdr,AC1       ; Load A into floating-point
                               ; accumulator 1
         MULF  @CAdr,AC1       ; Multiply it by C
         LDF   @BAdr,AC2       ; Load B into floating-point
                               ; accumulator 2
         MULF  @DAdr,AC2       ; Multiply it by D
         SUBF  AC2,AC1         ; Calculate A*C - B*D
         STF   AC1,@RPAdr      ; Move this value to RealPart

         LDF   @AAdr,AC1       ; Load A
         MULF  @DAdr,AC1       ; Multiply A by D
         LDF   @BAdr,AC2       ; Load B
         MULF  @CAdr,AC2       ; Multiply B by C
         ADDF  AC1,AC2         ; Add to get B*C + A*D
         STF   AC2,@IPAdr      ; Move this result to ImagPart
         MOV   Temp,R0         ; Restore R0
         RTS   PC

         .End  Start
```

The floating-point hardware of the PDP-11 will also check for the occurrence of any of the following floating-point error conditions which were described in detail in Section 5.2.

1. Floating-point overflow.
2. Floating-point underflow.
3. Negative 0 (an undefined quantity).
4. Division by 0.
5. Illegal operation code.
6. Conversion error (floating $\rightarrow$ integer).

If any of these errors occurs and the floating-point interrupt system is enabled, an interrupt will occur and the program execution will be suspended. This type of interrupt, called a *trap,* is described in detail in Section 18.4.

18.2
Additional Addressing Modes

The addressing modes available on the PDP-11 are the basic eight, and the four special modes that use the program counter. We have already described eight of these modes: seven in Section 11.2, and one (absolute addressing) in Section 15.2.1. In this section we introduce the remaining four. All of these new modes are the deferred variant of an addressing mode introduced previously.

18.2.1 Autoincrement Deferred Mode (Mode 3)

In autoincrement deferred mode, the register specified in the address field is a pointer to yet another address, which contains the effective address used by the instruction. Thus there are *two* levels of indirection. After the effective address has been determined, the contents of the register specified in the address field are incremented by 2, for *both* word and byte instructions.

$$Syntax: \qquad @(Rn)+ \qquad n = 0, 1, \ldots, 7$$

$$Effective\ address: \quad CON(CON(Rn)); \quad then\ Rn \to Rn + 2$$

EXAMPLES

(a) CLR @(R0)+ Internal representation: **005030**

	Before	*After*
R0:	100	102
100:	200	200
200:	33	0

The contents of register R0 are 100. We go to memory location 100 and pick up its contents, the value 200. This is the effective address, and the contents of memory location 200 are cleared to 0. After this operation has been completed, register R0 is incremented by 2. Notice the two levels of indirection. If we had simply written CLR (R0)+, which is autoincrement mode, the contents of cell 100 rather than 200 would have been cleared.

(b) In general, autoincrement deferred mode is useful for going through a table of addresses and processing the locations pointed at by those addresses. Assume register R0 points to a memory block of one hundred addresses:

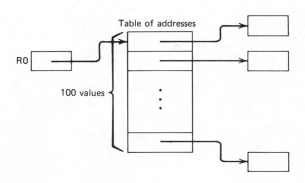

The following code fragment goes through the table and adds up all the values pointed at by the one hundred addresses in the table.

```
SUM:      .WORD    0
           .
           .
           .
          CLR      SUM
          CLR      R1           ; R1 contains the loop count
AGAIN:    ADD      @(R0)+,SUM   ; Here is an example of mode 3
          INC      R1
          CMP      #100.,R1     ; See if we are done
          BGT      AGAIN
```

18.2.2   Autodecrement Deferred Mode (Mode 5)

As with autoincrement deferred, in autodecrement deferred the specified register is a pointer to an address, and the contents of that address are the effective address. However, before we determine this effective address, the contents of the indicated register must be decremented by 2, for both byte and word instructions. Only then is the effective address evaluated. Just as in the preceding case, there are two levels of indirection.

$$Syntax:\qquad @-(Rn)\qquad n = 0, 1, \ldots, 7$$

$$Effective\ address:\quad Rn \rightarrow (Rn)-2$$
$$CON(CON(Rn))$$

EXAMPLES

(a)   INC @$-$(R2)   Internal representation: 005252

	Before	*After*
R2:	0070	0066
66:	0002	0002
2:	1234	1235

The contents of R2 are initially decremented by 2, from 70 to 66. Then we go to memory location 66 and pick up its contents, a 2. Thus, the effective address is location 2, and the contents of memory location 2 are incremented by 1, from 1234 to 1235.

(b)   Register R4 points to the end of a table of subroutine addresses. The fragment illustrated jumps in turn to each subroutine pointed at in the table, and gets back one output parameter, called FLAG. If FLAG is ever set to 1, the program will halt immediately. Otherwise, it will keep going until it has reached the end of the table, which is pointed at by R5.

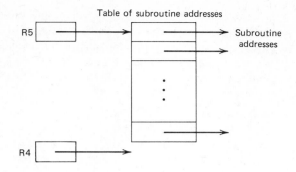

```
NEXTCALL:   JSR     PC,@ — (R4)   ; Activate the next subroutine
            .WORD   FLAG          ; This is the output parameter
            TST     FLAG          ; Are we done?
            BNE     DONE          ; Yes
            CMP     R4,R5         ; No, see if we have processed
                                  ; all of the routines
            BNE     NEXTCALL      ; No, more routines to activate
            JMP     DONE
```

18.2.3   Index Deferred Mode (Mode 7)

In index deferred mode, we add a base address to the contents of the specified register exactly as we did with index mode (mode 6). However, the resulting sum is not the effective address, but a pointer to an address. The *contents* of that address are the effective address. The base address value is stored in the word immediately following the instruction.

$$\textit{Syntax:} \qquad @X(Rn) \qquad n = 0,1, \ldots , 7$$

$$\textit{Effective address:} \quad CON(X + CON(Rn))$$

EXAMPLES

Assume that A is memory location 2000.

(a)   COM   @A(R0)   Internal representation: **005170**

002000

	Before	*After*
R0:	2	2
2002:	150	150
150:	177765	000012

The value A (address 2000) and the contents of register R0 are added to get 2002. We go to memory location 2002 and pick up its contents, 150. This is the effective address, and the contents of memory location 150 are complemented.

(b) Register R3 points to the beginning of a table containing three word entries. The first two words of each entry are integer values; the third is a subroutine address. The code fragment illustrated adds up the two integer values and, if the sum is negative, jumps to the subroutine whose address is in the third word. The fragment continues executing until it reaches the end of the table, which is pointed at by register R4.

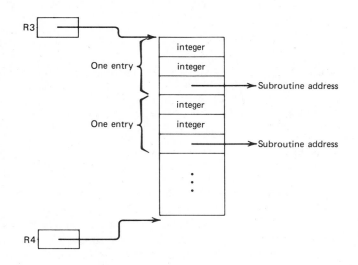

```
NEXT:   MOV   0(R3),TEMP   ; Get first integer
        ADD   2(R3),TEMP   ; Add in second integer
        TST   TEMP         ; See if result is negative
        BGE   OK           ; No
        JSR   PC,@4(R3)    ; Yes, branch to subroutine
OK:     ADD   #6,R3        ; Move on to next entry
        CMP   R3,R4        ; See if we are all done
        BLT   NEXT         ; No, do the loop again
```

18.2.4 Relative Deferred Mode (Mode 7, Register 7)

In relative deferred mode, the symbol used in the address field is considered a pointer to an address. The contents of that address are the effective address. For relative deferred mode, the assembler will compute an offset exactly as it does with relative mode. The offset will be a value such that, when it is added to the current value of the program counter, it will produce the address of the symbol in the address field. The *contents* of that symbol form the effective address.

Syntax: @symbol

Effective address: CON(offset + CON(PC))

EXAMPLES

Assume that LOOP is location 400, and the CLR instruction itself is stored in locations 200 and 202.

(a)   **CLR   @LOOP**   Internal representation: **005077   (200)**
000174   (202)

	Before	After
PC:	200	204
400:	22	22
22:	177777	0

The offset value in the word following the CLR instruction (174_8) is added to the current value of the PC, which is 204 after the offset has been fetched. The addition of 174_8 and 204_8 gives the value 400. The contents of address 400 is 22. Thus 22 is the effective address, and its contents are cleared to 0.

(b)   The variable TABLE points to the head of a table positive integers. The fragment illustrated searches through the table and finds the largest integer. The end of the table is marked by the value 177777.

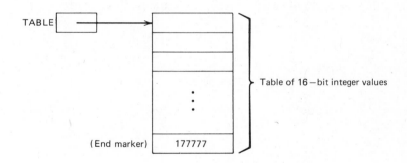

```
          BIG: .WORD    0
                  .
                  .
                  .
NEXT:     CMP      @TABLE,#177777    ; See if we have reached
                                     ; the end marker.
          BEQ      DONE              ; Yes
          CMP      @TABLE,BIG        ; No, see if this is the
                                     ; biggest value
          BLE      SMALL             ; No, it isn't
          MOV      @TABLE,BIG        ; Yes, this is the new one
SMALL:    ADD      #2,TABLE          ; Move to next entry
          JMP      NEXT
DONE:
```

This completes our discussion of the twelve addressing modes (eight regular modes and four program counter modes) available in MACRO-11.

18.3
Extended-Precision Arithmetic

The PDP-11 performs integer arithmetic on 16-bit quantities. This allows signed integer values in the range:

$$-32768 \le I \le +32767$$

For many applications this range is too small, and users frequently need to develop routines that handle larger integer quantities (e.g., thirty-two, forty-eight, or even sixty-four bits). These routines perform *extended-precision arithmetic,* by adding sixteen bits at a time, starting with the low-order digits. After each 16-bit "chunk" has been added, we must ascertain whether there was a carry (i.e., the C bit is 1). If there was, we must add a 1 to the next 16-bit unit to be added. This process is diagrammed in Figure 18-5.

The approach to extended-precision subtraction is quite similar, since in integer subtraction, the C bit is used to represent a borrow.

To facilitate writing these extended-precision routines, the PDP-11 includes two special arithmetic operations, called Add Carry and Subtract Carry.

Mnemonic	Name	Effect	N	Z	V	C
ADC addr	Add Carry Bit	CON(addr)+C→ CON(addr)	*	*	*	*
SBC addr	Subtract Carry Bit	CON(addr)−C→ CON(addr)	*	*	*	*

FIGURE 18-5   Model of an Extended-Precision Add.

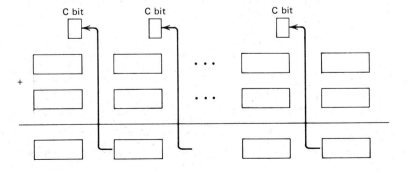

The subroutines presented in Figure 18-6 shows a 32-bit (2-word) add performed using the ADC operation. The addresses of the low-order word of the two operands are in registers R0 and R1, respectively. The result will be put back in the two words pointed at by R1.

This approach can be generalized to handle arbitrary N-word integer addition (Exercise 10) and subtraction (Exercise 11).

There is one other operation code available in MACRO-11 to facilitate multiple-precision arithmetic. If we have 16-bit single-precision values that we want to convert to double precision, then we must extend the sign bit throughout the high-order sixteen bits. Thus, if the number is positive, we can make it double precision by appending sixteen 0s. If it is negative, we append sixteen 1 bits because when we take the complement, they will become zeros. The process does not change the magnitude of the resulting value.

The following routine takes a 16-bit single-precision value called SPREC and converts it to a 32-bit value called DPREC so that it can be operated on by the double-precision add routine in Figure 18-6.

```
DPREC:  .WORD   0,0                 ; The double precision
            .                       ; value will go there
            .
            .
        MOV     SPREC,DPREC+2
        BMI     NEG                 ; See if it is negative
        CLR     DPREC               ; No, fill out with 0s
        JMP     DONE
NEG:    MOV     #177777,DPREC       ; Yes, fill with 1s
DONE:
```

This 5-instruction sign extension procedure can be reduced to one new instruction, called SXT, for *sign extension*.

Mnemonic	Name	Internal	Effect	N	Z	V	C
SXT addr	Sign Extension	0067aa	The N bit is copied into all 16-bit positions of the effective address	—	*	0	—

With the SXT instruction, the preceding operation can be recoded as:

```
DPREC:  .WORD   0,0
            .
            .
            .
        MOV     SPREC,DPREC+2
        SXT     DPREC
```

FIGURE 18-6   Double-Precision ADD.

```
ADDDOUB:    ADD     (R0),(R1)       ; Add the low-order 16 bits
            SUB     #2,R0           ; Move to high-order 16 bits
            SUB     #2,R1
            ADC     (R0)            ; Add the carry
            ADD     (R0),(R1)       ; Add the high-order 16 bits
            BVS     ERROR           ; Check for overflow
            ADD     #4,R1
            RTS     PC
```

This approach can be generalized to create integers of arbitrary length. Using SXT, we can convert a single-precision 16-bit integer to a multiple-precision, N-bit integer with the same magnitude and the correct sign. (Exercise 12 asks you to write this program.)

18.4
Traps

In Section 15.3, we introduced the external interrupt and showed how it can be used to increase the efficiency of input/output operations. Another type of interrupt is also extremely useful in assembly-language programming: the *internal interrupt,* or *trap.* An external interrupt is caused by a signal (e.g., a key struck on a CRT) that is generated external to the processor and whose timing is totally asynchronous with the execution of the program. Simply put, for an external interrupt, we have no idea when the signal will occur and when the interrupt will be generated.

A trap, however, is an interrupt generated by the program itself. The interrupt occurs when the processor attempts to execute an instruction in the program and encounters a condition that activates the trap. Therefore, an internal interrupt will always occur at precisely the same place and time in your program, whenever it is executed. The sequences of events that occur during an internal interrupt and during an external interrupt are exactly the same as those that occur during an external interrupt.

Associated with each type of trap is a 2-word *trap vector,* which is directly analogous to the interrupt vector described in Section 15.3.1. The first word contains the address of a routine, called a *trap handler,* to be executed when a particular condition occurs. The second word contains the new value of the processor status register (PS), to be loaded when the trap handler is executed. The exact sequence of events that occurs during a trap is:

1. Interrupt the current program being executed by the processor.

2. Save on the system stack the current values of the PC and PS.

3. Load the PC and PS from the trap vector associated with this type of trap condition.

4. Execute the trap handler.

5. Return from the trap handler via the special instruction RTT (return from trap), which restores the PC registers.

The RTT is exactly like the RTI instruction (return from interrupt) except that it will prevent another trap from occurring for at least one instruction. Otherwise, under some conditions, it is possible to get into an infinite loop of traps, each one occurring as soon as you return from the last one.

Traps generally fall into two different classes: error conditions and user requests. The trap mechanism is the PDP-11's way of handling fatal run-time error conditions. Associated with each of the possible error conditions that can be encountered during execution of a user program is a trap vector and a trap handler. Trap vector addresses are listed in Figure 18-7.

Whenever one of the conditions listed in Figure 18-7 is encountered, your program will be interrupted and the system will branch to the trap handler whose address is located in the corresponding trap vector. In general, these error-condition trap handlers perform the following steps. (The exact information produced varies slightly from implementation to implementation. However, it will always be similar to what is described here.)

1. Print an error message that states that a trap has occurred and what condition caused it.

•••ERROR—TRAP TO ADDRESS 4 •••
ODD ADDRESSING ERROR

2. Produce some information to assist in debugging. This will typically be a post-mortem dump of the memory and registers.

3. Suppress the further execution of your program and return instead to the operating system.

FIGURE 18-7   Trap Vector Addresses.

Trap Vector Addresses	Error Condition
4–6	Illegal operation code
	Stack overflow/underflow
	Odd address error
	Illegal address
10–12	Reserved instruction
24–26	Power failure
244–246	Floating-point exceptions
250–252	Memory management or parity errors

For example, if you incorrectly write the following instruction in your program:

JMP   @#101   ; This is illegal

you will generate an "Odd Address Trap" and cause the preceding sequence of events to take place. This trap will always occur at exactly the same location whenever the program containing this instruction is executed.

Similarly, if you are working on a multiuser system and cannot execute a halt instruction, the occurrence of a 0 op code (HALT) will cause a "Reserved Instruction" error and a trap to the reserved instruction trap handler, whose address is contained in memory location 10. Finally, if you generate any of the floating-point error conditions listed in the preceding section, you will generate a floating-point trap, usually called a *floating-point exception* to address 244.

Traps are not limited to handling error conditions; they can also be used to request services from the operating system that users are not allowed to perform themselves. These are called *user-initiated traps,* or, on some machines, *supervisory calls.* These are instructions that users code directly into their programs to generate a trap, cause a trap handler to perform some needed service on their behalf, and return to continue execution of the program.

The format and associated trap vectors of the four user-initiated trap instructions on the PDP-11 are listed in Figure 18-8.

Both the EMT and TRAP instructions allow you to include as part of the instruction an 8-bit parameter value that is passed directly to the trap handler. Thus, in a sense, it appears to the user as if there are 256 different EMT and TRAP instructions:

EMT 0, . . . , EMT 255
TRAP 0, . . . , TRAP 255

The primary purpose of the EMT is to allow users access to a special part of the operating system called the *supervisor.* This is the resident part of the operating

FIGURE 18-8   User-Initiated Trap Instructions.

Vector	Name	Mnemonic
30–32	Emulator Trap	EMT value
34–36	User Trap	TRAP value
14–16	Breakpoint Trap	BPT
20–22	I/O Trap	IOT

FIGURE 18-9   Hierarchy of Hardware/Software.

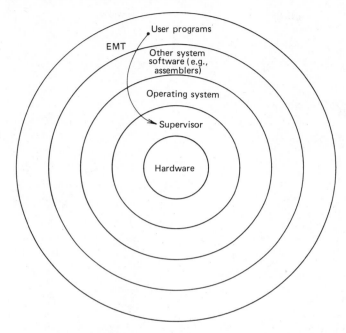

system that handles such critical tasks as I/O control, error control, and diagnostics. The hierarchy of the hardware and software is diagrammed in Figure 18-9.

It is absolutely critical that the supervisor and its tasks be protected from accidental or intentional change by user programs. One way to ensure this is to have two processor *states.* In *user state,* or *user mode,* only a subset of all MACRO-11 instructions can be executed, and only certain memory addresses can be referenced. An attempt to execute an instruction not in this subset or to reference a memory location that is out of bounds will result in an error trap to memory location 10 or 4, respectively.

In *supervisor state* (also called *privileged state* or *privileged mode*), all instructions can be executed and all addresses can be referenced without restriction. This 2-level approach effectively protects the supervisor from intrusion or modification during execution of a user program, since user programs always execute in user mode. The memory occupied by the supervisor is marked as inaccessible in user mode.

The instructions that are executable only in privileged mode on most PDP-11 computers are SPL, MTPS, MFPS, FADD, FSUB, FMUL, FDIV, RESET, and HALT. Except for HALT, these instructions have not been discussed in this text. (They are described in the PDP-11 Processor Handbook.) In multiuser mode, any

FIGURE 18-10   Memory Addressing in User Mode and
Privileged Mode.

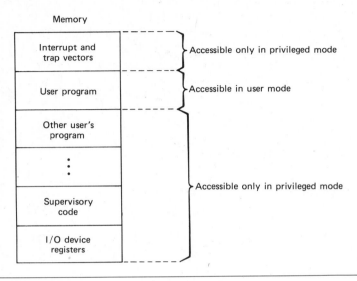

reference to a memory address outside of your own program's address space can be made only in privileged mode, as shown in Figure 18-10.

How can we execute a privileged instruction or access a forbidden section of memory? We must stop execution of our program (which executes in user mode), and enter the supervisor, which executes in privileged mode. This is the function of the EMT instruction. This instruction traps to a routine within the supervisor, which will analyze our request, determine what we want done, do it (if it's legal), and return us to our program. The EMT instruction is the only entry point back and forth between a user program and the supervisor (see Figure 18-9).

We communicate our needs to the supervisor through the 8-bit value field of the EMT instruction. Some of the 256 possible values have been assigned fixed meanings and will cause a particular operation to take place.

EMT op code	Parameter value
8 bits	8 bits

When the supervisor EMT trap handler becomes active, it simply looks at the parameter value, which it can access via the program counter value on top of the system stack, and determines exactly what is to be done. For example, in multiuser mode, the HALT instruction is illegal. Instead, the instruction:

EMT   60

is used to request that the supervisor terminate execution of the program normally.

Because trying to remember exactly what code produces what operation can be confusing, most of the EMT instructions have been recoded as system macros with more helpful and mnemonic names. The above "EMT 60" instruction is more commonly referred to as .EXIT. The macro .EXIT and the EMT instruction are exactly the same thing, since the definition of the macro .EXIT is simply:

```
.MACRO     .EXIT
EMT        60
.ENDM
```

Likewise, the type of I/O described in Chapter 15 may not be directly allowed on your system. The sequence:

```
LOOP:     TSTB      @#177560
          BPL       LOOP
          MOVB      @#177562,CH
```

accesses memory locations 177560 and 177562. On some systems, this access, which is outside of your program's address space, may be allowed only in privileged mode. In that case, I/O must be implemented via system macros such as .TTYIN and .TTYOUT, described in Figure 17-13, which expand into EMT calls with the proper parameter value.

The other three trap instructions—TRAP, IOT, and BPT—are similarly used for communicating between a user program and other software packages. IOT is frequently used for communication with privileged I/O software routines, device controllers, and I/O error-recovery packages. BPT is used for communication with debugging packages and software associated with testing and error analysis. Finally, TRAP is a general, unspecified trap instruction available for communication with arbitrary software packages. These trap-type instructions are used heavily in the development of system software, such as operating systems, linkers, loaders, and I/O packages. Their capabilities will be more fully exploited in advanced courses in computer science.

18.5
Reentrant Code

Sometimes in a multiuser system two or more users want to use the same program at the same time. One way to handle this is to give each user a personal copy of the code. This approach would be unrealistic, however, if the routine in question were very large (e.g., a Pascal compiler). In such cases, we would like to be able to *share* a single copy of the program among all users. This would significantly reduce the amount of memory that would be needed to execute these programs, as shown in Figure 18-11.

In a multiuser environment, code sharing is generally implemented as follows.

FIGURE 18-11   The Advantages of Sharing Software: (a) Using Separate Copies (b) Using a Single Copy

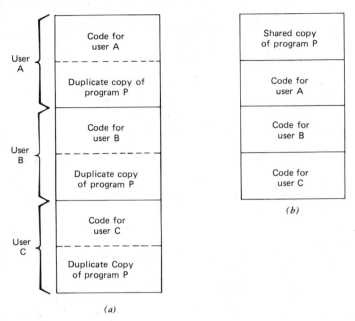

(a)

(b)

Assume that user A and user B are sharing a single copy of program P. User A's program executes the shared code until it is interrupted by a time-out signal telling A that his or her time is up. (The time unit allocated for each program is called a *time slice* or *quantum.*) The supervisor then performs a *context switch.* Registers R0, . . . , R7, PS, and the contents of the system stack of user A are stored and then reloaded with the values saved from the last execution of user B. User B then begins execution from wherever he or she last left off. Thus, while many people may be sharing the same copy of code, they will be at different points in the computation and will have different data and results.

A program that can be shared in this way is called *reentrant.* A reentrant program has the following two characteristics.

1. The code does not modify itself in any way.

2. The code and the data are separate, and all storage references to data are made through registers or through the system stack.

A program that meets these two requiremetns is also said to be *pure code.*

The first restriction means that an instruction cannot modify any other instructions within the program. For example, the code shown in Figure 18-12 adds up integer

FIGURE 18-12   An Example of Self-Modifying Code.

```
SUM:          .WORD    0
TABLE:        .BLKW    50.
              .
              .
              .
              CLR      SUM
              CLR      R1
NEXT:         ADD      TABLE,SUM
              ADD      #2,NEXT+2   ; This modifies an instruction
              INC      R1
              INC      R1
              CMP      R1,#100.
              BLT      NEXT
```

values in a 50-word table by modifying the actual addresses. Therefore, this program is nonreentrant.

Obviously, this code could not be shared because, when a second user tried to execute it, the ADD instruction located at address NEXT would be changed and would most likely not be pointing to the correct location.

The second restriction is that you cannot store any data local to the code itself. (Note that you can have fixed constants as part of the code, but you cannot have any values that are defined or changed during execution.) Referring again to Figure 18-12, we see that this restriction is violated by the inclusion directly in the code of the definition of the data value SUM.

The reason for the second restriction is that during a context switch, only register values are restored from their previous condition; memory locations that may have been changed are not restored. Thus, if you had computed a partial SUM of 123 and were then interrupted by a time-out, the next program sharing this code would reference the same memory location called SUM and would wipe out your value of 123. Each subsequent user would wipe out the work of the previous user.

To avoid this problem, all changeable data must be in a separate data block, so that each user can have his or her own separate copy, called a *local data block*. The local data block is pointed at by a register (e.g., R0) and all references to data items are made by offsets from the value contained in R0. When a context switch is performed, the new value loaded into R0 will point to the local data block for the current user. Any changes made to a variable now affect only this user's data, in his or her own local data block. A reentrant program can thus be interrupted and restarted at any point without affecting the computation. This approach is diagrammed in Figure 18-13.

To code the example in Figure 18-12 as a reentrant routine, we could use register R0 as a pointer to a local 51-word data block. The first word will be the SUM, and

FIGURE 18-13   Re-entrant Code and Local Data Blocks.

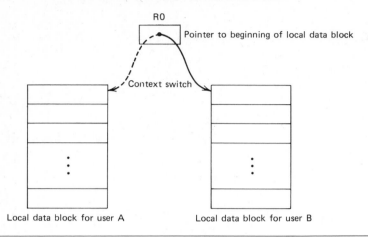

the next fifty words will be the TABLE. Before executing the shared routine called ADDUP, we must properly set up the local data block and its pointer, R0.

```
SUM:    .WORD   0        ; This is the local
TABLE:  .BLKW   50.      ; data block
           .
           .
           .
        MOV     #SUM,R0  ; R0 contains the address
        JSR     PC,ADDUP ; of the start of the
                         ; local data block
```

The reentrant routine called ADDUP is shown in Figure 18-14.

Notice that we never refer directly to the value SUM, but only to the word whose location is zero words past the address in R0 (lines 1 and 5 of the program). Likewise, we never refer directly to the location called TABLE, but only to the word whose location is two bytes beyond the address in R0 (line 5). When we perform a context switch and change the value in R0, these addresses will correctly reference each user's own local copies of SUM and TABLE.

The programming techniques just described are very important in the development and coding of programs that will be used frequently and by many different users. The ability to share a single copy of a program can dramatically reduce the memory demands placed on a system. Almost all important multiuser software—compilers, editors, file systems, operating systems, debugging packages, and loaders—is reentrant. In fact, the MACRO-11 assembler, which you have been using now for quite a while, is itself reentrant. Regardless of how many people are simultaneously assem-

FIGURE 18-14 Re-entrant Routine for Adding Up a Table.

```
ADDUP:   CLR   0(R0)       ; This clears SUM
         CLR   R1          ; R1 is a loop counter
         MOV   R0,R2       ; This initializes R2 to
         ADD   #2,R2       ; the beginning of the table
NEXT:    ADD   (R2),0(R0)  ; This adds the next table entry
         ADD   #2,R2       ; Move to the next entry
         INC   R1
         CMP   R1,#50.     ; Are we done?
         BLT   NEXT        ; No, go back
         RTS   PC
```

bling programs, there will be only one copy of the assembler in memory. Because the complete assembler/macro preprocessor package is a very large program, this approach results in quite a significant savings.

The frequent and widespread practice of sharing code makes the word *program* a poor choice for describing a sequence of instructions being executed. A single program may be used simultaneously by many different users, for totally different purposes, and with totally different data. A better term to describe a sequence of instructions being executed on behalf of a user is *process*. One program may simultaneously be part of many different processes. This distinction between the terms "program" and "process" is one of the most important ideas in computer science.

18.6
Conclusion

This completes our discussion of assembly-language programming in general and of MACRO-11 in particular. For additional details on advanced features that we have not discussed, refer to the reference materials listed in Section 10.1.

Higher level languages like FORTRAN, COBOL, Pascal, and Ada are relatively independent of any particular computer and are portable across a number of systems. As new computers are developed, compilers for these languages are written for them. Because of this portability, higher level languages have relatively long lives, even in the presence of major hardware advances and changes. FORTRAN, which was developed in 1957, and COBOL, designed in 1959, are still widely used and probably will continue to be used well into the 1990s, despite future dramatic changes in both hardware and software.

The same is not true of assembly languages. An assembly language is integrally related to one specific processor, as MACRO-11 is to the PDP-11. In today's volatile computer industry, new computer systems are being developed all the time, and each system has its own unique machine-language instruction set. A professional programmer may only have to learn two, three, or four high-level languages during an entire career, but he or she may come in contact with ten or twenty different assembly languages. The MACRO-11 material being studied now will become obsolete when a generation of computers is developed to replace the PDP-11 family. (In some respects, this is already happening with the smaller scale VAX computers, like the VAX-11/730 and 750. These are possible alternatives to the larger members of the PDP-11 family.)

Therefore, you must not develop "tunnel vision" about one particular assembly language, such as MACRO-11. You must not be so exclusively concerned with the specific details of the language that you fail to extract the more important general concepts of assembly language. It is highly likely that in a few years, you will move from MACRO-11 on the PDP-11 to another assembly language on another computer. Then such details as the rules for setting the C bit in a MOVB instruction will be less important than a thorough understanding of such fundamental ideas as instruction sets, addressing modes, subroutine linkage, register structures, I/O structures, and stacks.

In this portion of the text we have attempted to impart an understanding of the basic principles of assembly-language programming. Some of these essential principles are:

- Families of Operation Codes
  Register Transfer, Arithmetic, Compare, Branch, Logic, Shift, I/O,
  Assembler Directives
- Addressing Techniques
  Register, Deferred, Literal, Absolute, Symbolic, Indexed
  Autoincrement, Autodecrement, Location Counter
- Registers
  Accumulators, Index Registers, Program Counters, Stacks, Status
  Registers, General-Purpose Registers, Special-Purpose Registers,
  Carry and Overflow Indicators
- Subroutines
  Linkage Techniques, Parameter-Passing Mechanisms, Macros
- Assembly-Language Data Representations
  Binary, Octal, Hexadecimal, Integers, Characters, Floating Point
- I/O, Interrupts, Traps

An understanding of these and other important principles of computer organization will help you adapt to the new machines and new assembly languages that inevitably will be developed during your career.

Exercises for Chapter 18

1. Show the internal octal representation of the following real constants in single- and double-precision real modes as diagrammed in Figure 18-2.

   a.   1.0
   b. −2.0
   c.   5,000
   d. −0.001

2. Show the instructions needed to perform the following operations.
   a.   Reserve a block of memory for ten double-precision real numbers.
   b.   Generate the double-precision real constants 3.14159 and 2.71828.
   c.   Generate the single-precision real constant 6.02 * 10^{23}.

3. Write MACRO-11 program fragments to evaluate the following expressions in single-precision real mode. (Show the definition of all variables.)
   a. $[a * (b/c)] - 1$
   b. $(a^2 + b^2)/(a^2 - b^2)$
   c. $a^2/(b + 1.75)$

Note: Exercises 4–6 ask you to write and execute floating-point instructions. Be sure to check on the availability of these instructions on your system before attempting to execute these programs.

4. Write a subroutine called sum_real with the following four parameters:

   Table: The address of the beginning of a table of double-precision real values.

    Size: The number of elements in the table.

     X: A double-precision real value.

   Count: The answer computed and returned by the subroutine sum_real.

The subroutine should keep adding up the elements in the array called Table (i.e., Table(1) + Table(2) + · · ·) until one of the following conditions is met.
   a.   sum > X. Return in Count the number of elements added into sum.
   b.   The end of the table has been reached and sum is still ≤ X. Return a 0 in Count.

5. Write a subroutine that solves quadratic equations in single-precision real mode using the quadratic formula:

$$\frac{-b \pm \sqrt{b^2 - 4ac}}{2a}$$

Your subroutine should check the following two special cases.
   a. $a = 0$
   b. $(b^2 - 4ac) < 0$

Assume there exists a subroutine call SQRT which takes the single precision real value in register AC3 and returns, also in AC3, its square root. The subroutine is called by executing JSR PC, SQRT.

6. Write a subroutine that computes the following sum in double-precision mode.

$$f(x) = 1 + x + x^2 + x^3 + \cdots$$

The procedure has two input parameters corresponding to the value x and the number of terms N. The one output parameter is the sum of the first N terms.

7. Show the effective address and the before and after values in any affected registers for each of the following instructions. Assume the following initial values in the indicated registers.

Register	Value	Address	Contents
		1:	176
R0:	100:	76:	2
R1:	200	100:	120
R2:	300	120:	60
		200:	300
		300:	400
		400:	1

Assume that X is memory location 300.

    a.   CLR   @(R0)+
    b.   CLR   @(R1)+
    c.   CLR   @−(R0)
    d.   CLR   @X
    e.   CLR   @X−100
    f.   CLR   @X(R0)
    g.   CLR   @0(R2)

8. Modify the program fragment in Example b in Section 18.2.3 so that it jumps to the subroutine in the third word of the entry if and only if both of the integer values in the first two words of the entry are zero.

9. Modify the program fragment in example b in Section 18.2.4 so that it sums the positive integers pointed at by the pointers contained in the table array.

10. Modify the 2-word extended-precision Add shown in Figure 18-6 so that it adds two N-word blocks, where N is a value defined through a direct-assignment pseudo-op. The registers R0 and R1 still point to the low-order words of the two blocks.

11. Write a program to implement N-word subtraction using the extended-precision techniques described in Section 18.3. The value N is defined through a direct-assignment pseudo-op, and the addresses of the low-order word of the two operands are contained in registers R0 and R1, respectively. For example:

```
        N = 10.              ; The length, in words, of
                             ; the two operands
   A:   .BLKW        N       ; The left operand
   B:   .BLKW        N       ; The right operand
        .
        .
        .
      MOV   #A+2·(N−1), R0   ; Low-order word of A
      MOV   #B +2·(N−1), R1  ; Low-order word of B
```

12. Write a subroutine that takes a 1-word value X, and an integer value N greater than 1. The subroutine should extend the sign of X into the N words located immediately before X. For example, if $CON(X) = 100123$ and $N = 3$, the subroutine should perform the following operations:

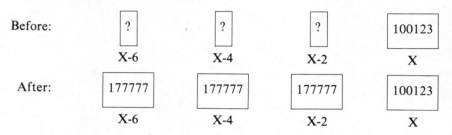

Before:

    X-6   X-4   X-2   X

After:

    X-6   X-4   X-2   X

13. Discuss the operations a trap handler might perform for each of the following traps:
  a. Illegal op code.
  b. TRAP 60.
  c. Accessing another user's memory space.

14. Looking at the following fragment:

```
SUM:     .WORD  0
TABLE:   .BLKW  10.
NEWVAL   .WORD  0

              .
              .              ; Assume that this section of the
              .              ; program fills Table with ten data
                             ; values
         CLR  R0
NEXT:    ADD  TABLE,SUM
         INC  NEXT+2
         INC  NEXT+2
         INC  R0
         CMP  R0,#10.
         BLT  NEXT
         MOV  SUM,NEWVAL
```

explain exactly why the program is NOT reetrant. Rewrite it so that it is reentrant and could be shared by a number of users simultaneously.

PART FIVE

AN INTRODUCTION TO SYSTEM SOFTWARE

CHAPTER 19

THE ASSEMBLY PROCESS

19.1
Introduction

Everything we have discussed so far in this text has been directed at the *hardware* organization of a computer—instruction sets, registers, memory, processors, buses, and the like. However, it would be very difficult to accomplish anything useful using only the hardware that we have described, without any software support—a so-called *naked machine.*

It is the job of the *system software* to facilitate user access to the hardware resources of a computer system. This software can be viewed as a "buffer" or "interface" between the hardware resources (i.e., the instruction set, memory, disk drives, etc.) that exist on the computer system and the high-level operations that the typical user wants to perform—compile programs written in high-level languages, execute packages, or save information. This interface responsibility is diagrammed in Figure 19-1.

The system software can be thought of as creating a *virtual machine,* or *virtual environment,* that presents the user with a simple, friendly, easy-to-use set of computational services. The user is freed from having to worry about most of the "messy" hardware details discussed previously. The operating system or system software level of abstraction is the highest and most machine independent, and its job is to allow the user to think in terms of problems and solutions, ignoring the underlying hardware organization (see Figure 1-2). Because of the central importance of software support to the overall operation of a computer, no discussion of computer organization would be complete without an introduction to this topic.

The main piece of system software is the *operating system,* which controls the operation of the hardware, allocates the resources of the system, and interfaces with users to determine their needs. The operating system acts as a "dispatcher": deter-

437

FIGURE 19-1   The Interfacing Responsibility of System
Software.

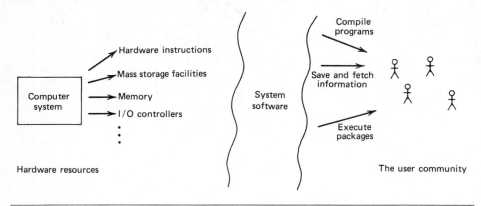

mining what needs to be done and activating and scheduling the software module
that will accomplish it (see Figure 19-2).

In addition to interpreting user commands and activating software packages, the
operating system has numerous other responsibilities. Among them are:

> *Resource Allocation:*   The operating system monitors, allocates, and
> retrieves the resources (printers, tape drives, memory, and I/O channels)
> of the computer system.

FIGURE 19-2   Role of the Operating System in System
Software.

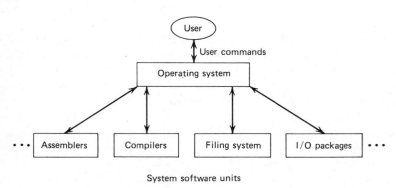

Process Scheduling: In a multiuser system in which processes are competing for processors, the operating system schedules the execution of processes in a fair and equitable manner.

Error Recovery: Operating system routines handle such common error conditions as illegal operation codes, addresses out of bounds, attempted execution of privileged instructions, and infinite loops.

Security, Protection: The operating system is responsible for guaranteeing the security and integrity of the information and resources of the computer and the filing system.

Operating system design and implementation is a topic much too extensive and complex to be addressed in this text. Instead, we briefly introduce two other important components of system software—the *assembler,* which translates your assembly-language source program into machine-language code, and the *linker/loader,* which links your program with other units and loads the resulting module into memory for execution. By studying these two pieces of software, we can describe the entire life cycle of a source program, from creation to its successful execution on a "PVM-like" computer system (Figure 19-3).

The topic of system software is discussed at length in numerous advanced courses in computer science. In addition to assemblers, linkers, and loaders, the following important classes of system software occupy significant portions of advanced courses and textbooks (see Figure 19-2):

Operating systems
High-level language compilers and interpreters
Database systems
Communications software and network protocols
Editors and formatters
I/O systems and device handlers
File systems
Programming support systems

Our purpose here is to introduce the topic so that you will appreciate the importance of software support in the overall organization and operation of a computer. Modern computer systems represent a cooperative design, with close working relationships between the hardware specialist, the computer architect, and the software systems engineer. To truly understand the behavior and operation of a computer, a computer scientist must be knowledgeable about the basic concepts of both hardware and software.

This chapter discusses the assembly process as representative of language translation operations in general. Chapter 20 deals with linking and loading, and describes in more technical detail the overall life cycle of a program as diagrammed in Figure 19-3.

FIGURE 19-3   Life Cycle of a Program.

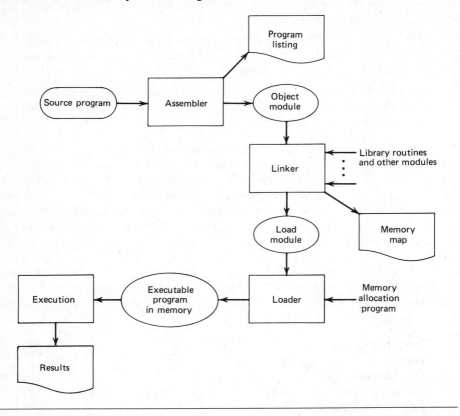

19.2
The Assembler

Although you need to understand the inherent concepts of a machine language, you would never want to program in it. As the following fragment clearly demonstrates:

```
016700     ; Move A to R0
177020
016701     ; Move B to R1
000400
060001     ; Add R0 and R1
005701     ; Test if R1 is 0
001420     ; Branch to LOOP if 0
000060
```

machine language is nonmnemonic, unfriendly, confusing, and extremely difficult to modify. For this reason, *language translators* are among the most important software support tools available. In this group are *assemblers, compilers, emulators,* and *interpreters,* which allow you to write directly in assembly language or a high-level language that is then translated into machine-language code for you. In this chapter, we describe the operation and construction of an assembler as representative of language translator packages. The topic of compiler construction, which is significantly more complex, is covered in other courses in computer science.

Almost all assemblers are implemented as *2-pass assemblers*. That is, they make two complete passes over your source code to produce the machine code. (Some assemblers make additional passes for purposes of optimization or to provide macro capabilities of the type described in Chapter 17. It is also possible, as we shall see later, to get by with "one-and-a-half passes.") The division of work between the two passes is somewhat arbitrary, and certain operations can be performed at either time. Thus, in considering the specific responsibilities of the assembler during each of the two passes, we have a good deal of flexibility in exactly how we partition the work. The steps involved in assembly are scanning, table generation, parsing, and code generation.

19.2.1 The Scanner

The *scanner* is the subsystem of the assembler that separates, isolates, and returns the indivisible *tokens* of each assembly-language statement. A token is simply a language element that is treated as a single indivisible entity and is not further separated or simplified. For example, given the following MACRO-11 command:

LOOP: MOV   R0,DELTA

we probably would not want to view that line as being composed of the sixteen separate characters:

'L' 'O' 'O' 'P' ':' 'M' . . .

Instead, we would probably view the line as being composed of the following six syntactic units:

LOOP
:
MOV
R0
,
DELTA

We do not need to break these six elements down any further to determine whether they have been put together into a valid MACRO-11 instruction.

In addition to locating and building tokens, a scanner must classify these tokens into *syntactic equivalence classes*. A syntactic equivalence class is simply the set of tokens that behave identically in terms of determining the syntactic correctness of a statement. For example, in the preceding MACRO-11 command, the grammatical correctness of the statement is not affected by the specific name that is used in the label field, as long as the label is formed correctly and is not used twice. So, all user-created names can be placed in the same equivalence class, called ⟨identifier⟩. In fact, a syntactically correct label field can be described in general as:

⟨label field⟩ ::= ⟨identifier⟩ ⟨colon⟩
⟨colon⟩   ::= :

This definition applies regardless of the specific token encountered.

Similarly, all of the following address expressions are syntactically equivalent, not in the sense of producing the same result, but in terms of correctness:

⟨identifier⟩ + 100
⟨identifier⟩ − 1420
⟨identifier⟩ + 2
etc. . . .

From the point of view of the syntax of address arithmetic, the + sign and the − sign behave equivalently, and all address arithmetic can be defined as:

⟨address⟩ ::= ⟨identifier⟩ | ⟨identifier⟩ ⟨sign⟩
                                    ⟨unsigned integer⟩
⟨sign⟩   ::= + | −

We could continue in this way, building up sets of equivalence classes of tokens and assigning a class number to each class. To show more clearly what we are talking about, Figure 19-4 lists a possible set of equivalence classes for MACRO-11.

Using the classification scheme of Figure 19-4, we are now in a position to describe exactly what the scanner does. It begins scanning the current input line, character by character, looking for the beginning of a token. When it finds a character that can begin a token, it starts storing characters and looking for the end of the token that it is building. When it reaches the end, indicated by the appearance of a character that cannot possibly belong to the token being constructed, the scanner classifies the token into the appropriate syntactic equivalence class, typically one of the types listed in Figure 19-4. The scanner then returns the character string making up the token, its length in characters, and its classification number. A typical calling sequence for a scanner might be:

FIGURE 19-4 A Possible Set of Token Classifications for
MACRO-11.

Class Number	Name		Elements
1	⟨identifier⟩		All valid used identifiers
2	⟨op code⟩		MOV, CLR, . . ., all valid MACRO-11 op codes
3	⟨number⟩		Any valid unsigned integer
4	⟨sign⟩		The symbols that can appear in address expressions, namely +, −, *, and /
5	⟨colon⟩	:	The symbol that ends labels
6	⟨comma⟩	,	The symbol that separates fields
7	⟨semicolon⟩	;	The symbol that begins comments
8	⟨left paren⟩	(	The symbol that begins indirect addresses
9	⟨right paren⟩	)	The symbol that ends indirect addresses
10	⟨literal⟩	#	The symbol that introduces literals
11	⟨at sign⟩	@	The symbol for indirection
12	⟨equal⟩	=	The direct-assignment operator
13	⟨period⟩	.	The symbol for pseudo-ops and the location counter
14	⟨undefined⟩		Any token or symbol that does not fit into classes 1–13

scanner (line, ptr, token, length, classification, notfound)

where:

line: The input line being scanned.

ptr: The position on the input line at which the scan should begin. On
return, ptr, has been advanced to the position at which the scan
ended.

token: The characters making up the next token found on the line (if
notfound = F).

length: The length, in characters, of the token.

classification: The equivalence class number of the token.

notfound: T if no token was found on the line; F otherwise.

A broad outline for the construction of such a scanner is presented in Figure 19-5.

As you can tell from a close examination of Figure 19-5, a scanner is simply a
fancy character handler. It packs characters into tokens and passes them on to the
next piece of software down the line. In spite of its relative simplicity, it is a very
important component within the assembler, and a scanner is in fact the necessary
front end of any system that deals with character-based input or a symbolic user

interface. This includes command-language interpreters, compilers, editors, and numerous applications packages. The scanner handles all of the messy details associated with input devices, control characters, character codes, end-of-line detection, end of file, and parity checking. It allows all succeeding software components of the assembler to operate only in terms of higher level syntactic components. Thus, using the notation in Figure 19-4, whenever a MACRO-11 statement begins with a class-1 object followed by a class-5 object (i.e., ⟨identifier⟩ ⟨colon⟩), we know that we have a valid label field, and we can make that decision without being concerned with the enormous amount of character processing that had to take place to isolate and create those two objects.

EXAMPLE

Input: **A:**   **CLR**   **(R0)+**

Scanner output:

Token	Class (Using Figure 19-4)
A	1
:	5
CLR	2
(	8
R0	1
)	9
+	4

19.2.2. Pass One: Building the Symbol Table

The primary function of the first pass made by an assembler is to assign a value to all symbols used in the program. The value of a symbol during assembly is the value of the location counter at the time the symbol is defined (i.e., used as a label or in a direct-assignment pseudo operation). The meaning of the location counter (LC) can be interpreted in two different ways.

An Absolute LC: The LC value corresponds to an absolute memory address.

A Relative LC: The LC value represents a relative distance from the beginning of the program.

To illustrate this difference, assume that we encounter the following instruction at the time the location counter has a value of 100.

LOOP: MOV   R0,R1   ; The LC is currently 100

If the location counter was interpreted as absolute, then the symbol LOOP would correspond to the actual physical memory address 100. Furthermore, the translated MOV instruction (010001) would be placed in memory location 100.

FIGURE 19-5   General Outline of a Scanner.

```
i = ptr
while line(i) = "blank" and not (end_of_line) do
    i = i + 1
end of loop

if not (end_of_line) then
    notfound = F
    length = 1
    token(length) = line(i)
    repeat
        i = i + 1
        if "line(i) could belong to this token" then
            length = length + 1
            token(length) = line(i)
        else
            end_of_token_found = true
        end if
    until end_of_token found
    "classify this token into its correct equivalence class"

else
    notfound = T
end if

ptr = i
```

If instead the location counter was interpreted as a relative value, the symbol LOOP would correspond to the memory address that is one hundred locations beyond the start of the program (i.e., $X + 100$, where X is the address of the first instruction). Because the address X will not be known until the program is loaded, we do not know the physical address of LOOP at assembly time when we use a relative location counter. However, the machine code produced by the assembler will be identical in both cases. The differences will occur in future interpretations of these addresses. We return to this discussion of absolute versus relative location counter values in Chapter 20, where we introduce the software package that is responsible for loading programs. During that operation, the different possible meanings of the addresses produced by the assembler become extremely important.

The minimal assembler responsibilities during Pass One come down to the following two operations:

1. Managing the location counter.
2. Defining all symbols used in the program.

These two responsibilities in turn reduce to a single operation: creating a *symbol table*.

The symbol table is the most important data structure generated during the language translation process. It contains the name, value, and characteristics of all symbols used within the program. The exact information kept in the table will depend on the rules and semantics of the particular language. The following are some of the fields that may appear in a typical symbol table.

1. *Symbol Name:* This is the actual character string used to name the object. The name may be stored directly in the symbol table, but in the more likely case the table simply contains a pointer into a *string space* where the actual characters are stored. This is a much more efficient representation if the identifier names can be of arbitrary and unbounded length as is the case in such languages as Pascal, Ada, or PL-1. For example, if we had used the names A, XYZ, HELLO, and LONGLONGNAME in our program, a symbol table that used the pointer and string space method of storage might look like Figure 19-6.

2. *The "Defined" Field:* This is a boolean value that is used to indicate whether the symbol has been defined yet. If the field contains a 'YES' then it has been given a value, either by being used in the label field of an instruction or in a direct-assignment pseudo-operation:

```
A:    MOV      R0,R1   ; This defines A
      A = 100          ; So does this
```

If this field contains a 'NO' then the symbol has only been referenced; it has not yet been defined. A symbol is referenced by being used in the address field of an instruc-

FIGURE 19-6   Name Storage in a Symbol Table.

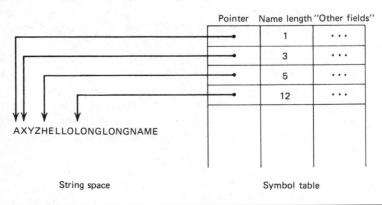

Pointer	Name length	"Other fields"
	1	· · ·
	3	· · ·
	5	· · ·
	12	· · ·

AXYZHELLOLONGLONGNAME

String space   Symbol table

tion. A symbol may get into the symbol table without being defined simply by being referenced *before* it is given a value.

        MOV   R0,X   ; This references X
                 .
                 .
                 .
    X: .WORD   0   ; This defines X

During the time between the processing of the first line above (MOV) and the second line (.WORD), the symbol X will be in the symbol table with the Defined field set to 'NO'. This type of reference is called a *forward reference,* and it is perfectly acceptable in all assembly languages.

Naturally, when the assembly process is finished, every value in the Defined field should be 'YES'; otherwise there is an *undefined symbol* error, abbreviated U. This means that you have used a name without having given it a value.

3. *The Value Field:* If the Defined field is 'YES' then this field holds the value of the symbol. The value of a symbol is, as we have mentioned, the value of the location counter at the time the symbol is defined (except in the case of the = pseudo-op, where the value of the symbol is the value of the expression on the right-hand side of the equal sign). If the Defined field is 'No', the value field has no meaning and should not be referenced.

4. *The Error Field:* This field is used to keep track of any errors associated with a symbol. For example:

   a. *Undefined Symbol Error (U Error):* caused by referencing a symbol but not defining it.

   b. *Doubly Defined Symbol Error (D Error):* caused by defining a symbol two or more times.

    A: MOV R0,R1
                 .
                 .
                 .
    A: MOV R2,R3   ; This will cause an error

   c. *Range Error (R Error):* caused by assigning a value to a symbol that is out of range. For example, on a 16-bit machine:

    A = 777777   ; This requires eighteen bits

The Error Field will keep track of whether there has been an R, D, or U error (or some other error) associated with this symbol. A complete list of MACRO-11 error codes appears in Appendix D.

There may be a great deal of additional information kept in the symbol table aside from what we have described here. For example, in a strongly typed, block-structured language like Pascal, we would probably keep the following information in our symbol table.

1. Type Information
   Is it an integer, real, array, record . . . ?
2. Bounds Information:
   If it is an array, what are the bounds on its subscripts?
3. Scope Information:
   In what program unit was this symbol declared?

However, for the sake of this discussion, we assume a symbol table with only the four fields: name, value, defined, and error. A Pascal-like description of the structure of such a symbol table is shown below.

```
type
    symbol_table = array(1..max_symbol) of symbol_records;

    symbol_records = record

            name : record
                    pointer :   0..max_string_space;
                    length  :   integer
                end;

        value :     0..max_address_space;

        defined :   boolean;

        error :     set of ('U', 'D', 'R')

            end;
```

The purpose of Pass One is to construct a symbol table for ultimate use by Pass Two. The rough outline of an algorithm to implement Pass One is shown in Figure 19-7. This algorithm is quite broadly sketched and a number of low level details are omitted.

When Pass One is finished, we will have a symbol table that we can use to generate code during Pass Two.

19.2.3   A "One-and-a-Half-Pass" Assembler

Before considering Pass Two, we should explain why most assemblers are composed of at least two full passes over the source code and why we described ours in that fashion. In the preceding section, we described the outline of a hypothetical first pass, in which we did the least amount of processing possible. In fact, all we did was build

FIGURE 19-7   Algorithm for Pass One.

1. Set the location counter (LC) to 0.

2. Get the next assembly-language statement.

3. Process the label field.
    3.1   Call the scanner to get the label field.
    3.2   If there is no label, go to step 4.
    3.3   We have a valid symbol in the label field. Look up this token in the symbol table.
          3.3.1   If the label was not found, then, in the next available slot of the symbol table, set:

          name ← token
          defined ← 'YES'
          value ← LC
          error ← none

          3.3.2   If the label was found, and defined = 'NO' then set:

          defined ← 'YES'
          value ← LC
          error ← none

          3.3.3   If the label was found, and defined = 'YES' then set:

          error ← 'D'

4. Process the operation code field.
    4.1   If necessary, call the scanner to get the next token.
    4.2   Process only the operation codes or pseudo-ops that affect either the location counter or the symbol table. Other op codes are not processed yet. For example:
          4.2.1   If the op code is an '=' then get the address field and reset the value field of this symbol in the symbol table to the value found in the address field.
          4.4.2   If the op code is .BLKB or .BLKW, increase the location counter by the value found in the address field.
          4.2.3   Process any other op code or pseudo-op that modifies the symbol table or location counter.

5. Process the address field.
    5.1   Call the scanner to get the next token. This will be the address field.
    5.2   If the token is a symbol, look it up in the symbol table.
          5.2.1   If the symbol was found, then nothing need be done.

FIGURE 19-7   Algorithm for Pass One. (*continued*)

5.2.2   If the symbol was not found, then in the next available slot in the symbol table, set:

name   ← token
defined ← 'NO'
value   ← undefined
error   ← none

6.   Update the location counter.

We have finished processing an instruction. Update the location counter.

LC := LC + length of this instruction

7.   Repeat steps 2–6 until we come to the end of the assembly process, indicated by the operation code .END.

8.   Finish up the Pass One operations by looking through the defined field of all entries in the symbol table. Wherever you encounter a 'NO,' set:

error ← 'U'

a symbol table. What if, instead, we wanted to do the *maximum* amount of processing possible? In fact, what if we wanted to do everything (i.e., symbol table generation, code generation, and listing) on the first pass and only look at the source code once? In a sense, we would be trying to eliminate Pass Two entirely. Would that be possible?

Not quite. On Pass One, we could perform almost every step needed to assemble a source statement into object code, but one construct would cause us trouble, namely the *forward reference*, mentioned previously. Look at this code fragment:

MOV   R0,DATA
.
.
.
DATA: .WORD   0

When we encounter the MOV instruction, we do not as yet know the address associated with the symbol DATA. Therefore, we cannot correctly assemble the second address field of that instruction. Not until we have encountered the symbol DATA in the label field can we correctly assemble the MOV instruction or, indeed, any other instruction that references the symbol DATA before its definition. This is why we build a symbol table first. When we have the value associated with every symbol in the program, we can go back over the source code a second time and correctly assemble all address fields, even those with forward references.

However, we can handle forward references without a full second pass by using a technique called "chaining." In chaining, we keep in the symbol table a pointer to all symbols that have been referenced before they have been defined. The pointer is kept in the value field of the symbol table. (We can tell the difference between a forward reference pointer and an actual value by looking at the Defined field of the symbol table. If it is 'YES', the Value field represents an actual value. If it is 'NO', the Value field is a pointer to a list of forward references.) Let's trace through exactly what happens using the following sequence of instructions.

LC Value		Instruction		
a_1		MOV	R0,DATA	; Forward reference
.		.		
.		.		
.		.		
a_2		MOV	R1,DATA	; So is this
.		.		
.		.		
.		.		
a_3		MOV	R2,DATA	; So is this
.		.		
.		.		
.		.		
a_4	DATA:	.WORD	0	; Here is the definition

When the first forward reference is encountered (line a_1 above), we put the name (DATA) in the symbol table and use the value field to point to the location in memory containing this instruction. In the second address field of this MOV instruction, we do not assemble an address. Instead, we store a special "End of Chain" value, represented as a "Λ" in the following diagrams. (The actual internal bit pattern corresponding to the symbol Λ is not really important.)

First Encounter

SYMBOL_TABLE(name_field) ← the name (DATA)
SYMBOL_TABLE(value_field) ← LC value (a_1)
SYMBOL_TABLE(defined_field) ← 'NO'
address field of instruction ← Λ

Pictorially:

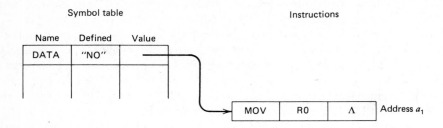

With each succeeding forward reference to the same symbol, we attach the address of the instruction containing that reference to the pointer chain beginning in the value field of the symbol table. We do this by appending the most recent reference to the head of the chain.

All Succeeding Encounters

$$\text{end\_chain} \leftarrow \text{SYMBOL\_TABLE (value)}$$
$$\text{SYMBOL\_TABLE(value)} \leftarrow \text{LC value } (a_2, a_3)$$
$$\text{address\_field(LC)} \leftarrow \text{end\_chain}$$

Pictorially:

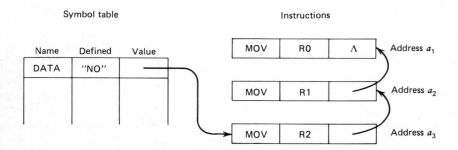

We have chained together every forward reference to the symbol DATA. This chain can be as long as desired, and the technique works for an arbitrary number of forward references for each symbol.

When we finally encounter the definition of the symbol DATA (at location counter value a_4 in the preceding diagram), we can go back and follow the chain to correctly assemble the address field of all instructions that referenced this symbol. That is, the value of DATA, which is address a_4, must be inserted into the address field of every instruction in the chain.

On Definition

```
end_chain ← SYMBOL_TABLE(value)
SYMBOL_TABLE(defined) ← 'YES'
SYMBOL_TABLE(value) ← LC (a₄ in this case)
Repeat until (endchain = Λ)
    next ← address_field(end_chain)
    address_field(end_chain) = SYMBOL_TABLE(value)
    end_chain ← next
End of loop
```

Pictorially:

Symbol table

Instructions

Name	Defined	Value
DATA	"YES"	a_4

| MOV | R0 | a_4 | Address a_1 |

| MOV | R1 | a_4 | Address a_2 |

| MOV | R2 | a_4 | Address a_3 |

All of the address fields have now been correctly assembled.

The use of this chaining algorithm would allow us to complete the entire assembly process in a single pass, except for the extra work of going back and fixing up the address fields of forward references. This is why the technique is sometimes called "one-and-a-half-pass" assembly. Everything described with respect to Pass One (Section 19.2.2) and Pass Two (Section 19.2.4, below) could be done in a single pass.

The only limitation imposed by this technique is that we cannot do *address arithmetic* on forward references. That is, if we write:

```
CLR    X+1  ; Address arithmetic on a forward reference
    .
    .
    .
```

> CLR   X+2   ; So is this
> .
> .
> .
>
> X: .WORD 0   ; Here is the definition

and X is a symbol that is defined later in the program, then it is not enough to chain together foward references to the symbol X. We must also keep track of all of the different arithmetic expressions that must be evaluated when the value of X is finally known. This is generally too difficult an operation to realistically implement, and the problem is avoided by outlawing forward references in address expressions.

Another problem associated with 1-pass assemblers is that listings must be produced on the first pass. However, the value of forward references is not immediately known, and the value actually stored in the address field of an instruction is not yet an actual address, but a set of pointer chains of the type just described. Thus, the listing that is printed will be misleading and confusing. (For the following example we are using a 6-bit op-code, 12-bit addresses, and an internal code of 05 for the mnemonic INC.)

LC	Object	Source Code	
100	057777	INC	X
104	050100	INC	X
110	050104	INC	X
.	.	.	
.	.	.	
.	.	.	
200	000000	X: .WORD	0

The listing does not properly show the address 200 assembled in place of the symbol X in locations 100, 104, and 110. When the first three INC commands were encountered, we did not know this value. Therefore, the listing simply shows the three forward references chained together. The symbol table contained a pointer to the last forward reference encountered, at location 110. This instruction points to location 104, the next forward reference, which in turn points to location 100. (The value 7777 in location 100 is the bit pattern being used to symbolize the end of the chain "Λ".) When the definition of the symbol X is ultimately encountered at location 200, these three instructions will be correctly reset, but it will be too late to correct the printed listing and it will appear as shown above.

In spite of these problems, a number of one- (and one-and-a-half-pass) assemblers have been designed and built.

19.2.4 Pass Two: Parsing and Code Generation

The second pass of the assembler has four basic responsibilities.

1. To *parse* the tokens of the assembly-language statement. This pass determines whether the tokens that have appeared were combined in a syntactially valid manner according to the grammatical rules of the language.

2. To *generate code*. If the parsing phase indicated that the statement is syntactically correct, then we must generate the machine-language equivalent of the symbolic command. During this process, we make use of information discovered during parsing as well as information contained in the symbol table.

3. To print the *listing*, which typically includes:

Error flags
Location counter
Binary code
Source code

A sample listing is shown in Figure 13-4.

4. To create an *object module*. This is the output of the assembly process and the input to the next software package, the linker/loader, described in Chapter 20. In addition to the object code, this object module may contain:

The address of where to start loading the program
The size of the program
The address of where to start executing the program
Information on external references
Relocation information

The role of the object module in the overall translation process is shown in Figure 19-3.

The main component of Pass Two is an extremely complex piece of software called a *parser*. The study of parsing techniques for high-level languages can (and does) occupy the major share of numerous advanced courses in computer science; here we simply make you aware of some of the key issues involved in the construction of these software units.

The design of a parser is based on a theoretical structure called a *finite-state machine* (FSM). An FSM, sometimes called a *state transition diagram*, is an idealized computational model composed of *states, inputs, actions,* and *transitions* between states. A transition is represented as shown in Figure 19-8. If you are cur-

FIGURE 19-8   State Transition.

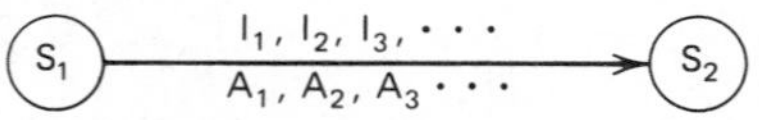

rently in state S_1 and you receive input I_1, input I_2, or input I_3, . . . , then you simultaneously make a transition to state S_2 and take actions A_1, A_2, A_3, ... A complete FSM is composed of a possibly large number of these states (S_1, S_2, . . .) and a possibly large number of transitions between these states. So, for example, Figure 19-9 shows an FSM with four states (S_1, S_2, S_3, S_4), three inputs (I_1, I_2, I_3), and three actions (A_1, A_2, A_3).

Given the machine in Figure 19-9, along with an initial or starting state and an input sequence, we can describe the exact sequence of actions that will result, as well as the final state in which we will end up. For example, if we start in state S_1 and receive an input sequence of $I_2I_2I_1I_1$, the resulting sequence of actions will be $A_3A_3A_2A_1$, and we will finish in state S_3.

The FSM model is used in parsing because as the various tokens come in from the assembly-language statement, we proceed from state to state based on which tokens have arrived and what we expect to happen next. The inputs to the FSM are the tokens on the line. The states of our FSM represent out current knowledge about what is happening, and the actions are the operations we wish to perform when we definitely recognize a specific construct (e.g., generate machine code, put something into the symbol table).

Illustrating these concepts using MACRO-11 would be much too difficult because it is such a large and complex language. An FSM to parse MACRO-11 code would have hundreds of states. Instead, let's use a highly simplified assembly language that only contains statements in the following format:

[label:] op-code address

where the label field is optional, the only op codes are MOVE (code 1) and JUMP (code 2), and the address field could be either a symbol or an unsigned integer. The syntax of this simplified assembly language is summarized in Figure 19-10.

FIGURE 19-9   Typical Finite State Machine.

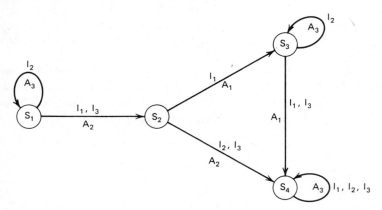

As we begin to parse a line, we are in a "Start" state because we have no information at all about the current instruction (i.e., a "clean slate" state). If the first input found by the scanner is an ⟨identifier⟩ (i.e., a class-1 object using the numbering scheme of Figure 19-4), then we may have a label field, although we will not know for certain until we find the succeeding colon. Therefore, we must move to a state colloquially called the "I think I have a label" state, because this is the extent of our current knowledge. We cannot yet take any action. If we are in this state and next receive as input a colon (a class-5 token, using the numbering notation of Figure 19-4), then we know we have a label and can move to the "I have a label" state. The action that might be caused by this transition could be a call on a procedure to put that label and its value into the symbol table (unless this was already done during Pass One).

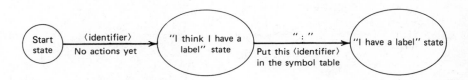

If we are in the "I have a label" state, then the only input we should receive is MOVE or JUMP, the two legal operation codes. These codes correspond to input of class 3, using the notation of Figure 19-4, and this input would take us to a new "I have an op code" state. The action taken would be to generate the correct binary pattern for this op code in the op-code field of the assembled instruction. Any input other than MOVE or JUMP would be an error and would take us to the "illegal op code" state. The appropriate action then might be to generate an illegal-op-code error flag.

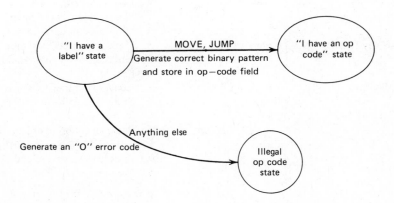

FIGURE 19-10   Syntax of Our Assembly Language.

⟨statemeht⟩ :: = ⟨label field⟩ ⟨op code⟩ ⟨address⟩
⟨label field⟩ :: = "none" | ⟨identifier⟩ :
⟨op code⟩   :: = MOVE | JUMP
⟨address⟩   :: = ⟨identifier⟩ | ⟨unsigned integer⟩

FIGURE 19-11   Finite State Machine.

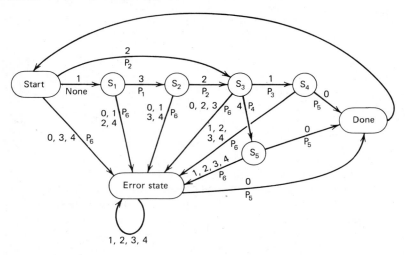

Inputs	States	Actions
0: no more tokens	S_1: I think I have a label.	P_1: Put label into the symbol table.
1: ⟨identifier⟩	S_2: I have a label.	P_2: Look up the op code to find its binary value. Store binary value of op code in op-code field.
2: MOVE,JUMP	S_3: I have a valid op code.	P_3: Look up symbol in symbol table. Store its value in address field.
3: ⟨colon⟩	S_4: I have a valid symbolic address.	P_4: Convert number to binary. Store that value in address field.
4: ⟨integer⟩		
	S_5: I have a valid numeric address.	P_5: Put instruction in object module and print a line in the listing.
		P_6: Print error message and put all 0s in the instruction.

We would continue constructing our FSM in this fashion, describing all the possible states and the transitions that can occur for all of the possible combinations of inputs. A complete FSM for the hypothetical language of Figure 19-10 is shown in Figure 19-11.

Now, how do we implement the theoretical model diagrammed in Figure 19-11? The answer is twofold. First, we must construct a data structure, let's call it PARSE_TABLE that contains information about states, inputs, transitions, and actions. We can make PARSE_TABLE a 2-dimensional array in which the rows represent the *states* of the FSM (S_1, S_2, ... , in Figure 19-11), and the columns represent the set of all possible *inputs* (the 0, 1, ... , 4 of Figure 19-11). The contents of the $[i,j]$th entry of PARSE_TABLE are two values.

1. A new state number. This represents the state to which we will move.
2. A list of actions to take (i.e., procedures to be called). These are the actions that occur during the transition.

The PARSE_TABLE for the finite state machine in Figure 19-11 is shown in Figure 19-12.

Given this data structure, we can describe how a parser works. If you are in state S_i and the next input token provided by the scanner is I_k, then you do the following.

1. Go to the new state contained in PARSE_TABLE[i,k].
2. Perform all actions contained in PARSE_TABLE[i,k].

Referring to Figure 19-12, if you are in state S_3 and you get input of type 4, then the table says to go to state S_5 and perform action P_4. What just happened is that you had a valid operation code (state S_3), received a valid integer constant (input of type 4), decided that this was a valid numeric address (state S_5), and stored that value in the address field of the instruction (action P_4).

Slightly more formally, we can sketch out the behavior of a parser algorithm in Pascal-like notation.

```
var
    parse_table = array(1..statecount, 0..input_count) of
            record
                new_state   :   1..state_count;
                actions     :   array(1..k) of proc_names;
            end;
            .
            .
            .
```

```
procedure parse_a_line (parse_table);

begin
  current_state := "START";
  repeat
    call scanner(token,input_class);
    for i := 1 to k do
      activate parse_table (current_state,input_class) .actions(i);
    current_state := parse_table(current_state,input_class).new_state;
  until current_state = "DONE"
end;
```

FIGURE 19-12   Parse Table for the FSM of Figure 19-11.

		Input 0	1	2	3	4
	START	Error / P_6	S_1 / —	S_3 / P_2	Error / P_6	Error / P_6
	S_1	Error / P_6	Error / P_6	Error / P_6	S_2 / P_1	Error / P_6
	S_2	Error / P_6	Error / P_6	S_3 / P_3	Error / P_6	Error / P_6
Current State	S_3	Error / P_6	S_4 / P_3	Error / P_6	Error / P_6	S_5 / P_4
	S_4	Done / P_5	Error / P_6	Error / P_6	Error / P_6	Error / P_6
	S_5	Done / P_5	Error / P_6	Error / P_6	Error / P_6	Error / P_6
	Done	Start / —	Start / —	Start / —	Start / —	Start / —
	Error	Done / P_5	Error / —	Error / —	Error / —	Error / —

where S = New state (from Figure 19-11)
      P = Action to take (from Figure 19-11)

For example, given the parse table in Figure 19-12 and the above procedure, the statement:

MOVE   100

would result in the following sequence of states: START, S_3, S_5, DONE, and the following actions: P_2, P_4, P_5. If the procedures P_i performed the operations described in Figure 19-11, then the three actions P_2, P_4, and P_5 would result in the following internal operations.

P_2: Look up MOV to find its binary operation code.
    Store that binary code in the op-code portion of the instruction being built.

P_4: Convert 100 (decimal) to binary.
    Store that binary value in the address field of the instruction being built.

P_5: Store the completed instruction in the object module.
    Print a line in the listing.

The instruction has been correctly *parsed*, the code has been properly *generated*, the instruction has been *stored* in the object file, and the listing has been *printed*. These are the four responsibilities of Pass Two that we described at the beginning of this chapter.

You might find it instructive to trace through the parsing of these two additional hypothetical instructions:

L: MOVE   A
L: MOVE: A

List the exact sequence of inputs, states, and actions that occur during parsing. Exercises 7 and 8 at the end of the chapter contain some additional examples of parsing.

19.3
Conclusion

Language translators are the most widely used and important support tools available to the programmer. Assemblers provide you with mnemonic assistance, additional addressing capabilities, and some useful assembler directives. Compilers and high-level languages create an entire "virtual environment," with its own set of problem-solving primitives, data structures, and subprogram facilities that are totally independent of the underlying hardware. The programmer is freed from the "tyranny of hardware," that is, from having to think, design, and code directly at the hardware level, using binary representation and absolute addresses. Instead, an environment is created that is more friendly to the user and more conducive to error-free program development. The primary purpose of system software is to facilitate the effective use of the hardware resources available. Without an assembler or a compiler, our programs would look like this:

$$010011101011110$$
$$10011011011111$$
$$000100111100111$$

.

.

and we would have difficulty getting anything useful done. Language translators are among the most important and critical components of system software. Courses in compiler design and formal languages expand greatly on the theoretical material presented in this chapter.

We now have an *object module* that is the result of the language translation process. Let's see what happens to that module as it is processed by the next piece of system software—the *linker/loader*.

Exercises for Chapter 19

1.   Design, code, and implement a scanner that locates tokens and classifies them according to the following table.

Class Number	Name	Elements
1	⟨identifier⟩	All valid user identifiers
2	⟨op code⟩	The reserved identifiers JUMP, MOVE, ADD
3	⟨colon⟩	The symbol ":"
4	⟨integer⟩	All valid unsigned octal integers
5	⟨unknown⟩	All tokens that do not fall into classes 1–4

The calling sequence for your scanner should be identical to the one described in Section 19.2.1.

2.   Write two routines called ENTER and RETRIEVE that enter and locate symbols in a symbol table using the string space name storage technique described in Section 19.2.2. The calling sequence should be:

ENTER (name, defined, value, error)

where name is the name of the token, defined is the value "YES" or "NO", value is the address value of the token, and error is one of the characters: blank, "D", "U", or "R". ENTER should look up the name in the symbol table. If it is not there, enter it into the table in the next available slot and set the defined, value, and error fields to the values passed in as parameters. If ENTER finds the name, reset the defined, value, and error fields in the symbol table to the value of the parameters.

RETRIEVE (name, found, defined, value, error)

RETRIEVE should look up the name in the symbol table. If it is not there, set the parameter found to false. Otherwise, set found to true and set the defined, value, and error parameters to the values stored in the symbol table fields for that symbol.

3. Use your scanner from Exercise 1 and your symbol table handlers from Exercise 2 to write a miniature assembler for a language with the following syntax:

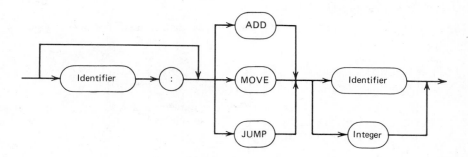

The op code can be ADD (op code 0), MOVE (op code 1) or JUMP (op code 2). The address can be either an unsigned octal integer or a symbol. If it is a symbol, use the address associated with that symbol in the address field. Instructions are eight bits long and in the following format:

Op code	Address
2	6

Here is an example of an assembled program in this simple language:

Location Counter	Instruction			
0000	102	A:	MOVE	2
0001	000	B:	ADD	A
0002	001		ADD	B
0003	220		JUMP	20

4. Make your assembler more realistic by making some (or all) of the following changes.

    a. Add enough instructions so that you have a somewhat realistic instruction set. Use Figure 9-10 as a guideline.

    b. Enlarge the instructions to accommodate a reasonable number of op-codes and memory addresses. One possibility is a 6-bit op-code field and a 10-bit address.

    c. Allow some additional addressing modes. This may include address arithmetic, indexing, or indirection.

    d. Add the ability to locate and detect errors. Print out error flags if any errors are detected.

Upon completion of Exercises 1–4, you will have implemented a realistic (albeit extremely simplified) assembler.

5. Using any familiar high-level language (Pascal, FORTRAN, COBOL), describe the information you think should be kept in the symbol table to provide the services of that language.

6. What impact would the following language features have on building a symbol table?

    a. Local variables.

    b. Symbolic constants.

    c. Reserved words.

7. Show the parse table that would determine whether you have a correctly formed phone number. The syntax for a phone number is:

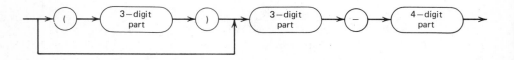

Assume that you have a scanner that returns as input the following seven classes of information.

Input Class	Value
1	"("
2	")"
3	A collection of three decimal digits
4	A collection of four decimal digits
5	"–"
6	Any other token not belonging to classes 1–5
7	No more tokens found

Try to make the determination of syntactic correctness with the smallest possible number of states.

8. Show the parse table to determine whether you have a correctly formed name. The syntax of a name is:

Assume that you have a scanner that returns as input the following six classes of information.

Input Class	Value
1	A string of characters of length > 1
2	A single character
3	" , "
4	" . "
5	Any token not belonging to classes 1–4
6	No more tokens found

Try to determine syntactic correctness with as few states as possible.

9. Using Figure 19-12, parse the following assembly-language instructions:
   a. **L: MOVE A**
   b. **L: MOVE: A**
   c. **L MOVE A**
   d. **MOVE A:1**
   e. **MOVE MOVE**

Describe exactly what happens when each of these instructions is parsed according to the rules specified in Figure 19-12.

10. Translate the following two operations into:
   a. PDP-11 machine language.
   b. MACRO-11 assembly language.
   c. Pascal.

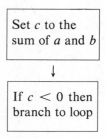

Using this example, discuss the "virtual programming environment" created by assembly languages and high-level languages as it relates to ease of implementation, avoidance of errors, future modifications, legibility, and power.

CHAPTER 20

LINKING AND
LOADING

20.1
Introduction

In Chapter 19 we described the assembly process, which produces the *object file*. The object file contains translated machine-language code that cannot be directly executed by the processor until the object file has been processed by two system software packages, the *linker* and the *loader*. Before we can describe the complete life cycle of a process from initial coding to final execution, as diagrammed in Figure 19-3, we must study these two final packages in detail.

20.2
The Loader

The loader is a software package that takes translated machine-language instructions from the object file and places them in the proper physical memory location inside the computer. This loading responsibility is diagrammed in Figure 20-1.

The one responsibility that every loader has, namely, the loading of instructions, is shown in Figure 20.1. However, a loader may also be responsible for *address binding*. This step involves changing a logical address in a program into the physical memory address where it will be stored in the computer. Thus, for the following instruction:

        X: MOV   #1,COUNT

binding occurs when we determine which physical memory address will contain the integer constant 1, and which physical memory addresses will correspond to the user-defined symbols X and COUNT.

FIGURE 20-1   The Loading Process.

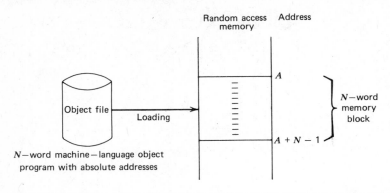

Binding can occur at four different stages in the life of a program. The earliest point at which binding can occur is *programming time.* In this case, all actual physical addresses are directly specified by the programmer within the program itself. Examples of binding at programming time include programming directly in machine language or using only absolute memory references in MACRO-11 program. For example:

Address		Instruction
200	MOV	@#100,R0
204	ADD	@#102,R0
210	MOV	R0,@#104
.	.	
.	.	
.	.	
220	JMP	@#200

In this example, the programmer has done the binding of logical addresses to physical addresses. Instead of using symbolic names like LOOP, A, DELTA, or PAY, the programmer has already mapped these names onto physical locations 100, 102, and 104 and has coded directly in terms of these addresses. Code of this type is very rarely used because it is so inflexible. If the code in the example were changed (e.g., if new statements were added or existing statements deleted), all of the physical addresses probably would be changed and the old references would be incorrect. Thus, the entire program would have to be rewritten every time the program was modified.

Instead of binding addresses at programming time, we can postpone this operation until *assembly* time, or compile time if we are working in a high-level language. This is the condition we assumed in Chapter 19 in our description of an assembler. The symbol table we constructed mapped a symbolic address selected by the programmer into a physical address determined by the assembler via its location counter. Thus, when we write:

```
LOOP:   MOV   X,R0
        ADD   #2,R0
        MOV   R0,Y
          .
          .
          .
        JMP   LOOP
```

we are not worried about the physical addresses associated with the symbols X, Y, or LOOP, or the location of the constant 2. The assembler determines those values during assembly and performs the binding. To change the program (e.g., to add a new statement), we simply *reassemble* the program to bind the symbols to their correct new addresses; it is not necessary to rewrite the code above.

When binding is performed at either programming time or assembly time, the loader has no binding responsibility at all. It merely loads the translated instructions into memory, one by one, exactly as shown in Figure 20-1. This type of loader, which is by far the simplest, is called an *absolute loader*. Examples of the use of absolute loaders are given in Section 20.2.1.

One problem with this approach to binding is that once a program has been assembled, its addresses are fixed. Referring to Figure 20-1, the program would be bound to occupy the N memory locations $A, A + 1, A + 2, \ldots A + N - 1$. However, what if we wanted to *move* the program? What if, when we were ready to execute the program, memory locations $A, A + 1, \ldots$, were in use, but locations $B, B + 1$, $\ldots$ were available? The assembled program could not be moved as is. Instead, it would have to be reassembled with a new initial value for the location counter—address B instead of A. Because of this early binding we still lack total flexibility in moving and relocating programs.

A better approach is to implement address binding at *load time*. To do this, we have the assembler translate our symbols not into absolute addresses, but into *relative addresses*. These addresses will be relative to some known point such as the start of the program, which is typically considered to be location 0. Thus, if the symbol table says that the symbol LOOP has the value 40, this does not mean that LOOP is to be bound to physical memory location 40. Instead, it simply means that this symbol will be found in the fortieth memory location beyond the beginning of the program (location 0).

If all of our addresses are represented in this relative format, moving a program around becomes much easier. To load a program into physical memory locations A, $A + 1, A + 2, \ldots$, the loader simply adds the constant A to each instruction as it is loaded into memory. To move the program to memory location $B, B + 1, B + 2$, $\ldots$, we would simply repeat the loading process, adding the constant B to each

FIGURE 20-2   Relocatable Loader.

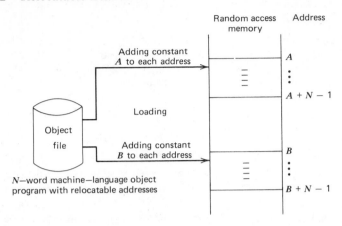

instruction instead of the value A. We would not need to reassemble the original program. This type of loader is called a *relocatable loader* and is diagrammed in Figure 20-2.

Relocatable loaders are very common and are described further in Section 20.2.2. They increase flexibility significantly by making programs easier to move around to wherever memory is available.

But we can do even better. We can postpone binding until the last possible moment by doing it at *execution time*. The address field that is loaded into memory is not yet bound to a physical address. It is not until the statement has been executed that we finally determine the address of the physical location that will be referenced. We have now gained complete and total flexibility. Since binding is not done until the code is executed, we can move a program to whatever locations we want, whenever we want, even when it is executing!

Systems that do binding at execution time use many different approaches and go by many different names: *paging systems, demand paging systems,* and *virtual memory systems.* These systems are discussed briefly in Section 20.2.4. However, they are extremely sophisticated and a fuller discussion is beyond the scope of this book. These systems are discussed at length in courses on operating systems design and computer architecture.

Our discussion has showed that as binding is postponed later and later, we gain more and more flexibility in our programs and the use of resources. This effect is seen over and over again in many applications in computer science. The longer we can postpone the mapping of a logical entity onto a physical resource, the more beneficial it will be. When you have to firmly and irrevocably fix a value to an object, you will always benefit by postponing the decision as long as possible.

20.2.1 Absolute Loaders

The simplest type of loader is called an *absolute* loader. Its job is simply to load absolute binary instructions into memory after the binding operation has been completed by the assembler. Because the binding operation has already fixed all addresses, the absolute loader must load the instructions into a specific and predetermined set of memory locations. We do not have any choice about where to put these instructions.

The absolute binary object file contains the machine-language instructions themselves, along with at least three other pieces of information.

1. The number of instructions in the object file (the *program length*), typically expressed in terms of the number of memory words occupied by the program.
2. The *load address*. This is the physical memory address of where to begin loading the instructions (the address *A* in Figure 20-1).
3. The *execution address*. This is the physical memory address of the first instruction to be executed. In MACRO-11, this will come from the address field of the .END pseudo-operation.

Absolute object files vary in the exact format from system to system, but they generally include the information just listed. Figure 20-3 shows the layout of a typical absolute object file.

The absolute loader that would process an object file in the format of Figure 20-3 is quite easy to specify. The algorithm for such a loader is shown in Figure 20-4. It assumes that each machine instruction occupies one word of memory. Notice that the last thing the loader does is load the address of the first executable instruction into the program counter. The next instruction to be fetched will be the first instruction of the newly loaded program, which will then begin executing. This is how we might typically handle the transition from the program-loading phase to program execution.

Absolute object files and absolute loaders are not very common for the reasons

FIGURE 20-3　Typical Absolute Object File.

FIGURE 20-4   Algorithm for an Absolute Loader.

```
START
    read in N, the number of instructions
    read in the load address
    for i : = 1 to N do
        begin
        read in a machine-language instruction
        store that instruction in memory
            location "load address"
        load address ← load address + 1
        end
    read in execution address
    store execution address in the program counter
END
```

mentioned earlier. Programs must be kept in source form and reassembled and reloaded every time they are run because assembly binds their addresses to a fixed location in memory. One area in which absolute loaders *are* used is "student-oriented" compilers, sometimes called *load-and-go* compilers. In this case, the program is compiled directly into absolute locations reserved for student use; it is then loaded and immediately executed exactly as shown in Figure 20-4. Since student programs tend to be small and are run infrequently, we usually do not mind paying the price of reassembling or recompiling them every time they are run.

Another example of this approach is called a *bootstrap loader*. We know that a loader can load another program, but what loads the loader? The answer is a bootstrap, which is a very small and simple loader. The bootstrap's only job is to load the full loader, which in turn loads the other essential pieces of the system. The bootstrap loads the full loader into fixed and known locations in memory. Figure 20-5 shows how a simple bootstrap loader might operate. (Note: This fragment assumes that the input device containing the full loader is a DMA device with three registers called

FIGURE 20-5   A Typical Bootstrap Loader.

```
BOOT:     MOV    #LOADER,BA   ; Address where loader is to be
                                loaded
          MOV    #N,WC        ; Size of full loader
          BIS    #1,DEVICESR  ; Input device status register
LOOP:     BIT    #200,DEVICESR ; Wait till loader is loaded
          BEQ    LOOP
LOADER:   .BLKW  N            ; The full loader goes here
```

DEVICESR, BA, and WC, as described in Section 15.4.) Notice that the bootstrap loads the full loader into the fixed and predetermined locations LOADER, LOADER + 2, ... Also notice that after the bootstrap program is finished, it "falls" directly into the full loader program, which then begins executing.

In the "olden days," the 6-line bootstrap shown in Figure 20-5 would occupy fixed memory locations in RAM and, if the code were destroyed or overwritten, it would have to be rekeyed in at the operator's console. Today, bootstrap loaders are always placed in read-only memory (ROM) of the type described in Section 6.6. The process of initiating the execution of a bootstrap loader in ROM, usually accomplished by pushing a START button, is called a *cold start* or *dead start,* and this is how computer systems are initially started. The bootstrap loader loads the full loader, the full loader loads the operating system (or some part of it), and the operating system then asks what should be done next and loads the appropriate software unit.

20.2.2 Relocatable Loaders

A program is said to be *relocatable* if its addresses are not bound at translation time and the instructions can be loaded into any section of memory for execution as shown in Figure 20-2. To make a program relocatable, we must do two things.

1.   Both the location counter values and the address field(s) of all instructions must be assigned values *relative* to a fixed base point, typically the beginning of the program, which is considered address 0. Thus a location counter value of 24 does not refer to physical address 24 but, rather, to the twenty-fourth byte beyond the start of the program. Similarly, a CLR 100 does not mean to clear physical address 100 but to clear the hundredth byte of the user's program.

2.   The assembler must append to each instruction a set of special flags, called *relocation bits,* telling how that instruction and its addresses are to be relocated at load time. The set of all relocation bits is called a *relocation dictionary.* There will be one relocation bit for the location counter and one for each address field in the instruction. In Figure 20-6, a typical relocatable object module, we have assumed that all instructions are in 1-address format.

The possible values of the relocation bits shown in Figure 20-6 will depend on the number of different "base points" we wish to have in our program. That is, from how many different memory locations do we wish to load our program? For example, assume that we wished to assemble and load our program in two pieces. All data would be assembled and loaded relative to a "data origin" point, and all code would be assembled and loaded relative to a "program origin" point. Thus, in memory, our program might resemble Figure 20-7. To achieve this, the assembler would need values for the relocation bits, identified in Figure 20-8.

On the PDP-11 and VAX-11, a program is allowed to have *many* origins, called *control points* or *control sections*, not just the two shown in Figure 20-7. These sections, which are loaded separately, are created using the .PSECT and .ASECT

FIGURE 20-6   Relocatable Object File.

program section length, data section length

| lc, | instruction, | lc reloc. bit, | addr. reloc. bit |
| lc, | instruction, | lc reloc. bit, | addr. reloc. bit |

.   .   .
.   .   .
.   .   .

| lc, | instruction, | lc reloc. bit, | addr. reloc. bit |

execution address, ea reloc. bit

where:

$$lc = \text{location counter value}$$

lc reloc. bit = the flag describing how to interpret the location counter value

addr. reloc. bit = the flag describing how to interpret the address field in the instruction

ea reloc. bit = the flag describing how to interpret the execution address

FIGURE 20-7   Program Loaded Relative to Two Origin Points.

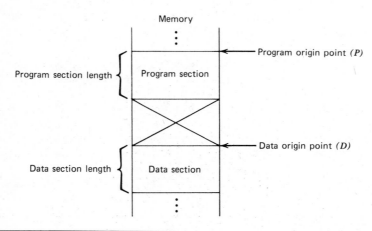

FIGURE 20-8   Typical Interpretation of Relocation Bits.

Value	Meaning	Example
0	Do *NOT* relocate this address The logical address in the program is either a fixed constant or an absolute address that should not change when the program is loaded.	CLR @#100
1	The logical address is given as a relative value. Relocate this address relative to the program origin point, P. That is, physical address = program address + P, where P is the point shown in Figure 20-7.	JMP LOOP LOOP:
2	The logical address is a relative value. Relocate this address relative to the data origin point, D. That is, physical address = program address + D, where D is the point shown in Figure 20-7.	CLR X . . . X: .WORD 0

pseudo-operations, which are described in Section 6.8 of the MACRO-11 Language Reference Manual. The ability to create many separate and independently loaded program segments allows a MACRO-11 program to be loaded as a number of separate noncontiguous pieces, thus making more efficient use of memory.

Assuming that the assembler has assembled our program using the three relocation bit values described in Figure 20-8, we are ready for the algorithm for a typical relocatable loader (Figure 20-9). This algorithm assumes that there is a procedure called get_memory(size,address) that finds a memory block of "size" words and returns the starting "address" of that block. Such a "memory allocation manager" program exists as part of every operating system. The algorithm assumes that the relocatable object file is laid out as shown in Figure 20-6.

20.2.3   An Example of the Loading Process

Let's follow a simple but complete example of a process through assembly, loading, and execution. We will use the simple 1-address instructions shown in Figure 9-10 and assemble the program shown in Figure 20-10. Assume that the translated machine-language instructions for our computer contain eighteen bits, with the first six bits for the op code and the next twelve bits for the address.

Our relocatable assembler will assemble the three data words (X, Y, and Z) into a separate data segment, and the five actual data instructions (LOAD, ADD, STORE, BR, HALT) into a program segment. The relocatable object file will look like Figure 20-11. (Assume that the op-code values are LOAD = 0, STORE = 1, ADD = 2, BR = 3, HALT = 4.)

FIGURE 20-9   Algorithm for Typical Relocatable Loader.

```
START      {relocatable loader}
Read the object file to get the program section length, P_SIZE,
  and data section length, D_SIZE
Get_memory(P_SIZE, prog_address)
Get_memory(D_SIZE, data_address)
j : = prog_address
k : = data_address

Repeat until all instructions have been read
   Read in LC, instruction, LC relocation bit, address
     relocation bit

   Case address relocation bit of {this is the binding phase}
      0   : Nothing needs to be done
      1   : Address field : = address field + prog_address
      2   : Address field : = address field + data_address
   End

   Case LC relocation bit of   {this is the loading phase}
      0   : *ERROR* This is an illegal absolute reference.
      1   : Store the instruction in memory location LC + j
            j := j + 1
      2   : Store the instruction in memory location LC + k
            k := k + 1
   End
End or repeat loop

Read execution address, EA relocation bit
Case EA relocation bit of
      0   : PC ← execution address
      1   : PC ← execution address + prog_address
      2   : PC ← execution address + data_address
END   {relocatable loader}
```

In Figure 20-11, the first instruction in the object file (the constant 5) is loaded at location 0 relative to the *data origin,* relocation flag 2. The value itself is the constant 5 and should not be relocated; that is why the second relocation flag is 0. The constant 6 is handled in the same way. The first actual instruction (LOAD X) on the third line is loaded into location 0 relative to the *program origin,* relocation flag 1. It refers to cell X, which is in the data segment, so the address field of that instruction will be relocated relative to the data origin, relocation flag 2. Thus all program instructions will be loaded relative to the program origin, and all data-generation pseudo-ops will be loaded relative to the data origin. All references to data will use the data origin, and all references to other instructions will use the program origin.

FIGURE 20-10   Sample Assembly-Language Program.

```
        X:      .WORD  5
        Y:      .WORD  6
     START:     LOAD   X
                ADD    Y
                STORE  Z
                BR     DONE
        Z:      .WORD  0
     DONE:      HALT
                .END   START
```

To load the object file from Figure 20-11, we need two blocks of physical memory 5 and 3 words long, the final size of the program and data sections, respectively. Assume that we made two calls on get_memory (see Figure 20-9) and that the procedure returned the following two values:

prog_addr : 600
data_addr : 700

Then, after processing by the relocatable loader in Figure 20-9, the instructions in memory will look like Figure 20-12.

We are now ready to execute the program. The program counter contains the value 600, and if we begin the fetch/execute phase we will fetch and execute the complete sample program.

The advantages of a relocatable loader should now be readily apparent. To move the program around we do not need to reassemble it. Instead, we simply keep the

FIGURE 20-11   Relocatable Object File for the Sample Program.

```
        5       3           (program length, data length)
 0000   000005   2   0      (lc, instruction, lc rel. bit, addr.
                            rel. bit)
 0001   000006   2   0
 0000   000000   1   2      (The LOAD instruction)
 0001   020001   1   2      (The ADD instruction)
 0002   010002   1   2      (The STORE instruction)
 0003   030004   1   1      (The BRanch instruction)
 0002   000000   2   0      (The variable Z)
 0004   040000   1   0      (The HALT instruction)
        0000     1          (execution adddress)
```

FIGURE 20-12   Sample Program After Loading.

Address	Op Code		Address	
600	0 0	¦	0 7 0 0	
601	0 2	¦	0 7 0 1	
602	0 1	¦	0 7 0 2	Program section
603	0 3	¦	0 6 0 4	
604	0 4	¦	0 0 0 0	
			.	
			.	
700	0 0	¦	0 0 0 5	
701	0 0	¦	0 0 0 6	Data section
702	0 0	¦	0 0 0 0	

```
0600
```
Program
counter

object file from Figure 20-11. Then when get_memory returns new addresses for the program and data sections, we reapply the loader shown in Figure 20-9, and the object file addresses will be rebound to their new locations.

20.2.4   Dynamic Run-Time Loaders

The one drawback of the relocatable approach just described is that, once loaded, all program addresses are bound to fixed locations. Therefore, once a program has begun execution, it must occupy exactly the same memory locations until it has completed execution. This can be a very severe restriction. Many times we would like to interrupt the execution of a running program, take it out of memory, and start it up again later. This is true, for example, in the following two situations.

1.   We want to have many users in memory and give each one a small unit of time on a round-robin basis. This is called *time-sharing.*

2.   The user initiates an I/O operation that will take a great deal of time. It is senseless to leave the program in memory when there is nothing it can do.

In both cases, we might like to remove one program from memory, put it out on a mass storage device like a disk, and replace it temporarily with a different program.

The process of removing one program and replacing it with another is called *swapping*. Using the loading scheme just developed, however, we could not swap programs because we probably could not guarantee that exactly the same memory locations would be available when the program was ready to be restarted.

For these situations we need to delay binding even further. We need to postpone it until the instruction itself is executed. This is called *dynamic* or *run-time binding*. In this case, the instruction loaded into physical memory is still the relative address as shown in Figure 20-6 or 20-11. Only when the instruction is actually fetched and executed by the processor during the fetch/execute cycle do we convert that relative address into a physical memory location.

One simple way to do run-time binding is by using a *base register*. This is a hardware register that contains the origin point of a program or data segment (i.e., the points P or D in Figure 20-7). Now when an instruction is executed, the processor will automatically add the contents of the base register to the contents of the address field before it determines the effective address.

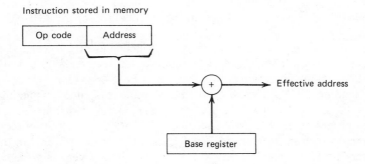

To move a program around, we simply reload the contents of the base register with a new value. Moreover, we can do this *during* execution because the address in the address field of the instruction has not yet been bound.

Referring to Figure 20-2, moving a program from locations $A, \ldots, A + N - 1$ to $B, \ldots, B + N - 1$ can be easily implemented. Initially we load the value A into the base register. When the relative addresses in the program are determined during execution, they will be bound to locations A through $A + N - 1$. If the program is swapped out and must be brought back into locations B to $B + N - 1$, we merely load the new value B into the base register. This new approach allows us to handle the two situations described at the beginning of this section.

This has been only the briefest introduction to dynamic run-time binding. There are many other techniques available such as *multiple-base register schemes, paging,* and *demand paging,* also called *virtual memory.* The VAX-11 computer system makes extensive use of the dynamic memory management scheme called virtual memory.

20.3
The Linker

If every program written were totally "self-contained" (i.e., if it contained every line of code to be executed), then our discussion would be complete. A program would be written (Chapters 11–18), assembled (Chapter 19), loaded into memory (Sections 20.1 and 20.2), and, finally, executed by a typical Von Neumann-like processor as described in Chapter 9.

However, most programs are not self-contained. They reference other program units (procedures, functions, data blocks) that were separately written, separately translated, and stored in a separate *program library*. These routines, which are not included in the source program text, are called *external routines* or *external data blocks*. We make use of external routines often. For example, the following Pascal statement:

x := sqrt(sqr(abs(y)) + sqr(abs(z)));

makes use of three external routines: sqrt, sqr, and abs. The texts of these routines are not included in our program. Instead, they reside in a separate Pascal run-time library.

The operation of *linking* involves combining independently translated program units into a single overall module so that references between units refer to the proper locations. This linking operation is summarized in Figure 20-13.

As with loading, linking can be handled at a number of times. If linking is done at *coding time,* it essentially means that there are no external routines in the language. The programmer must find and place into the program the source code for all subprograms that are referenced. Thus, a subprogram is replicated in the source code of every program that references it. This technique is very inefficient because we could wind up with dozens of copies of the same subroutine stored in our file system.

When linking is done at *assembly time,* the assembler must fetch (at assembly time) the source code of every subroutine referenced, and reassemble them as a unit every time the program is run. Although the problem of having duplicate copies of the source program is eliminated, this approach is very inefficient because it does not take advantage of a library of assembled routines that can be used directly without the need for translation.

The most popular approach is to perform the linking operation after assembly but just before loading. This way, we take all of the program units, which have been assembled relative to location 0, and put them together into a single module that still has its addresses translated relative to location 0. We now resolve all of the inter-module references in terms of the relative position of these calls within the overall module. When this resolution has been accomplished, all external references have been satisfied, and the module can be passed on to the loader to be loaded exactly as described in Section 20.2. This single module in which all references have been

FIGURE 20-13 The Linking Process.

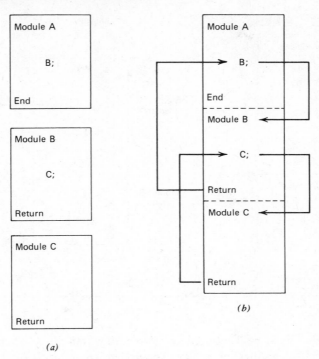

(a)

(b)

resolved in terms of relative addresses is called a *relocatable load module* because it can be relocated and loaded as a unit anywhere in physical memory. This is the type of linker we investgate in the upcoming sections, and it is diagrammed in Figure 20-14. A linker that produces a relocatable load module for processing by a loader is frequently referred to as a *linkage editor*.

Linking, like loading, can also be postponed until *execution time*. In this case we do not resolve the external references until the external call is executed by the processor. At that time, the program is temporarily suspended (actually it is interrupted, using the interrupt mechanism described in Chapter 15). Then the desired external routine is located in a library, loaded into memory, and linked to the calling module. The original program is then allowed to continue executing. These *dynamic linkers* are extremely powerful because they do not require memory to be allocated for program units unless those units are referenced. That is, if you have the following sequence in your program:

```
         BEQ   AROUND
         JSR   PC,SUB
AROUND:
```

FIGURE 20-14   A Relocatable Load Module.

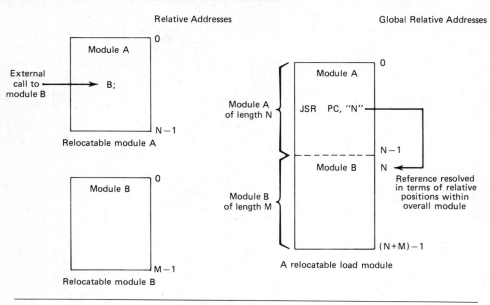

then a linker that links in all subroutines referenced within the program will include the code for SUB, regardless of whether you branch around it. If SUB is very long, this could lead to a very inefficient use of memory. A dynamic linker would only load the program SUB if the JSR instruction were executed. It would not load SUB if you branched around it.

These dynamic linking procedures go by the names *segmentation systems, chaining,* or *dynamic overlays.* A discussion of their implementation can be found in courses in operating systems design.

20.3.1 External References and Calls

A linkage editor has one main function: to match *external calls* with their corresponding *external definitions.* An external defintion identifies a symbol in such a way that the value of that symbol can be made known to program units outside the scope of the current unit. The exact syntax of an external definition will vary from language to language. For example:

1. COMMON /A/X,Y
2. EXTERNAL FUNCTION F(A,B)
3. A: .ENTRY ; This is called an *entry point*
4. #A: ... ; The '#' indicates a global symbol

In MACRO-11, the pseudo-operation that is used to declare that a symbol is external is .GLOBL. The following sequence:

```
            .GLOBL   A
        A:       .
                 .
```

declares the symbol A to be an external symbol that may be referenced (e.g., JSR
PC,A or CLR A) by other program units.

An *external call,* also called an *external reference,* is a reference to a symbol that
has been defined within another module not within the scope of the current module.
The assembler must be told that this reference is external and will not be found
within the unit. Otherwise, it will simply mark that symbol as "undefined" and flag
it as an error (the "U" error). Again, the syntax of external calls will vary from
language to language. For example:

```
    1.  procedure A(x,y); external;
                     .
                     .
                     .
        A(m,n)

    2.  CALL A(M,N)
    3.  .EXTERNAL   A
                 .
                 .
                 .
        JUMP       A
```

In MACRO-11, external calls are implemented using the same .GLOBL pseudo-op
described above. The following sequence:

```
            .GLOBL  A
                .
                .
                .
            JSR       PC,A
```

indicates that A is an external symbol whose value will not be assigned within this
program unit.

To link together these external definitions and calls, the assembler or compiler
must produce a special table called the *external symbol directory* (ESD). This table
contains the information that will be needed by the linker to resolve intermodule

references. For each external definition, we must store in the ESD the following three values:

1. The symbol name.
2. The fact that it is an external definition.
3. The relative value of that symbol (i.e., the location counter value of its definition within this module).

For each external symbol that is referenced within a module, we must store in the ESD the following three values:

1. The symbol name.
2. The fact that it is an external reference.
3. A pointer chain linking together every reference to this symbol within the module. The head of the chain will be in the ESD.

Figure 20-15a shows a hypothetical program unit containing two external definitions, the symbols C and D, and references to two externally defined symbols, A and B. In this example, the pseudo-op .ENTRY is used for external definitions, and .EXTERNAL is used for external references.

In Figure 20-15c, we show the ESD that would be produced by the assembler when translating this module. Symbols C and D have been marked as external definitions, and their value is equal to the location counter value at the time the definition (the .ENTRY command) was encountered: namely, 0 and 4, respectively. Symbols A and B have been marked as external references, and the value field in the ESD is the head of a chain pointing to every instruction that references that external symbol. In the case of external symbol A, the chain beginning in the ESD points to the instructions in locations 4, 3, and 0 (in that order). In the case of external symbol B, the chain points to location 1. (Also notice that the local symbol X, which is defined within this module, is not affected by any of these operations because it is not external.) The algorithm for building and searching these reference chains is virtually identical to the algorithms presented in Section 19.2.3 for chaining together all forward references to a symbol.

The assembled program shown in Figure 20-15b and the ESD shown in Figure 20-15c are the output of an assembler that provides and supports external programs. In the next section we describe the linking process that takes these modules, along with their external symbol directories, and produces a relocatable load module of the type shown in Figure 20-14.

20.3.2 The Linking Algorithm

The linker must bring in, one by one, all modules referenced in the program and combine them into a single unit. To do this it must construct a *global external symbol directory* (GESD). This data structure contains the same information found in the

FIGURE 20-15   The External Symbol Directory:
(a) Sample Module, (b) Assembled Program, and
(c) External Symbol Directory.

			Relative Address	Instruction	
A:	.EXTERNAL		0	LOAD	
B:	.EXTERNAL		1	ADD	
C:	.ENTRY		2	DIVIDE	6 (0)
	LOAD	A	3	STORE	(3)
	ADD	B	4	OUT	
	DIVIDE	X	5	HALT	
	STORE	A	6	00000	
D:	.ENTRY				
	OUT	A			
	HALT				
X:	.DATA	0			

(a)   (b)

Symbol	Type	Value/Pointer
C	External Def.	0
D	External Def.	4 (4)
A	External Ref	
B	External Ref.	(1)

(c)

local ESDs, but its values are given in terms of a *global location counter value* (GLOBAL-LC). The GLOBAL-LC represents the single relative base point for all relative addresses in the entire module (see Figure 20-14). The individual relative address of each module $0, 1, \ldots, M$ and $0, 1, \ldots, N$, and $0, 1, \ldots, P$ are converted by the linker, using the GLOBAL-LC, into global relative addresses $0, 1, 2, 3, \ldots, (M + N + P + \cdots)$. The linking algorithm is given below.

Step 1:   Set GLOBAL-LC = 0. The entire unit will be relative to this location 0.

Step 2:   Bring in the "next" module for linking. This includes the units automatically included in every translation of this language (e.g., the Pascal library), as well as the program units explicitly specified by the user.

Step 3:   Enter all external definitions from the local ESD of this module into the GESD. However, set the value field of the symbol to "local ESD value" + GLOBAL-LC.

Step 4: Now check all external references in the local ESD of this module to see if the corresponding external definition has been entered yet into the GESD. If not, go to step 6.

Step 5: For each symbol that is externally referenced follow the chain leading from the value field of that symbol in the local ESD. Replace the pointer in the address field of the instruction with the value field of that symbol stored in the GESD. Keep going until you come to the end of the chain of references. Repeat this step for every external reference whose definition has been encountered.

Step 6: Set GLOBAL-LC := GLOBAL_LC + length of the last program module.

Step 7: Repeat steps 2–6 until all modules referenced in this program have been processed.

Step 8: Make a second pass through the local ESD of all modules just processed looking for external references that were not satisfied on the first pass. This is necessary to handle the case in which a reference to a module is made before the module itself is encountered. This is called a *forward reference*. If any forward references are found, apply step 5 and satisfy all references.

Step 9: If any unsatisfied external references remain, this is a *linker error*. The user has referred to a nonexistent program unit. Typically, most linkers place the address of an operating system error routine in place of the nonexistent reference. Thus, if procedure A cannot be located, the statement:

JSR   PC,A

will become:

JSR   PC,$ERROR

where $ERROR is a location within the operating system that will produce helpful debugging information and abort the program.

What we have now produced is a relative image of the entire process with all externals satisfied relative to the process itself. This is ready to be passed to the loader.

When the linker has finished, it usually prints out, or stores in a file, the global external symbol directory. This allows the user to see what modules have been included in the program and where they have been placed in the relative address space of the relocatable load module. When the GESD is printed out in a nice user-oriented format, it is usually called a *memory map*.

For example, Figure 20-16a shows the linking together of four modules called MAIN, A, B, and C. MAIN is one hundred words long (decimal), while A, B, and

FIGURE 20-16   Example of a Memory Map.

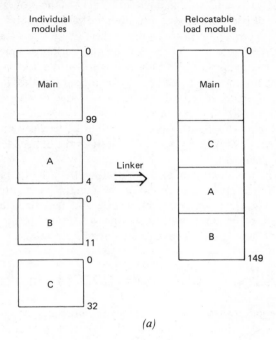

(a)

Memory Map

Module Name	Starting Point	Length
MAIN	0	100
C	100	33
A	133	5
B	138	12

(b)

C are five, twelve, and thirty-three words long, respectively. The entry point of all four of the modules is assumed to be the first word of the module. The memory map for one possible load module is shown in Figure 20-16b. Notice that the linker happened to link the units in the order: MAIN, C, A, B. The ordering of modules is generally immaterial and depends on the order in which the modules are encountered as the linker searches the various libraries.

   Access to a memory map is frequently crucial if we need to study or analyze the run-time behavior of a program. For example, let's assume that the 150-word relocatable load module in Figure 20-16a was ultimately loaded into physical memory locations 1401–1550 (all values are in decimal). Then, as the program was executing, it terminated abnormally with a program counter value of 1507. Where were we within the overall program? From the value in the PC, we know that we were about to execute the instruction located in the 107th word within our program. However, without access to the memory map in Figure 20-16b, we don't know what that 107th location represents, because the modules may be pieced together in any order.

However, with a memory map, and with the knowledge of where the loader began loading our program (1401 in this example), it is easy to see that the 107th word of the program represents the eighth word of module C, because module C occupies relative locations 100–132. We can now go directly to the desired location and determine the cause of the error.

A real memory map is usually much more detailed than the simple example shown in Figure 20-16b. It also contains information on such things as entry point locations, execution address locations, external references, and undefined external symbols. However, regardless of its complexity, it will provide the important information we have described here, and it will always be significant in program execution analysis.

20.4
The Life Cycle of a MACRO-11 Program

We have spent a good deal of time describing computers in general and the PDP-11 in particular. In this section we summarize the life cycle of a MACRO-11 process to tie together many of the concepts presented throughout. This was done informally in Figure 19-3. Here, in much greater detail, we show what operations are being performed and what information is being produced at each stage. Our commands are written using RSX-11 operating system syntax. The commands at your installation may differ slightly if you are using a different operating system, but the ideas will be the same.

1. $Edit f.MAC {f is any file name}

We first use a text editor to prepare a source file containing a syntactically valid MACRO-11 program. We may use any of the ninety-five or so operation codes or pseudo-ops introduced in Chapters 10 to 16 and listed in Appendices A and C. We may also use any of the advanced language features such as macros, extended precision, conditional assembly, or floating-point instructions (Chapters 17 and 18). The file name extension must be .MAC to indicate that it is a MACRO-11 source program.

2. $Macro/List f

This command activates the MACRO-11 assembler to assemble the source file called f.MAC. This 2-pass assembler will operate very much as described in Chapter

19 to produce two new files. The first file produced is f.OBJ, an *object file* that contains:

Machine code
Relocation dictionary
Program length   } Loader information (Section 20.2)
Execution address
External symbol directory } Linker information (Section 20.3)
"Other information"
      (owner, account number, restrictions on use, . . .)

The second file produced is f.LST, a listing file that contains a listing of the source program, the translated code, the location counter, and the symbol table (see Figure 13-4).

3. $Link/Map   f + A + B + . . .

This command activates the linking process described in this chapter. The linker will link the object modules of all files named in the link command. This example will link together files f.OBJ, A.OBJ, B.OBJ, ... The final relocatable load module, as shown in Figure 20-14, will be placed in the file called f.EXE. This file is ready to be loaded and executed. In addition, the linker will produce a file called f.MAP that contains a memory map of the type shown in Figure 20-16.

4. $run   f

This command causes the loader to load the relocatable load module called f.EXE into memory. To accomplish this, the loader is given a block of memory of size "program length" and starting address A. As instructions from f.EXE are loaded, the addresses are bound by adding the value A to each relocatable instruction. After loading, the execution start address is placed in the program counter, the fetch/execute cycle switch is set to "fetch," and execution of the newly loaded program is carried out exactly as discussed in Chapter 9. Each instruction is fetched and executed by the processor, either directly in hardware or via special microcoded commands called firmware. Execution continues either until a HALT (or .EXIT) command is executed or until a fatal error is encountered. Then program execution is ended and we return to the operating system to begin another process. The life cycle of this process is now ended.

20.5
Summary

This concludes our discussion of computer design, structure, and organization. These chapters on system software support the view of a computer and its overall organization as an integrated system in which hardware, software, and firmware (micro-programs) cooperate to process information.

We have, of necessity, looked mostly at computer hardware: memory, registers, buses, processors, I/O, interrupts, instruction sets, addressing techniques, and machine languages. However, we have also introduced, where appropriate, some important classes of system support software: assemblers, macro processors, inter-rupt handlers, linkers, and loaders. Future courses in computer science will expand on these topics and introduce new ones, including *compiler design, operating systems, telecommunications software,* and *database systems.*

In addition, courses in computer architecture will begin to investigate interesting alternatives to the typical Von Neumann machines described in Chapters 6 to 9, including *parallel processors, pipeline processors,* and *local networks.*

Finally, referring back to Figure 1-2, you may wish to "drop down" to a new level of abstraction and study computer systems not as hardware functional units or as software systems, but as a collection of gates, and discrete electrical components. If so, you will be interested in electrical engineering courses covering such areas as *hardware design, logic design, digital electronics,* and *device interfacing.*

As you reach the end of this text, it should be clear that you have not completed the study of computer organization. This text has served as an introduction to a good deal of fascinating new material about computer systems, their design, their struc-ture, and their use.

Exercises for Chapter 20

1. In addition to inflexibility, what drawbacks are there to binding at coding time with absolute octal addresses when you write MACRO-11 programs?

2. When using a direct-assignment pseudo-op to assign a value to a symbol, as in:

```
STREG = 177560
     .
     .
     .
BIS    #1,@ STREG
```

when is binding done?

3. The object file in Figure 20-3 contains only the program length, the execution address, and the translated instructions. What advantage would there be to adding the symbol table (as described in Chapter 19) to the object file of a program?

4. Referring to Figure 20-5, explain precisely why it is not incorrect to fall into the .BLKW data block and begin executing data.

5. Give some additional reasons for the acceptability of the relatively inflexible approach of absolute assembly and absolute loading ("Load and Go") in student-oriented environments.

6. In a relocatable environment, it is the job of the assembler to determine whether an address is relocatable, that is, whether its final physical memory address depends on where in memory the program is located. For the following instructions, state whether the address field represents a relocatable quantity that should be modified when the program is loaded. Assume X and Y are labels defined as follows:

```
X:  .WORD  0
    .
    .
    .
Y:  .WORD  0
```

```
a.  CLR  X
b.  CLR  X + 1
c.  CLR  X + Y
d.  CLR  X − 1
e.  CLR  Y − X
f.  CLR  R0
g.  CLR  X(R0)
h.  CLR  @#100
```

7. What would be the advantage of having more than three distinct values for the relocation field, as shown in Figure 20-8? If you had five possible values for relocation bits, how might you interpret those additional possibilities?

8. Referring to Figure 20-9, explain why value 0 of the second case statement, the absolute memory reference, should be considered an error.

9. The relocatable loader of Figure 20-9 uses an operating system routine called get_memory. This routine allocates memory blocks of size N to programs that request them. Not shown in Figure 20-9, but certainly essential, would be a companion program called return_memory(size,address) that returns a block of memory of length "size" beginning at location "address". Describe an algorithm for implementing the routines called get_memory and return_memory.

10. Using the simple 1-address commands from Figure 9-10, show what the relocatable object file for the following program would look like. Use the value of the relocation bits specified in Figure 20-8.

```
        A:    .WORD   1
        B:    .WORD   2
        C:    .WORD   3
    START:    LOAD    A+1
              ADD     B
              STORE   C
              HALT
              .END    START
```

11. Assume that the relocatable object file produced in Exercise 10 was loaded into the following memory locations:

program   load point :   20
data   load point : 100

Show what the final contents of memory would be after the program was loaded and all addresses were bound.

12. Some languages include a command called:

%include filename

in which the source file called "filename" is copied directly into the program that contains the %include command. What kind of linking does this exemplify?

13. Why is there no ambiguity in MACRO-11 caused by using one pseudo-op (.GLOBL) for two purposes—external definitions and external references?

14. Referring to Figure 20-15c, why is the symbol X not contained in the ESD? How would the linker handle the symbol X?

15. Assume that two modules A and B are each ten (octal) words long. Furthermore, assume that A and B have the following local ESD.

ESD for Module A			*ESD for Module B*		
Name	Type	Value	Name	Type	Value
A	Ext. Def.	2	B	Ext. Def.	0
B	Ext. Ref.	3	A	Ext. Ref.	7

Show the *global* ESD created when A and B are linked into a single relocatable load module.

16. Assume that you have a linker that always searches for unresolved external references by first looking in a private user library. If it does not find them there, it

then looks in a public library. What implications does this sequence have for a program that contains a subprogram with a name such as "sqrt"?

17.   The following is a memory map of a relocatable load module. (All values are octal.)

Name	Starting Address	Length
System Stack	0	1000
$MAIN	1000	104
SUB_1	1104	20
SUB_2	1124	20
SUB_3	1144	102

If this relocatable load module was loaded into memory beginning at physical memory location 017760, and the program was halted with the program counter containing the octal value 021070, describe exactly where you were in the program when it halted.

APPENDIXES

A
Permanent Symbol Table (PST): Macro-11 Operation Codes

B
Summary of Address Mode Syntax

C
Permanent Symbol Table: Macro-11 Assembler Directives

D
Diagnostic Error Message Summary

E
Routines for Input/Output

The material in Appendices A to D has been adapted in part from the following copyrighted publications of the Digital Equipment Corporation:

PDP-11 MACRO-11 Language Reference Manual, Copyright 1977, Digital Equipment Corporation, Maynard, Massachusetts

This material is the sole responsibility of the author.

APPENDIX A

PERMANENT SYMBOL TABLE (PST): MACRO-11 OPERATION CODES

The permanent symbol table (PST) contains the symbols that are automatically recognized by MACRO-11. These symbols consist of both op codes and assembler directives. The op codes (i.e., the instruction set) are listed here. The assembler directives are listed in Appendix C.

For a detailed description of the instruction set, see the appropriate PDP-11 Processor Handbook.

Mnemonic	Octal Value	Functional Name
ADC	005500	Add Carry
ADCB	105500	Add Carry (Byte)
ADD	060000	Add Source To Destination
ASH	072000	Shift Arithmetically
ASHC	073000	Arithmetic Shift Combined
ASL	006300	Arithmetic Shift Left
ASLB	106300	Arithmetic Shift Left (Byte)
ASR	006200	Arithmetic Shift Right
ASRB	106200	Arithmetic Shift Right (Byte)
BCC	103000	Branch If Carry Is Clear
BCS	103400	Branch If Carry Is Set
BEQ	001400	Branch If Equal
BGE	002000	Branch If Greater Than or Equal
BGT	003000	Branch If Greater Than
BHI	101000	Branch If Higher
BHIS	103000	Branch If Higher Or Same
BIC	040000	Bit Clear
BICB	140000	Bit Clear (Byte)

Mnemonic	Octal Value	Functional Name
BIS	050000	Bit Set
BISB	150000	Bit Set (Byte)
BIT	030000	Bit Test
BITB	130000	Bit Test (Byte)
BLE	003400	Branch If Less Than or Equal
BLO	103400	Branch If Lower
BLOS	101400	Branch If Lower or Same
BLT	002400	Branch If Less Than
BMI	100400	Branch If Minus
BNE	001000	Branch If Not Equal
BPL	100000	Branch If Plus
BPT	000003	Breakpoint Trap
BR	000400	Branch Unconditional
BVC	102000	Branch If Overflow Is Clear
BVS	102400	Branch If Overflow Is Set
CALL	004700	Jump to Subroutine (JSR PC,*xxx*)
CCC	000257	Clear All Condition Codes
CLC	000241	Clear C Condition Code Bit
CLN	000250	Clean N Condition Code Bit
CLR	005000	Clear Destination
CLRB	105000	Clear Destination (Byte)
CLV	000242	Clear V Condition Code Bit
CLZ	000244	Clear Z Condition Code Bit
CMP	020000	Compare Source To Destination
CMPB	120000	Compare Source To Destination (Byte)
COM	005100	Complement Destination
COMB	105100	Complement Destination (Byte)
DEC	005300	Decrement Destination
DECB	105300	Decrement Destination (Byte)
DIV	071000	Divide
EMT	104000	Emulator Trap
FADD	075000	Floating Add
FDIV	075030	Floating Divide
FMUL	075020	Floating Multiply
FSUB	075010	Floating Subtract
HALT	000000	Halt
INC	005200	Increment Destination
INCB	105200	Increment Destination (Byte)
IOT	000004	Input/Output Trap
JMP	000100	Jump
JSR	004000	Jump To Subroutine
MARK	006400	Mark
MFPI	006500	Move From Previous Instruction Space
MFPS	106700	Move From PS (LSI-11)
MOV	010000	Move Source To Destination

Mnemonic	Octal Value	Functional Name
MOVB	110000	Move Source To Destination (Byte)
MTPI	006600	Move To Previous Instruction Space
MTPS	106400	Move To PS (LSI-11)
MUL	070000	Multiply
NEG	005400	Negate Destination
NEGB	105400	Negate Destination (Byte)
NOP	000240	No Operation
RESET	000005	Reset External Bus
RETURN	000207	Return From Subroutine (RTS PC)
ROL	006100	Rotate Left
ROLB	106100	Rotate Left (Byte)
ROR	006000	Rotate Right
RORB	106000	Rotate Right (Byte)
RTI	000002	Return From Interrupt (Permits a Trace Trap)
RTS	000200	Return From Subroutine
RTT	000006	Return From Trap (Inhibits Trace Trap)
SBC	005600	Subtract Carry
SBCB	105600	Subtract Carry (Byte)
SCC	000277	Set All Condition Code Bits
SEC	000261	Set C Condition Code Bit
SEN	000270	Set N Condition Code Bit
SEV	000262	Set V Condition Code Bit
SEZ	000264	Set Z Condition Code Bit
SOB	077000	Subtract One And Branch
SUB	160000	Subtract Source From Destination
SWAB	000300	Swap Bytes
SXT	006700	Sign Extend
TRAP	104400	Trap
TST	005700	Test Destination
TSTB	105700	Test Destination (Byte)
WAIT	000001	Wait For Interrupt
XOR	074000	Exclusive OR

Operation Codes (Floating-Point Processor Only)

Mnemonic	Octal Value	Functional Name
ABSD	170600	Make Absolute Double
ABSF	170600	Make Absolute Floating

Mnemonic	Octal Value	Functional Name
ADDD	172000	Add Double
ADDF	172000	Add Floating
CFCC	170000	Copy Floating Condition Codes
CLRD	170400	Clear Double
CLRF	170400	Clear Floating
CMPD	173400	Compare Double
CMPF	173400	Compare Floating
DIVD	174400	Divide Double
DIVF	174400	Divide Floating
LDCDF	177400	Load And Convert From Double To Floating
LDCFD	177400	Load And Convert From Floating To Double
LDCID	177000	Load And Convert Integer To Double
LDCIF	177000	Load And Convert Integer To Floating
LDCLD	177000	Load And Convert Long Integer To Double
LDCLF	177000	Load And Convert Long Integer To Floating
LDD	172400	Load Double
LDEXP	176400	Load Exponent
LDF	172400	Load Floating
LDFPS	170100	Load FPPs Program Status
MFPD	106500	Move From Previous Data Space
MODD	171400	Multiply and Integerize Double
MODF	171400	Multiply and Integerize Floating
MTPD	106600	Move To Previous Data Space
MULD	171000	Multiply Double
MULF	171000	Multiply Floating
NEGD	170700	Negate Double
NEGF	170700	Negate Floating
SETD	170011	Set Double Mode
SETF	170001	Set Floating Mode
SETI	170002	Set Integer Mode
SETL	170012	Set Long Integer Mode
SPL	000230	Set Priority Level
STCDF	176000	Store And Convert From Double To Floating
STCDI	175400	Store And Convert From Double To Integer
STCDL	175400	Store And Convert From Double To Long Integer
STCFD	176000	Store And Convert From Floating To Double
STCFI	175400	Store And Convert From Floating To Integer

Mnemonic	Octal Value	Functional Name
STCFL	175400	Store And Convert From Floating To Long Integer
STD	174000	Store Double
STEXP	175000	Store Exponent
STF	174000	Store Floating
STFPS	170200	Store FPPs Program Status
STST	170300	Store FPPs Status
SUBD	173000	Subtract Double
SUBF	173000	Subtract Floating
TSTD	170500	Test Double
TSTF	170500	Test Floating

APPENDIX B

SUMMARY OF ADDRESS MODE SYNTAX

Address mode syntax is expressed in the summary below using the following symbols:

n   An integer between 0 and 7 representing a register number
R   A register expression
E   An expression
ER Either a register expression or an expression in the range 0–7

Format	Address Mode Name	Address Mode Number	Meaning
R	Register	0n	Register R contains the operand.
@R or (ER)	Register Deferred (indirect)	1n	Register R contains the address of the operand.
(ER)+	Autoincrement	2n	The contents of the register specified as (ER) are incremented after being used as the address of the operand.
@(ER)+	Autoincrement Deferred	3n	The register specified as (ER) contains the pointer to the address of the operand; the register (ER) is incremented after use.
−(ER)	Autodecrement	4n	The contents of the register specified as (ER) are decremented before being used as the address of the operand.
@−(ER)	Autodecrement Deferred	5n	The contents of the register specified as (ER) are decremented before being used as the pointer to the address of the operand.

Format	Address Mode Name	Address Mode Number	Meaning
E(ER)	Index	6n	The expression E, plus the contents of the register specified as (ER), form the address of the operand.
@E(ER)	Index Deferred	7n	The expression E, plus the contents of the register specified as (ER), yield a pointer to the address of the operand.
#E	Immediate (literal)	27	The expression E is the operand itself.
@#E	Absolute	37	The expression E is the address of the operand.
E	Relative (symbolic)	67	The address of the operand E, relative to the instruction, follows the instruction.
@E	Relative Deferred	77	The address of the operand is pointed to by E whose address, relative to the instruction, follows the instruction.

PERMANENT SYMBOL TABLE: MACRO-11 ASSEMBLER DIRECTIVES

Form	Operation
.ASCII /string/	Generates a block of data containing the ASCII equivalent of the character string enclosed in delimiting characters, one character per byte.
.ASCIZ /string/	Generates a block of data containing the ASCII equivalent of the character string enclosed in delimiting characters, one character per byte, with a zero byte terminating the specified string.
.ASECT	Begin or resume the absolute program section.
.BLKB exp	Reserves a block of storage space whose length in bytes is determined by the specified expression.
.BLKW exp	Reserves a block of storage space whose length in words is determined by the specified expression.
.BYTE exp1,exp2, . . .	Generates successive bytes of data; each byte contains the value of the corresponding specified expression.
.CSECT (name)	Begin or resume named or unnamed relocatable program section. This directive is provided for compatibility with other PDP-11 assemblers.
.DSABL arg	Disables the function specified by the argument.
.ENABL arg	Enables (invokes) the function specified by the argument.
.END (exp)	Indicates the logical end of the source program. The optional argument specifies the transfer address where program execution is to begin.
.ENDC	Indicates the end of a conditional assembly block.
.ENDM (name)	Indicates the end of the current repeat block, indefinite repeat block, or macro definition. The optional name, if used, must be identical to the name specified in the macro definition.

Form	Operation
.ENDR	Indicates the end of the current repeat block. This directive is provided for compatibility with other PDP-11 assemblers.
.EOT	Ignored; indicates end-of-tape (which is detected automatically by the hardware). Symbol is included for compatibility with earlier assemblers.
.ERROR exp;text	User-invoked error directive; causes output to the listing file or the command output device containing the optional expression and the statement containing the directive.
.EVEN	Ensures that the current location counter contains an even address by adding 1 if it is odd.
.FLT2 arg1,arg2, . . .	Generates successive 2-word floating-point equivalents for the floating-point numbers specified as arguments.
.FLT4 arg1,arg2, . . .	Generates successive 4-word floating-point equivalents for the floating-point numbers specified as arguments.
.GLOBL sym1,sym2, . . .	Defines the symbol(s) specified as global symbol(s).
.IDENT /string/	Provides a mean of labeling the object module with the program version number. The version number is the Radix-50 string appearing between the paired delimiting characters.
.IF cond,arg1	Begins a conditional assembly block of source code that is included in the assembly only if the stated condition is met with respect to the argument(s) specified.
.IFF	Appears only within a conditional assembly block, indicating the beginning of a section of code to be assembled if the condition upon entering the block tests false.
.IFT	Appears only within a conditional assembly block, indicating the beginning of a section of code to be assembled if the condition upon entering the block tests true.
.IFTF	Appears only within a conditional assembly block, indicating the beginning of a section of code to be assembled unconditionally.
.IIF cond,arg, statement	Acts as a 1-line conditional assembly block where the condition is tested for the argument specified. The statement is assembled only if the condition tests true.
.IRP sym,⟨arg1,arg2, . . .⟩	Indicates the beginning of an indefinite repeat block in which the symbol specified is replaced with successive elements of the real argument list enclosed within angle brackets.

Form	Operation
.IRPC sym,⟨string⟩	Indicates the beginning of an indefinite repeat block in which the specified symbol takes on the value of successive characters, optionally enclosed within angle brackets.
.LIMIT	Reserve two words into which the Task Builder inserts the low and high addresses of the task image.
.LIST (arg)	Without an argument the .LIST directive increments the listing level count by 1. With an argument this directive does not alter the listing level count, but formats the assembly listing according to the argument specified.
.MACRO name,arg1,arg2, . . .	Indicates the start of a macro definition having the specified name and the following dummy arguments.
.MCALL arg1,arg2, . . .	Specifies the symbolic names of the user or system macro definition required in the assembly of the current user program, but which are not defined within the program.
.MEXIT	Causes an exit from the current macro expansion or indefinite repeat block.
.NARG symbol	Can appear only within a macro definition; equates the specified symbol to the number of arguments in the macro call currently being expanded.
.NCHR symbol,⟨string⟩	Can appear anywhere in a source program; equates the symbol specified to the number of characters in the specified string.
.NLIST (arg)	Without an argument, the .NLIST directive decrements the listing level count by 1. With an argument, this directive suppresses that portion of the listing specified by the argument.
.NTYPE symbol, aexp	Can appear only within a macro definition; equates the symbol to the 6-bit addressing mode of the specified address expression.
.ODD	Ensures that the current location counter contains an odd address by adding 1 if it is even.
.PAGE	Causes the assembly listing to skip to the top of the next page, and to increment the page count.
.PRINT exp;text	User-invoked message directive; causes output to the listing file or the command output device containing the optional expression and the statement containing the directive.
.PSECT name,att1, . . . attn	Begin or resume a named or unnamed program section having the specified attributes.
.RADIX n	Alters the current program radix to n, where n is 2, 8, or 10.
.RAD50 /string/	Generates a block of data containing the Radix-50 equivalent of the character string enclosed within delimiting characters.

Form	Operation
.REPT exp	Begins a repeat block; causes the section of code up to the next .ENDM or .ENDR directive to be repeated the number of times specified as exp.
.SBTTL string	Causes the specified string to be printed as part of the assembly listing page header. The string component of each .SBTTL directive is collected into a table of contents at the beginning of the assembly listing.
.TITLE string	Assigns the first six Radix-50 characters in the string as an object module name and causes the string to appear on each page of the assembly listing.
.WORD exp1,exp2, . . .	Generates successive words of data; each word contains the value of the corresponding specified expression.
direct assignment pseudo-op (=)	Assigns to the symbol on the left-hand of the = the value of the expression on the right hand side of the = .

DIAGNOSTIC ERROR MESSAGE SUMMARY

MACRO-11 ERROR CODES

A diagnostic error code is printed as the first character in a source line that contains an error detected by MACRO-11. This error code identifies a syntactical problem or other type of error condition detected during the processing of a source line. An example of such a source line is shown below:

    Q   26 000236 010102   MOV R1,R2,A

The extraneous argument A in the MOV instruction above causes the line to be flagged with a Q (syntax) error.

Error Code	*Meaning*
A	Assembly error. Because many different types of error condition produce this diagnostic message, all the possible directives that may yield a general assembly error have been categorized to reflect specific classes of error conditions:

Category 1: Illegal Argument Specified

.RADIX—A value other than 2, 8, or 10 is specified as a new radix.

.LIST/.NLIST—Other than a legally defined argument is specified with the directive.

.ENABL/.DSABL—Other than a legally defined argument is specified with the directive.

.PSECT—Other than a legally defined argument is specified with the directive.

.IF/.IIF—Other than a legally defined conditional test or an illegal argument expression value is specified with the directive.

.MACRO—An illegal or duplicate symbol found in dummy argument list.

Category 2: Null Argument or Symbol Specified

.TITLE—Program name is not specified in the directive, or first nonblank character following the directive is a non-Radix-50 character.

.IRP/.IRPC—No dummy argument is specified in the directive.

.NARG/.NCHAR/.NTYPE—No symbol is specified in the directive.

.IF/.IIF—No conditional argument is specified in the directive.

Category 3: Unmatched Delimiter/Illegal Argument Construction

.ASCII/.ASCIZ/.RAD50/.IDENT—Character string or argument string delimiters do not match, or an illegal character is used as a delimiter, or an illegal argument construction is used in the directive.

.NCHAR—Character string delimiters do not match, or an illegal character is used as a delimiter in the directive.

Category 4: General Addressing Errors
This type of error results from one of several possible conditions.

1. Permissible range of a branch instruction, i.e., from -128_{10} to $+127_{10}$ words, has been exceeded.

2. A statement makes invalid use of the current location counter, e.g., a ".=expression" statement attempts to force the current location counter to cross program section (.PSECT) boundaries.

3. A statement contains an invalid address expression. In cases where an absolute address expression is required, specifying a global symbol, a relocatable value, or a complex relocatable value results in an invalid address expression. Similarly, in cases where a relocatable address expression is required, either a relocatable or an absolute value is permissible, but a global symbol or a complex relocatable value in the statement likewise results in an invalid address expression. Specific cases of this type of error are those which follow:
.BLKB/.BLKW/.REPT—Other than an absolute value or an expression that reduces to an absolute value has been specified with the directive.

4. Multiple expressions are not separated by a comma. This condition causes the next symbol to be evaluated as part of the current expression.

Category 5: Illegal Forward Reference

This type of error results from either of two possible conditions:

1. A global assignment statement (symbol = = expression) contains a forward reference to another symbol.

2. An expression defining the value of the current location counter contains a forward reference.

Error Code	Meaning
B	Boundary error. Instructions or word data are being assembled at an odd address. The location counter is incremented by 1.
D	Doubly defined symbol referenced. Reference was made to a symbol that is defined more than once.
E	End directive not found. When the end-of-file is reached during source input and the .END directive has not yet been encountered, MACRO-11 generates this error code, ends assembly pass 1, and proceeds with assembly pass 2.
I	Illegal character detected. Illegal characters that are also nonprintable are replaced by a question mark (?) on the listing. The character is then ignored.
L	Input line is longer than 132_{10} characters in length. Currently, this error condition is caused only through excessive substitution of real arguments for dummy arguments during the expansion of a macro.
M	Multiple definition of a label. A label was encountered that was equivalent (in the first six characters) to a label previously encountered.
N	A number contains a digit that is not in the current program radix. The number is evaluated as a decimal value.
O	Op-code error. Directive out of context. Permissible nesting level depth for conditional assemblies has been exceeded. Attempt to expand a macro that was unidentified after .MCALL search.
P	Phase error. A label's definition of value varies from one assembly pass to another or a multiple definition of a local symbol has occurred within a local symbol block. Also, when in a local symbol block defined by the .ENABL LSB directive, an attempt was made to define a local symbol in a program section other than that which was in effect when the block was entered. A P error code also appears if an .ERROR directive is assembled.
Q	Questionable syntax. Arguments are missing, too many arguments are specified, or the instruction scan was not completed.
R	Register-type error. An invalid use of or reference to a register has been made, or an attempt has been made to redefine a standard register symbol without first issuing the .DSABL REG directive.
T	Truncation error. A number generated more than 16 bits in a word, or an expression generated more than 8 significant bits during the use of the .BYTE directive or trap (EMT or TRAP) instruction.

Error Code	*Meaning*
U	Undefined symbol. An undefined symbol was encountered during the evaluation of an expression; such an undefined symbol is assigned a value of zero. Other possible conditions that result in this error code include unsatisfied macro names in the list of .MCALL arguments and a direct-assignment (symbol = expression) statement that contains a forward reference to a symbol whose definition also contains a forward reference; also, a local symbol may have been referenced that does not exist in the current local symbol block.
Z	Instruction error. The instruction flagged is not compatible among all members of the PDP-11 family.

ROUTINES FOR INPUT/ OUTPUT

```
        .MCall  .TTYIN,.TTYOUT

LF        =    12      ; 10 decimal is a line feed character
CR        =    15      ; 13 decimal is a carriage return
                       ; character
Asc0      =    60      ; 48 decimal is "0"

Temp1:   .Word  0      ; These locations save the values
Temp2:   .Word  0      ; of the registers
Temp3:   .Word  0

; Here is InChar, which gets a character from the user and
; returns it in R0

InChar:  .TTYIN
         RTS  PC

; Here is OutChar, which prints the character in R0 on the
; screen

OutChar: .TTYOUT
         RTS  PC

; Here is In, which gets a 6-digit octal number from the user
; and returns it in R0

In:      MOV  R1,Temp1    ; Save the value of R1
         MOV  R2,Temp2    ; Also save R2
In0:     CLR  R1          ; R1 counts each octal digit (6
                          ; maximum)
```

```
         CLR    R2            ; R2 is the sum as it is accumulated

         MOV    B#76,R0       ; 76 is the prompt character ">"
         JSR    PC,OutChar    ; Print the prompt

ILoop:   JSR    PC,InChar     ; Get a character
         CMP    R0,#CR        ; Is it a carriage return?
         BEQ    IEOL          ; Yes, return the sum

         SUB    #Asc0,R0      ; Is the number less than zero?
         BLT    IllChar       ; Yes, Illegal character
         CMP    R0,#7         ; Is the number greater than 7?
         BGT    IllChar       ; Yes, Illegal character

         ASL    R2            ; Multiply the sum by 8
         ASL    R2
         ASL    R2
         ADD    R0,R2         ; Add in this new octal digit
         INC    R1            ; Increment the number of digits
                             ; read in
         CMP    R1,#6         ; Have we read in 6 octal digits?
         BLT    ILoop         ; No, get another digit

IEOL:    JSR    PC,Flush      ; Flush the input buffer
         MOV    R2,R0         ; Move the sum into R0
         MOV    Temp1,R1      ; Restore the values of R1
         MOV    Temp2,R2      ; and R2
         RTS    PC            ; Return with the number in R0

IllChar: JSR    PC,Flush      ; Flush the input buffer
         MOV    #IllMsg,R1    ; Put the address of the message in R1
         JSR    PC,OutMsg     ; Print the message
         BR     In0           ; Now get the number
```

; Here is Out, which prints out the octal number in R0

```
Out:     MOV    R1,Temp1      ; Save the value of R1
         MOV    R2,Temp2      ; Also save R2
         MOV    R3,Temp3      ; And R3
         CLR    R1            ; R1 is the loop counter (6 digits)
         MOV    R0,R2         ; Move the value to be printed into R2

         MOV    #1,R3         ; One bit for the first octal digit
         CLR    R0            ; Clear the digit to be printed

OLoop:   ASL    R2            ; Shift a bit out of R2 into the carry
         ROL    R0            ; Move it into R0
         DEC
```

```
          BNE     OLoop          ; No, move another bit

          ADD     #Asc0,R0       ; Yes, Add the ASCII bits to get the
          JSR     PC,OutChar     ; correct character and then print it

          MOV     #3,R3          ; Put 3 bits in the next octal digit
          CLR     R0             ; Clear R0 for the next digit
          INC     R1             ; Increment the digit counter
          CMP     R1,#6          ; Have we printed all 6 octal digits?
          BLT     OLoop          ; No, print another digit
          MOV     Temp1,R1       ; Yes, restore the values of
          MOV     Temp2,R2       ; the registers and
          MOV     Temp3,R3       ; return to the caller
          RTS     PC
```

; Here is OutMsg, which prints the message whose address is in
; R1, terminated by a 0

```
OutMsg:   MOVB    (R1)+,R0
          BEQ     OMDone
          JSR     PC,OutChar
          BR      OutMsg

OMDone:   RTS     PC
```

; This illegal message is used by the subroutine In

```
IllMsg:   .Ascii  /Illegal character/
          .Byte   CR,LF,0
          .Even

Flush:    CMP     R0,#CR         ; Is this character a carriage return?
          BEQ     FDone          ; Yes, all characters have been
                                 ; flushed
          JSR     PC,InChar      ; No, discard this character and
          BR      Flush          ; keep flushing

FDone:    JSR     PC,InChar      ; Discard the carriage return
          RTS     PC
```

INDEX

Page numbers followed by an f refer to a figure on that page.